An Age of Melodrama

An Age of Melodrama

FAMILY, GENDER, AND
SOCIAL HIERARCHY IN THE
TURN-OF-THE-CENTURY
JAPANESE NOVEL

Ken K. Ito

STANFORD UNIVERSITY PRESS
STANFORD, CALIFORNIA

Stanford University Press
Stanford, California

©2008 by the Board of Trustees of the Leland Stanford Junior University.
All rights reserved.

No part of this book may be reproduced or transmitted in any form or by any means,
electronic or mechanical, including photocopying and recording, or in any information
storage or retrieval system without the prior written permission of Stanford University Press.

Printed in the United States of America on acid-free, archival-quality paper

Library of Congress Cataloging-in-Publication Data

Ito, Ken K.
An age of melodrama : family, gender, and social hierarchy in the turn-of-the-century
Japanese novel / Ken K. Ito.
p. cm.
Includes bibliographical references and index.
ISBN 978-0-8047-5777-5 (cloth : alk. paper)
1. Japanese fiction—Meiji period, 1868-1912—History and criticism. I. Title.
PL747.6.I796 2008
895.6'34209355—dc22
2008011776

Portions of Chapter 1 were published in *Harvard Journal of Asiatic Studies* 60.2 (December
2000).

Portions of Chapter 3 were published in *Journal of Japanese Studies* 28.2 (Summer 2002).

Frontispiece by Takeuchi Keishū from the first edition of *Konjiki yasha*. Kan'ichi kicks
Miya to the ground after she has revealed her intention to leave him and marry a
wealthy man. SOURCE: *Konjiki yasha, zenpen* (Tokyo: Shun'yōdō, 1898).

Typeset by Bruce Lundquist in 11/14 Adobe Garamond

For Liz, Ella, Maile, and Ilima—my family

Contents

Figures

Acknowledgments

My life at the University of Michigan has nurtured this book in many ways. The research was begun during a year supported by a Michigan Humanities Award and continued over a sabbatical. Faculty Research Grants from Michigan's Center for Japanese Studies allowed me to devote time to writing key parts of the study. The College of Literature, Science, and the Arts; the Office of the Vice President for Research; and the Department of Asian Languages and Cultures jointly provided a subvention toward publication.

My longtime friends and colleagues—Esperanza Ramirez-Christensen, Hitomi Tonomura, Shuen-fu Lin, Luis Gomez, and the late Gary Saxon-house—have been generous with their encouragement. Markus Nornes introduced me to the film criticism on melodrama. And I've been grateful to have in Jonathan Zwicker a colleague also interested in melodrama. Nancy Florida has shouldered the administrative burdens in our department, giving the rest of us more time for our research. Michigan's Asia Library provided the books for this study; Kenji Niki, the able steward of its Japan Collection, has found everything I've ever requested.

I was lucky to start thinking about this project when I taught an extraordinary group of graduate students, now all accomplished researchers and teachers on their own. Nothing can be more gratifying than to acknowledge that I've learned more from these young scholars than I ever managed to teach them. James Reichert, Richi Sakakibara, and Atsuko Ueda will find traces of our discussions in the pages that follow. I have to single out Timothy Van Compernolle, because he fearlessly critiqued every chapter in this study. Later students have continued to help me with my thinking: Alex Bates, Heather Bowen-Struyk, David Henry, Jason Herlands, Hoyt Long, Mimi Plauché, David Rosenfeld, and Kristina Vassil. I'm grateful to them for listening to half-baked ideas and challenging me to do something with them.

I was also able to test the arguments presented here at talks given at Stanford's Department of Asian Languages, the Center for Japanese Studies at the University of Michigan, the Department of Asian Languages and Literatures at the University of Washington, the Department of East Asian Languages and Literatures and the Center for East Asian Studies at Yale University, the Department of East Asian Languages and Literatures at Ohio State University, the Middlebury Summer Language Schools, and the annual conferences of the Association of Asian Studies, Association for Japanese Literary Studies, and the University of Colorado East Asian Graduates Association. Mark Jones and Andrew Gordon gave me the opportunity to discuss the material that became Chapter 3 in a seminar at Harvard's Reischauer Institute of Japanese Studies. An earlier version of Chapter 1 appeared as "The Family and the Nation in Tokutomi Roka's *Hototogisu*," *Harvard Journal of Asiatic Studies* 60.2 (December 2000), and an earlier version of Chapter 3 has been published as "Class and Gender in a Meiji Family Romance: Kikuchi Yūhō's *Chikyōdai*," *Journal of Japanese Studies* 28.2 (Summer 2002). I'm grateful to the editors of the journals that carried this work, Howard Hibbett and John Treat respectively, for their encouragement, for giving me an early forum for this research, and for rigorous and helpful comments. I wish to thank Joanna Handlin Smith and Martha Walsh for wrangling with my writing and for permission to use the material here. The Department of East Asian Languages and Literatures and the Center for Japanese Studies at the University of Hawai'i at Mānoa were my gracious hosts as I completed editing the manuscript for this book. Joel Cohn, Robert Huey, and Lucy Lower made my stay in Hawai'i a pleasure, and Tokiko Bazzell gave me access to the University of Hawai'i Library's Japan Collection. Mahalo nui loa.

Aside from the University of Michigan Library and the University of Hawai'i Hamilton Library, research for this study was conducted at the National Diet Library, the Dōshisha University Library, the Ritsumeikan University Library, and the University of California at Berkeley Library. At Berkeley, Yuki Ishimatsu let me use materials from the incomparable Murakami Collection. I am grateful to all librarians, practitioners of a profession based on sharing.

This study has been enriched by criticisms, reading suggestions, information, encouragement, prodding, and offhand comments from numerous friends and colleagues, some of whom have probably forgotten how they've helped. I wish to thank Christopher Hill, Charles Inouye, Edward Kamens, William Kelley, Maryellen Mori, Emiko Ohnuki-Tierney, Sharalyn Orbaugh, Ann Sherif, Alan Tansman, William Tyler, Dennis Washburn, and Louise Young. I'm grateful to Jordan Sand for many hours of conversation on the Meiji ideology of domesticity. Richard Torrance and an anonymous reader provided good and tough advice during the final revision of the manuscript. As I wrote this book I was often reminded of lessons learned from my own teachers: Edwin McClellan, and the late Etō Jun and Kawashima Itaru.

As the book took its final form, I benefited from the help of many at Stanford University Press: Muriel Bell, Rob Ehle, Alan Harvey, Judith Hibbard, Bruce Lundquist, Kirsten Oster, Joa Suorez, and Stacy Wagner. Richard Gunde was my copy editor; I've learned from the dialogue on language he initiated. David Luljak skillfully assembled the index. Kendra Strand, a current Michigan student, was my patient and sharp-eyed proofreader. I am deeply grateful to Nemoto Akio, who graciously allowed me to use the illustration by Kaburaki Kiyokata on the cover of this book.

My thinking about the protean nature of affiliations has been aided by Kalyan Dutta, Kris Seifert, Arno Kumagai, Mieko Yoshihama, Stephen Sumida, Gail Nomura, Ruth Gomez, Brian and Sheryl Woo, Kathryn Williams, Chris Wilson, and the late Edith and Henry Gomberg.

My parents, Kenzo Ito and the late Hisako Ito, gave me my first insights into struggles against the *ie*. The book in its entirety was made possible by Elizabeth Sumi Hokada, whose patience, kindness, level-headed wisdom, and endless moral support have taught me the meaning of family. Elizabeth Kainani Ito has affected my writing in more ways than she will ever know. But perhaps I should mention that before she came along I was thinking of writing a book about fathers and sons in the Meiji novel. Her arrival has slowed this project, but I know that both the book and I have changed for the better in the interval. Thank you.

Ken K. Ito
Honolulu, July 2007

A Note on Names

In Japanese names mentioned in this book, the family name has been placed first. In writing the names of authors, I have followed the Japanese convention of relying on pennames when both first and last names are not used: thus, I refer to Ozaki Kōyō (where "Ozaki" is the surname, and "Kōyō" is the penname) as "Kōyō."

An Age of Melodrama

Introduction

Melodrama and the Family in Meiji Japan

Night enfolds the beach at Atami. Voices rise above the sound of waves. A young man and a young woman cling to each other in the moonlight. They had been raised together and had pledged their love, yet Miya's desire for wealth had led her to betray Kan'ichi and accept the marriage proposal of a banker's son. Kan'ichi tries to make her see what is right. But her mind cannot be changed, and they are left in a despairing final embrace:

> He held tight to Miya, as though trying to save her from danger. His hot tears fell on the fair skin of her neck, and his body shook like a withered reed in the wind. Miya trembled too, holding him as though she could not let him go. She sobbed, biting the sleeve of his coat.
>
> "Oh, what can I do? Please, won't you tell me? What will you do if I marry him?"
>
> Kan'ichi thrust Miya away; the two fell apart like the halves of a log being split. "You've finally made up your mind to go! So you won't listen to me no matter what I say. You're rotten inside! You whore!"
>
> With these words, Kan'ichi raised his foot and suddenly kicked her slender waist. She fell sideways with a shudder; she could not speak, and, quietly enduring her pain, she sobbed into the sand.

"Miya, you, you whore! Your unfaithfulness has driven a man called Hazama Kan'ichi to madness, to unbearable despair. His precious life will go astray. Forget about education and all the rest. This bitterness will make me a living demon determined to eat the flesh of beasts like you." . . .

Miya suddenly tried to rise, but she fell, her injured leg made useless by pain. She slowly crawled toward Kan'ichi and clung to him; her voice fought back tears as she said, "Kan'ichi, please . . . please wait. Where . . . where are you going?"

Kan'ichi was surprised in spite of himself when he saw Miya's kimono in disarray and a snow-white knee laid bare, trembling and covered in blood.

"You're hurt," he said.

When he bent closer, she stopped him, saying, "Don't worry about this. I want to know where you're going. I have something to tell you, so please come home with me tonight. I beg you, Kan'ichi."

"If you have something to say, say it here."

"No, not here."

"What could you possibly have to say to me? Let go."

"I won't."

"If you're stubborn, I'll kick you again."

"I don't care if you kick me."

When Kan'ichi tore himself away with all his might, she crumpled to the ground.

"Kan'ichi," she cried.

Kan'ichi had already sped some distance away. Miya desperately got to her feet and followed after him, staggering in pain. "Kan'ichi, I won't stop you anymore, so please once more . . . once more . . . I have something left to say."

Miya had fallen again. She no longer had the strength to stand, and all she could do was call out Kan'ichi's name. She saw his shadow, gradually growing dim, rushing up the hill. Miya writhed on the ground and continued to call his name. The dark shadow, finally reaching the top of hill, seemed to be looking back toward her. Miya wrung out her voice and called. The man's voice came back to her from far away.

"Miya!"

"Oh, oh, oh, Kan'ichi!"

Miya craned her neck and peered into the night, but after his voice sounded the dark shadow vanished as though erased. The lonely trees she had mistaken for him stood unmoving, the waves sent forth their mournful murmurings, and the moon of the 17th of January shed its pale, heartsick light.

With longing, Miya again called out Kan'ichi's name.[1]

This outpouring of exorbitant emotion and violence occurs in what was arguably the most popular of Meiji novels, *Konjiki yasha* (The golden demon, 1897–1903), by Ozaki Kōyō (1867–1903). Serialized in major daily newspapers, reprinted repeatedly as books, and adapted to the stage and to movies, *Konjiki yasha* and novels like it penetrated the imaginations of men and women of all classes, young and old, in the cities and the countryside.

Kan'ichi and Miya are led to this wrenching moment by a moral vision that structures their conflict as a polarized battle between pure love and filthy lucre. Miya has forsaken love for money, and both she and Kan'ichi will pay for this choice throughout a chronicle of intense suffering that consumes the rest of the novel and confirms the precious value of what has been lost. Such emotional extravagance was common in the novels of the Meiji period (1868–1912). At the turn of the last century, Japanese fiction pulsed with an urge to view the world as a moral drama in which good ceaselessly clashed with evil. Men and women fought desperate moral battles, confronted searing ethical dilemmas. Narratives were designed to wing the breathless reader from one superheated scene to another, in which no outpouring of emotion was too excessive. It was an age of melodrama.

Most students of melodrama see its host environment as a society and a culture in flux. The disappearance of former verities and the challenges of new ethical discourses breed a desire for moral certitude answered by the melodramatic mode. Japanese melodramatic fiction grapples with the traumatic discontinuities of the Meiji period: the replacement of the Tokugawa order with a nation-state wedded to industrial capitalism, the destruction of an established status system and the arrival of uncontrolled social mobility, the disturbance of gender roles by new discourses and beliefs, the dislocations in the family where modernity collided with flesh and blood. It is Meiji melodrama's portrayal of the family upon which I will focus. In part, this is because the family is a prime setting for melodrama in general. But, more importantly, this focus reflects the significance of the family within the mid- to late-Meiji ideological field, where it was seen as a key locus for the cultivation and expression of moral sentiments.

Through readings of *Konjiki yasha* and three other enormously popular novels—*Hototogisu* (The cuckoo, 1898–99) by Tokutomi Roka (1868–1927), *Chikyōdai* (Raised as sisters, 1903) by Kikuchi Yūhō (1870–1947), and *Gubijinsō* (The poppy, 1907) by Natsume Sōseki (1867–1916)—I seek to examine how the stark lighting of the melodramatic imagination illuminates the Meiji family. Turn-of-the-century novels did more than portray established models of family; with impressive fecundity they generated newer forms that responded to the discontinuities of their time. The polarized morality of melodrama not only tears apart the budding family of Miya and Kan'ichi, it also replaces it with ever more inventive and emotionally fraught alternatives. The story I tell involves the forms of family left to the devastated young man rushing into the shadows and the brutalized young woman calling his name, the moral and ideological forces engaged by these fictive families, the social exigencies they address, and the narrative feats required to bring them into being.

LOCATING MEIJI MELODRAMATIC FICTION

We should begin by acknowledging that melodramatic fiction is not an accepted category in modern Japanese literary history. "Melodrama" is not a term that would have been applied to these works in the Meiji period, nor is it used with any frequency by Japanese literary critics today.[2] The works I examine were, in their day, called *shinbun shōsetsu* (newspaper fiction) and, in one instance, *katei shōsetsu* (home fiction). Critics would now think of most of these novels as *taishū shōsetsu* (popular fiction), although they do so aware of the anachronism involved in using a term that achieves currency only in the 1920s. I wish to argue forcefully, however, that "melodramatic fiction" is an appropriate and productive framework for thinking about these works, and that, in fact, melodrama is an important concept for understanding Meiji culture.[3]

The terms "melodrama" and "melodramatic" are, as nearly every critic working with them points out, often used pejoratively to refer to narratives damned by crass appeals to sentiment, cheap sensationalism, exaggerated coincidences, and simplistic moral values. Peter Brooks undertook a major act of redemption in his 1976 book, *The Melodramatic Imagination: Balzac, Henry James, Melodrama, and the Mode of Excess*, which resituates the "melodramatic" as a broad and powerful sensibility that courses through the drama and fiction of the nineteenth and early twentieth centuries.[4] He does this by drawing a distinction between "melodrama" as a theatrical genre and the "melodramatic" as a mode of imagination. While Brooks begins with the former and delineates the features of theatrical melodrama as they were developed by François-René Guilbert de Pixérécourt and others in early post-Revolution France, his thrust is to show how these features help to illuminate the "melodramatic imagination" found in later nineteenth-century novelists, principally Honoré de Balzac and Henry James, but also many others. It is the melodramatic as a mode of imagination or sensibility that concerns me as I address Meiji fiction.

For Brooks, the melodramatic mode is first and foremost characterized by its moral or ethical vision. Underlying it is the claim that, somewhere beneath the exterior of quotidian manners and relations, there lies a realm of extravagant moral demand in which men and women must respond, either unwillingly or by choice, to powerful moral forces. Melodrama digs beneath the mundane appearances of everyday life in order to reveal and dramatize the hidden moral core of experience:

> Such writers as Balzac and James need melodrama because their deep sub-ject, the locus of their true drama, has come to be what we have called the "moral occult," the domain of spiritual forces and imperatives that is not clearly visible within reality, but which they believe to be operative there, and which demands to be uncovered, registered, articulated. In the absence of a true Sacred . . . they continue to believe that what is most important in a man's life is his ethical drama and the ethical implications of his psychic drama.[5]

The drama of moral revelation is played out on a resolutely dualistic moral terrain, where good and evil are locked in combat. Melodramas stage "a heightened and hyperbolic drama, making reference to pure and polar concepts of darkness and light, salvation and damnation."[6] The moral posi-tions are starkly arrayed, exhibiting what Brooks calls the "excluded mid-dle"; for the melodramatic imagination, the choices are either/or and the middle ground is denied. This moral polarization underlies melodrama's hyperbolic sentiments, where emotions are supercharged by the unequivo-cating demands of moral opposition. Characters are put under constant emotional pressure as they face ethical confrontations that brook no easy compromises.

Additional facets of the mode are emphasized by later critics working on melodrama. Linda Williams, for example, stresses that moral legibility is established through the simultaneous presence of "pathos *and* action—the sufferings of innocent victims *and* the exploits of brave heroes or mon-strous criminals."[7] Ben Singer points to the importance of sensationalism, because emotionally charged spectacle—the train rushing toward the help-less heroine—reveals the connection of melodrama to the "hyperstimulus" of the modern urban environment.[8] Other critics point to qualities such as melodramatic narrative's reliance on coincidence, episodic plotting, and deus ex machina climaxes, or the melodramatic character's undivided nature, an attribute that allows the illustration of specific moral coordinates. Perhaps the wisest overall approach is Singer's: melodrama is a "cluster concept," in which these various characteristics are capable of appearing in many combinations. Here, melodrama is defined not by the occurrence of all possible identifying characteristics, but rather by the differing combinations of constitutive elements.[9] In this study, I will refer to many of the components of the melodramatic cluster, but I return repeatedly to moral dualism, because this strikes me as the key to understanding Meiji melodramatic fiction and the cultural work it undertakes.

Although a dualistic moral vision can suggest a world of abstract categories, Brooks emphasizes melodrama's connections to the specifics of a social milieu. Because melodrama seeks to excavate the moral significance of everyday life, its extravagant moral claims are made in texts that also attempt to reproduce the textures of quotidian experience and the material solidity of physical settings. Of particular import for my study is Brooks's assertion that certain melodramas attempt to uncover moral polarities through the detailed depiction of social relations. Writers whom Brooks calls the "social melodramatists"—Balzac and James, but also Dickens, Gogol, Dostoevsky, Proust, and Lawrence—undertake a "dual engagement with the representation of man's social existence, the way he lives in the ordinary, and with the moral drama implicated by and in his existence. They write a melodrama *of* manners."[10] The texts I study are very much melodramas of manners: they concern themselves with the ethical implications of commonplace problems in Meiji society.

The other facet of melodrama's engagement with the social has to do with the historical role it fulfills. Melodrama, as Brooks conceives it, is a socially and politically active mode that seeks to articulate morality in response to specific historical situations. Brooks makes this point most powerfully when he describes the rise of theatrical melodrama following the French Revolution:

> It comes into being in a world where the traditional imperatives of truth and ethics have been violently thrown into question, yet where the promulgation of truth and ethics, their instauration as a way of life, is of immediate, daily political concern. . . . We may legitimately claim that melodrama becomes the principal mode for uncovering, demonstrating, and making operative the essential moral universe in a post-sacred era.[11]

Melodrama arises amidst epistemic rupture. It speaks at historical moments when prior structures of belief have given way and where ethical positions must be located in fluid and contingent circumstances. Its function is to illuminate, with its stark and polarized lighting, the moral significance of human endeavor.[12]

Brooks's arguments on the social functions of melodrama have enabled much of later melodrama criticism. Students of melodrama have frequently sought to discover the cultural work it undertakes by locating specific manifestations of the mode within their social and historical settings. Marsha Kinder, for example, interprets Spanish melodramatic cinema as an expression of a shifting search for national identity.[13] And Linda Williams uncovers the melodrama in representations of American race relations ranging from *Uncle Tom's Cabin* to the media coverage of the O. J. Simpson trial.[14] My study, too, finds melodrama's significance in the way it responds to particular social and cultural circumstances. Positioning Meiji melodramatic fiction within the ideological contestations of the Meiji period, I investigate how it marshals the morally exorbitant trope of family to mediate anxieties over social mobility and new expectations of gender.

One implication of Brooks's insights demands extension, and this concerns melodrama's ultimate potential for achieving what it seeks. What chance does melodrama ultimately have of establishing moral certitude, if it is, as Brooks says, "constructed on, and over, the void, postulating meanings and symbolic systems which have no certain justification because they are backed by no theology and no universally accepted social code"?[15] What are the consequences for melodrama when it undertakes its cultural work in the face of absent transcendent standards? If Brooks does not explicitly explore this question, a rich line of thinking has developed, particularly in film studies, to theorize the ambivalence of melodrama's relations to a contested ideological terrain. Much of this discussion has focused on 1950s Hollywood melodramas, whose moral platitudes frequently seem self-contradictory. Thomas Elsaesser famously called attention to this problem in a foundational essay in studies of film melodrama:

> There seems a radical ambiguity attached to melodrama, which holds even more to film melodrama. Depending on whether the emphasis fell on the odyssey of suffering or the happy ending, on the place and context of rupture . . . melodrama would appear to function either subversively or as escapism—categories which are always relative to the given historical and social context.[16]

Film melodrama, then, is an ideologically slippery form; a movie's conclusion may restore a happy family, rescue a beleaguered heroine, or reunite a separated couple, but differences in perspective or emphasis can produce subversion and "radical ambiguity." In earlier film criticism on melodrama, the tendency was to locate these effects in music or mise-en-scène[17]—for example, in the fantastic, hard-edged lighting and saturated colors that assert an ironic visual counterpoint to the conventional resolutions in Douglas Sirk's films—but this left ideological subversion as a hidden implication that could be gauged only by the discerning critic. Laura Mulvey pushed the argument one step further; for her, melodrama displays not subverted ideological coherence but a fundamental and motivating ideological inconsistency:

> Ideological contradiction is the overt mainspring and specific content of melodrama, not a hidden, unconscious thread to be picked up only by special critical processes. No ideology can even pretend to totality: it must provide an outlet for its own inconsistencies. . . . The strength of the melodramatic form lies in the amount of dust the story raises along the road, a cloud of over-determined irreconcilables which put up a resistance to being neatly settled in the last five minutes.[18]

Geoffrey Nowell-Smith reiterates this point in his characteristically pithy prose: "The importance of melodrama . . . lies precisely in its ideological failure."[19]

Although there is a vast difference in the specific ideological contents of Hollywood movies and Meiji fiction, my reading of the latter bears out the insight that the melodramatic imagination is shot through with contradictions. The Meiji melodrama attempts to install, in a fluid moral universe, a dualistic morality clearly defining good and evil. In every text I encounter, however, this endeavor is beset by ideological inconsistencies and crosscutting ethical discourses. This leads me to argue that Meiji melodramatic fiction strains toward unquestionable moral oppositions and hierarchies, but finds itself thwarted by ideological irreconcilables. My project is to study the "dust the story raises along the road."

In their attempts to chart melodrama's ideological complexity, other critics have generally agreed with Brooks that the mode surges to the cultural forefront in moments of turmoil. Elsaesser, for example, notes that "historically, one of the interesting facts about this tradition is that its height of popularity seems to coincide (and this remains true throughout the 19th century) with periods of intense social and ideological crisis."[20] Although he too foregrounds the importance of French theater after the Revolution, he finds precursors in eighteenth-century sentimental novels that record the struggle of the bourgeois consciousness against the remnants of feudalism.[21] In her study of English domestic novels, Martha Vicinus locates Victorian melodramatic fiction in the unsparing social transformations of nineteenth-century England, where the values of the family came under the economic and social assault of industrial capitalism.[22]

Melodrama, then, finds its element in ideological contestation, particularly as this occurs in recently transformed socioeconomic or political environments. With its distinctive dualistic vision, it attempts to discover and articulate moral values amidst changes that have destroyed older values or concealed the moral valences of human life. These general characteristics apply to Meiji melodramatic fiction. The last decade of the nineteenth century and the first decade of the twentieth were a time of impassioned ideological activity.[23] The Meiji Restoration had brought to Japan epistemic rupture and social transformation every bit as stunning as the French Revolution. The first twenty years of the Meiji period were filled with rapid and disorienting change—the replacement of the Tokugawa shogunate with a modern nation-state engaged in perpetual self-invention, the abolition of the quadripartite Edo status system in favor of a putative egalitarianism, the displacement of the Neo-Confucian and Buddhist worldviews by a flood of new ideologies, the construction of a modern education system and a modern military, an initial wave of industrialization fueled by aggressive entrepreneurial capitalism. By contrast, the following two decades bracketing the turn of the century were a time of consolidation: "The late Meiji period was less a time of upheaval than one of settlement, less of structural drama than functional adjustment, a time when change was absorbed and some sort of stability was wrested from the aftermath of crisis."[24] Yet, if the crisis of structural change had somewhat abated, there was still an "atmosphere of crisis" bred partly by an apprehension of the human consequences of radical socioeconomic change.[25] Carol Gluck's catalog of the "social problems" (*shakai mondai*) perceived by commentators of the time is instructive:

> Society, they said, was in disarray, afflicted with ills, beset by economic difficulties, roiled by the struggle for survival, upset by labor problems, exposed to dangerous thought, threatened by socialist destruction, rent by gulfs between rich and poor, city and country, worker and capitalist. . . . Cities were sinks of iniquity leading young people astray and fomenting social strife,

even revolution. Customs were degenerating, morals in decline. And the middle classes, the "root and branch" from whom so much civic stability had been expected, had developed "social problems" of their own.[26]

Meiji melodramatic fiction participates in the broad crisis consciousness suggested by such a list. It locates itself in the variegated and contested terrain of late Meiji perceptions of social problems. The book that follows is concerned with how these problems appear when they are refracted through the dualistic lens of the melodramatic imagination.

Most studies of melodrama now begin with the assumption that it is a modern mode. This is certainly true of Brooks's work, which positions melodrama as a response to a "post-sacred era." Ben Singer has stated his view succinctly: "Melodrama was quite literally a product of modernity."[27] My own view is closest to that of Martha Vicinus, who has written that "melodrama is best understood as a combination of archetypal, mythic beliefs and time-specific responses to particular cultural and historical conditions."[28] As I will shortly show, Meiji melodrama was deeply indebted to prior paradigms. But my study argues for the modernity of Meiji melodramatic fiction because of its specific concerns.

The texts I study deal with problems taken from a catalog of the modern experience. They are all set against the background of wrenching social and cultural discontinuity. The characters in these novels do not live in the same world as their parents—they grope their way toward new values, they struggle to assume gender, class, and occupational identities just now coming into being: military officers, "new aristocrats," students, bourgeois wives, and more. These identities are conditioned upon the existence of the modern nation-state and a capitalist economy. The construction of gender identities and models of family supportive of the nation-state turn out to be a central concern for *Hototogisu*. The problem of locating the "moral occult" in capitalism's cash nexus preoccupies *Konjiki yasha*, but this problem is actually at issue in all of the works I study. These novels are also absorbed with another frequently mentioned marker of modernity, which Pitrim Sorokin calls "vertical mobility."[29] Characters are either frightened of losing the status that they have or inflamed by the desire to improve it. *Chikyōdai* deals with the complications of gender and class that arise when a girl of modest background succumbs to the siren call of *risshin shusse*, the Meiji cult of self-advancement. The mark of melodrama here is the linking of social mobility to moral instability. The modern preoccupation with individualism and its clash with the needs of the group is also a pervasive concern. In *Gubijinsō*, for example, a young woman's desire to marry whom she wishes endangers male designs to build alliances through a "traffic in women." Other key features of modernity crop up with regularity in these works: urbanization provides a crucial context, with the textures of Tokyo life often being contrasted against those in other areas; new technologies of communication such as the telegraph and the newspaper play important roles in the plots; the pervasiveness of the clock, which Lewis Mumford has called the "key-machine of the modern industrial age," shapes the sense of time;[30] railways and trains speed "horizontal mobility," radically expanding the spatial range of human relations;[31] and modern laws and judicial systems are repeatedly invoked by the characters. These features make inescapable the conclusion that Meiji melodrama's commitment is to mirror and wrestle with the social dimensions of modernity. The Meiji melodramatic novel articulates the moral significance of the transformations lived by the men and women of turn-of-the-century Japan; the extent to which it does this with an attention to their social behaviors and practices renders it a "melodrama of manners."

MEIJI MELODRAMA AND ITS ANTECEDENTS

Why the melodramatic became the predominant mode for engaging social issues in turn-of-the-century narrative is a question that cannot be fully answered. But part of the explanation lies with prior paradigms for conceptualizing and narrativizing the social order—in Vicinus's terms "archetypal, mythic beliefs." Neo-Confucianism, the official ideology of the Tokugawa shogunate, relentlessly viewed social and political issues within a moral framework. Social and economic hierarchy, the right to rule, and gender relations were all ostensibly weighed on the scales of virtue.[32] The Confucian worldview found its narrative expression in late-Tokugawa fiction's preoccupation with *kanzen chōaku*, the encouragement of good and the chastisement of evil. *Kanzen chōaku* had initially been a critical term rooted in Chinese Confucian thought, where it was used to underline the moral credentials of canonical texts. The *Zuo Commentary* (*Chunqiu Zuozhuan*), for example, says that the *Spring and Autumn Annals*, "in the appellations which it uses, is clear with an exquisite minuteness, distinct through obscurity, elegant by its gentle turns, and full without descending to the low, condemning what is evil, and encouraging what is good—who but the sage could have compiled it as it is?"[33] When the concept of *kanzen chōaku* began to appear in Japanese literary commentaries during the medieval period, it was applied, following Chinese usage, as a standard for evaluating or defending texts according to their didactic utility.[34] The utilitarian defense of literature, however, can be variously utilized, and during the early Edo period it was not uncommon to see the concept of *kanzen chōaku* used either conveniently to legitimize texts with no apparent salubrious effect on public morals or parodically as a means of tweaking Tokugawa authority's concern with moral rectitude. Scores of Edo kabuki plays paid lip service to *kanzen chōaku*, adding a veneer of respectability to scripts whose main dramatic interests lay elsewhere.

It was Takizawa Bakin (1767–1848) who made *kanzen chōaku* a serious undertaking toward the end of the Edo period. Bakin sought to rearticulate Neo-Confucian virtue as the core of a grand narrative at a time when the Tokugawa order was fissuring under the strains of a commercializing economy, peasant rebellions, the ideological challenges of *kokugaku* scholars, and new forms of media that quickly publicized social discontents.[35] He made *kanzen chōaku* his watchword, saying, "For the most part, fiction is not worth troubling with if it does not establish as its principle the encouragement of good and the chastisement of evil."[36] And, in his *yomihon*, "books for reading" in an age when the prominence of illustration meant many books were looked at rather than read, he constructed works of historical fiction that dramatized *kanzen chōaku* through epic plots of virtue imperiled yet finally victorious.[37] In his magnum opus, *Nansō Satomi hakkenden* (Biographies of eight dogs, 1814–42), eight heroes who are the avatars of the eight Confucian virtues battle and finally triumph over evil figured in baroque and various ways. At the end of the Tokugawa period, then, Japanese fiction was well acquainted with a morally conscious fictional practice that viewed the world in dualistic terms.

There was another genre that defined the fiction of the first half of the nineteenth century along with the *yomihon*, and this was the *ninjōbon*, or "books of sentiment." The *ninjōbon*, too, exhibited a dualistic morality, but unlike Bakin's *yomihon*, which thematized the heroism of past warriors, these stories focused on the love lives of contemporary commoners. As inheritors of *sewamono* puppet plays that dealt with domestic dilemmas, the *ninjōbon* specialized in discovering the intensity of feeling flowing beneath the quotidian surface of plebeian urban life. The textures of commoner experience were rendered with great accuracy through both the careful portrayal of manners and mores and the painstaking transcription of various Edo dialects. The stock in trade of the *ninjōbon* was a triangular love affair in which two women loved the same man; this structure generated frustration, jealousy, and self-sacrifice so wrenching—not only for the characters but presumably also for the largely female readership—that these books were known alternatively as *nakihon* or crying books. Late-Edo fiction, then, had also featured a kind of writing that combined hyperemotionalism with the specific portrayal of social manners.[38]

The standard view among literary historians has been that Tsubouchi Shōyō's *Shōsetsu shinzui* (Essence of the novel, 1885–86), the critical essay usually regarded as the point of origin of modern Japanese fiction, pushed such Edo genres as the *ninjōbon* and the *yomihon* to the margins.[39] Indeed, Tsubouchi did profess an evolutionary view of literary history whose telos was the "novel," and he preached the need to leave Edo literature behind. He was particularly hard on Bakin's writing, whose dependence upon the paradigm of *kanzen chōaku* he considered inimical to the true portrayal of human feelings:

> The eight heroes in *Hakkenden*, Bakin's masterwork, are monsters of benevolence, righteousness, and the eight virtues, and can in no way be said to be human beings. The author's intention was, from the very first, to create a novel by modeling people after the eight virtues, and he made the behavior of his heroes perfect and unblemished in order to represent the idea of encouraging good and chastising evil. Thus, if one were to judge this work with the encouragement of good and the chastisement of evil as the main objective, then *Hakkenden* might be said to be an admirable work of fiction unequaled either in the East or the West, in the past or in the present, but if one were to evaluate this in another manner, making human feeling (*ninjō*) the main point, then it would be hard to call the work a flawless jewel. . . . This problem arises because the eight heroes are based upon Bakin's ideals and are not true representations of human beings in this world.[40]

Bakin's reliance upon polarized idealization prompts Tsubouchi to judge his *kanchō shōsetsu* (a term derived from the common abbreviation of *kanzen chōaku*), which he glosses as the "didactic novel," to be far inferior to the *mosha shōsetsu*, which he glosses as the "artistic novel," but which might more literally be translated as the "mimetic novel." Tsubouchi argues that once a writer has inserted a fictional character in a work, "he should regard him as a living person. In describing a character's emotions, the writer should not use his own preconceived designs to construct a character's feelings as good or evil, but rather endeavor to set things down as they are (*arinomama ni mosha suru*) from the position of an onlooker."[41]

These kinds of pronouncements have caused literary historians to declare that Tsubouchi was attempting to install modern realism as the goal of fiction. One of the things that gets lost in such a sweeping view is the complexity inherent in Tsubouchi's effort to say something new using the critical vocabulary available in the Japan of the 1880s, a vocabulary that necessarily owed a great deal to preceding literary usage. The difficulty of Tsubouchi's project is apparent in his often-quoted declaration regarding the aims of fiction: "The main emphasis of fiction is human feeling; close behind follow the state of the world and manners" (*Shōsetsu no shugan wa ninjō nari, setai fūzoku kore ni tsugu*).[42] Although this statement is sometimes interpreted as representing Tsubouchi's investment in psychological depiction and the representation of social experience, it is worthwhile noting that his term for human feeling here is the *ninjō* of *ninjōbon*.[43] Linguistically and conceptually Tsubouchi must reach backward in order to make his enunciations for the future.

The ambivalence of this dynamic is nowhere more evident than in Tsubouchi's statements on Bakin, which, rather than being dismissive in a straightforward way, act out a tangled love-hate relationship. After deriding Bakin for creating one-dimensional characters embodying moral absolutes, he later revisits *Hakkenden*, this time to comment with great admiration on its prose, which he sees as an ideal mixture of elegant and vernacular language. Much more important, in the section of his essay devoted to the benefits of fiction, Tsubouchi reveals that he has been deeply and personally touched by the very didacticism that he abhorred:

> I have a friend born in Tokyo, whose scholarship ranges from China and Japan to the West. He is known for his upright heart, his sense of honor. Yet he once said to me: "When I read *Hakkenden* and see the communion between the eight warriors I cannot but feel a secret shame." For one such as myself, this experience is all the more frequent. If readers do not have these feelings, it is not so much that the novel lacks the moral power to encourage good and chastise evil, but rather that readers lack the eyes to really read.[44]

For all of his disapproval of Bakin, Tsubouchi turns out to be a moral reader who responds to moral fiction. Despite his championing of the "artistic novel" based upon social observation, Tsubouchi continues to believe that fiction exists, in part, to instruct and enlighten its readers on good and evil. This contradictory position is significant when we consider the later development of Meiji melodramatic fiction. *Shōsetsu shinzui*'s mixed messages contain strains that support Meiji melodrama just as much as they encourage the writing usually considered its offshoots, such as Futabatei Shimei's portrait of an anguished intellectual in *Ukigumo* (Drifting clouds, 1887–89) or the Naturalists's numerous autobiographical texts. Tsubouchi's identification of *ninjō* as the proper content of fiction, his emphasis on portraying social conditions and manners, and his support for fiction's moral benefits can all be read to authorize the melodramatic fiction that would arise in the decade after the publication of his influential criticism.

Tsubouchi's ambivalent responses to Bakin must be seen in light of certain facts about the Meiji literary field. To begin with, he was hardly the only Meiji reader to be moved by Bakin's visions of virtue. Late-Edo fiction continued to be read enthusiastically during the first few decades of Meiji. In fact, during the early 1880s, the arrival of moveable-type printing resulted in the frequent republication of late-Edo fiction; Bakin's works proved to be among the most popular reprints, with *Hakkenden* appearing in seven editions.[45] Early Meiji writers were steeped in the moral aesthetic of *kanzen chōaku*, and they produced stories of their own that led to victories of virtue. In fact, Tsubouchi had been motivated to write his essay by the very proliferation of such fiction in his time. In the introduction to *Shōsetsu shinzui*, he had bemoaned how writers remained mired in "thinking that the encouragement of good and the chastisement of evil was the main aim of fiction, and labored to invent plots that fit within the prefabricated mold of morality."[46] When he attacked *kanzen chōaku* fiction, Tsubouchi was by no means beating a dead fictional paradigm. Many early-Meiji genres were written to fit the *kanzen chōaku* framework, including the enormously popular *dokufumono*, or "poison-women tales," in which femmes fatales met their just desserts after amply demonstrating their carnality and wickedness. It is noteworthy that the plots of these works were set against the background of contemporary social and historical developments. Although the crimes attributed to the poison women were astonishing and sensational, their stories were often serialized under the guise of being "actual records" (*jitsuroku*) in *koshinbun*, the plebeian newspapers of the day. One purported "actual record," Kubota Hikosaku's *Torioi Omatsu kaijō shinwa* (New seaborne tales of Torioi Omatsu, 1878), tells the story of a temptress and extortionist belonging to the abjected *eta* group who negotiates her way through historical changes that reclassified *eta* as "new commoners." There were clear precedents in Meiji, then, for the dualistic vision to be turned upon the social fabric.

Literary developments of the mid-1890s, the period following the Sino-Japanese War, were also important in shaping Meiji melodrama. This era has the appearance of a cornucopia of new genres, as writers and critics announced one new category of fiction after another. One of these genres was the *kannen shōsetsu*, or "concept fiction." The concepts addressed were various—adulterous love, social hypocrisy, and the inhuman demands of duty were some of the issues explored—but what these stories shared was a conviction that Meiji modernity contained contradictions so severe that they could lead only to tragic and spectacular outcomes. Lurid sensationalism was the stock in trade of another genre of the time, known as *hisan shōsetsu*, "misery fiction," or alternately as *shinkoku shōsetsu*, "grim fiction." Writing of this type related the ordeals of protagonists who suffered dire social disadvantages: poverty, indenture to prostitution, mental incapacity, and physical deformity. In these stories, dreadful predicaments led to deadly obsessions and moral transformations; there was a precedent for an embrace of the extreme in the 1890s. One last genre from this period of flowering genres bears mentioning, and this is the *shakai shōsetsu*, or "social fiction," a category clearly inspired by the crisis consciousness regarding *shakai mondai* that roiled the Meiji ideological field. This genre was brought to the attention of the reader by the *Kokumin no tomo* magazine, which in 1896 trumpeted its intention to publish a series addressing social issues:

> Our national destiny has expanded and social phenomena have become ever more varied and complex. It is the duty of novelists to relay accounts of the undersides of such phenomena. This is not a time for writers to rest easy in themes of traditional elegance. Indeed, the recent preoccupation is for writers to fix their gaze on society, human beings, ways of life, and the current era.[47]

The announcement actually failed to call forth very many works, and so the genre turned out to be more important for its aspirations than its achievements. Nonetheless, there was a call for fiction that grappled with social upheaval and investigated its "undersides."

The proliferating genres of the 1890s cannot and should not be set into a linear history leading toward Meiji melodramatic fiction. The works in each of these genres are actually more varied in themes and narrative features than the critical urge toward nomination suggests, and they contain a wide range of potential connections to later writing. In fact, some of these genres have been linked by critics to the eventual rise of Japanese Naturalism, which becomes institutionalized in standard histories as Meiji's most important literary movement. My point here is to note that features such as sensationalism, a fascination with extremes, and a concern for social exigencies were coursing through the literary environment that produced the melodramatic fiction of the turn of the century.

In thinking further about backgrounds and constituents, we cannot ignore the presence of Western melodramatic fiction in Meiji Japan. All four writers of the novels I study were readers of fiction written in English (in Sōseki's case, a broad and incisive reader), and they were familiar with the works of Western writers imbued with the melodramatic imagination. Sōseki, Ozaki Kōyō, and Tokutomi Roka had read Dickens; in fact, Roka claimed that his *Omoide no ki* (Footprints in the snow, 1900–1901) had been directly inspired by *David Copperfield*.[48] By his own admission, Sōseki had read and digested almost all of the works of George Meredith.[49] Japanese scholars have discerned the impact upon *Gubijinsō* of Meredith's *Diana of the Crossways*, a work noted for its use of the melodramatic mode.[50] We cannot, moreover, ignore the many volumes of now forgotten melodramatic popular fiction that entered Japan in an undiscriminating age (Victorian fiction, after all, was contemporary fiction for Meiji writers, with all that this implies about the lack of an established canon). Hori Keiko has recently found close resemblances between *Konjiki yasha* and *Weaker Than a Woman*, a popular novel by Bertha M. Clay.[51] My chapter on Kikuchi Yūhō's *Chikyōdai* explores how another piece of popular fiction, attributed to Clay, was rewritten in a Japanese context. But my general orientation is not to emphasize the "influence" of specific Western works upon Japanese melodramatic fiction. As Martha Vicinus has pointed out, "melodrama can be found in virtually every Victorian writer."[52] The Western melodramatic imagination was all too readily and widely available to the authors I study.

MELODRAMATIC FICTION
PRODUCED AND CONSUMED

One final element of the literary environment needs to be considered, and this is that the works I study were produced for mass consumption by a modern publishing industry. The four novels I take up were all initially serialized in daily newspapers at a time of burgeoning circulations. The turn of the century in Japan witnessed the convergence of a newly literate mass audience produced by universal education and a capitalist publishing industry built on new technologies of print and marketing.[53] The Sino-Japanese War of 1894–95 and the Russo-Japanese War of 1904–5—the modern nation's first foreign wars—fanned a voracious nationalistic news appetite that publishers were all too eager to feed.[54] Papers competed for shares of a growing market, often by aiming their contents at such emerging groups of readers as urban workers, students, and women.[55] The results are apparent in the circulations of some of the newspapers that serialized the novels I study. The *Osaka mainichi shinbun*, which carried *Chikyōdai*, pushed its circulation from 68,475 to 289,699 between 1895 and 1907, and the combined circulations of the two sibling newspapers that simultaneously carried *Gubijinsō*—the *Osaka asahi shinbun* and the *Tokyo asahi shinbun*—rose from 151,597 to 222,717 over the same period.[56]

The salient fact to be kept in mind about the serialization of melodramatic works is that they were meant to attract readers to newspapers in the struggle for increased circulation. Fiction had been a part of Japanese newspapers since the 1870s, when *koshinbun*, the "small newspapers" specializing in local and human-interest stories, carried *tsuzukimono* serials, the docunovels of their day that chronicled in semi-fictionalized form the transgressions of "poisonous women" as well as various other crimes and scandals.[57] The *ōshinbun*, the "big newspapers" that concentrated on political coverage and editorials, had serialized political novels in the 1880s. When these two streams of journalism merged in the 1890s and publishers began to concentrate on increasing circulations and profitability, it led, among other things, "to the serialization of novels by even the most respectable publications."[58] The types of fiction carried in newspapers varied and included translated Western literature, transcriptions of various forms of theater and oral narrative (of which *kōdan* recitations of samurai valor were the most frequent), and detective stories, as well as melodramas. Newspaper fiction achieved what Takagi Takeo calls its "initial peak" with the blockbuster publication of Ozaki Kōyō's *Konjiki yasha* in 1897–1903.[59] Although other forms of narrative, particularly *kōdan*, continued to be carried in newspapers, melodramatic novels addressing contemporary social issues became the dominant and most visible segment in newspaper fiction after *Konjiki yasha*'s enormous success. Newspapers jockeyed to recruit noteworthy writers; in 1907 the *Asahi* newspapers created a sensation by luring Natsume

Sōseki away from his prestigious teaching post at Tokyo Imperial University and installing him as a well-paid house writer whose first serialization was *Gubijinsō*. This kind of recruitment happened only because fiction helped to sell newspapers.

The cultural impact of Meiji melodramatic novels far exceeded their initial publication in daily newspapers, for they were quickly put out in book versions, sometimes while later chapters were still being serialized. Three of the works studied here—*Konjiki yasha, Chikyōdai,* and *Gubijinsō*—were published in book form by Shun'yōdō, the leading literary publisher of the time. The fourth, *Hototogisu,* became one of the runaway bestsellers of the Meiji period when it was put out by Min'yūsha, the publisher of the *Kokumin shinbun,* in which it was first serialized. After its initial release in 1900, the book went through a hundred printings by 1909. By 1927, there were 192 printings, which added up to some 500,000 copies.[60]

These kinds of sales records were related to the fact that melodramatic fiction appeared before there was a clear demarcation between popular fiction and high-culture art fiction. One of the deans of modern Japanese literary studies, Katsumoto Sei'ichirō, has said that "for the concept of popular literature to become apparent, there needs to be a split in the concept of literature."[61] Japanese literary historians generally hold that this sort of split did not appear until the end of the period that I study, when, beginning around 1907, Japanese Naturalism established itself as a school of self-consciously serious art fiction. Before then, fiction was a commercial undertaking, more or less by definition. Without a clear demarcation between high and low fiction, readers of both genders and various social backgrounds read stories in what was—in comparison to later, more segmented times—a broad, shared reading culture. One indication of such a readership appears in a later statement on *Konjiki yasha* by Ozaki Kōyō's disciple, Izumi Kyōka, who recalled that "women old and young, girls with their hair parted in the middle, and retired gentlemen with tortoiseshell spectacles all fought to be the first to pore over and recite the installments delivered in the morning editions of the *Yomiuri shinbun.*"[62] Another indication of a relatively unsegmented literary culture is that the author of *Chikyōdai,* Kikuchi Yūhō, now largely forgotten and considered a hack writer by the few literary historians who take up his work, was published by the same publishers as Ozaki Kōyō, a literary lion of his time, and Natsume Sōseki, who now occupies the dead center of the canon, though most assuredly not because of *Gubijinsō*. In the decades bracketing the turn of the century, all three were writing works deemed suitable for wide dissemination by a major commercial publishing house. Meiji melodramatic fiction was consumed by an overarching reading public of a sort that would begin to disappear shortly afterward. Such fiction maintained its appeal even as the literary market became more divided. *Konjiki yasha* went through 189 printings when it was republished during the Taisho period, the heyday of the autobiographical high-culture fiction of *shishōsetu* (personal fiction).[63]

Moreover, the audience affected by melodramatic fiction went well beyond the reading public. Like *Uncle Tom's Cabin*, which Henry James once said was less a book than a "wonderful 'leaping' fish" jumping from one cultural medium to another,[64] Meiji melodramatic fiction quickly leapt into other forms of cultural presentation. *Konjiki yasha* provides a good example. As Seki Hajime has shown in his groundbreaking study of the incarnations of this story, theatrical adaptations began to appear very quickly, some even while the novel was still being serialized.[65] All of these adaptations were in the *shinpa* mode, combining kabuki conventions of staging and acting with elements of Western theatrical realism in a brew that closely resembled Western theatrical melodrama.[66] There were five stage versions of *Konjiki yasha* already by 1903, and many more followed as the story became an enduring *shinpa* favorite. Artists, too, found *Konjiki yasha* a sympathetic subject and published pictorial retellings toward the end of the Meiji period.[67] There were also repeated efforts to "translate" *Konjiki yasha* into narrative poetry, with at least six poetic versions extant.[68] When moviemaking took hold in Japan, one of the *shinpa* versions was quickly filmed in 1911.[69] Nineteen film versions of *Konjiki yasha* followed, with the last being produced in 1954. This kind of afterlife, in which texts were adapted in various genres and media, was not unusual for the most popular works of Meiji melodramatic fiction; a similar, if not quite so extensive, record can be traced for the other works I take up. The Meiji melodramatic mode unfolded not in singular and stable texts, but rather in fluid, multiple cultural products continually transformed and recycled in response to the desires of audiences, the demands of various media, and the dictates of a capitalist entertainment industry. Within the limits of this study, I cannot address how melodramatic fiction was transformed to meet generic, commercial, ideological, and historical contingencies—there is still much work to be done to follow up on the implications of Seki's admirable study. But what I would like to note is that, because of a modern publishing industry and the translation of melodramatic fiction to other forms, the texts I study had a social penetration unequaled by anything written in Japan before this time and perhaps unparalleled by anything else published in Japan before World War II.

What I call Meiji melodramatic fiction was an immense cultural phenomenon whose audience comprised both men and women, crossed class and regional barriers, and included generations of readers. Melodrama's doomed efforts to find firm moral bearings in an uncertain world, to clearly define right and wrong in a way that answered sentiment, was an endeavor that resonated through the modern Japanese experience.

THE FAMILY IN MEIJI IDEOLOGY

The moral field of force with which I am primarily concerned involves the family. Meiji melodramatic fiction abounds with clashes between family and love, dastardly deceptions that threaten lineages, contested inheritances, and rival courtships. Men and women flout or fulfill the family roles demanded by their genders. These enactments are, in the melodramatic manner, played out as emotionally wrenching encounters with moral choice. The emphasis upon families in Meiji melodrama can be partially explained by the prominence of families in melodrama generally. Critics writing about Western melodramatic theater, fiction, and film invariably comment upon the thematization of family as a hallmark of the mode.[70] This is not surprising since the family readily lends itself to portrayals that depend on the simultaneous engagement of morality and sentiment. In Meiji melodramatic fiction, however, this general tendency was magnified by the presence of a powerful ideological movement, initiated and supported by ideologues allied with the state, that sought to construct the family as the moral foundation of the nation. Meiji melodramatists were responding to an ideological field in which the family had already been relentlessly and repeatedly portrayed as an institutional bulwark of morality.

The family was recruited to serve this purpose amidst the general crisis consciousness of the 1890s, which saw "social problems" rending the fabric of the nation. If modernity had brought the social dislocations attendant upon industrialization and urbanization, as well as the ideological challenges posed by such new concepts as popular rights, individualism, and socialism, then the "traditional" family could be used as a force for order, an institution for the proper location and training of citizens within the national hierarchy. In addition to the generalized sense of crisis, however, the family was brought to the attention of ideologues by a more specific perception that the family itself was being endangered by the forces of modernization.[71] The family was being torn apart by the very forces whose impacts it was supposed to help contain—by industrialization, urbanization, social mobility, and new ideas about individual rights. By 1906 a young Yanagita Kunio, who was then a director of the National Agricultural Association, was complaining that heavy out-migration was resulting in farm families committing "domicide," a neologism signifying the killing of families.[72] The very institution that ideologues wanted to use as a line of defense was itself under attack.

Ie-seido (the *ie* system) and *kazoku kokka kan* (the family-state concept) are the terms used by historians to retroactively refer to the constellation of ideas regarding the family developed in the 1890s by state-aligned ideologues such as Hozumi Yatsuka and Inoue Tetsujirō.[73] The Meiji iteration of the *ie* and its nationalistic and authoritarian application in the *kazoku kokka* cannot be disentangled, because the two developed in contiguous, mutually dependant circumstances. The ideological construction of the *ie* would not have been articulated in the way it was without the presence of statist and authoritarian demands, and the *kazoku kokka* could not have been synthesized without reference to the *ie* as the "traditional" form of family in Japan. For clarity, however, there is some utility to discussing these concepts sequentially.

In this study, I am most interested in how melodramatic fiction responds to the concept of *ie* as it was developed by Meiji ideologues.[74] The focus is not so much the *ie* as it operated historically as a structure for family organization, or even as a set of lived relations in the Meiji period, but rather the ideological construction of the *ie* and the state's tying of ideology to juridical practice through the Meiji Civil Code of 1898.[75] Kawashima Takeyoshi, one of the first postwar analysts of the *ie*, provides a threefold definition that serves as a useful framework.[76] First, he notes that the *ie* is constituted as a "lineage group that has nothing to do with domicile, involving a belief in the continuity of its identity despite changes in its membership through deaths, births, and marriages."[77] This characteristic—the *ie*'s status as a diachronic entity persisting through generational replacements—played a central part in the Meiji definition of the *ie* and is prominently noted by virtually every scholar who has written on the subject. It is the most obvious feature that distinguishes the *ie* from the synchronous household and the nuclear family. Patrilineality through male primogeniture is the form of descent in the *ie*, which is structured as a stem family, in which the male successor continues the family line together with his wife, while younger males are spun out into branch families and female siblings are married away. Kawashima is careful to point out that descent is achieved not only through birth lineage but also through the "fictive blood lineage" (*giseiteki kettō*) established through adoptions; his emphasis here is worth noting because, in contrast to others who have viewed the *ie* as a corporate rather than a lineage group, he recognizes that adoption in the *ie* functions to support rather than supplant lineage. The patrilineal *ie* is buttressed, according to Kawashima, by a certain consciousness that includes a powerful respect for the continuity of the male line and an attendant devaluing of women in general and non-reproductive women in particular, a belief in the unity of ancestors and descendants, the valorization of tradition, the privileging of the *ie* over the individual, and the ranking of people outside the family according to the status of the *ie* to which they belong. It is implicit in Kawashima's definition that ancestor worship, embedded in both Japanese Buddhism and Shintoism, reinforces the diachronic qualities of the *ie*. The ideologues of the *ie* system were more explicit about the prominence of ancestor worship in their thinking: Hozumi Yatsuka, an important legal theorist for the emperor system who influenced the drafting of the Meiji Civil Code, famously declared in 1891 that "Our country is a country of ancestor worship. It is a land of the *ie* system. All power, all law is born in the *ie*."[78]

The second part of Kawashima's definition points out that each *ie* has a specifically appointed househead or *koshu*, who has the right to command and expect obedience from other members of the family. The *ie* organizes a hierarchy of power based upon gender and seniority. Because the *koshu* was nearly always male, this hierarchy placed men over women, but the *ie* also placed younger males under the control of the househead. Kawashima argues that the compliance of family members was gained through using a myriad of "tools," among them the training of children in *ie* ideology, the underscoring of hierarchy in family life, the control of family property, and an emphasis upon upholding the "face" of the family head. We will later see how the state's moral education programs and the Meiji Civil Code forged some of these "tools." For now, we should note that the Meiji ideologues themselves were frankly approving of the authoritarian aspects of the *ie*. Hozumi Yatsuka again provides a ready example:

> When children are young, the father is clearly superior both in terms of intellect and physical strength. This is usually the case, no matter who the father is. It is the most clearly discernible standard by which superiority and inferiority are naturally divided. This is to say that the standard has to do with a relationship of power, and that power is the logic involved in issuing a command and compelling obedience. I believe that this is where the relationship of command and obedience is taught and where it grows. Thus the veneration of parents is a veneration of power.[79]

This bald and chilling view of family relations shows why the patriarchal model of the family was so attractive to those who favored an authoritarian state.

The final element in Kawashima's view of the *ie* considers the dynamics made possible through the combination of a belief in lineage and the power relations of patriarchy. This combination "sacralizes the power of the family head, supports it through the power of tradition, and makes relations of power and subordination outwardly invisible, or outwardly acceptable."[80] Kawashima's insight here is that the *ie* functions as ideology by making markedly unequal relations of power seem inevitable and right, by wreathing them in the mists of tradition and lineage.

The issue of "tradition" requires some additional comment because the Meiji ideologues themselves represented the *ie* as a model of the family inherited from ages past. In their thinking, the *ie* needed to be preserved at all cost because it was *the* essential and transhistorical model of the Japanese family, whose rules had applied to all Japanese since time immemorial. This ideological view has been subjected to an evolving series of scholarly interventions. The earlier trend was to emphasize the roots of the *ie* in the past, perhaps because the interest of scholars working in the immediate postwar period was to identify the "feudal" and atavistic elements of a model of family that had been mobilized in the war and thus needed to be repudiated after the defeat.[81] The first scholars to critically engage Japanese family ideology, including Kawashima, pointed out that the *ie* of the Meiji period was an attempt to sustain the patriarchal and patrilineal structure of samurai families of the Tokugawa period. They further argued that the ideology of the *ie* drew its key concepts, including that of filial piety, from Tokugawa Confucianism. Even a somewhat later scholar such as Itō Mikiharu offers a variation on this position when he asserts that, whatever its

origins, *ie* ideology found acceptance in Meiji Japan because the popu-
lace was intimately familiar with notions of lineage and filial piety.[82] What
should be recognized, however, is that, even at the start of this stream of
argument, some scholars were very much aware that Meiji *ie* ideology was
a construction with a distinct historicity. Kawashima, for example, argued
that the *ie* model had historically *not* applied to the vast majority of Japanese.[83] He stresses that patriarchy was not nearly so absolute in premodern
commoner and farmer families. And he emphasizes that male primogeniture had not been the universal model of inheritance for all of Japan in
the years before Meiji; there were, in fact, regions where commoners and
farmers practiced the division of family holdings or sole inheritance by
the *youngest* son.[84] The Meiji model of the *ie*, then, had been imposed
upon a familial field that displayed marked regional and status-demarcated
variations. To recognize that Meiji ideologues sought to universally install a
samurai model of family at a time when samurai status had been abolished
is to already be aware of the enormous endeavor involved in representing
the *ie* as the essential form of family for Japan.

In the last ten years, scholars have come to increasingly stress this direction of argument. Muta Kazue has argued that the Meiji *ie* was distinct
from any prior version of the *ie* in being free from feudal obligations or
entanglements with a larger extended family; it was thus specifically designed to function as a direct component of a nation-state and participate
independently in a capitalist economy.[85] For Muta, the *ie* is Japan's version
of the "modern family." Ueno Chizuko, too, argues for the *ie*'s modernity
and, drawing upon Eric Hobsbawm's ideas on the "invention of tradition,"
asserts that the *ie*'s purported ties to the past are largely imagined:

> Many historians have regarded the *ie* as a "remnant of feudalism" without
> investigating its historical origins. In this sense, they themselves can be said
> to be entrapped within *ie* ideology. This is so because ideology functions to
> conceal its own origins and to naturalize its own existence. Far from decon-
> structing the ideology of the times in which they live, they have lent a hand
> to the strengthening of ideology by seeing the *ie* as "tradition." . . . But there
> is a diversity to tradition depending upon region or class, and we must be
> aware that, at every change in its context, history has continually worked
> to redefine as "tradition" cultural elements—taken from within the diverse
> matrix of culture—that are appropriate for the age. Thus what has lived on
> as "tradition" has experienced change in accordance with the times. "Tradi-
> tion that transcends its time" does not exist. All we have is ideology naming
> certain things "tradition" and concealing its origins.[86]

The emphasis now is on the energetic fabrication involved in the Meiji ideologues' representation of the *ie*. Whatever the historical derivation of the constituent elements of the *ie*, we cannot but acknowledge the enormous inventiveness involved in recruiting these elements for modern ideological needs. The *ie* was part of the grand Meiji experiment of building a national identity out of a mélange of cultural components creatively separated from—yet made to gesture toward—their original contexts. It served the interests of a state seeking to standardize and rationalize a form of family that would serve its ends.

The ingenuity of Meiji ideologues was most prominently on display in *kazoku kokka* ideology, which joined the *ie* with the state. This alignment was represented through a series of overlapping analogies.[87] To begin with, the family was bound to the nation in a synecdochic relationship. It was regarded as the nation's smallest constituent unit, which represented in microcosm the power relations within the state. The family ruled by its patriarch operated on the same principles as the nation ruled by the emperor; the observance of hierarchy and the enactment of proper roles, based upon position and gender, were paramount in each. An often-stated component of the master analogy was the idea that the relationship of subject to emperor mirrored the relationship of son to father. This identification became so commonplace that the ruling principles of the two relationships in Confucian ideology, respectively *chū* (loyalty) and *kō* (filial piety), were, despite their manifest differences, collapsed into the frequently encountered compound principle of *chūkō*. The *ie*'s investment in lineage was also inscribed into the national framework through emphasis upon the continuity of the imperial line; if each *ie* was important for its existence through time, then the imperial family (and, by extension, the nation) was owed veneration because it was the oldest lineage, unbroken through the ages. This assertion was frequently augmented with the observation that the imperial family was a kind of main family line, to which all other Japanese *ie* were branch families. The most literal readings of lineage saw the Japanese people as all sharing a common ancestor in the Sun Goddess; thus the nation actually was a family, a gigantic *ie* with its origins in the mythical past proceeding through the generations into the future.

Although variants of such ideas had been present in Japanese thought well before the Meiji era, it was in the 1890s, the period Carol Gluck associates with the swelling of an "ideological chorus,"[88] that they coalesced into the ideological and juridical definition of the *kazoku kokka*. This decade was framed by the promulgation of the Imperial Rescript on Education in 1890 and the enactment of the Meiji Civil Code in 1898. The Imperial Rescript was, as Gluck has argued, a compromise document that could be read in many ways,[89] and its statements about the family—which included injunctions regarding filiality toward parents, affection between siblings, and harmony between husbands and wives—were merely vague repetitions of commonplace notions. But when Inoue Tetsujirō, a Tokyo Imperial University professor and a government ideologue, wrote a quasi-official commentary on the Rescript at the invitation of the Ministry of Education, such homilies took on a specificity that displayed a developed vision of the *kazoku kokka*.

> The emperor to his subjects is like a father and mother to their offspring. Which is to say that a country is an expansion of the family and that for a ruler to direct and command his subjects is not at all different from parents giving compassionate guidance to their children. Thus, now that his majesty, our emperor, speaks to us as his subjects, we his subjects must all listen respectfully and attentively, with the feelings of children toward a strict father or a loving mother.[90]

A number of the overlapping analogies used to define the *kazoku kokka* are evident here: the nation is a family expanded, the ruler is a parent and subjects are children, and the emperor is due the feelings of filial piety owed a parent.

Similar expressions found their way into various publications directed at the citizenry, foremost among them school ethics textbooks. A primary level *shūshin* (moral education) textbook approved for use the very year of the Rescript, contained the following:

> The emperor . . . in the way he troubles his soul over the people is no different from a father who worries over his children, never letting them out of his thoughts. . . . We must always adore him, as though thinking of a distant father. . . . Do not forget this feeling, not even for a moment.[91]

The analogy of the emperor to a parent has been restated for pedagogical effect with an emphasis upon the affective duties of the child. Another volume in the same series promotes the lineage-based view of the nation as a single family:

> Our imperial family constitutes for ourselves, the people, the ancestral main line of our families, and just as the feelings between father and children are

natural, the great bonds between ruler and subject originate in *nature*. Thus the depths of loyalty we feel toward his majesty is a special *natural* trait possessed by the Japanese people.[92]

The repeated emphasis on the "natural" in this passage confirms Anne McClintock's observation that the "family trope . . . offers a 'natural' figure for sanctioning national *hierarchy* within a putative organic *unity* of interests."[93] The unifying rhetoric of lineage allows the hierarchy of emperor and subject to be read as innate and essential, and indeed as a key component of Japanese national identity. Loyalty to the emperor is removed from the specific historical moment of Meiji and turned into something as natural and eternal as the family. What this assertion elides is that the particular model of the family to which it refers, the *ie*, was one specifically supported by the Meiji state and thus historically coeval with the modern emperor system.

The state's most decisive action regarding the family occurred when the Meiji Civil Code was enacted after long debate in 1898. An earlier civil code, based on French law and premised on the individual as the unit for the conduct of civil law, had been promulgated in 1890. But it had been withdrawn before enactment when it drew heavy fire from conservatives led by Hozumi Yatsuka, who considered the emphasis upon the individual inimical to the nation's investment in family. Hozumi famously coined the battle cry, "the Civil Code appears, and loyalty and filiality disappear" (*minpō idete, chūkō horobu*).[94] The revised Civil Code that was finally enacted in 1898 treated the *ie*, rather than the individual, as the key unit in civil law. Under its provisions, every Japanese was required to belong to an *ie*, even if it comprised only himself or herself, as it might in the case of an orphan. The Civil Code juridically established the position of *koshu*, or *ie* headship, and granted the head of an *ie* wide-ranging powers over subordinate members of the family, including the right to approve marriages or adoptions, the authority to determine where family members lived, and the capacity to control family property. It encoded elaborate rules of succession and inheritance, based on male primogeniture but designed to respond to various contingencies in order to ensure continuity of the *ie*. Both marriage and adoption were defined as legal relationships within the *ie* framework. The Civil Code functioned to standardize and rationalize—and to bring under state control—what had largely been determined by custom and had differed according to status and region. That the *ie* was meant to be a component of the nation was made clear in the stipulation that only a Japanese citizen could hold *ie* headship. With the Civil Code's enactment, the Meiji state had achieved the juridical means to enforce a model of the family that served the nation.

FICTIVE FAMILIES AND
MELODRAMATIC ALTERNATIVES

In the scholarly writing about the "family-state," there is a continuing insistence on its "fictive" nature. Irokawa Daikichi, for example, writes that the "only way the communal character of the 'family' can be extended beyond itself is as a 'fiction.'"[95] And Ishida Takeshi observes that: "Submission to the househead did not end in itself, but became submission to landowners through its expansion in the form of *fictive* filiation. This connection, moreover, led to absorption into the village collective, where landlords were the dominant power, and ultimately to submission to the nation-state."[96] *Gisei*, the Japanese term used by these scholars, generally refers to legal fictions, where a supposition is accepted as fact for legal purposes. But it is clear that these commentators are using the term beyond its narrow legal definitions. The scholar who makes this clearest is Kawashima, who deliberately glosses *gisei* with the English word "fiction":

> Let me quickly define the meaning of "fiction." "Fiction" refers to a situation where two things (A and B) are clearly not the same, but are viewed as similar for certain purposes and within certain limits. Fictions are frequently employed in law, but they are also often used in actual social life. In particular, the fiction of family relations is applied to many kinds of social relations in Japan, beginning at the top with the formation viewing the emperor as the family head of the nation and leading at the bottom to formations organizing yakuza and street vendors into "families" and "kin" (I call this the family-based structuring [*kazokuteki kōsei*] of Japanese society). It is no exaggeration to say that this constitutes the backbone of Japanese behavioral patterns.[97]

Kawashima, then, removes the notion of *gisei* from narrow legal definitions and places it in the realm of what anthropologists would call "fictive kinships," relationships (such as the assigning of godparents or the swearing of blood brotherhoods) in which the terminology and the affective bonds of kinship are extended to those who are technically not kin. In making such an observation, Kawashima follows the work of pioneering ethnologists such as Yanagita Kunio and Aruga Kizaemon, who observed the prevalence of hierarchical relationships expressed in the quasi-filial terms of *oyako nari*.[98] His point is that the ideological construction of the *kazoku kokka* must be seen in the context of social practices of fictive kinship that permeate discourse and social organization in Japan. From this perspective, Meiji family-state ideology has much in common with *iemoto* performance lineages in Japanese music and the patterns of loyalty in yakuza gangs.

In this book, I am expanding the concept of "fictive families" and using it in a double sense. The families I study live within fictional narratives; they are fictive because they are imaginary. But the agency of fiction is employed in Meiji melodramatic writing to generate *alternative families*—families that are not sanctioned by conventional notions of family relations or by the ideological complex of the *ie* and the "family-state." Meiji melodramatic novels are about "fictive families" because they repeatedly dramatize situations in which the affect and vocabulary of family are transferred to relations that do not constitute "family" in any biological or legal sense. This book argues that these fictive families are constructed in response to the pressures and challenges of modernity. Although the Meiji state may have conceived its version of the family, the *ie*, as a bulwark against the social dislocations of the era, writers of the time created, with an impressive fecundity of imagination, other versions of the family reflecting and responding to these very social dislocations. The "cultural work" of Meiji melodramatic fiction involved using the trope of family to imagine the myriad and shifting ways in which human beings could be connected in a modern era.

The dynamic I analyze in my texts repeats the transition from *filiation* to *affiliation* that Edward Said finds in numerous examples of late-nineteenth- and early-twentieth-century Western literature. In Said's conception, this transition is accomplished through a three-part pattern. The pattern begins with an anxiety over family continuity linked to larger social processes: "The failure of the generative impulse—the failure of the capacity to produce or generate children—is portrayed in such a way as to stand for a general condition afflicting society and culture together."[99] The disruptions of modernity erupt in fiction as interruptions of biological filiation. This failure of family continuity can be stated not only from the parent's position but from the child's as well, for Said mentions "orphaned children" as part of his schema. The second part of the pattern, following from the first, involves

the pressure to produce new and different ways of conceiving human relationships. For if biological reproduction is either too difficult or unpleasant, is there some other way by which men and women can create social bonds between each other that would substitute for those ties that connect members of the same family across generations?[100]

Said's term for this kind of alternate social connection is *horizontal affiliation*. The turn from filiation to affiliation is completed in a third step, which manifests "the deliberately explicit goal of using that new order to reinstate vestiges of the kind of authority associated in the past with filiative order."[101] The pattern is completed, then, with a kind of "restored authority."[102]

When I explore *filiation* and *affiliation*, I use the former to mean biological descent within a family and the latter a constructed social bond. By using these terms, however, I hope to retain Said's insight that there is an "echo" between the words *filiation* and *affiliation*. When affiliation works to restore authority in the third part of Said's schema, it functions as a *re-presentation* of the filiative order: "Filiation gives birth to affiliation. Affiliation becomes a form of representing the filiative processes to be found in nature, although affiliation takes validated nonbiological social and cultural forms."[103] Affiliation, then, involves the discourse, the affects, and the hierarchies of biological families. It resembles the Japanese social practice of fictive families identified by Kawashima and others. We might reasonably expect that the dynamics of modern affiliation are authorized in Japan by preexisting paradigms and practices.

Elements of Said's three-part pattern repeatedly emerge in the texts I study. Anxieties about the continuity of the biological family—anxieties over paternity and filiality—typically initiate the plot in Meiji melodramatic fiction. Compromised and displaced in numerous ways, the fathers in this kind of writing are a far cry from the steadfast father-househeads imagined in Meiji family ideology. They are either dead (Kan'ichi's father in *Konjiki yasha*, Kōno and Fujio's father and Ono's father in *Gubijinsō*), separated from their offspring (the marquis in *Chikyōdai*), unfit for the paternal role because morally compromised (Shigizawa in *Konjiki yasha*), or characterized by a combination of these factors (Takeo's father in *Hototogisu* is both dead and tainted by the Meiji elite's greed for money). As a result, the fact or the rhetoric of orphanage arises repeatedly in these works. The young adults who are the protagonists often feel lost, abandoned, or betrayed to the point of desperation. Yet the separation of these characters from biological filiation is also a source of opportunity, for orphanage, either actual or metaphorical, launches a search for affiliations figured as alternative families.

This movement of the plot in Meiji melodramatic fiction resonates not only with Said's schema but also with the problems of paternity that Peter Brooks identifies as a central concern of modern Western fiction: "Paternity is a dominant issue within the great tradition of the nineteenth-century novel (extending well into the twentieth century), a principal embodiment of its concern with authority, legitimacy, the conflict of generations and the transmission of wisdom."[104] Brooks finds this engagement present in works—including *Le Rouge et le noir*, *Le Père Goriot*, *Frankenstein*, *Great Expectations*, and *The Brothers Karamazov*—occupied with what he calls the "key problem of transmission":

> the process by which the young protagonist of the nineteenth-century novel discovers his choices of interpretation and action in relation to a number of older figures of wisdom and authority who are rarely biological fathers—a situation that the novel often ensures by making the son an orphan, or by killing off or otherwise occulting the biological father before the text brings to maturity its dominant alternatives. The son then most often has a choice among possible fathers from whom to inherit, and in the choosing—which may entail a succession of selections and rejections—he plays out his career of initiation into a society and into history, comes to define his own authority in the interpretation and use of social (and textual) codes.[105]

Like the characters in the works discussed by Brooks, the young male protagonists of Meiji melodramatic fiction often attempt to discover their place in the world and in history by allying themselves with an alternative father—sometimes a succession of alternative fathers. To the extent that this kind of fiction is melodramatic, the candidates for fathers illuminate points in a moral universe.

Adoption is the plot element most often used to resolve issues of paternity and filiality. The frequency of fictional adoptions of various kinds is especially significant because orthodox *ie* ideology reserved a prominent place for adoption as a means of allowing the all-important continuance of the family line when nature did not provide a proper successor. In the Meiji Civil Code of 1898, nearly as much attention was devoted to regulating adoption as to codifying marriage, another important ingredient of *ie* continuation (in fact, the Civil Code uses the term *engumi*, literally the "joining of bonds," to refer to both kinds of unions). A key article, located near the beginning of the code's section on family law, stated: "As between an adopted child and the adoptive parents and the latter's blood-relatives, the same relationship as between blood-relatives arises as from the day of adoption."[106] This provision tacitly recognizes blood relations as the constituting force in the *ie*, but it also establishes adoption as functionally duplicating them. Another article makes clear that provisions of this sort were not motivated solely by the wish to protect adoptive children: "After an adopted child has become head of the house his (her) adoption may no longer be dissolved."[107] The indisputable purpose here is to insure *ie* continuity by preventing an adopted successor from bolting the headship of an *ie*. The Civil Code's effort to make adoption a means of *ie* perpetuation is most clearly evident in the many articles designed to juridically recognize and govern *mukoyōshi* or "adopted-husband" marriages.[108] These provisions were used by sonless families to adopt male successors who were simultaneously married to a family daughter. The Civil Code's heavy investment in adoption is summarized by Hozumi Nobushige, Yatsuka's older brother and Japan's first doctor of laws, who wrote in 1912 that "adoption may be regarded as the corner-stone of Family Law. Without it, the continuity of the House, upon which rests the perpetuation of ancestor-worship, cannot be maintained."[109]

Meiji melodramatic fiction contains legally constituted adoptions that would warm the hearts of those who framed the Civil Code. But the far greater preponderance of "adoptions" in the texts I study takes place outside of official and juridical boundaries. These adoptions, consummated as fictive kinships of various sorts, produce alternative families that testify to both the diversity of human needs and the flexibility of interpersonal bonds. Such families demonstrate the second step of Said's pattern, where people are joined "under pressure to form new and different kinds of human relationships." In *Hototogisu*, a young naval officer, devastated by the death of his wife and the domestic aridity of the *ie* that he heads, finds solace by establishing a bond with his former father-in-law, an army general. This connection, figured as that between a father and a son, brings together two grieving men—but it also produces an alternative family of men who fight in the service of the empire. The male protagonist of *Konjiki yasha*, an orphan, is initially slated to assume the headship of a family planning to adopt him and have him marry their only daughter. When this *mukoyōshi* adoption is ruined by the daughter's decision to marry a richer man, the protagonist too throws himself into the pursuit of filthy lucre by becoming a moneylender. He does this by forming an affiliation with an established usurer, an affiliation that is explicitly described in familial terms. Toward the end of this unfinished work, the protagonist enters yet another alternative family when he rescues and becomes a father-figure to a young couple on the verge of a love suicide. His circuitous course through a mercenary world is figured as a journey through a series of constructed families.

These examples bear out the third step in Said's pattern, where an affiliation becomes the means of *re-presenting* filiation. Male protagonists form new bonds reflecting the exigencies of a modernizing culture, but they do so in ways that mobilize the vocabulary and the emotional weight of family. In so doing, these new families reinstate the hierarchy of the parent-child relationship.

The narrative plot I have been describing shows the complex and contradictory stance of Meiji melodrama's affiliative families vis-à-vis *ie* ideology. On the one hand, melodramatic fiction generates countless options to filiation. It undercuts the claims to universality of the model of family supported by Meiji ideologues and juridically empowered by the Meiji Civil Code. Melodrama's families acknowledge the diverse human connections forged amidst social transformations. On the other hand, by employing the rhetoric of adoption, a practice encouraged by the state for the purposes of family continuity, melodrama's fictive families simultaneously repeat as well as subvert family ideology. Instead of taking egalitarian forms, the affiliations in these stories create new hierarchies. Moreover, as we see in the example of *Hototogisu*, which ends up investing the affect of family in a relationship between imperial soldiers, the new families of melodrama can serve nationalist ends. Given these dynamics, it is impossible either to condemn Meiji melodramatic fiction's complicity with state ideology or celebrate its resistance. Written in an era suffused with discussions of *ie* ideology, the texts I study cannot exist outside of the prevailing discourse. Yet, by using the discourse of family in unconventional ways, they show that, if the family is inescapable, it could be recycled in radically altered versions. If melodrama in general is a mode marked by ideological contradiction, one of the specific roots for ideological contradiction in Meiji melodramatic fiction lies in its tangled relationship with family ideology.

A deeper undercurrent in this relationship becomes apparent when we more closely examine the discourse of adoption in Meiji fiction. Despite its support by the state, adoption has a way of undercutting essentialist views of family structure because, as a practice, it is situated precisely at a point of anxiety created by the lack of biological filiation. It exists where culture must fill in for nature. Unlike nature, which can claim to be ruled by a set of biological laws, culture is a collection of endlessly malleable and historically contingent beliefs. If alternative versions of adoptions can be discursively produced in fiction, does this not call attention to the discursive character of official adoptions and, by extension, the *ie*? Adoption can highlight ways in which all kinds of families are fictive.

An observation from a contemporary commentator demonstrates how this was especially true for the Meiji family. In a 1905 publication, the British Japanologist Basil Hall Chamberlain had the following to say about the make-up of the Japanese family:

> It is strange, but true, that you may often go into a Japanese family and find half-a-dozen persons calling each other parent and child, brother and sister, uncle and nephew, and yet being really either no blood relations at all, or else relations in quite different degrees from those conventionally assumed. . . . Though genealogies are carefully kept, they mean nothing, at least from a scientific point of view—so universal is the practice of adoption, from the top of society to the bottom. This it is which explains such apparent anomalies as a distinguished painter, potter, actor, or what not, almost always having a son distinguished in the same line:—he has simply adopted his best pupil. It also explains the fact of Japanese families not dying out.[110]

Chamberlain affirms that adoption works in the interests of family continuity. But what a family it is! The Japanese family he describes is almost devoid of biological kinship, being held together by adoptive bonds. Furthermore, when Chamberlain begins to talk about the families of painters, potters, and actors, it becomes clear that there is no real dividing line here between legally constituted *ie* and those affiliative relationships given filiative form in artistic lineages.[111] To a keen contemporary observer, there is no distinction between juridically recognized *ie* and fictive kinships. Families, both juridically approved and fictive, exist in a continuum conditioned by the prevalence of adoption—and hence of cultural construction. Melodramatic fiction's alternative families, then, call attention to this phenomenon, where the official *ie* is but one model in a world crowded with various kinds of families created to meet social needs.

GENDER, STATUS INCONSISTENCY,
AND THE FICTIVE FAMILY

In talking about filiation and affiliation, we have been speaking largely of fathers and sons, that is, of men. This is the prevailing tendency among male critics, including Said and Brooks. We might, then, legitimately ask how fictive families respond to pressures placed upon women by modernity. A simple answer would be that melodrama's alternative families do not work as well for women as they do for men. But this does not do justice to the range or the prominence of female fictive families in Meiji melodramatic fiction. In *Chikyōdai*, for example, a woman's desire for upward mobility possesses her, in an action both thrilling and dastardly, to "adopt" a family in keeping with her self-image. In the process, the novel raises the possibilities of a "milk lineage," an alternate line of descent based upon female nurturance rather than male "blood." *Gubijinsō* portrays a mother and a daughter attempting to use the *mukoyōshi* institution to displace the rightful male heir of an *ie* and establish another kind of family ruled by female power. But these alternative families ultimately fail to provide the advantageous connections, the emotional rewards, or the social mobility that male characters achieve through their affiliations.

The vexed relations of women to alternative families in Meiji fiction has partly to do with the fact that, for young women, marriage rather than adoption was the most obvious means of inter-family and social mobility.[112] Social redefinitions through marriage, however, were different in a number of key ways from male adoptions, both official and unofficial. This comparison is facilitated in Meiji melodramatic fiction because the protagonists in these works tend to be young men and women who are either on the verge of marriage or who have very recently married. Questions regarding the choice of marriage partners repeatedly occur alongside the trope of adoption. These contexts reveal that, although women might hope to gain social advantages through marriage, they remain stuck in the gender hierarchy. Women are subject to male power whether they are in their father's house or their husband's. Miya's decision to wed the wealthy Tomiyama in *Konjiki yasha* demythologizes upward marriage by showing that a woman who commodifies her beauty on the marriage market ultimately ends up treated as sexual chattel. The assymetries of gender are powerfully exposed in *Gubijinsō*, where Fujio is killed because of her refusal to be trafficked between men for the purposes of marriage. The force of patriarchy also intrudes when a woman is married to a kindhearted man; in *Hototogisu*, Namiko and Takeo's struggle to form a *katei*, a model of family defined by domestic love, briefly puts forward an alternative to the *ie*, but it is quickly overwhelmed when Namiko comes down with a disease that threatens the male lineage of her husband's family. These portrayals show that the gender hierarchies of heterosexual marriage afford less social flexibility than male adoption.

Another aspect of the troubled relationship of women to alternative families is that they tend to function, within melodramatic fiction, as threats to social order. The moral crises in Meiji melodramas are commonly precipitated by women. This is true even when they are virtuous, like Namiko in *Hototogisu*, the wifely paragon who endangers the continuity of her husband's family by contracting tuberculosis. But, much more often, women end up on the side of villainy in a dualistic moral universe. And they frequently do so by embodying desires and sentiments associated with modernity. The mercenary Miya of *Konjiki yasha* sends herself and Kan'ichi spinning toward moral degradation when she chooses money over love. Kimie in *Chikyōdai* rushes headlong after her dream of upward mobility and betrays a woman who considers her a sister. Fujio of *Gubijinsō*, portrayed as the epitome of modern female willfulness, reaches for both love and power by plotting to replace the rightful male heir of her family with the man she loves. There is a temptation here to conclude that women in these works are the vessels of displaced modern desires and, perhaps, that Meiji melodramatic fiction is fundamentally misogynistic. Such a view would be reinforced by the fact that many melodramatic novels, including the four studied here, end with the death of the woman who has destabilized the social order—a death that is invariably spectacularly staged.[113] Whether ethereally consumed by tuberculosis or run through with a knife blade, the heroines of melodramatic fiction breathe their last in scenes of high sentiment that drive home the moral lessons of the text.

A consideration of the female role in melodramatic fiction would be incomplete without touching on mothers. In this body of texts, the good mothers tend to be dead, and living mothers and especially stepmothers exhibit moral failings of various sorts. The virtuous Namiko is caught between two cruel mothers representing extremes of cultural allegiance: her Westernized stepmother regards her as a rival for her husband's love and her traditionalist mother-in-law views her as a rival for her son's affection. Neither mother has a shred of sympathy for a young woman unwillingly trapped in these triangulations. Fujio's mother in *Gubijinsō* emerges as the main instigator of the plot to separate her stepson from his rightful inheritance; for this transgression she is made a helpless witness to her daughter's death. In *Konjiki yasha*, Miya's mother grows so fond of the material advantages of her daughter's marriage that she purposely ignores the latter's growing distress. Kimie's mother in *Chikyōdai* has the most mixed role; she is kind enough to adopt and raise the orphan Fusae, but she also sets into motion the social striving that will mark her daughter's life. Mothers in Meiji melodramatic fiction, then, are no more able than fathers to offer clear moral direction. In fact, they contribute to the moral disturbance faced by the protagonists.

There is something missing, though, in a reading that reduces women in these texts to sirens of disorder whose destruction mends the social fabric. It is important to keep in mind the scale and the prominence of female characters in Meiji melodramatic fiction. Every example I have encountered of this type of writing contains at least one strong and meaty female part; many works have a female lead and some rely upon a female ensemble to carry forward the action. This differentiates melodramatic fiction from most later canonical Meiji novels, which tend to foreground male characters, relegating women to bit parts.[114] If Meiji melodramatic fiction attracted female readers, one simple reason was that women mattered in this kind of writing.

More importantly, women matter because they have moral agency. The female protagonists of Meiji melodrama make significant moral decisions and they live out the consequences of their choices. They are distinguished, in this regard, from the villainesses in an earlier form of Meiji narrative—the *dokufumono*, or "poison-women tales." The *dokufu* was essentially evil; she engaged in vice because this was her nature. In contrast, even when they end on the side of villainy, the women in melodramatic fiction are morally active beings whose choices express responses to the exigencies they face. The ethical engagement of female characters holds as true for Kimie in *Chikyōdai*, who ignores the voice of conscience, as it does for Namiko in *Hototogisu*, a martyr to domestic love. Perhaps the most forceful revelation of the "moral occult" in Meiji fiction occurs in *Konjiki yasha*, where Miya's belated discovery of her love for Kan'ichi provides an affirmation of the moral value of love expressed as regret, suffering, and unendurable longing. In Meiji melodramatic fiction, female characters are full participants in the exorbitant moral universe of melodrama.

This female moral capacity underlies one of the key contradictions driving this kind of fiction. Women are subject to the same extravagant moral demands faced by men. They confront similar moral challenges—new discourses of love and marriage, imported ideas about individualism and self-fulfillment, social aspiration bred by transformations in social hierarchy, a desire for wealth fed by a growing capitalist economy. Yet they are constrained by layers of social disadvantage—beginning with the gender hierarchy in marriage and the family, and extending to exclusion from higher education and from the workplace, except in its lowest reaches. The contradictions of a morality enmeshed in an unequal gender system, then, are among the problems that the Meiji melodrama attempts to mediate and negotiate.

Aside from gender, one other site of contradiction recurs in the works I study: Meiji melodramatic fiction's alternative families repeatedly confront the issue of stratification and mobility in Meiji society. Writing in this mode exhibits a heightened awareness of social instability. There are two different, but deeply interconnected, levels to this instability. First, Meiji melodrama depicts a world of social discontinuity where the status system has become unmoored and transformations have begun toward a social structure not yet fully determined. The status categories that ordered Edo society have become extinct (leaving their traces in designations such as *shizoku*, a term referring to former samurai) and in their place there has emerged, seemingly overnight, a welter of new social categories and identities that protagonists must negotiate. The second level concerns not the status system itself, but the nature of the individuals inhabiting that system. Meiji melodramatic fiction depicts a world of extreme social mobility for the individual and the family. Social status is usually not inherited in this world, and, if it is, only with a deep anxiety about the propriety of such inheritance. The ever-present danger of social descent breeds uneasiness about the future. But the melodramatic imagination was more passionately engaged with the opposite potential for social ascent. The ideal of self-advancement, known as *risshin shusse*, was a powerful social dynamo in the Meiji period, when men and women eagerly sought to push themselves forward in the wake of vast social reorganization, the development of new credentialing mechanisms in the school system, and the creation of immense wealth by industrial capitalism.[115] Melodramatic fiction was fascinated by the possibility for *risshin shusse*, but it raised questions about it as well, asking whether the race to get ahead left room for family, love, and virtue.

The melodramatic novel's concern with social mobility is tightly connected to the fact that its protagonists are young adults. This is the age at which characters reap the consequences of their earlier self-cultivation and education, and consolidate their social status either through employment or marriage.[116] This is also the age at which protagonists most frequently seek or enter fictive families formed in response to social desires that cannot be otherwise addressed. The affiliative alternative family, then, is one destination of characters who travel up and down a hierarchy that is itself in flux.

I cannot argue, as Ian Watt does for the English novel, that the rise of a certain group of texts is tied to the rise of a certain class. We still do not know enough either about the Meiji novel and its readership or about formations of class and status at the time to make such a claim convincingly. But I will propose that Meiji melodramatic fiction addresses what Michael McKeon has called "status inconsistency."[117] In contrast to Watt, who connects the rise of the novel to the rise of a middle class, McKeon views the English novel as an attempt to mediate and explain the transition of society from one organized by hereditary status to one demarcated by socioeconomic class. He argues that a status-oriented society—stratified with an aristocracy at the top—produces an ideologically consistent overlap:

> In aristocratic culture, it is not only that power, wealth, and honorific status most often accompany each other; honor also is understood to imply personal merit or virtue. Thus the social hierarchy is a great system of signification: the outward forms of genealogy and social rank are taken to signify an analogous, intrinsic moral order.[118]

This kind of consistent mapping had been dislodged in England of the late seventeenth and early eighteenth centuries. Instabilities in socioeconomic categories and an explosion of social mobility made it impossible to support an ideology that viewed power, wealth, and virtue as coalescing within a single group. The contradictions of status inconsistency resulted when these qualities no longer coincided.

McKeon's analysis provides considerable purchase in understanding changes that occurred in the transition from Edo to Meiji in Japan, although the situation here is complicated. The "rule by status" of the Edo period had been founded on the belief that social order demanded adherence to a model of hierarchy that regulated occupations and privileges.[119] The manifestations of status so permeated all of the facets of everyday life—work, family, residence, names, clothing, manners, and language—that one historian has observed that "*all* social relations in the Tokugawa period can be understood at some level as an expression of the institutions of the status system."[120] This system upheld the view that both power and wealth belonged in the hands of samurai, a hereditary military aristocracy. Samurai rule was justified by the principle, founded on Confucian ideology, that the status hierarchy reflected a moral hierarchy, in which samurai "naturally" functioned as the guardians of social morality.[121] The ruling Confucian ideology, then, put forth a vision of status consistency.[122]

The transformations of the Meiji period transported the issue of status to an entirely different register. The central change was the total elimination of the institutions of the Edo status system, accomplished through a series of reforms in the first decade of Meiji. The official hierarchy that had been ideologically defined as the source of moral order disintegrated almost overnight. The status inconsistencies of the Meiji period were experienced in a fluid context as the new social order took form in piecemeal fashion. The state's approach toward status was contradictory, on the one hand rhetorically proposing imperial subjecthood as *the* singular status enjoyed by all Japanese, and on the other hand busily manufacturing new status categories such as the modern aristocracy, the *shizoku*, and the *shin heimin* (the "new commoners" constituted by former outcasts). The expansion of a capitalist economy also had massive effects on social hierarchy. Employing the classic Weberian distinction between status, defined by honor and privilege, and economically determined class,[123] David Howell observes that, in the Meiji period, economic relations, and thus class, came to play a greater role in ordering society.[124] I would not argue with the truth of this observation, for every one of our texts will demonstrate a sharp engagement with the economic positionality of its protagonists. But I would also add that, if the effects of the capitalist economy were being intensely felt, a vocabulary for identifying social positions within a class structure was highly unstable through most of the Meiji period. Class could only be experienced and expressed through multiple, half-formed discourses. When we add to this the effects of a social mobility demanded by the needs of capitalism and the nation-state, and encouraged by modern ideologies of egalitarianism and individualism, then we can begin to glimpse an overall social fluidity that resists encapsulation. Under such conditions, no group could be deemed to be the proper possessor of power, wealth, and virtue.

The evidence from fiction is that this bred a gnawing awareness of status inconsistency. Through their alternative families, Meiji melodramatic novels undertook the cultural work of mediating and proposing solutions to the problems of status inconsistency that arose when the powerful or the wealthy were far from virtuous, when social mobility complicated moral categorization. A key problem addressed by *Hototogisu* is the legitimacy of a "new aristocracy" tainted by recently acquired wealth; Takeo's union with the general, his former father-in-law, allows the construction of a lineage of morally upright aristocratic men. *Konjiki yasha* seemingly identifies higher school students and graduates as a new moral elite, united by a rhetoric of fraternity, but when this status group, too, is shown to be tainted by the money economy, the novel must reach elsewhere for morally defensible alternative families.[125] *Chikyōdai* addresses the contradictions of aspiration, aptitude, and virtue, by portraying a remarkably talented lower-class girl who uses deception to choose an aristocratic family for her own. And Sōseki's *Gubijinsō* describes how social mobility through the educational system gives a man of uncertain background and questionable ethics access to a family above his origins. These portrayals clearly reveal a restricted class perspective: a consideration of the experience of the poor or the working class is largely missing. In the sense that the focus is on socioeconomic elites and their aspirants, Meiji melodramatic fiction may be said to be a bourgeois literature. But it is precisely this orientation that allows the memorable portraits of social striving that characterize these texts.

Meiji melodramatic fiction, then, repeatedly recruits fictive families to address a social morality that must be articulated in the face of status inconsistency as well as gender inequality. Drawn with melodrama's trademark dualism, these fictive families attempt to produce solutions for socially located moral problems, but these problems, as we will see, are so intractable that they cannot but lead to ideological contradiction.

A MELODRAMATIC AGE

Although I will be dealing almost exclusively with fictional writing, I would like to at least raise the proposition that a strong strain of melodramatic sensibility runs through Meiji discourse broadly conceived. The moral dualism of melodrama may well echo structures of feeling present in Meiji politics, historiography, and ideology. My observations here parallel those of Wylie Sypher, who argues, in reference to European intellectual history, that the "aesthetic category of melodrama becomes a modality of the 19th Century mind."[126] Sypher observes that the dualism of melodrama crops up not only in literature, but in nineteenth-century science and thought:

> The view of the world as a diagram of polar forces encourages not only a melodramatic ethics (the strong and the weak, the hard and the soft, the good and the bad) but also emotive history and emotive science. . . . Having done with a personal God, the 19th Century could now displace the drama in its mind into the universe itself by means of the laws of geology, biology, energy, and more immediately, economics.[127]

The reference to economics here points to the trajectory of Sypher's argument, which goes on to claim that even Marxism, with it dualistic opposition of proletarians and capitalists, is a product of the nineteenth century's pervasive melodramatic consciousness (which Sypher sees as being inescapably bourgeois).

I cannot venture into science or Marxism, but I can point out that a melodramatic dualism suffuses the extra-literary discourse of Meiji ideology. For example, in his commentary on the Imperial Rescript on Education, Inoue Tetsujirō explicated the Rescript's injunction to "perfect moral powers" in the following way:

> If an evil man reforms his heart, he becomes a good man overnight. If a good man does not correct his errors, he immediately changes into an evil man. This being the case, good men must strive all the more to proceed toward the good. And the evil, as long as they have life remaining in which to reform, must move toward the good and practice virtue, attempting to atone for the transgressions of their former lives, with the feeling of one who has through good fortune safely reached shore after being shipwrecked and forced to make his way through stormy seas. . . . If one practices virtue, his days will be blessed with an eternal ease. If he loses sight of virtue, his body will become but a prison for his soul, and he will often face unbearable suffering and the idle scorn of others.[128]

What we see here is the structure of the excluded middle: there is good and evil and nothing in between. There is a perpetual struggle in the name of virtue and the potential for both bliss and extreme suffering. This is the stuff of melodrama. It is particularly noteworthy, moreover, that this structure is applied by Inoue to developments within a single person. This contrasts with analyses of classic theatrical melodrama that view the paradigmatic personality in the genre as purely good or purely evil, victims or villains.[129] In Inoue's view, the individual swings between the poles depending upon how he or she exercises moral agency. This version of dualism is worth keeping in mind given the dramatic moral reversals exhibited by characters in Meiji melodramatic fiction as well as in Natsume Sōseki's *Kokoro* (1914), a work whose connections to the melodramatic mode I briefly examine in my conclusion.

A melodramatic sensibility is particularly evident in Meiji family ideology. When Hozumi Yatsuka attacked the civil code promulgated in 1890 with his famous phrase, "The Civil Code appears, and loyalty and filiality disappear," his rhetoric was thoroughly dualistic. The version of the code written on individualist principles was, in his view, totally antithetical to Japanese "tradition." His argument is built on the dualism of either/or, in which upholding one means destroying the other. His language reflects the hyperbolic sense of crisis generated by polar opposition: "In our country, ancestor worship has not yet been swept away by another faith. Yet the text of the Civil Code would start with rejecting our national religion and would be founded on a spirit that would ravage the family system."[130]

A similar binarism is apparent in Yanagita Kunio's statements, made in 1906, regarding the devastation of rural families by migration to urban areas. In order to make his point, Yanagita unfolds an exemplary narrative of tradition destroyed, and in a hyperbolic verbal gesture coins the neologism "domicide" to refer to the ruin of rural *ie*. His account of the endangered farm family is worth quoting at some length to register the melodrama of its plot:

> Whether it is having one's dwelling at the foot of the hill, or plowing a field on the river bank, or settling in a certain village in a certain district, when one lives in the country, everything is determined by the will of the *ie* rather than the will of the individual. The descendants carry out the will of the ancestors, who had desired prosperity for the *ie*. This goes without saying for noble houses and lineages, but even small farmholders and tenant farmers each have their family legends, as faint as these may be. This partly has to do with the fact that country life is conducive to health, but it is only after ten or twenty generations have had such a consciousness that an *ie* can be said to have persisted. In contrast to this, once one lives in the city, old records and lineage charts are burned in fires or lost amid moves, surnames become nothing more than signs distinguishing those with the same name from others, and the ties between the self and ancestors are immediately severed. . . . Even if living members of the family raise no objection, when one takes into account the descendants as yet unborn, then domicide, or the killing of the house, is not suicide—it is murder. If killing one's own children is homicide, then is it not equally criminal to forever deprive our living descendants of the awareness of their lineage? Is the *ie*, which is second to the nation in the length of its existence, to be destroyed overnight at the discretion of the head of the household? And yet, today, moving one's permanent residence to a big city nearly always results in just this kind of domicide, the killing of an *ie*. . . . In Japan, the connection between a person and his ancestors, in short, the awareness of the existence of the *ie*, is at the same time the link between the individual and the nation. Today, if we but probe a little, we realize that the faithful subjects and loyal retainers of history are our ancestors, and we are aware, not just vaguely but in a concrete way, of the intentions of our ancestors. The awareness that our

ancestors have lived and served under the imperial family for thousands of generations forms the surest basis for the feelings of loyalty and patriotism. If the *ie* were to disappear, it might even be difficult for us to explain to ourselves why we should be Japanese. As individualism flourished, we would come to view our history no differently from the way we view that of foreign countries.[131]

Yanagita's vision, which reveals adherence to orthodox family-state ideology, is nothing if not melodramatic: with the mode's characteristic extravagance, he counterpoises a nostalgic picture of pastoral family continuity, warmly shared by all classes of rural residents, against the destructive powers of modern urban individualism, which displays a homicidal hostility toward the *ie*. This dualistic opposition invites an overheated rhetoric that foretells a calamity just around the corner that will mean death not only for families but for Japanese identity. In this hyperbolic representation, migration to urban areas becomes a moral transgression, a murderous crime, rather than a necessary response to the economic forces of capitalism and industrialization. The only thing that stands in the way of evil is the moral force of rural householders, to whose sentiments Yanagita appeals by offering a poignant account of all that stands to be lost.

Statements like these show that the crisis consciousness of Meiji ideologues was often formulated and expressed in the melodramatic mode. Meiji melodramatic fiction, then, must be seen as resonating with and circulating within a melodramatic age. While echoing the tenor of Yanagita's sensational claims, the melodramatic fiction studied in the chapters that follow produced a host of alternatives to the orthodox vision of the *ie* he held so dear. The rhetoric of good and evil locked in mortal combat, of fullness and loss, of profound joy and suffering could be used as well to narrate the many ways in which the family could be conceived in Meiji Japan.

But There's Your Mother and Your Work

The Family and the Nation in *Hototogisu*

National ideals must have penetrated the family as well, although again we know very little about this process. Just how the father used appeals to nationalism in order to strengthen his patriarchal powers we can only glimpse in the novels of the age and the memoirs of those who revolted against such discipline.[1]

When George Mosse made these comments in his groundbreaking study *Nationalism and Sexuality*, he was referring to Germany and England during the nineteenth and early twentieth centuries. Had he been a scholar of Japanese history, he would have found that the penetration of national ideals into the family had been very well studied indeed. Kawashima Takeyoshi, Ishida Takeshi, and others pioneered the study of *ie* ideology in the postwar years. There are now enough books on the ideological and juridical history of what is variously called the *ie-seido* (the *ie* system) or the *kazoku kokka* (the family-state) to fill more than a few library shelves. This research confirms that the Japanese father's patriarchal powers were reinforced by nationalism, but it shows even more forcefully that the state benefited mightily from the mobilization and manipulation of patriarchy. We can more than glimpse this dynamic in fiction, for fiction is not merely a reflection of some prior reality; it participates actively in the ideological and discursive processes that produce, among other things, the sense of the nation. As Timothy Brennan puts it, "nations . . . are imaginary constructs that depend for their existence on an apparatus of cultural fictions in which imaginative literature plays a decisive role."[2] Such a formulation draws upon the influential ideas of Benedict Anderson, who has stressed the cultural work involved in the nationalizing process. Specifically, Anderson has pointed out that the "imagined communities" of nationalism are supported by the emergence of "national print languages" and by the apprehension of time and geography allowed by two types of print commodities—the newspaper and the novel.[3]

In this chapter I analyze the imbricated models of family and their relationship to the nation in one of the most popular of Meiji novels (which incidentally first appeared in a newspaper). My intent is to locate Tokutomi Roka's *Hototogisu* (The cuckoo, 1898–99) in extra-literary discourses on the family constructed by ideologues both within and outside the Meiji government. By examining how the novel negotiates among these discourses, both on the thematic level—involving representations of family, gender, and status—and on the level of narrative, specifically its treatment of temporality, I hope to arrive at a deeper reading of its place in the national imagination. Viewing this novel as a melodrama—a text that represents and evokes extreme sentiments through mobilizing binary moral structures—allows us to take full account of its mediation of competing ideologies of family.

Hototogisu was a true phenomenon in the history of Meiji publishing. When the novel was written, its author, Tokutomi Roka, was toiling obscurely as a staff journalist in the Min'yūsha, the publishing house that had been established by his more famous older brother, Tokutomi Sohō. *Hototogisu* brought Roka quick recognition. Although the novel drew favorable attention when it was serialized in the Min'yūsha's newspaper, the *Kokumin shinbun*, from November 1898 to the following May, it was when a revised version of the work appeared in book form in 1900 that it became one of the runaway hits of Meiji, reproduced in hundreds of printings.[4] The work attracted readers from a broad range of backgrounds. The haiku poet Takahama Kyoshi, the son of a samurai, sent Roka a piece of fan mail that included one of his less distinguished lines of poetry: "At my hibachi, tears fall on the novel."[5] Readers came from humbler backgrounds as well; the socialist critic and writer Takakura Teru observes that *Hototogisu* was read by female workers in the thread mills.[6] Roka's novel, moreover, had a vigorous afterlife that spilled over into other genres. It inspired a book of poetry, it was adapted for the *shinpa* stage, where it became a stalwart of the repertoire, and it was eventually made into over a dozen movies.[7] *Hototogisu* is clearly a story that made its way into the popular consciousness.[8]

There is a line in the novel that penetrated into the Japanese collective memory. Elderly Japanese can still recite the famous lament over the burdens of gender uttered by the work's heroine on her deathbed: "Aa tsurai! tsurai! Mō—mō—mō onna nanzo ni—umarewashimasenyo" ("It's more than I can bear. It's more than I can bear. I'll never, never, never be born a woman again.").[9] On her way toward making this plaintive declaration, Namiko, the beautiful and gentle young heroine, has been first abused by a domineering mother-in-law and then divorced when the tuberculosis she contracts endangers her husband's *ie*. *Hototogisu* is thus most often remembered as a novel that depicts the victimization of women, particularly the victimization of young brides, in the Japanese family. Namiko's misfortune and mistreatment is one mark of *Hototogisu*'s melodramatic thrust. In her writing on film melodrama, Linda Williams has observed that "the key function of victimization is to orchestrate the moral legibility crucial to the mode, for if virtue is not obvious, suffering—often depicted as the literal suffering of an agonized body—is."[10] Suffering as a marker of moral worth will be a memorable part of every melodramatic novel taken up in this study; but it appears in its most elemental form in *Hototogisu*. Namiko suffers the emotional agony of being torn away from Takeo, the husband whom she deeply loves, and the physical torture of a disease that wracks her body with bloody coughs. The doubled anguish of the martyred heroine attests to her virtue and to the moral value of the cherished ideal of marital love.

The institution held responsible for Namiko's suffering is the *ie*. Nakano Yasuo, the author of the standard three-volume biography of Roka, reads *Hototogisu* as a work that "protests against and sympathizes with the unfair fate of women under a feudalistic family system."[11] The critic Hiraoka Toshio has argued that *Hototogisu* is a novel in which the demands of an *ie*, invested in lineage and hierarchy, destroy a happy *katei*, a competing model of family based on the Western ideal of "home" and emphasizing the affective bonds of a married couple.[12] When Namiko's tuberculosis threatens Takeo's life and the continuity of his *ie*, his *katei* must be sacrificed while being romanticized as the locus of conjugal and personal happiness. Although neither scholar would use the term, both Nakano and Hiraoka have identified a melodramatic binary functioning within *Hototogisu*. In

FIGURE 1.1   Kuroda Seiki's painting of Namiko—used as the frontispiece for the first edition of *Hototogisu*—erases all traces of her aristocratic status, emphasizing instead her suffering as a victim of tuberculosis and the *ie*. Source: *Hototogisu* (Tokyo: Min'yūsha, 1900).

this novel, the opposition between the *ie* and the *katei* works in the interests of moral legibility. The harsh demands of the *ie* and the villainous machinations of its agents throw into relief the sweet comforts of the *katei* and the virtue of the couple it enfolds.

Roka himself had suggested something of this sort in an advertisement for *Hototogisu* that appeared in *Kokumin shinbun* shortly before the novel's publication in book form. These comments belong to what Gérard Genette would call a "paratext," which comprises materials—such as a text's title, the name of its author, illustrations, book jacket blurbs, author's interviews, and advertisements—that surround a text and present it, that is "assure its presence in the world, its 'reception' and its consumption."[13] Roka's paratextual statements attempt to lay the groundwork for reading his novel as a morally upright piece of writing:

> Although the measure of Meiji now exceeds thirty years, in the very fiber of society there are more than a few outdated practices that exist with frightful force. This writer has merely endeavored to capture one of the nearest at hand. Although the writer wishes not to beat his own drum or blow his own horn, he is confident that this book resolutely eschews unhealthy words and can be admitted into the purest of homes (*fukenzen no moji o tachite seijō naru katei ni mo iriubeki wa mizukara shinzuru tokoro nari*).[14]

Although Roka does not name it in his statement, the contents of his book make plain that the *ie* is the dreaded anachronism he has in mind. His mention of "outdated practices" shows he has absorbed the state's position that the *ie* was the "traditional" form for family organization in Japan, though with an opposite and negative evaluation. His stipulation of the *katei* as the proper locus for the apprehension of the "frightening force" of the *ie* suggests that the *katei* exists in contradistinction to the *ie*. Roka's statement, then, can be read to support the argument that *Hototogisu* mobilizes a melodramatic binary in an act of moral protest.

The unexpected turn in this statement, however, gives it a somewhat schizophrenic tone. After the assertion that the text exposes certain obsolete and harmful social practices, we expect the writer to "beat his drum" about the protest quotient of his work. Yet it turns out that what makes the writer proudest is that his novel can be offered for family consumption. The odd twist suggests something of the significance in Meiji of the idea of *seijō naru katei*, the "purest of homes." The *katei* was a model of the family in which a protest against anachronism could be consumed, but also one in which such protest had to take the form of utter respectability. The view of the *katei* as the moral opposite of the *ie* must be tempered with the understanding that the *katei* itself was shot through with limitations and paradoxes.

Roka's statement, then, hints that *Hototogisu*'s quest for moral certitude may need to be examined in light of its inherent ideological contradictions. In my reading of the novel, I will point out that the protest quotient of the book is very much circumscribed by its treatment of various models of family, its attitudes toward social status, its flag-waving, and its support of imperial ventures abroad. A fuller interpretation needs to take account of the work's portrayal of gender roles within the family—specifically involving the death of the domestically inclined heroine and the "adoption" that socially reintegrates the hero at the conclusion of the novel—and their implications for the national project. To decode these interrelations, we must begin by examining how a vigorous stream of discourse in the 1890s attempted to install the *katei* as a model of family that competed with the *ie*.

KATEI AS AN ALTERNATIVE MODEL OF FAMILY

Roka's claims about his novel found an echo in a somewhat unlikely quarter. Sakai Toshihiko, who later became the first chairman of the Japanese Communist Party, lauded numerous facets of the novel in a review published in the *Yorozu chōhō* newspaper in 1900.[15] The review began by praising the novel's prose, which Sakai found "healthy" and "fresh as well as judicious" in contrast to the "vulgar tone that has become a kind of standard among our so-called novelists."[16] It becomes clear that there are certain assumptions about gender and social status in Sakai's criticism of current novelists, for he goes on to say that most fictional prose was "effeminate and indecent, lacking in force and will, and appears to be neither the product of a man's hand nor the issue of a gentleman's brush." The term I have translated as "gentleman," *shijin*, was used in the Meiji era to refer to a man of substance, a cultured person with a certain status in society, but it could also refer specifically to someone who was of samurai birth (as Roka was). What Sakai imagined as he read Roka's prose was an author who upheld a certain image of upright, samurai manhood. Sakai was also pleased by *Hototogisu*'s "accurate portrayal of current society," particularly its depiction of the home lives of military officers and merchants, and by the setting of its plot in a certain historical reality, namely the Sino-Japanese War. Both of these comments are rooted in Sakai's belief that fiction should reflect social and historical contexts. But they also reveal more than a little about his political views at this time, for he adds that "something like the passage on the battle in the Yellow Sea deserves to be read." As I will show later, the descriptions of battle in *Hototogisu* are aggressively nationalistic; we can only conclude that Sakai was still far removed from the pacifism that he would advocate during the Russo-Japanese War. Sakai closed his review by observing that "the book contains no unhealthy attitudes" (*henchū sukoshimo fukenzen no shisō naki o yorokobu*) and that "a volume of this nature should fill the void in reading matter for the home" (*katei no yomimono no ketsubō wa mata kono gotoki hen ni yori mitasarubeki o shinzuru*).

What Sakai saw in *Hototogisu*, then, was a book that glowed with healthy attitudes and healthy prose. It embodied a proper male voice, yet it would appeal to women and children and would embarrass no one by being on the bookshelf in a genteel *katei*. Statements like this have led literary historians to sometimes classify *Hototogisu* as a precursor of a genre called *katei shōsetsu*, or "home fiction," that flowered in the fourth decade of Meiji.[17] This genre did not necessarily get its name because it comprised stories set in the home, although this was often the case. Rather the reference to "home" was to a locus of reading or to an audience. The *katei shōsetsu* was a genre expressly written by male authors to be read in the home for the enjoyment and edification of women and children.[18] As such, it was defined by a thematic and ideological restriction; respectability was its standard, and anything too threatening or too challenging was out of bounds.

I do not wish to overemphasize the connection of *Hototogisu* to the *katei shōsetsu*, because the work contains elements that diverge from the genre; there are more typical examples, including *Chikyōdai* (Raised as sisters, 1903), which I take up in a later chapter. My objective here is to show that there was widespread awareness of the model of the family called the *katei*, which arose in contradistinction to the idea of the *ie*. Both Roka and Sakai write with reference to a preexisting discourse on the *katei*. Their statements show that this model of family—associated with health, a progressive outlook, respectability, and proper gender roles—may provide one discursive key to understanding the family conflicts in *Hototogisu*. It would seem worthwhile, then, to step back and briefly trace the discursive history of the *katei*.

The idea of *katei* was prefigured in Meiji discourse by the concept of *hōmu*, or "home," lovingly put forth by Iwamoto Yoshiharu, Uchimura Kanzō, and others of like mind during the 1880s.[19] These Christian ideologues were affected by mid-nineteenth-century American devotional writing and women's literature, which viewed the "home" as a castle of comfort containing an angelic woman characterized by her piety, purity, submissiveness, and domesticity,[20] and they began to conceive of a *hōmu* that would offer them solace from their daily labors at converting and modernizing the multitudes. They explicitly contrasted the *hōmu* against the sternly hierarchical Japanese *ie*, devoid of *waraku danran*, a key term that came to connote the harmony and joys of family togetherness.[21] The *hōmu* was held together not by duty or loyalty but by love. This emotional bond centered on a married couple; the Christian thinkers frowned upon the cohabitation of different married generations because it inhibited the all important expression of marital affection.[22] In their role as proselytizers, Iwamoto and others pointed out that the harmonious, emotionally rich *hōmu* was conducive to piety, and that it was indeed "modeled on Heaven."[23] This refuge of devotion had as its moral center a wife who strove to encourage family togetherness through her "kindness, endurance, self-denial, and her love for others."[24] Aside from the practice of these feminine virtues, the woman of the house was also required to plunge herself into her domestic duties. It is in the writing of Meiji Christians that we see some of the earlier examples of the term *shufu*, the mistress of the house, whose charge it was to undertake the interior, domestic running of the house while her husband turned his energies toward the exterior world. Iwamoto believed strongly enough in his visions of *hōmu* and femininity that in 1885 he started Japan's first magazine for women, *Jogaku zasshi* (Journal of female learning), to spread his ideas.[25] Yet the Christian ideologues clearly knew that *hōmu* was an ideal, a figment of their longing that could not be found on Japanese soil; when Uchimura Kanzō stated that *hōmu* could not be translated into Japanese he was acknowledging that no Japanese analogue existed.[26]

If an idealistic thinker like Uchimura could not imagine translating the term into Japanese, however, less-exacting propagandists were bound to try. In the late 1880s and 1890s *katei* evolved into a widely accepted translation for *hōmu*, and it is at this point that the new ideas on family became a key concern in public discourse.[27] The major *sōgō zasshi*, or "general magazines," which then as now served as key nodes for the formation of public opinion, began to run numerous articles advocating the transformation of the Japanese family toward the model of the *katei*.[28] An especially influential magazine, *Taiyō*, even began to carry a *katei ran*, or "home column," starting in 1894. The *sōgō zasshi* were aimed at an educated, mostly male audience, and their attention to the *katei* shows that the family was viewed as an important social issue deserving of the attention of males, as well as of the occasional educated female reader. Less advantaged female readers, too, were well served by the adherents of *katei*. The two decades following the publication of *Jogaku zasshi* saw the appearance of numerous women's magazines filled with advice for homemakers.[29] The investment of these magazines in new concepts of the family is evident in some of their titles: *Katei zasshi* (Home magazine), *Katei no tomo* (Friend of the home), *Nihon no katei* (Japanese home).

With the translation of *hōmu* into *katei*, the concepts attached to the earlier ideal were translated as well. Piety was stripped out of the equation as non-Christians began to advocate the *katei*, but the emphasis on the married couple joined by powerful emotional bonds remained. Various concrete proposals were put forth to strengthen the marital ideal.[30] Advocates of *katei* opposed the age old practice of socially privileged men keeping mistresses, and they supported the *ippu ippu* (one husband, one wife) marital structure. Like the adherents of *hōmu*, they opposed young married couples living with their parents. And they proposed that in determining marriages the feelings of the couple needed to be considered along with the opinions of their parents. The monogamous, affectively determined *katei* was assigned supreme value; one writer wrote that "peace in the home (*katei no heiwa*) was the goal of all humanity."[31]

The *katei* gained a progressive cachet through being connected to the Western associations of the *hōmu*. Indeed, some writers emphasized the enlightened nature of the *katei* by conversely linking the coresidence of married children and parents with the "East," or more specifically "Shina," the China viewed through Japanese eyes that was doomed by its unthinking adherence to the old.[32] The progressivism of *katei* ideology was also linked to ideas of national progress. Some writers turned on its head the state's insistence that the *ie* was the preferred structure in the nation-building enterprise. "If one regards absolute adherence to a household as a virtue," one writer said, "how can one encourage virtues having to do with the society and the nation?"[33] Another made the success of *katei* a precondition for national advancement: "Without happy homes national prosperity can never be achieved."[34]

These statements show that ideologies, such as those existing respectively around the *katei* and the nation, do not exist in splendid isolation, but rather mediate social experience through their various combinations and juxtapositions. Such interaction means that the study of social ideologies must constantly attend to contexts, combinations, and contradictions. The rationalizing of progress and nationalism in the statements above suggests how closely the progressive impulses in *katei* ideology could run to the conservative and authoritarian ones that underlay the government's support of the *ie*. Muta Kazue shows her awareness of the contradictions possible in such dynamics when she speaks of the "paradox" present in the evolution of thinking on the *katei*. For her, this paradox is especially apparent in the *katei*'s treatment of women. If the *katei* was meant as a progressive alternative to the *ie*, it also advocated—in the guise of progressivism and in tune with the nineteenth-century Western discourse on home and womanhood—the domestication of women. In order for the *katei* to function as the warm, emotionally satisfying site of comfort promised by its advocates, it needed to enfold at its center a woman defined as a *shufu*, a specialist in the affairs of the home. The *shufu* could quickly become a *ryōsai kenbo*, the "good wife, wise mother" advocated by government propagandists, as she did when the "home column" in *Taiyō* declared, during and just after the Sino-Japanese War, that the *katei* constituted the battlefront for Japanese women and that its prime function was the forging of citizens for victory.[35] In such an instance, the *katei* was not far in its functions from the *ie*.

THE MIN'YŪSHA ON THE KATEI

This paradoxical nature of the *katei* was very much in evidence in the discursive environment surrounding Roka as he wrote *Hototogisu*, for Min'yūsha ideology reflected the Meiji debate on the family. The Min'yūsha, led by Roka's brother Tokutomi Sohō, is known for having initially advocated a liberal and egalitarian program called *heiminshugi* or "commonerism," which it discarded over the course of the 1890s in favor of a nationalist and expansionist agenda that became especially evident around the time of the Sino-Japanese War.[36] This ambivalent history clearly affected the Min'yūsha approach to the family. The Tokutomi brothers, who had attended Dōshisha, the Christian college in Kyoto, were most likely exposed there to Christian views of the *hōmu* as an alternative to the *ie*. In his earlier writings, Sohō exhibited genuine hostility toward the *ie*, which he saw as the repository of a feudal mentality, inimical to egalitarianism in its support of inherited wealth and social position, and, with its myriad obligations, repressive in its effect upon ambitious young men. To him, the traditional family was "a breeding ground of every abuse: servility, double-dealing, mistrust, hypocrisy, jealousy, alienation, and treachery."[37] The *ie* also led to women being treated as "natural slaves" who had no choice except to serve their husbands and bear sons to carry on the family line. To reform the family, Sohō developed a five-point plan.[38] First, he proposed having property belong to individuals rather than to families, thus making individuals economically more independent. Second, in order to end what he saw as a kind of economic parasitism, he advocated the abolishment of early retirements that made parents premature dependents of adult children. Third, he insisted that parents and married children should live separately, each managing their own affairs. Fourth, he recommended that young men should not marry until they were self-supporting, again to foster independence. And fifth, he recommended that relations with distant relatives should be minimized.

Taken together, the plan was aimed at cutting the networks of intergenerational obligations and lineage ties that defined the *ie*. As an alternative model of family, the Min'yūsha supported the *katei*. One characteristic of the Min'yūsha was a strong pedagogical strain, and in order to spread his message to a popular audience and to women in particular Sohō started a magazine called *Katei zasshi,* or "Home Magazine," in 1892. The stated purpose of this magazine was to "reform the foundations of society and to encourage the creation of harmonious and enlightened *katei*."[39] The Min'yūsha also published a series of popular self-help books called the *Katei sōsho,* or "Home Library." The volumes in this series are advertised prominently in the back of the first edition of *Hototogisu*, composing a paratext suggestive of both the intended audience of the book and the kind of ideological context that surrounded a contemporary reading of the novel.[40] The titles in the series include: *Katei no waraku* (Harmony in the home), *Katei eisei* (Home hygiene), and *Katei kyōiku* (Education in the home).

The last of these books, *Katei kyōiku*, published in 1894, exhibits some of the vagaries that creep in when the Min'yūsha's ideas on family are translated into practical or pedagogical form.[41] On the one hand, *Katei kyōiku* conscientiously exhibits a progressive and cosmopolitan outlook. It makes a show of quoting the latest Western experts on family education and advocates teaching the alphabet along with *hiragana*. It stresses the need for parents to respect their children's differences and encourage a sense of self-determination, albeit controlled by self-discipline. On the other hand, the brand of progressivism the book advocates also involves the observation of a rigid gender hierarchy. Although the following passage on the division of labor in the family cites a foreign authority (this is a favorite rhetorical strategy of the text), what is being emphasized is clearly a central vision of the work itself:

> According to Professor Kern, the mother might be called the center of family and family life because she devotes herself wholeheartedly and earnestly to domestic duties, serving her husband and caring for her children, avoiding no labor, indeed with no thought for her own life. With her love, she creates harmony among the members of the household and unifies the disparate hearts of various individuals. But, given her innately gentle nature, she submits to her husband, the head of the family, and administers family matters according to his will. The husband spends much of his time outside of the house because of his profession. He goes to work; represents the family toward the rest of society, attending to its relations with the families of others; and establishes its place in society, the nation, and the church. For this reason, the authority of the father, who is the master of his house, arises naturally.[42]

The family as envisioned in this Min'yūsha tract is hierarchically organized by certain "innate" and "natural" dynamics. It is affectively rich and comforting, assigning a self-sacrificing specialist to undertake the emotional management of the home. This specialist subordinates herself willingly to a husband who is freed to attend to, and gain authority from, his connection with larger institutions, including the nation. If women were no longer to be "natural slaves" to the *ie*, they were now required to be domestic angels, whose presence allowed men to take on the important work of their sex.

The *katei*'s positioning within patriarchy, then, complicates the binary opposition between the *ie* and the *katei* posited in early Min'yūsha writings. The representation of the *katei* as a model of family more in keeping with Min'yūsha egalitarianism is undercut by the desire to view it as a source of hierarchy that mediates connections with an external order. The ideological contradictions that we see here are reflected in *Hototogisu*'s assertion of the moral superiority of the *katei* as a model of family. The *katei* in *Hototogisu*, while romanticized, is not necessarily a progressive alternative to the *ie*. In ways that echo its treatment in the Min'yūsha's pedagogical works, the *katei* in the novel binds Namiko and Takeo to gender roles they cannot escape. These gender roles are shown in the novel to support the state, and thus the defense of *katei* in *Hototogisu* implies that it can serve the nation just as well as can the *ie*. What is more, the novel's ending suggests that Namiko and Takeo's *katei* has ultimately contributed to the formation of an alternative version of *ie*, which can carry on the work of empire.

FAMILY AND GENDER IN HOTOTOGISU

Hototogisu opens idyllically with a newly married couple spending a few days amidst the natural beauty of the resort of Ikaho. There is much to suggest that the couple are well matched. He is a navy officer, manly and vigorous. She is beautiful, refined, and gentle. There is a clear affection and an erotic tie binding the young couple—in a telling detail, the wife kisses her husband's coat as she hangs it up. The narrator deliberately obscures the exact identities of the protagonists: she is referred to as the "woman" (*fujin*) and he as the "man" (*otoko*) or the "youth" (*wakamono*).[43] As the novel begins, then, the emphasis is upon a man and a woman who care about each other, spending time together in a pastoral topos far from the social obligations of the city.[44]

The first third of the novel repeatedly alludes to the potential implied in this romantic interlude—the potential for a man and a woman to share an innocent enjoyment of the affective bonds that underlie a *katei*. We are told that the bride had looked forward to her marriage as an opportunity for "freedom and pleasure she had heretofore been denied" (232).[45] When the young naval officer must leave on a voyage, he sends back letters filled with longing in which he says that he constantly carries his wife's photograph in an inner pocket of his uniform. The wife replies that she has been tracing his ship's route on a map of the world and checking the newspapers for weather reports for his ports of call. When she goes to her room and sees her husband's photograph, the heroine "gently takes it into her hands and gazes steadily at it. She kisses it, rubs it against her cheek, and whispers 'Please come home quickly,' as though the person in the picture were there beside her" (267). This devotion is rewarded when the husband returns and sighs that his homecoming seems like a "second honeymoon" (278). The text orthographically emphasizes that there is something new about the relationship depicted here; both *kissu* and *honimūn* appear as transliterated glosses. The young couple then are shown as being joined in a marriage of the new style, marked by mutual affection and by a surprising physical demonstrativeness.

Yet, even as the romantic portrayal of the *katei* is being drawn, the boundaries of the *ie* are being fixed tightly around it. When the main characters are formally identified at the beginning of the second chapter, they are framed in the context of their families and their social positions:

> The character referred to in the preceding chapter as "the youth" is Navy Ensign Baron Kawashima Takeo. It was only last month that, with the help of an able go-between, he was wed to Namiko, the eldest daughter of Lieutenant General Viscount Kataoka Ki, an army commander whose fame resounds throughout the land. (230)

Once we know Namiko and Takeo's full names they become figures enmeshed in various social institutions: the military, the aristocracy, the family, and the nation. The narrative moves on to quickly flesh out this matter of social location and does so by describing the two protagonists as members of their respective *ie*.

To begin with Namiko's family, the Kataokas are headed by the general, a former Satsuma samurai who rose to become a minister in the Meiji government. The general is portrayed as a gentle giant, a father who lavishes attention on his children but also an officer who is known throughout the army as the "impregnable fortress" on whom the nation can depend in times of need. At the beginning of the novel, the general is in the reserves, but his concern with the nascent empire is evident in the maps of the continent spread out upon his desk along with books with such titles as *The Current State of the Siberian Railway*. These interests are rewarded later in the novel when he is called back to active duty and given command of the Second Army during the Sino-Japanese War. The general's loyalty to the state is evident in the portrait of the emperor and the empress that stares down at him in his study.

Of the novels discussed in this book, *Hototogisu* most clearly displays the classic form of melodramatic characterization, in which the dramatis personae represent pure moral states arrayed in a binary opposition. Robert Heilman, an early critic of the mode, has written that, in the melodrama, "man is bad—that is, a villain—or good, whether as victor over evil or as a victim who does not deserve his fate."[46] *Hototogisu* defines good and evil through an unsubtle coding of Meiji discourses on gender and cultural identity. The general's cultural leanings are suggested by an item that hangs in his study along with the imperial portrait, a piece of calligraphy by Saigō Takamori that reads *jin o nasu*, which might perhaps be translated "Practice

Virtue." This slogan, with its Confucian ring, and the image of Saigō, the Restoration leader who was lionized as an exemplar of samurai integrity despite losing his life in a rebellion against the Meiji oligarchy, is clearly important in Kataoka's portrayal. The general is manly, incorruptible, decisive. He is also repeatedly described as being "generous" (*kandai*) or "large-hearted" (*ōyō*), qualities the text views as being "Oriental" (*tōyōteki*). The general is a model of modern samurai manhood, a practitioner of virtue who can yet be a leader of a modern army and contribute to the building of a modern empire.

Directly opposed to the general's "Oriental" positioning is his second wife and Namiko's stepmother, Kataoka Shigeko, a case of Westernization gone amuck: "Though born in an established samurai family, she had been sent away to be educated in England from an early age and thus, on top of being as strong-minded as a man, was dyed through and through in the Western style" (230). It seems, then, that if the "Oriental" man is valorized, the "Western" Japanese woman is seen as a transgressor of the rules of both culture and gender; Shigeko bosses around her husband, the general, and is selfish and cold in a way that the text explicitly associates with the "West." She is also a poor practitioner of the domestic arts and a laughingstock across class lines: "Valuing the Western in everything, she eagerly tried to practice exactly what she had learned abroad in the management of her house and the education of her children; but the servants merely snickered at her gullibility behind her back" (255). Her culturally determined emotional parsimony makes Shigeko a minor villain in the story, for she allows her relationship with Namiko to be colored by "the pride in academic accomplishment of an inexperienced self-server, by suspicion, and even jealousy" (231). The suspicion and jealousy stem from a displaced and barely submerged erotic triangle, in which Shigeko mistreats Namiko because of a rivalry she feels for Namiko's dead mother, the general's first wife. Shigeko wants to be "the only one to occupy her husband's heart, the only one to exercise the authority of the mistress of the house," yet Namiko, who looks like her mother, "had invaded her territory by calling forth the traces of the woman who had passed away" (256–57). The triangle takes on the appearance of an allegory of cultural contestation, for the general's first wife is described as having been "from a proper samurai house and thus well mannered in everything that she did" (230). The Western and the Japanese war over the soul of Meiji manhood in General Kataoka's household. It is not entirely clear who wins, but it is obvious which of the general's two wives was warmer and more sympathetic. Although we learn only a little about the first wife, what comes through in Namiko's memories is telling: "Since she had only been eight, she could clearly remember neither her mother's face nor form, but a day did not go by that she did not recall . . . that her mother had always had a smile on her face" (230).

Meiji fiction is filled with male characters whose destinies involve multiple fathers and father-figures—Kan'ichi in *Konjiki yasha*, the young narrator in *Kokoro*, or, as we will see, Takeo in this novel. Like the male characters who must choose between the alternatives presented by their fathers, Namiko is marked by her relationship to the cultural models presented by her mothers. At first glance, Namiko would seem to be closer to her birth mother in her values. She is, to begin with, a faithful and obedient daughter. Unusually attached to her father, she had happily let him arrange her marriage to Takeo. Her sense of propriety also makes her a supporter of multi-generational families. She had disagreed with her Westernized stepmother's assertion that young married couples should live apart from their parents because she believed that "this is out of tune with our national customs" (*waga kokufū ni awazu* [294]). The notion of a "national custom" presupposes the nation as a source of identity and of custom as its agent of perpetuation. Namiko, then, is a supporter of the state's ideological position on the *ie*, while at the same time believing in the romantic possibilities of the *katei*. Despite the difficulties she faces, Namiko genuinely strives to meet her mother-in-law's expectations once she moves into the Kawashima household. All of this makes her an unlikely victim for the sanctions of the *ie*. And perhaps this is one of the reasons why her fate is so poignant.

It would be a mistake, however, to interpret Namiko as a woman wholly aligned with "tradition." Yoshiya Nobuko, the early-Showa writer of popular fiction, observed in a 1927 interview that "while Namiko seems like a passive, Japanese-style woman, there is something quite different about her."[47] Yoshiya mentions the physicality evident in the way Namiko kisses her husband's coat and the forthrightness with which she expresses herself when the occasion demands. While Yoshiya thinks that there is "something of the advocate of women's rights" present in Namiko's directness, I cannot help noticing that, in the scene Yoshiya has in mind, Namiko's boldness is being used to defend her sense of propriety against an unscrupulous former suitor. What is new in Namiko's portrayal is the combination of a fierce sense of respectability with a deep capacity for affection, physical and otherwise. It is no surprise to find that Namiko is also deeply invested in domesticity, having "naturally gained an interest in home management because of the teachings of her father, the lieutenant general" (294). In many scenes, she is shown either knitting or sewing. Namiko is the domestic angel in Japanese guise, a specialist in the affairs of the heart and home. She is a woman who believes in the *ie*, but whose personal qualities make her the perfect wife in a *katei*.

The force of the *ie* is represented in this novel by the third of Namiko's mothers, her mother-in-law, the widow Kawashima Keiko.[48] This mother's installation as the central villain of the work is associated with two aspects of her characterization: her cultural positioning as someone who cannot escape the past and her psychological depiction as a victim turned tormentor who crosses gender lines in the process of her transformation. The first of these qualities is immediately obvious to Namiko when she marries Takeo. She notices that, in comparison to the Westernized atmosphere of her stepmother's household, everything at the Kawashimas is "old-fashioned, or rather countrified. One might generously call this a sense of taste that recognized the past, but actually the sensibility and the logic were those of the widow, who had not changed at all since she had had to pound her own rice" (265). I will return later to the elements of regional and status identity implied by these judgments and for now only note that a provincial background and humble beginnings help to reinforce Kawashima Keiko's portrayal as an antediluvian creature. All of this, of course, resonates with Roka's paratextual statement that his intention was to write about "old practices that exist with frightening force." Keiko is portrayed to stress that *ie* ideology is something antiquated and anachronistic; what is elided is that this ideology was utilized by a modern state in its nation-building project.

The second element in Keiko's characterization as an unbending supporter of the *ie* involves a personal history of domestic violence. Keiko's late husband—a man who had started out in life as a low-ranking Satsuma samurai but had amassed a fortune while serving as an appointed governor in various prefectures—had been famous for his short temper. Only Takeo was exempt from his fits of anger, and "beginning with his wife, Keiko, but also extending to servants and subordinates, and even including the pillar in the sitting room, there was none spared a taste of the master's iron fist" (262). The Keiko who had suffered these regular batterings had been a thin and sickly wraith. But upon her husband's death, she had undergone a remarkable physical metamorphosis, "expanding like a compressed rubber ball being let loose" (261). To underscore the imposing nature of the widow's current physical proportions, the narrator at one point uses a metaphor from sumo, saying that she qualifies to be a *sekiwake*, or junior champion, in the ranks of the aristocracy. This physical transformation is accompanied by a psychological one. The formerly timid Keiko had become domineering and had gained a temper rivaling that of her late husband. The metaphorical association of Keiko's girth with that of a sumo wrestler already implies the gender complications in her transformation; this implication is confirmed in terms that suggest a cross-gender spirit possession: "Her appearance and her gestures these days, the way she held her pipe in one hand and glared at people while twitching her dark eyebrows, and, what was more, the roughness of her behavior and above all the same temper—there were some indeed who said that she was the living image of her husband" (263). By taking on her late husband's traits Keiko becomes a female who is not fully "feminine." Although her beliefs and tastes are poles apart from those of Namiko's cruel stepmother, Keiko shares with Shigeko a tendency for gender-crossing behavior. In this text's melodramatic binary, gender purity (of the sort exhibited by Namiko and Takeo) signifies virtue, while breaching gender lines is associated with villainy.

What is interesting about Kawashima Keiko is that her bad-tempered behavior aligns not only with masculine irascibility but also with ethical defects coded as peculiarly feminine. For example, she engages in the stereotypical behavior of the Japanese mother-in-law who visits upon her son's bride the indignities she had suffered as a young wife. Keiko's sexual jealousy toward Namiko, which I will discuss subsequently, is another trait associated with the feminine. This overabundance of gendered faults betrays the text's anxiety over female power, an anxiety that is inherent in the treatment of mothers in *ie* ideology. While the *ie* and *kazoku kokka* ideologies were patriarchal and preached the superiority of men over women, they also routinely emphasized obedience to mothers in their emphasis upon filial piety. Simply put, the discourse of *ie* elevated mothers at the same time that it denigrated women. In his commentary on the Imperial Rescript on Education, Inoue Tetsujirō had said that the "emperor to his subjects was like a father and mother to their offspring" and that subjects should listen attentively to the emperor "with the feelings of children toward a strict father or a loving mother."[49] Statements of this nature do more than expand the gender of the emperor, allowing him to be both the mythical father and mother of the people; they confer a privileged position on the "loving mother" redefined as an imperial presence in the home. The turn-of-the-century *shūshin* textbooks bluntly stated what was required of children in light of this analogy: "In all things, follow what your father and mother say, and do not disobey them, even for a moment."[50] Kawashima Keiko benefits from these ideological prescriptions, and she expects obedience from her son. This is especially true because of her husband's early death, which had caused Takeo to develop habits of reliance on her. Although Takeo has officially gained *ie* headship—he has assumed his father's baronetcy—his mother continues as the de facto househead, making the major decisions and carrying on the family's external relations with kin and acquaintances. Takeo acknowledges his mother's authority through the use of two metaphors that demonstrate that this exponent of *katei*, too, links the family to the nation. He refers to her variously as the "prime minister" of the family and as its "queen," the latter using the English term as a loanword (315, 295). Takeo sees his mother as either a male source of political authority or a regal female symbol, but his acquiescence to her power is clear.

For being descended from his parents, Takeo is remarkably unaffected. He is loving and gentle toward his wife—not a sign here of an inherited tendency toward domestic violence. He is something of a model young officer. Unlike his father, who had enriched himself in the process of serving the nation, Takeo is ethically fastidious, placing duty and integrity above the pursuit of money. (Of course, he can afford to do this, for the fortune his father had amassed makes the Kawashimas wealthy even among the aristocracy.) He later proves to be tough in battle and at one point, while on shore leave, even manages to save his father-in-law's life by throwing himself on a Chinese assassin. He also exhibits a cultural syncretism proper to an officer in a navy that is modern and Japanese: Serving on a steam-powered battleship, he dreams of restoring moral fiber to a military that has lost the "bearing of the samurai of old" (280). These ideological affiliations are apparent in the eclectic furnishings of his study, done in the *wayō setchū* style, which mixes the Japanese and the Western. Tables and chairs stand in a room where a green carpet has been put over tatami. His father's sword, a Kanemitsu, stands in the *tokonoma*, not far from a pair of binoculars and the cutlass issued to officers in the Westernized navy. The pictures and photographs that fill the room bespeak the male institutions and the male lineage to which he belongs. A portrait of his late father, the baron, stares down from the lintel. Among the photographs are those of his ship and his classmates at the naval academy, and, perhaps most significantly given later developments, a portrait of his father-in-law, General Kataoka, in full uniform. There are, however, a few feminine touches in this relentlessly male space. Its order, its cleanliness, and a graceful flower arrangement bespeak the presence of someone "with a warm heart, attentive to detail, and with a practiced hand" (276). This someone smiles winsomely from a silver, heart-shaped frame placed next to the flower arrangement. The meaning of this interior is unmistakable: Takeo is a Japanese comfortable with the West, a samurai's son who has become an officer in a modern navy, a male heir to his *ie* who can appreciate the feminine presence in his newly formed *katei*. This combination struck one Meiji reader as a representation of ideal manhood: an anonymous reviewer for the literary journal *Bunko* in 1900 wrote that a real pleasure of the work was the "manly deportment of the male protagonist Takeo."[51] *Hototogisu* awards virtue to the proper alignment of gender ideals and cultural syncretism.

THE IE AND SOCIAL HIERARCHY

A description of the Kawashimas as an *ie* would not be complete without mentioning those who are at its borders. This is important because the *ie* in history (rather than in Meiji ideology) was, as many anthropologists have observed, not so much a strict kinship unit as a corporate group with fluid boundaries capable of including, to varying degrees, relatives and in some cases non-kin, like family retainers. The presence in the novel of Chijiwa Yasuhiko, who is literally a poor cousin, and Yamaki Shōzō, a merchant with deep ties to the family, exemplifies this aspect of the *ie*.

The narrator begins his description of Chijiwa's background with a terse observation: "Chijiwa Yasuhiko was an orphan" (240). This remains the single most important factor in his life. Chijiwa's father, a Satsuma samurai, had been killed in battle at the time of the Restoration, while his mother had died in a cholera epidemic when he was six. He had been taken in by the Kawashimas because Keiko was his aunt. Takeo is fond of observing that he and Chijiwa were raised together like brothers, but the text makes very clear that Takeo's father viewed Chijiwa as a burden and treated him like the poor relation that he was. This treatment had a profound effect on Chijiwa's outlook: "He realized early on that he was not like Takeo, blessed with parents, money, and status to spare, but rather someone who needed to make his own way in the world with his fists and his wits. He hated Takeo and despised his uncle" (241). This outlook makes Chijiwa a type of character that recurs in Meiji fiction—the man of disadvantaged origins, often an orphan but always with tenuous ties to family, who is willing to forego moral scruples in his pursuit of wealth and self-advancement.[52] Chijiwa's nose for the main chance has made him seek out an appointment with the army chief of staff following graduation from the military academy. He uses this position to collect bribes and to secure information that he can use for his own advantage.

Given this kind of background, Chijiwa's relationship with the institution of the *ie* is a twisted one. He often functions as a member of the extended Kawashima family—for example, becoming Keiko's main advisor when Namiko's tuberculosis arises as a family problem. Yet he uses his family connections and the rhetoric of the *ie* with utmost personal calculation. Although he pretends a concern for the House of Kawashima when he argues for a divorce, his real motives include taking revenge on Takeo and punishing Namiko, who had once rejected his advances. Chijiwa, then, is a character who shows that the *ie* can be put to cynical and self-serving uses.

Yamaki, the merchant, matches Chijiwa in his self-aggrandizing nature. But he is less repellent because he is a comic character. Filled with vulgar energy, he advertises his own philistinism and relishes his role as a Meiji parvenu. In his business as a supplier to the military, he leaves no financial opportunity unexplored, no palm ungreased. He uses the money thus gained to build a fancy house and a villa by the Sumida River and keep a slew of mistresses. He plots to gain social advancement, sending his son abroad to an unnamed university in Boston and enrolling his daughter in the girl's division of the Peer's School. The text employs a distinctly Meiji appellation when it somewhat ironically calls Yamaki a *shinshō*, or "gentleman-merchant," a combination that would have been unthinkable during the Edo period. Yamaki lives in a Meiji world where social position can be bought.

Though the text is not absolutely clear about the origins of Yamaki's connection with the Kawashimas, it suggests that he was initially a moneylender who had served Takeo's father as a lackey while the latter used his membership in the Meiji elite to build his personal wealth. Yamaki's own fortune had grown along with that of the Kawashimas, and his services had made him a *deirimono*, a merchant with close enough ties to an *ie* to come and go on a regular basis. A merchant or an artisan who is a *deiri* is expected to serve a House in many ways beyond that of his specific trade, and so it is that Yamaki becomes Keiko's ally in the scheme to divorce Namiko. He is the one called upon to act as a go-between in negotiating a divorce with the Kataokas.

The presence of Chijiwa and Yamaki in the vicinity of the Kawashimas emphasizes that the *ie* organizes hierarchies not only of age and gender, but also of class and status. The poor, self-aggrandizing cousin and the venal merchant serve, by means of contrast, to highlight the aristocratic bearing of characters such as Takeo and Namiko. The plot elements recruited to emphasize this point involve marital scheming that threatens to disrupt Takeo and Namiko's fitting union. These machinations indeed raise the specter of marriage across class and status lines. The calculating Chijiwa had determined that the best way for a young army officer to enhance his prospects was to marry a general's daughter, and he had once sent Namiko a love letter before her marriage to Takeo. The proper young woman, however, had been incensed that a suitor would approach her without her father's knowledge; not only had she ignored Chijiwa's advances, she had also later reproached him for his unseemly behavior in the most ringing terms. Her comment on his love letter drips with contempt: "I have burned that piece of filth" (*kegarawashii mono wa yakisutete shimaimashita*, 239).[53] It was this scene of Namiko putting Chijiwa in his place that had convinced Yoshiya Nobuko that the novel's heroine could not be understood as a passive and acquiescent woman. Needless to say, Namiko's rejection earns Chijiwa's permanent enmity, an enmity sharpened by his fear that discovery of his advances will lose him his connection with the Kawashimas. Yamaki's marital scheme involves his daughter Otoyo. He dreams of having his daughter marry Takeo after Namiko's divorce, creating a union that will give Otoyo a title and himself access to the Kawashima family fortune. This is never achieved because the pouty and brazen Otoyo, another broadly drawn comic character, is summarily dismissed by Takeo. In both these instances, the rejection of any possibility of miscegenation across status boundaries helps to define Takeo and Namiko's inviolate standing. The two young aristocrats are made for each other because they are more noble and virtuous than their undeserving suitors.

The functions of status and class in *Hototogisu*, however, are more complicated than they would initially appear. For if the text plays upon the young lovers' aristocracy, using their status to heighten their claims on virtue, it also makes clear that this status is of very recent vintage. Takeo and Namiko are aristocrats as a direct result of Meiji social upheavals, which created new classes and status categories and caused the violent movement of individuals and families up and down the social hierarchy. At one point Yamaki, the *shinshō* who should know something about Meiji social fluidity, explicitly points to these historical contexts by referring to the Kawashimas as *shinkazoku*, or "new aristocrats." This was a term of Meiji coinage applied to those families who were not members of the hereditary nobility based in Kyoto but rather were awarded titles by the Meiji government in recognition for their services to the newly formed state.[54] General Kataoka and Takeo's father were not, by any stretch of the imagination, born to a patrician background. They were lower-ranking provincial samurai who had demonstrated their loyalty to the state, which in turn had rewarded them in the process of producing a peerage mirroring that of the West. The Kawashimas and the Kataokas bear the burden of showing that they possess a nobility of bearing and of moral comportment befitting their new status. Any chink in their social armor—Keiko's clinging to the old-fashioned parsimony of her upbringing, for instance—immediately bares the status inconsistency produced when members of low-ranking samurai families are suddenly elevated to the aristocracy.

The roles played by Chijiwa and Yamaki in the text call attention to these social dynamics. Chijiwa is an example of what could go wrong in the social mobility of Meiji; his father had started out with the same lower-samurai status as General Kataoka and Takeo's father, but he had died before achieving any position in the new order, leaving his son dependent upon the charity of relatives. Chijiwa is a reminder that the same historical forces that created aristocrats also created paupers. Only a paper-thin line separates the social stations of the hero and the villain in this tale.

For his part, Yamaki serves to suggest some of the ways status interacted with class in the 1890s. When a rich merchant can send his daughter to the Peer's School, we see a world in which social standing can to a certain extant be bought; economically determined class has started to compromise the privilege conferred by status. Moreover, in a reflection of the historical context, the novel makes clear that Yamaki is not merely a merchant of the old school but a more than budding capitalist; as a military supplier during the Sino-Japanese War he is a link between big industry and government. He is an emblem in the novel of the immense wealth created by the alliance between capitalism and the nation-state. His association with Takeo's father underscores that the latter too was implicated in the capitalist world of greed and cozy deals. Such a portrayal was very much rooted in contemporary discourse regarding aristocrats. In a fascinating article, Nagatani Ken has argued that in the fourth decade of the Meiji era there was a merging in the media of the previously separate stereotypes of the "sneaky merchant" (*kanshō*) and the noble aristocrat; both came to be seen as social groups marked by economic superiority in an increasingly money-conscious society.[55] Status categories once far apart were being pulled together through their association with wealth. The merchant and the aristocrat looked closer when viewed through the lens of class. The creation of the category of the "gentleman merchant" had been part of this phenomenon; another expression had been press coverage of "thieving gentlemen," who took advantage of their status to acquire personal assets. There was considerable hostility at this time toward aristocrats as "parasites" who had parlayed being in the right place at the right time during the Restoration into vast, ill-gained riches.[56] For all of Takeo's disdain for Yamaki and his anger about the corrosive effects of money upon military officers, the fact remains that he is a beneficiary of the mercenary ethos of the age. His "noble" lineage ties him to a family that owes its wealth to very recent avarice. Takeo's characterization must negotiate the status inconsistency of aristocratic wealth and virtue being linked with aristocratic greed; the novel will need to resolve the contradiction of a noble hero who benefits mightily from capitalism.

There is also a distinct regional inflection to the class and status dynamics of the novel. While the second generation of aristocrats, Takeo and Namiko, exhibit the refined metropolitan manners proper to their station (Namiko had attended the girl's higher school established in Tokyo for daughters of the peerage), the members of the first generation are clearly drawn as the products of provincial upbringing. The text emphasizes this through the use of dialect. General Kataoka's dialogue contains a heavy dose of Satsuma speech, while his London-educated wife, who generally speaks in a polite "standard" or Tokyo style, is said to break into Chōshū dialect when she becomes angry.[57] Takeo's mother, too, constantly speaks using Satsuma dialect. In the context of the novel, the new aristocrats' rural roots are evaluated in contrasting ways, depending upon their overall cultural positioning. For General Kataoka, who shares in the cultural syncretism prized by the text, the provincial samurai background is a positive attribute that lets him bask in the reflected glory of Saigō Takamori's heroic simplicity. It is another matter entirely for Takeo's mother. Keiko's roots only explain and amplify her outdated values; when a servant observes that "she started out digging potatoes in Satsuma," the implication is that Keiko has not escaped her origins, whatever her current station in life (341). Keiko's belief in the *ie* is made to seem all the more obsolete—and harmful—because it belongs to a woman with dirt still clinging to her hands, a woman both temporally and spatially disconnected from the elite Tokyo world in which she lives.

THE IE AND THE KATEI IN CONFLICT

As I have already suggested, Takeo and Namiko start out believing, or at least trying to believe, that their dreams of *katei* can be accommodated within the *ie*. In the very same letters from foreign ports in which he proclaims his longings for Namiko, Takeo admonishes his young bride to take good care of his arthritic mother. Out at sea, he is able to nurse his illusion of a home that contains a loving wife devotedly serving his mother. But the cracks in such an illusion are more immediately apparent to Namiko, who has to stay and live in the Kawashima house. Takeo's mother finds fault with everything she does and gives her little recognition for her efforts to learn the *kafū*, or house customs, of her new family.[58] When Takeo comes home, Namiko is glad to have him near, but she also observes that his presence leads to an uncomfortable tension in the family:

> Although it seemed unthinkable that a parent would feel jealousy over a child, Namiko had noticed, since her husband's return, that a certain odd relationship had cropped up between herself and her mother-in-law. Upon coming back from distant seas, Takeo saw how thin his wife had become. Despite his stout, manly heart, he had been filled with sympathy for the cares she had borne during his absence, and he had renewed his efforts to comfort her. It did not escape Namiko's perceptive eyes that her mother-in-law found this more than a little distasteful. At times she silently agonized over the fact that the paths of filial piety—namely toward her mother-in-law—and love might diverge such that it would be difficult to travel both at once. (291)

Namiko thinks she is caught in the bind between filial piety and love, that is, loyalty toward the *ie* or the *katei*, and this is indeed the case. But she has seen something more through her perception that Keiko feels "jealousy"; she is at least dimly aware that she has become caught in another barely disguised triangle. Once again, she has become a rival to her own "mother," a woman who will fight for the primacy of her relationship to a man. If Keiko's possession by the ghost of her husband makes her gendered position at times ambivalent, in her rivalry with her daughter-in-law she is all "woman," a creature who cannot stand to share male affection with another female. Namiko realizes that the more Takeo loves her, the more reason there will be for Keiko to despise her. Namiko's *katei*, based on conjugal love, is threatened not only by the *ie*'s bonds of obligation but also by passions that lie just below its surface.

The plot element that sets off this explosive situation is Namiko's contraction of tuberculosis. There have been some excellent recent studies that cogently locate *Hototogisu* in Japanese historical discourses on the disease, and so I will not delve into the matter here.[59] But it is worthwhile briefly noting some elements of the cultural construction of tuberculosis as they relate to status and the family. First, tuberculosis was associated with the privileged. Although, in fact, mortality from the disease was highest in industrial centers or lower-class urban neighborhoods, there was a considerable discourse describing tuberculosis as a disease of the wealthy and the talented.[60] This association, which was already present from the Edo period, was abetted by the arrival of Western Romantic writing that connected consumption with beauty, sensitivity, or desirability (in the ways that Susan Sontag has shown in *Illness as Metaphor*).[61] Thus, by having Namiko die of tuberculosis, *Hototogisu* gives her a disease that confirms her aristocratic status and leaves her ever paler, more gentle, more ethereal as she proceeds toward death.

Second, in turn-of-the-century Japan, there was no agreement regarding the etiology of the disease. Epidemiologists had yet to reach the current understanding of tuberculosis as a multifactorial disease, in which infection tends to occur when the presence of the tuberculosis bacillus combines with certain conditions having to do with the patient (his or her age or sex) and the environment (population density).[62] Although Robert Koch had isolated the tubercle bacillus in 1882, the implications of this discovery were not widely recognized during the Meiji period. The notion of contagion was present generally in the discourse, but how contagion was accomplished was not specifically known. In the absence of concrete information, many Japanese regarded tuberculosis as hereditary. What can be said is that the lay population had recognized the frequent clustering of the disease in people who lived in close proximity. Because the disease was so often fatal, they feared it as something that could wipe out entire families. It is this fear that erupts during a critical scene, where Takeo's mother argues that extreme measures are necessary for the preservation of the *ie*. When Keiko begins to urge her son to divorce his wife, she initially recalls that Namiko's mother had died of the disease and suggests an etiology based on heredity:

"Couldn't this illness be handed down from mother to daughter?" she asks (315). But she quickly turns to another etiology when she recalls a family that has been wiped out by tuberculosis:

"Také, even among diseases, this is an especially terrible one. You must know about this, too, but do you remember Governor Tōgō, whose son you used to fight with all the time? How about that child's mother? She died of consumption—that was last April—and then at the end of the year the governor died too. Are you listening? On top of that, the son—he was working as an engineer somewhere—he just recently died of consumption as well. They both caught it from the mother. There are lots of stories like this. Také, that's why when it comes to this disease you can't let your guard down. If you do, it'll soon be a crisis." (316)

We can see how the doubled etiology of tuberculosis constructs it as an illness devastating to the family. As a hereditary disease, it kills off descendants; as a contagious disease, it kills off spouses.

Having established the character of tuberculosis, Keiko proceeds to press Takeo to accept a divorce. As her argument moves forward, it begins to widen to include the *ie* and the state. In admonishing her son to do his duty, Keiko calls upon the power of interlocking institutions:

"Listen to me. Perhaps it isn't so bad just now, but I've made it a point to find out from the doctors. When it comes to this disease, you might improve for awhile, but it soon gets worse again. It comes back when it gets warm or cold. There's not a single person who's ever been cured of tuberculosis; that's what the doctors say. Granted, Nami might not die now, but she'll surely get worse again soon. And there's no doubt it'll get transmitted to you. Isn't that so, Také? You'll get it, and then when you have children, they'll get it. It's not only Nami we're talking about. If you, the precious master of the House (*daiji na shujin*), and your children, the precious heirs (*daiji na atotori*), become consumptives and die, the House of Kawashima will be destroyed. Listen to me. You got where you are because of your father's care. And now, the House of Kawashima, upon which the emperor has bestowed his personal favors, will end in your generation.—I do feel sorry for Nami, and I know it's hard for you. It's not easy for me to be a parent and to bring up something like this. It's awful. But, no matter what you say, the disease is what it is. I can't give you up, or give up the House of Kawashima, just because I feel sorry for Nami. You need to think deeply about this and resign yourself to what has to be done." (318)

In Keiko's logic, Takeo's wish to remain married to Namiko is self-destructive and, worse, destructive of the *ie*. His wish makes Takeo, the sole male heir, a killer of his unborn children and of the future lineage of his House, an ingrate not only toward his parents but toward the emperor, who has given the *ie* its present aristocratic status. Keiko's rationale, which conflates loyalty to the emperor and filial piety, is that of the *kazoku kokka* or the "family-state," which regarded the *ie* as a constituent unit of the nation.

Faced with his mother's monolithic argument, Takeo attempts to address the ethics of the situation by replying that divorcing Namiko would be inhuman and wrong, and that taking such a step might kill her immediately. Keiko's response is to speak more specifically about the social practice of divorce. When she does this, it becomes clear that she has thoroughly absorbed the ideology that women are replaceable commodities who must be jettisoned if they do not help to reproduce the *ie*: "There's a lot of this sort of thing in life. Women are divorced if they don't fit in with the customs of the house, they're divorced if there are no children, they're divorced if they get a serious illness. That, Také, is the way it is in life. There's nothing improper or cruel about it" (319–20).

This argument evokes Takeo's most impassioned response: "You say that's the way life is, that's the way life is, but there's nothing that says we're free to do what's wrong just because everyone else does. Divorcing a woman just because she's ill is something out of the past. If I'm wrong, and that's what's being done in our society now, then perhaps we should, we *must*, destroy that society" (320).

Peter Brooks has written that "one of the most immediately striking features of melodrama is the extent to which characters tend to say, directly and explicitly, their moral judgments of the world."[63] This stems, of course, from melodrama's endeavor to impart moral legibility on human experience. Here, the mother has declared in no uncertain terms her willingness to sacrifice Namiko for the *ie*. And Takeo has taken a principled stand that views the requirements of the *ie* as morally indefensible. He rejects custom as a model for the present and he codes *ie* ideology as an anachronism. His moral judgment calls for him to revolt against the *ie* even if this means doing violence to the world in which he lives.

Keiko recognizes the precipice at which Takeo stands, the choice that he is about to make, and she responds by turning to the argument of last resort. She grabs a memorial tablet from the family altar and thrusts it in Takeo's face:

"See if you can say that one more time in front of your father. Go ahead and say it. The tablets of all our ancestors are looking down at you. Say it again, you ingrate. . . . Someone who always sticks up for his wife and doesn't listen to his parents is an ingrate, isn't that so? Isn't an ingrate someone who disregards the body that his parents raised, someone who destroys the *ie* passed down through the generations? Takeo, you're an ingrate, a huge ingrate. . . . Is your wife more important than your parents? What a fool you are. Whenever you open your mouth, it's always 'my wife this, my wife that.' What about your parents? You're always talking about Nami, you ingrate. I'll disown you." (321)

This speech operates on multiple levels that cannot be fully reproduced through translation. On one level, the crisis here concerns *ie* continuity. By thrusting the ancestral tablet, a concrete symbol of the *ie*'s diachronic nature, in Takeo's face, Keiko is making the point that the *ie* must be secured through the behavior of each succeeding generation. Takeo owes his dead father and his other ancestors a debt for *ie* membership, which he can repay only by putting aside personal feelings. By translating the recurring term *oya* in the plural form "parents," I have emphasized the connection Keiko seeks to make between ancestors and parents, who are the most recent iterations of ancestors. But there is another level to her discourse, hidden in the fact that the Japanese language does not need to mark plurals. *Oya* can refer either to parents or to a parent in the singular. If we reread the passage with this in mind, the extent to which Keiko is foregrounding herself becomes evident. She is the parent whose advice Takeo is rejecting, she is the one who nurtured his body. Keiko is also asking more specifically: "Is your wife more important than me?" Boiling away alongside the ideological commitment to *ie* is the sexual jealousy that Namiko had noted.

The family seems ready to self-destruct in the confrontation between the son who wants to uphold feeling and moral judgment and the jealous mother who wants to protect the *ie* at all costs. This is a dangerous combination, and there appears to be a real possibility that the House of Kawashima will end, that real violence will be done to the *ie*. But, in a suggestive interruption, a telegraph arrives ordering Takeo back to his ship. War is brewing in China, and the fleet has suddenly been ordered out on maneuvers. The state intervenes to bring a temporary halt to the battle between mother and son. Takeo departs after making his mother promise that she will do nothing until his return.

This is a promise the mother will not keep. Advised and aided by such henchmen as Yamaki and Chijiwa, she approaches Namiko's family and asks them to accept a divorce. General Kataoka, a proud man who would not dream of having his daughter stay in a family where she is unwanted, quickly accepts her return. The divorce is complete before Takeo comes back. The palpably awkward narration of Takeo's thoughts after he learns of the divorce emphasizes the exclusion of the young couple from this crucial decision: "She was his wife for eternity. Yet his mother had divorced her in his name, and her father had acted for her in accepting her return" (371).[64] There is a lot of acting by proxy going on here. The *ie* has shown itself powerful. Parents have exercised their authority over their children and the eternal bonds of love underlying the *katei* have proven defenseless.

Faced with this fait accompli, both Takeo and Namiko enter realms of pain. Devastated by their separation, frustrated by their helplessness, and angered by the wrongs perpetuated against them in the name of *ie*, Takeo and Namiko become victims whose suffering serves as a sign of virtue.[65] Takeo heads back to China, where his bitterness makes him a reckless warrior. Namiko treads the path to death:

> The very next day after she had heard of the unexpected outcome, her illness grew visibly worse. From her writhing breast, she brought up the scarlet stuff of her soul, so much so that she was hardly conscious. Her doctors were silent, her family furrowed their brows, and she waited for a death that might come at any moment. Her life truly hung by a thread. Namiko awaited death with joy. Oh happy death. What pleasure was there, what worth was there in remaining in this world for someone so suddenly and unexpectedly thrust into the depths of darkness? Whom should she hate, and whom should she yearn for? Such thoughts hardly had a chance to form. All there was was a darkness that she feared and loathed, that she only wanted to escape. Death was truly her only route toward life. Namiko waited impatiently for death. (373)

The hyperbole of Namiko's suffering—the agony of her body, the torture of her soul—transforms her into a melodramatic heroine. Her virtue is validated. The spectacular pathos of her pain makes visible the cruelty of the *ie* and the sweetness of the *katei* destroyed.

RESISTANCE, THE NATION, AND TIME

It is the melodrama in *Hototogisu*—an insistence on the nomination of good and evil, an emphasis on suffering as a means of providing moral legibility—that allows the novel to be read as an oppositional or resistant text. A mother hidebound in the *ie* ideology separates a loving couple by force and deception. A son argues for an ethics based on feeling and finds himself devastated. A young woman who had wanted nothing more than to be a loving wife and a good daughter-in-law is cast out of the family and becomes a martyr to the idea of *katei*. There are, without a doubt, chords of protest being sounded here against the treatment of women in the *ie* system, against the transcendent value attached to the continuity of the family line, against the sacrifice of feeling in an ideology based upon duty.

Yet we need to keep in mind, too, the Meiji view of the novel as the very model of respectability, as a "healthy," morally upright work suitable for consumption in the *katei*. Whatever its protest quotient, the work was not ultimately dangerous or revolutionary. Women and children could be safely exposed to its contents. Examined from such a perspective, *Hototogisu* quickly emerges as a work whose protest is purposely blunted and shown to be no threat to existing patterns of authority. Indeed, the novel demonstrates that some of the newer configurations of family it advocates can be even more helpful to established authority than the aspects of the *ie* it regards as outmoded.

To begin with, the Kawashima's *ie* and the world around it are left more or less intact. Takeo never acts on his outcry—"We must destroy that society"—and returns rather meekly to his own house after the war.[66] There is more than a suggestion of residual tension over his mother's actions, but the fact remains that he does go back once his initial fury has been exhausted. The *ie* still has its heir.

I do not want to overemphasize Takeo's return, however, because I think the novel's protest quotient has already been severely compromised by making Kawashima Keiko the most virulent supporter of *ie* ideology in the novel. It is important to recognize, in this respect, that she is not the only character in *Hototogisu* to operate within the *ie* system. Although General Kataoka is portrayed as occasionally being bested in argument by his Westernized second wife, there is no doubt that he functions as a patriarchal househead. He made the decision to give Namiko to Takeo, and when he is approached about the divorce, he agrees on the spot to the dissolution of his daughter's marriage. The text, however, avoids the question of his power in the *ie* by depicting him as a loving father who constantly worries about his daughter's welfare, sympathizes with her trials, and does his best to comfort her in her illness. Similarly, Takeo, the proponent of sentiment over institution, is clearly shown to be a beneficiary of the *ie*. As the comparison with Chijiwa indicates, Takeo's inherited social position and wealth have clearly given him advantages in life. These advantages only make him all the more appealing as a romantic hero, and it is Chijiwa, the poor cousin locked in a marginal position, who is portrayed as having been twisted by the *ie* institution. Despite this considerable evidence that the *ie* favors the interests of many others, it is Takeo's mother who takes the villain's role when it comes time to articulate and act upon the ideology. As we have seen, she is someone whose values are suspect because of her positioning in relation to various hierarchies of gender, status, culture, and region. Not only is she a woman, she is a woman who expresses male aggression and remains tied to her dirt-poor Satsuma origins. She is, moreover, a mother motivated by an incestuous jealousy that she cannot fully acknowledge. This portrayal allows *ie* ideology to be read as the belief of a particularly backward woman, who has turned from being victim to victimizer and who acts against her son and her daughter-in-law in a fit of submerged erotic rage. Coding the *ie* as an anachronism has also meant compartmentalizing it, eliding the participation of good, modern Meiji men. The novel never engages the historical fact that the *ie* was supported not only by neurotic old women but also by leaders of the state. *Hototogisu*'s protest against the *ie* system, then, begins to appear compromised if we take into account the gender bias present in the way it assigns responsibility.

The blunting of protest in *Hototogisu* also extends to its portrayal of newer domestic configurations. If the novel offers the *katei* as an alternative to the *ie*, then it is being offered as a relatively unthreatening alternative. The *katei* does not possess the power to fundamentally challenge the *ie*, let alone the nation-state that the family system served. There are signs that Namiko recognizes this even when she is most desperately clinging to the idea of the *katei*. The following dialogue takes place on the beach at Zushi, where Namiko has been sent during her convalescence. She has been contemplating the possibility of never recovering from her illness when Takeo takes her hand, adorned with the diamond engagement ring that he gave her, and presses it to his lips:

> Namiko smiled through her tears. "I will get well. I'll do my best to get well. Why is it that human beings have to die! I want to live! I want to live for a thousand years, no ten thousand. If I have to die, let's the two of us die together! The two of us together!"
> "Namiko, if you die, I won't live on."
> "Truly? How happy that makes me! The two of us together!—But there's your mother and your work. Even if that's what you intend, you're not free

to do what you want. When the time comes, I'm going to have to go on ahead and wait for you—after I die, will you think of me from time to time? Will you, dear? Will you?"

Takeo swept away his tears. He stroked Namiko's hair and said, "Let's not talk like this anymore. You'll take care of yourself and get well quickly, Namiko. And we'll both live long lives, and then we'll celebrate our golden anniversary."

Namiko grasped her husband's hands firmly between her own. She threw herself against him, and her warm tears fell upon his knees. "Even if I die, I will be your wife. No matter what anyone does to us, no matter what happens with my illness, no matter if I die, forever and ever into the future I am your wife." (308–9)

The words and images in this exorbitant love scene partake of layered cultural discourses. The diamond ring, the golden wedding anniversary, the promise of eternal union all derive from Western ideals of domestic love. But the suggestion of double suicide comes from somewhere else; Namiko and Takeo brush up here against the Edo world of *shinjū*, where death is the only culturally sanctioned escape for socially shackled lovers. The proponents of domestic love, it seems, are forced to reach back toward a narrative plot from the past when they contemplate a foreclosed future. What is most significant here, however, is that even amidst her fantasies of a love that transcends death, Namiko knows that her husband must live to attend to the demands of *ie* and the state: "But there's your mother and your work," she says. "You're not free to do what you want." She is more than a little clairvoyant here, for even before she dies her husband will be divorced from her and on his way to fight in the Sino-Japanese War.

Beyond its relative powerlessness, there is also an indication that the *katei* can serve the interests of the state. When Namiko receives a visit from Chizuko, her cousin and best friend, the two engage in girlish fantasies about the future. Namiko's imagination takes flight as she envisions her own husband and her friend's fiancé, a bureaucrat in the Foreign Ministry, taking part in the work of the nation:

> "When I'm in bed like this, I think about all kinds of things. . . . Please don't laugh at me now. Many years from now, imagine there's a war against some foreign country and Japan wins. Then your husband will be the foreign minister, and he'll march into wherever and negotiate a peace treaty. And my husband will be the commodore of the fleet, and he'll lead dozens of warships into their port. . . ."
>
> "If that's the case [Chizuko broke in] then your father will be the com-

mander in chief, and my father will be in the House of Peers where he'll appropriate tens of millions of yen."
"With all this going on [Namiko added] you and I will head out with a Red Cross flag before us." (297)

All of this talk is for the fun of it, and Namiko and Chizuko burst out laughing when they are done. But it is significant that, when their imaginations run free, the two young women fantasize about a Greater Japan and the highly gendered roles they will play in it. Namiko is proud of being a military officer's daughter and wife; she regards foreign wars as a route to glory for both her nation and her men; and she sees herself as a potential female auxiliary in the work of the nation.

The kind of nationalism we glimpse here grows ever more intense as the novel proceeds; this trajectory explains why the work stops short of implicating the state in its indictment of the *ie*. To analyze the particular configuration of *Hototogisu*'s nationalism, let me adapt from Bakhtin the notion of the "chronotope," the intersection of historical time and space in a narrative. With uncommon elegance, Bakhtin has defined the chronotope in the following way: "In the literary artistic chronotope, spatial and temporal indicators are fused into one carefully thought-out, concrete whole. Time, as it were, thickens, takes on flesh, becomes artistically visible; likewise, space becomes charged and responsive to the movements of time, plot, and history."[67]

In the first two-thirds of the novel, *Hototogisu* exhibits a chronotope of geographical shifts accomplished within a relatively linear timeline. Although there are analepses, or flashbacks, to fill in backgrounds, time keeps moving forward in the main as the scene shifts from Ikaho, the site of the honeymoon, then to Tokyo, and on to the seaside town of Zushi, where Namiko is sent when she falls ill. One thing can be said about the significance of topography in these earlier scenes. The space of innocence, where Takeo and Namiko enjoy the domestic bliss of the *katei*, is already marginalized, first being set at Ikaho and later at the villa in Zushi. There are only a few happy moments for the couple in Tokyo, which is overwhelmingly a space dominated by the difficulties of family interactions and the plotting of such characters as Yamaki and Chijiwa. The budding *katei* or "home" of Takeo and Namiko is largely homeless.

In the last third of the novel, the chronotope of temporal and spatial progression gives way to a different chronotope, where a series of returning analepses, flashbacks that reach backward and then return to the narrative present, show events occurring at the same time in very different locales. A substantial part of this section of the novel follows Takeo as he goes to war in the fall of 1894 and takes part in the decisive battle in the Yellow Sea, where much of the Chinese fleet is destroyed. The narrative here attempts to provide both a bird's-eye view of the strategic maneuvers of the two opposing fleets, as well as an account of Takeo's bravery. The tone is unapologetically nationalistic:

> Our main fleet headed toward the right, the advance fleet to the left, and, having captured and surrounded the enemy, our forces commenced firing. The fighting approached its zenith. As the battle grew heated Takeo no longer took notice of himself. . . . He was not aware of his voice growing hoarse from shouting repeated commands, the sweat pouring down his face. The enemy shells, aimed toward the flagship, rained down upon the *Matsushima*, and the ship's armor was pierced, the woodwork burned, and blood ran on the deck—all of this Takeo failed to register. His entire being was consumed by the heat of battle, so that his heart seemed to beat in time with the booming of the cannons, both friendly and unfriendly, and he found strange the silence around his ears during lulls in the firing. Since this was the case with Takeo, the gunners under his command took no notice of the enemy rounds flying around them. They loaded, took aim, fired and loaded again. . . . When fire threatened to strike, they extinguished it; they transported ammunition without being ordered; they carried away the dead and wounded as soon as they fell. Hardly waiting for an order from an officer, their hands and their legs moved of their own accord. The fighting machine ran smoothly and relentlessly. (355–56)

The narrative calls out to a Japanese narratee using the rhetoric of "ours" versus "the enemy." Such a rhetoric ties narration to the nation and assumes support for Japanese military actions abroad. The content of the passage is similarly nationalistic: Takeo is deprived of the consciousness with which he feels the personal pain of his divorce and is welded, together with his men, into a single, mindless fighting unit. The emotional attachments of the *katei*, it would seem, do not hinder the work of men in the service of the nation.

The battle sequence ends with Takeo suffering a serious wound. He is evacuated to the Japanese port of Sasebo, a main staging area for the war, and recovers slowly. At this point, the narrative engages in a series of analepses to describe what has been happening on the home front during Takeo's months aboard ship off China and his recovery. A short sequence summarizes how his mother back in Tokyo had been shocked by her usually obedient son's furious response to the news that Namiko had been divorced without his knowledge. Keiko had briefly agonized over whether she had done the right thing, but this pang of conscience had only made her angrier at both her son and Namiko. As a way of steadying the *ie*, she had begun to think of a second marriage for Takeo, even considering the merchant Yamaki's daughter as a prospective bride. Another much longer analepsis describes how Namiko, following her divorce, had returned to her family's villa in Zushi. She had continued to long for Takeo. Her despair had brought her close to suicide, but she had found solace in the friendship of a devoutly Christian older woman. Learning of Takeo's injury, Namiko had sent him a care package, which he had immediately recognized as being from his former wife, although she had deliberately omitted any identification of the sender.

This chronotope I have been describing, where returning analepses knit together what happens during the same months in the Yellow Sea, in the Kawashima home in Tokyo, and at the villa in Zushi, is necessary for some practical reasons. War and divorce pull apart the main characters, and thus the novel must describe their separate experiences. But there is something else going on as well, for the narrative clearly shows the interdependence, the emotional relevance of things that happen at the same time in distant places. Here, let me add to the idea of the chronotope by referring to Benedict Anderson's concept of "simultaneity."[68] Anderson has argued that the capacity to "think the nation"—to imagine as a community people living at the same time in far flung locales—is crucial to the development of modern nationalism. According to Anderson, there are two mediums that most encourage the apprehension of this kind of simultaneity. The first is the newspaper, which gathers on a single page events occurring across the country at the same time. Significantly, Namiko is shown as an avid newspaper reader, who peruses the daily papers for information as mundane as the weather in Takeo's ports of call and as momentous as news of battle. The other medium Anderson points to is the novel, whose generic techniques of analepsis equip it to show many events happening at the same time. The simultaneity pictured in *Hototogisu* pulls together Tokyo, the metropole, with the oceans at the reaches of Japanese imperial ambition and a small seaside town where a young woman is slowly dying. Events in these varying locales are associated within the same space of time and within the same pages. *Hototogisu* is a text that allows its reader to "think the empire." It is no accident that the battle scenes employ the rhetoric of "our fleet" and the "enemy." For this is a text that posits a narratee that is "us," the Japanese of the turn of the century beginning to imagine Japan as a colonial power.

The idea of simultaneity inscribed here involves certain assumptions of gender, for it is men who go off to fight in foreign seas and women who wait for them at home. The novel allows the reader to envision in a nationalist framework not only events that occur at the same time in different topographies, but also events that occur at the same time to men and women. Many years later, Roka wrote an autobiographical novel in which he suggests, in another layer of paratextual commentary, that he had written the battle scenes because of his desire to engage in a certain kind of gendered discourse.[69] (In the following quotation, the Roka character is called Kumaji.) "But Kumaji found something wanting in a simple tale about the home, aimed only at the tears and smiles of women and children, and . . . he could not help expressing something of his masculine tastes. Thus, at the beginning of the third part of the work, he inserted the scene of the naval battle in the Yellow Sea."[70] If we are to follow this condescending explanation, the simultaneity captured in the novel exists because the author wanted to engage in some macho chest beating. Tired of writing about the *katei* for female readers, he had written about the nation at war in order to indulge his masculinity.

The gender dynamics expressed here bear out Linda Williams's observation that moral legibility in the melodrama is achieved through a combination of "pathos *and* action." If the suffering of the victim, conventionally assigned to females, is one aspect of melodrama, then there is another side typified by male action films—Westerns, gangster films, Clint Eastwood movies, and the *Rambo* series—in which outbursts of violent agency reveal moral worth:

> The suffering of the victim-hero is important for the establishment of moral legitimacy, but suffering, in these examples, is less extended and ultimately gives way to action. Similarly, the recognition of virtue is at least partially achieved through the performance of some deed. Here pathos mixes with other emotions—suspense, fear, anxiety, anger, laughter and so on—experienced in rescues, chases, gunfights, fistfights, or spaceship fights of the various action genres.[71]

We might readily add battle to the list of situations faced by male heroes in action-oriented melodrama. Takeo's bravery in war adds another gendered layer to his portrayal as a melodramatic hero. His commitment to courageous action, in fact, is coextensive with his suffering, for it is desperation bred by the latter that makes him fearless. In effect, suffering and action make each other visible in his portrayal, and both serve to highlight his virtue. We should note, however, that if Takeo's suffering is related to the loss of his *katei*, his actions, despite being partially motivated by his suffering, are undertaken not in the interests of the *katei*, but of the nation.

This slippage persists right through to the closing scene of the novel, which takes place after Namiko has died. Finally home from his service abroad, Takeo goes to his wife's grave with a bunch of white chrysanthemums grasped in his hand. Suffering spectacularly, he murmurs "Oh Namiko, why did you have to die?" as he reads to himself her deathbed letter in which she writes that her soul will be with him forever. He is standing at the grave grief-stricken when he hears someone approaching:

> With Namiko's testament still in his hand, a startled Takeo turned around, wiping his tears away. He was face to face with Lieutenant General Kataoka, who was standing at the gate to the family plot.
>
> Takeo hung his head. He suddenly felt his hands being grasped firmly, and when he looked up his eyes met those of the general, which welled with tears.
>
> "Takeo, it was hard for me too."
>
> As the two men held each other's hands, the tears fell drop by drop at the foot of the grave marker.
>
> After a while, the general dried his tears. He patted Takeo's shoulder and said, "Even though Nami has died, I am still your father. You've got to be strong now. There's still a long way to go. Everything that happens serves to forge a man's heart. It's been awhile, Takeo. Why don't you come with me and tell me all about Taiwan." (417–18)

In the last paragraph of the novel, a new lineage of men has been formed. The "father" and the "son," whose relationship has ironically been cemented rather than severed by Namiko's death, go off together to engage in men's talk about Taiwan, which has just been ceded to Japan in the Treaty of Shimonoseki and where Takeo has been briefly assigned. The novel concludes with the comforting thought that all the suffering experienced by the male characters do not weaken, but rather make them stronger, strong enough, in fact, to carry on the work of empire. Roka's autobiographical novel again provides direction on how this final scene should be read:

> Kumaji finally allowed Namiko to die. Takeo was still alive. Kumaji was at a loss what to do with him. If he made Takeo commit suicide, then everything

would end with a trite tragedy. If Takeo turned desperate, that would not serve Namiko well. Takeo could not die. He had to live. Where would the strength to live come from? To make a man required a woman's love and, beyond that, a man's strength. Aside from a supportive, horizontal strength, there needed to be a vertical strength passed down from man to man. Kumaji finally hit upon the idea of having the father and the husband grasp hands before Namiko's grave.[72]

In this analysis, what allows Takeo to live is finding his place in a male hierarchy. In a clear instance of affiliation reproducing elements of filiation, General Kataoka's "adoption" of Takeo involves a *re-presentation* of the lineal descent that characterizes the *ie*. In the process, the many anxieties attendant upon Takeo's relations with family, gender, culture, status, and class have been transcended. His new af/filiative relationship absolves Takeo of any responsibility for the death of his *katei* and Namiko, and frees him from the backward beliefs of a gender-crossing mother. It also resolves the status inconsistency in his portrayal as a morally superior aristocrat benefiting from recently acquired wealth, for his adoption by General Kataoka removes any taint of the blood tie with the violent and mercenary prefectural governor who had been his father by birth. Takeo's manhood is now confirmed by a fictive lineage connecting him to a gentle patriarch who is both a general of a modern army and an exemplar of samurai ethics, a lineage of fighting men in the service of the nation.

In a way, the third of the triangles involving Namiko had presaged this resolution. This triangle, which binds Namiko to her father and her husband, differs from Namiko's rivalries with her mothers, for it is characterized by an eerie absence of jealousy and the emphasis of similarities between the potential rival parties. When Namiko thinks about her equally intense relationships with her father and her husband, she is struck by the resemblance between the two men:

Namiko's father had said he liked Takeo right from the start of the marriage negotiations. Having married Takeo, Namiko truly understood why. Generous and manly, plain spoken yet compassionate, and without a grain of vulgarity—Takeo was a younger version of her father. Indeed, the way he walked, swinging his shoulders and stamping his feet, and even his childlike laugh resembled her father, and Namiko clung to him with heartfelt and undivided joy. (266)

The two men in Namiko's life are joined through her in a relationship of mutual identity and mutual affection. While the emphasis in the passage above is upon the sense of fulfillment that Namiko feels in the neat resolution of her Oedipal desires, it is easy to see why the relationship between the two men might continue despite her death. The general had liked Takeo before Namiko had even met him, and Takeo had returned the affection—we might recall here that a photograph of the general had decorated Takeo's study along with the silver, heart-shaped frame holding a portrait of his wife. The male ties had been important even amidst Takeo and Namiko's brief domestic bliss. Now that Namiko is dead, there are reasons why this homosocial bond should grow all the stronger.[73] When the general refers to his daughter's death, saying "Everything that happens serves to forge a man's heart," he is referring to a new level of identity that the two men share. Both men have lost Namiko, and they are better men because of it. Suffering has validated their mutual virtue. At the conclusion of the novel, Namiko is most important for her absence, an absence that contributes to the cult of imperial manliness.

There is a passage in one of Namiko's letters to Takeo that resonates in fascinating ways with her famous deathbed declaration that she would never be born a woman again. When she writes to tell Takeo that she has been following his voyage on a map of the world and reading the newspaper for weather reports from foreign ports, Namiko says: "My heart is filled with the impossible fantasy that, had I been born a man, I could become a sailor and never leave your side" (271). Namiko's fantasies had told her that true happiness, a true bond with Takeo, lay not so much in the *katei* but in an alternative male relationship where desire is figured in the service of the nation.

Hototogisu, a novel that begins with an affirmation of domestic romance, must ultimately acknowledge the fragility of heterosexual love. Its despairing male protagonist finds solace in an alternative *ie*, built upon female absence, that can reproduce fathers and sons, willing soldiers for the empire, through the agency of adoptive male lineage. The Meiji state's version of the *ie*, as patriarchal as it was, had depended upon the participation of women for its formation and reproduction. The ideological contradiction of this melodrama traces a trajectory toward an exclusively male fictive family serving the interconnected needs of manliness and nationalism.

A Jewel Shining in the Mud

Love and Money in *Konjiki yasha*

Outbursts of violence punctuate *Konjiki yasha* (The golden demon), the blockbuster novel that Ozaki Kōyō wrote between 1897 and 1903. At the climax of what is perhaps the most famous scene in all of Meiji melodrama—the scene on the beach at Atami repeated in countless *shinpa* plays and movies, and reproduced in an endless succession of illustrations and photographs—the protagonist Hazama Kan'ichi topples with a well-aimed kick his wavering lover and fiancée Shigizawa Miya, who has decided to marry a richer man.[1] Later in the novel, Kan'ichi is beaten senseless by thugs, after he has become a hated moneylender in a perverse reaction to his loss. The loan shark who initiates Kan'ichi into his new trade is burned alive in a fire started by the aggrieved mother of one of his customers. In the most spectacular scene of violence in the novel, Miya wrestles over a knife with Mitsue, a female usurer in love with Kan'ichi, stabs her to death, and then pleads with Kan'ichi to run her through with the same knife:

> "After this, my life is already lost. I beg you, Kan'ichi, let me die at your hands. I can then die happily knowing you've pardoned me. Will you take revenge for all that's passed between us and give me your forgiveness? I beg

this of you, Kan'ichi. If you still won't forgive me, after I've died with these feelings, I'll hate you through seven cycles of death and rebirth. So don't let me wander. Just chant a sutra with your lips and kill me with one thrust."

Miya held Kan'ichi's hand in hers as she made him grasp the bloodstained knife, and she repeatedly rubbed her cheek against the hand she had missed so dearly. . . .

"They say one's final wish decides the life to come, and so I'll cling to this thought as I die. Kan'ichi, see my regret and forgive me!"

Miya's voice trembled and she seemed about to embrace him when she suddenly dropped forward aiming for the knifepoint held above the man's knees.

"What, what have you done!" Something let go in Kan'ichi's chest, and he was finally able to speak.

"Kan'ichi!" Horrible to behold, Miya's upraised throat was soaked with blood, its center pierced by the knife. Without loosening her hand, she opened her tortured eyes and looked up at the man's face.

Totally beside himself, Kan'ichi took her in his arms, crying, "Miya, what have you done!" He tried to pull out the deadly knife, but the determined woman would not lessen the strength of her grip.

"Let go, let go of this. I'm telling you to let go. Why won't you let go?"

"Kan . . . Kan'ichi."

"What is it?"

"I'm happy. There's . . . nothing more I want. You've forgiven me."

"Let go, loosen your hand."

"I won't! Now I can die in peace. Kan'ichi, I'm starting to fade away, so hurry, hurry, and let me hear you say you'll forgive me. Say it. Say that you'll forgive me!"

The blood pulsed out of her more rapidly, and the shadows of the hereafter seemed to draw darkly near. Kan'ichi could not bear to look. His heart was in total disorder.

"Miya, hold on."

"Oh."

"I forgive you! I've forgiven you at last; I . . . I . . . I pardon you!"

"Kan'ichi!"

"Miya!"

"I'm so happy! So happy!"

Kan'ichi's heart was about to burst. No words would come out of his mouth. Hot tears falling from his eyes soaked Miya's face, which he cradled in his arms, and he desperately kissed her icy lips. Miya painfully swallowed the man's saliva passed to her from lip to lip.[2]

Unlike the other instances of violence in *Konjiki yasha*, this explosion of blood and hyperbolic emotion—the reader is finally told toward the end of the scene—takes place in the realm of dream. Yet this dramatic moment of determined female action and male impotence, tortured atonement and sadomasochistic desire, is merely a slightly heightened extension of the all-consuming relations between Kan'ichi and Miya. In this work the melodrama's realistic surface is constantly broken by frenzied sentiments it cannot contain.[3] Violence is a marker of the passions generated by the melodrama's polarized morality, which defines a wrong that can be expiated only by death.

In a panel discussion on *Konjiki yasha*, held while the novel was still being serialized, Ozaki Kōyō said that his intent was to draw the "battle between love and gold."[4] This is a statement that points to melodramatic dynamics, for it attempts to install a binary designation of "love" as virtue and "gold" as vice. When Miya chooses the wealth of Tomiyama over the love offered by Kan'ichi, she makes a choice that dooms both of them to lives of longing, where the cold comforts of gold offer little compensation for the loss of love. The brilliant turn in *Konjiki yasha*'s melodramatic structure involves transforming both protagonists into villains: Miya is condemned by her mercenary choice and, as we will see, Kan'ichi becomes less than human through metamorphosing into a loan shark. Yet *Konjiki yasha* makes clear that both characters are being motivated by love. Miya is driven mad by the knowledge that she has thrown away the irreplaceable, and Kan'ichi is consumed by a betrayed lover's anger and pain. Throughout the novel neither character can escape the reality that they once loved each other and still do, each in their own twisted way. They both suffer mightily, and this suffering becomes a gauge of the love that will not let them go. *Konjiki yasha*, then, functions as a paean to love as virtue by demonstrating the frightening consequences of its loss. "Love" here acquires a special luminosity precisely because the characters' moral flaws render it forever out of reach.

I will examine how *Konjiki yasha*, like the texts studied in the other chapters, attempts to mobilize melodrama's binary morality. My analysis will show that the passions in the novel are produced as much by ideological failure as by ideological certitude. Both poles of the binary opposition in *Konjiki yasha* are riven by ideological complications. The "love" celebrated by the novel turns out to be fundamentally destructive, and the "money" denigrated by so many characters turns out to be all-encompassing, leaving no exterior site of resistance. These contradictions become clear in the way love and money impact families both conventional and affiliative. And they prove to be deeply connected to the gendering of success and the inconsistencies of status in Meiji Japan. The novel's gesture toward a transcendent morality is also complicated by its multitude of languages. Language is the *melos* of Meiji melodramatic fiction. Baroque combinations of highly stylized and lyrical languages carry forward the plot. Emotions heighten and crises crest with swelling chords of language. Yet the fact that no single language predominates undercuts the melodrama's endeavor to put forward a single set of moral values. Throughout my discussion, my central concern will be to limn the discursive and ideological contradictions capable of motivating the violent passions of Kan'ichi's dream.

SOCIAL AND DISCURSIVE LOCATIONS

In order to begin to understand the moral choices made by Kan'ichi and Miya, we need to understand how their relative social locations shape their responses to intertwined discourses of family and ambition, marriage and love, status and gender. These social locations are produced by historical forces we have already seen: the extinction of Edo status categories and their replacement by new identities, the growth of capitalism that fueled a concomitant fear of the morally corrosive effects of money, and the radical intensification of social mobility, both upward and downward, in a suddenly more fluid society.

Miya is the only daughter of Shigizawa Ryūzō, an ex-samurai and former bureaucrat who now supports himself through real estate investments. Ryūzō, we can gather, is someone who has weathered the social changes of Meiji relatively well, but not too well. This last point is important because future security will be an issue in determining Miya's marriage prospects. After the Restoration, Ryūzō had managed to gain a position in the Ministry of Agriculture and Trade, the government bureau responsible for setting industrial policy.[5] Although he had worked in an organ of the state directly connected to the growth of Japanese capitalism, Ryūzō himself had only achieved the marginal success of a lower-level civil servant, and he had never gained any substantial wealth. His real estate investments are described by another character as being "quite conservative and small." More to the point, he himself says, rather proudly, that he can pass on an inheritance of 7,000 yen. This figure has been carefully calibrated, for it is one that indicates security on a small scale. Seven thousand yen is a not inconsiderable sum of money. (We will later learn that a man's career and reputation can be ruined because he cannot repay a loan of 3,000 yen.) At the same time, a possible yearly income from this nest egg, approximately 700 yen (calculated at a generous 10 percent yield), is only slightly higher than that of a beginning civil servant in this period, whose annual salary would have been roughly 600 yen.[6] Ryūzō's income allows him to live with some respectability and to have aspirations for his daughter, but it does not provide luxury or freedom from financial worry.

Miya and Kan'ichi were raised together, because Ryūzō had taken care of Kan'ichi after the death of his parents when he was fifteen. The situation of an orphan being raised by a relative or some other benefactor, which we have already briefly encountered with Chijiwa Yasuhiko in *Hototogisu*, occurs repeatedly in Meiji melodramatic fiction.[7] Characters of this type reflect, on the one hand, the reality of a time when there were few public means of caring for orphans. Absorption into another family was an accepted way for such children to be reared in Meiji society. On the other hand, melodramas so often featured orphans because they offered opportunities for the exploration of certain themes. To begin with, they were, as Said would argue, convenient markers for larger social discontinuities figured as interruptions in biological filiation. The status of Chijiwa and Kan'ichi as orphans emphasizes their lost samurai patrimony and their abandonment in a world of intense social mobility. Orphans could also play a special role in moral fiction: in their defenselessness, they presented a vulnerability that tested the ethics of a family or a society. They could either be treated kindly, showing the moral stature of the benefactor, or they could be treated coldly. An orphan, in turn, could be easily inscribed into plots of virtuous or villainous repayment for prior care. Thus, in *Hototogisu*, Chijiwa, who grows up embittered as a poor relative in the Kawashima household, emerges as one of that novel's villains. Orphanhood, moreover, had particular poignancy and potential in the *ie* system. The orphan was both helpless and a free agent within a system that conceived of the family as the prime determinant of a person's social identity, the foundation of his or her economic security, and a bulwark of social control. The orphan might be isolated and unprotected, but he or she also possessed, by virtue of that isolation, a freedom that could be either exploited by others or exercised on his or her own behalf.

Kan'ichi's predicament displays many sides of the orphan's fate. The novel specifically situates his orphaning as occurring within the *ie* system by referring to him after his parents' death as an *osanaki koshu*, or "young househead." This was true to the Meiji Civil Code (promulgated in 1898 while *Konjiki yasha* was being serialized), which provided for *ie* continuity by allowing a surviving successor to be designated a househead at any age.[8] Such a provision cannot but betray a certain anxiety to rationalize every human being within the *ie* structure, even if it means designating an orphan like Kan'ichi as the child househead of an *ie* whose only living member is himself. The text is aware of the irony of this situation, for the passage calls Kan'ichi a "young househead," which emphasizes his utter helplessness.

> Did not the young househead face, before thinking of his education, the burden of having to eat; before thinking of eating, the burden of burying his parents; before burying his parents, the burden of nursing them and paying for their medicines? How was a person too young to support himself to be saved from burdens of this sort? (69)

A fifteen-year-old orphan worried about his own survival is not the head of very much. The *ie* is revealed here to be an abstraction out of touch with the real needs and sentiments of those who supposedly constitute it. Far from being a genuine source of social order, it merely generates expectations that cannot be fulfilled. This jaundiced view of the gulf between *ie* ideology and the lives of actual families colors *Konjiki yasha*'s depiction of the *ie*.

It is Ryūzō who steps into the breach in Kan'ichi's moment of desperation. Kan'ichi's father had been a past benefactor to Ryūzō in some unexplained way, and the latter offers help out of a sincere wish to repay old kindnesses. He had already aided Kan'ichi's parents with money for medicine and for school fees for their son. Upon the father's death, Ryūzō and his wife take Kan'ichi into their house and provide for his education. They even eventually decide to have him marry Miya, their only daughter, and carry on their *ie*. Although all of this is laudable as treatment for a penniless orphan, it is worth attending to the text's precise wording in describing this sequence of events, because it slyly suggests the element of calculation:

> He was the child of their late benefactor, and Ryūzō and his wife were truly devoted in caring for him. Seeing how much Kan'ichi was loved, there were those who thought the Shigizawas intended to make him the husband of their daughter. But, at the time, they had no such clear thoughts. The idea had slowly come to them as they saw how diligent he was at school, and their intentions had finally taken shape when he gained admission to higher school.
>
> The couple were secretly pleased. Kan'ichi was not only diligent; he was honest and his behavior was upright. Were this person to be crowned with a mortarboard, he would be a rare catch as a husband. (69–70)

More than the repayment of old debts, then, motivates Ryūzō and his wife. The idea of having Kan'ichi marry Miya occurs to them when they discover his academic gifts, and it coalesces when he is admitted to higher school, the public preparatory school for university admissions.[9] Some explanation of the place of the higher school in the Japanese educational hierarchy may be necessary to fully appreciate the contingencies in the Shigizawas' plans. It was during the third and fourth decades of the Meiji era that Japan evolved a system to produce an educated and credentialed elite. This was also when the ideology of *risshin shusse*, which fanned a mania for self-advancement, became centered upon educational attainment, and when a popular Social Darwinism saw survival of the fittest being enacted in a student's progression through ever more difficult admissions tests.[10] During this period, only a minuscule proportion of male students were able to proceed through the system to higher school (such schools never enrolled more than one percent of the male age cohort).[11] Graduation from higher school virtually guaranteed admission to an imperial university, which in turn was the point of entry to elite levels of the bureaucracy. In these contexts, it means a great deal that Kan'ichi is a student at the First Higher School, the most prestigious of the higher schools. He is in his final year as the novel begins, and he is looking forward to going on to Tokyo Imperial University. What the Shigizawas had waited to ascertain before offering their daughter to Kan'ichi was that he was securely on the route toward academic and social success.

Shigizawa Ryūzō had been situated to feel intensely the forces organizing Meiji social hierarchy. As a former samurai, he would have been all too aware that status and income were no longer hereditary, that they needed to be earned anew by each succeeding generation. As a minor bureaucrat in the Ministry of Agriculture and Trade, he would have witnessed the incursion into the bureaucracy of members of the "new middle class," identified by their educational background and professional credentials.[12] And, as a retiree living on a nest egg, he would have felt a need to augment family income, both to give his daughter a comfortable life and to gain security for himself and his wife at a time when government social security programs were nonexistent. For all of these reasons, a son-in-law on the educational fast track could be reckoned to be a good addition to the family.

Specifically, the Shigizawas intend to make Kan'ichi a *mukoyōshi*, or an adopted son-in-law. Kan'ichi's orphan status plays nicely into this plan. Unencumbered with family ties, he can be adopted into Ryūzō's family with relative ease. Had Kan'ichi's father still been alive, it would have been impossible for Ryūzō to think of adopting him, for he would have been expected to remain as the successor to his father's *ie*. We should note, however, that by adopting Kan'ichi, Ryūzō will be contradicting his reasons for taking care of the boy in the first place. Depriving the Hazama *ie* of its "young househead" and causing its certain demise is definitely no way to repay his debt to Kan'ichi's father. At this stage, we can already see that worldly calculations have overshadowed Ryūzō's good intentions.

This plan has a special gravity because of Kan'ichi's own status background. Although his father had apparently not done as well as Ryūzō in the post-Restoration period, the family had been of samurai stock. This no doubt makes the adoption even more attractive to the Shigizawas because they will have a son-in-law from the same social stratum. But it also means that they will be asking a young man to give up the *ie* of his birth within a status group where family and surname continuity meant the most. (A little later, we will have occasion to see Kan'ichi's views on this matter.)

One other aspect of Kan'ichi's origins is worth mentioning, and this has to do with his father's understanding of education's relationship to status. His father's oft-repeated words on this subject are revealing on many counts:

> His dead father had often said: Born, as it happens, in a samurai House (*samurai no ie*), what honor would I have were I to let my child Kan'ichi, too, be held in contempt by others. I would have him become a university graduate (*gakushi*) and stand once again atop the four estates (*shimin*). These words were used regularly to admonish Kan'ichi, and they were used as well to complain to Ryūzō whenever they happened to meet. (69)

Kan'ichi's father, then, had been a man keenly aware of status inconsistency. He had come from a group used to ruling over others on the basis of a moral discourse emphasizing "honor." Yet, in the Meiji world where samurai status had disappeared, he was now held in "contempt" by others because of his poverty, that is, his low position in terms of class. Educating Kan'ichi had been a means of resolving this status inconsistency. The terms employed by Kan'ichi's father, however, display both his recognition and misrecognition of modernity. He is attuned enough to realize that social priority now belongs to *gakushi*, or university graduates. But, using a phrase that is redolent of the samurai sense of entitlement, he reveals that he thinks social leadership still involves standing "atop the four estates" of the Edo period. This archaism suggests why Kan'ichi's father had fared less well than Ryūzō in the currents of Meiji social fluidity. The father had found it difficult to let go of Tokugawa assumptions, and the young Kan'ichi had been drilled in an ideology emphasizing family honor. This specific portrayal of the father makes inescapable the conclusion that the disruption of filiation marked by his death and Kan'ichi's orphaning points to the broader historical dynamics that disinherited the samurai and intensified social mobility.

Kan'ichi's responses show that he has absorbed his father's lessons. As we have seen, he becomes a high achiever in the educational system. It is instructive here that the text attributes his success to "diligence" (*tokugaku*) rather than brilliance; he is someone who has been motivated to work very hard. This motivation is multiplied once he is taken in by the Shigizawas, for, as we have seen, the approval of his benefactors hinges upon his performance. Once he becomes aware that marriage to Miya and adoption into the Shigizawa family is a possibility, these incentives become more complicated:

> Even if it meant inheriting the family fortune, he would have been ashamed to endure the unbearable humiliation of taking a different surname. Yet, in comparison with gaining for a wife the beautiful Miya, what import was humiliation or fortune? With this thought in mind, he was even more enthusiastic about the plans than Ryūzō and his wife, and he worked all the harder at his studies. (70)

Within this summary of Kan'ichi's feelings, we see the intersection of numerous ideologies. We can see that he has been affected by *ie* ideology, especially as interpreted by those of samurai stock, because he senses humiliation at abandoning the name of the *ie* to which he had been born. He is, however, quite unlike a samurai in being willing to suffer any humiliation for the right to marry a beautiful wife. Although we will have occasion later to examine in more detail Kan'ichi's attitudes toward "love," suffice it for now to say that he has grown up to become a man who valorizes romantic attachments. Finally, we can see that self-advancement is, for him, a means rather than an end. Academic and occupational success is most important for Kan'ichi because it is a condition for his prospective marriage to Miya. Another way to put this is to observe that there is a hierarchy to Kan'ichi's various motivations, with the desire for marital love at the top of the list and others either dependant or subservient. This hierarchy has allowed Kan'ichi to rationalize the various ideologies pulling at him. We will later see the moral consequences of a system of values structured in this particular way.

Miya, the object of Kan'ichi's attentions, has very different values. She has not been raised to believe in status or family honor in a way associated with samurai background. A product of a bourgeois upbringing—she has had, for example, violin lessons at a private music school—she is someone straining against her middling circumstances. The one attribute that feeds her aspirations is the breathtaking beauty emphasized from her very first appearance in *Konjiki yasha*. This happens at the famous opening of the novel, where the card games at a New Year's party become a synecdoche for a society degraded by uncontrolled competition and self-aggrandizement. Women with their kimonos askew and men with torn shirts reach greedily through a cloud of tobacco smoke to grasp the cards they want. Over this scene, Miya reigns like a "queen": "Even the hearts of the fiercest men softened before her, and in the end all came to worship her. The women felt a sense of awe, even as they writhed in envy" (57). The text makes clear that these reactions are a result of Miya's beauty and that her beauty comes from her physical gifts rather than any adornment. The latter point is important because it emphasizes her limited financial resources (her clothes are "no more than average") as well as the physical loveliness that makes her truly exceptional. The picture is drawn, then, of a woman whose beauty is inconsistent with her economic station.

Miya is aware of the effect she has on others, particularly men, and she had learned at an early age that her assets might be exchanged for social advancement. Older, accomplished men had thrown themselves at her feet, and her "little chest had pounded to the point of bursting" because of the upward aspirations inflamed by these conquests. The text analyzes Miya's desires in an unsparing passage that reads her aspirations against Kan'ichi's love for her as well as against the ideology of self-advancement:

Miya, for her part, found Kan'ichi not unlikable. But her thoughts for him were probably only half as strong as his for her. This was because she was aware of her own beauty. . . . Miya naturally knew what her beauty was worth. Given her beauty, merely inheriting a bit of wealth and marrying a university graduate like any other was hardly at the top of her desires. She had seen that the consorts of the mighty often came from the ranks of the lowly. And she had seen the rich forsake ugly wives and be drawn to beautiful mistresses. Just as a man could fulfill his wishes for self-advancement (*risshin*) as long as he was talented, she believed that a woman could gain wealth and position through beauty. . . . She constantly dreamed even during the daytime that a person of position or of wealth or of fame would seek her out. She believed and did not doubt that such a destiny, in which a jeweled palanquin (*tama no koshi*) would be sent to fetch her, was sure to come her way. It was precisely because of this that she did not feel so deeply for Kan'ichi. (70–71)

Poor, unsuspecting Kan'ichi, then, has fixed his thoughts on a woman who wants more than he can ever offer. The passage shows with incisive clarity that Miya responds very differently to the ideologies surrounding her and Kan'ichi. Whereas Kan'ichi orders his motivations by putting love first and self-advancement and the *ie* well behind, Miya wants social ascent before anything else and subordinates her feelings for Kan'ichi. Thoughts of *ie* continuity, which might have occurred to her as the only child of the family, do not seem to have any weight for her at all; she clearly has her heart set on a marriage outside of the restricted opportunities provided in the House of Shigizawa. We should also note that Miya has completely different standards by which to define self-advancement. While Kan'ichi is slaving away in order to get a university degree and thereby win Miya's hand, Miya herself views university graduates as dime-a-dozen drudges and wants to rise far above both Kan'ichi and her own family. Although fame and position are mentioned here along with wealth in Miya's understanding of success, her later statements and actions make clear that wealth is the center of her aspirations. She is one of the many characters in turn-of-the-century melodrama who signal the increasing hold of class, rather than status, upon the Meiji consciousness. Her sense of status inconsistency can only be resolved through acquiring a husband whose wealth matches her surpassing beauty; her goal is not status per se, but upward mobility in terms of class. Kan'ichi's efforts to deal with his own status inconsistency—by gaining an education and a bureaucratic job equal to his sense of moral superiority—is never going to suffice.

Perhaps what is most striking about Miya's portrayal is the way it so clearly delineates the gendering of success in Meiji Japan.[13] When Miya draws the equation that a woman's beauty can gain her wealth and position the way that a man's talent can gain him self-advancement, she reveals the conditions that defined female success at the time. The powerful ideology of *risshin shusse* was articulated in male terms, and it identified "talent" (*sai*) as desirable because it helped men get ahead in higher education and work. Miya shows that the siren song of advancement was heard by women as well, but that it came with different lyrics. If women were largely excluded from higher education and work, they could still attempt to better their social position through a good marriage, and for this the most desirable attribute was not talent, but beauty. Miya, then, responds to a female version of *risshin shusse*, different in means and requirements but sharing in the ambitions unleashed by the social mobility of the Meiji period. When she dreams of a "jeweled palanquin" being sent to fetch her, she resorts to an image enshrined in the Meiji discourse on female success.[14]

Given the hierarchy of Miya's values, it is not at all surprising that she accepts a marriage proposal from Tomiyama Tadatsugu. The latter's defining attribute is great wealth, a quality visible from the moment of his entrance at the New Year's party, where his enormous diamond ring causes a sensation.[15] Tomiyama is a proper capitalist, being the scion of the founder of the "Tomiyama Bank" and himself the director of a budding export firm. He also operates according to Miya's expectations, for he has been trolling for a beautiful wife ever since returning from England (this is the reason for his presence at the New Year's party). Tomiyama is a man tailor-made to fit a scenario where female beauty must be translated into success.

Although the text does not give us direct access to Miya's thoughts as she makes her fateful decision, it indicates that the decision has been hers to make. At one point, her mother says to Miya, "It's all been up to you. It's because you started out saying that you wanted to go through with the marriage that we settled things this way" (94). Miya's part in marriage negotiations differs significantly, then, from that of Namiko in *Hototogisu*. Instead of allowing a male parent to make a decision, Miya has taken the initiative in accepting Tomiyama's proposal. In this novel, female agency decides unions rather than a male "traffic in women." The crisis in this novel arises because female agency is tied to moral values that cherish wealth and position.

These values are actually shared by the Shigizawas, and this colors their approach to the *ie*. It will be recalled that by initially planning to adopt Kan'ichi as a *mukoyōshi* the Shigizawas sought to combine the twin demands of family continuity and financial security. When Tomiyama enters the scene, these two aims are brought into conflict. This becomes evident in the tense meeting where Ryūzō attempts to explain to Kan'ichi why he has changed his mind. Ryūzō's words make it clear that he has been swayed by an opportunity to gain security of a different magnitude: "The House of Shigizawa (*Shigizawa no ie*), as you know, has no relatives (*shinrui*) to speak of, and this makes me feel helpless about various matters. We keep on getting older, and you're both so young. If we had relatives we could count on, how reassuring it would be" (91). Ryūzō is seeking an alliance with able kin, and there is no doubt that the ability in question is financial, since Tomiyama's most distinguishing feature is wealth. What should not be missed is that Ryūzō is now willing to risk family continuity: Tomiyama, the son of a rich banker, is not a candidate for adoption. Although Ryūzō attempts to retain Kan'ichi as a potential adopted son ("It's not much," he later says to Kan'ichi, "but I am prepared to pass on this House to you in its entirety. You are still my successor." [88]), he has shown what is most important to him. For all his talk about the House of Shigizawa, he is willing to take the chance that the *ie* will have no inheritor in order to gain a promise of financial security. With the Shigizawas, we have a couple whose allegiance to the *ie* is overshadowed by their wish for comfort in their old age.

Kan'ichi's reaction is predictable. Adoption had struck this son of a former samurai as an indignity made palatable only by the prospect of marriage to the beauteous Miya. Now he faces a future where he will not only be deprived of Miya but become the adopted son of a man who has betrayed him. His connection to the ideal of self-advancement is also transformed. He had once been motivated to study by the knowledge that his academic achievements would lead to gaining Miya's hand. Now there is no reward. Extreme emotions wash over him—shock, hurt, disappointment over Ryūzō's mercenary weakness, frustration over the obligation he feels toward the Shigizawas.

It is clear, at this point, that Kan'ichi cannot continue along the route of self-advancement that he has trod so diligently. His sense of betrayal is too strong for him to remain with the Shigizawas, and, in practical terms, he cannot continue his education without their help. Kan'ichi is back to being an orphan, albeit one who is now a little older. His future will again be colored by the fact that he is both isolated and a free agent. All of this is not yet sufficient to understand the violence in the text; for this we must raise the issue of the "love" between Kan'ichi and Miya.

IDEOLOGIES OF "LOVE"

One way to start examining "love" is to take a closer look at Kōyō's often-quoted statement at the panel discussion. He describes the central opposition dramatized in his novel as follows:

> Generally speaking, in the human world there are two immense sources of POWER that support social linkages. To say what these are, they are love and gold. But, to my mind, the power of gold is MOMENTARY, and no matter

how intense cannot retain its force forever. In contrast to this, however, love's dominance of human life is eternal and unchanging. In other words, it is love that provides the closest linkages in human life. I undertook the work hoping to write about this. Hazama Kan'ichi demonstrates concretely in a single person the battle between love and gold.[16]

This statement has served as an influential paratext to the novel, and later critical discussions have often remarked on the structural opposition of love and money in *Konjiki yasha*. I am not going to dispute this characterization of the work's thematics. My argument will be directed toward exploring the consequences of such an opposition for melodrama.

It should be apparent that the structure of feeling Kōyō describes is laid out along melodramatic lines: two great sources of "POWER," one momentary, the other eternal, are locked in a struggle to order social relations.[17] What needs emphasis here is that Kōyō conscientiously constructs the opposition of love and money in binary terms. Love and gold are not opposites; they do not necessarily exist in the antonymical relationship of good and evil. One can conceive of situations in which love and money might be mutually supportive. Yet, in speaking of the "battle between love and gold," Kōyō posits a conflict between mutually exclusive essences.

This conflict generates the melodrama's hallmark hyperbolic emotions. Although the excess of sentiment engendered by the opposition of love and money can be illustrated with any number of passages from the work, it is convenient to examine how it operates in the scene where Kan'ichi responds to Ryūzō's rationalizations for giving Miya away in marriage:

> As Ryūzō proceeded with his explanations, Kan'ichi gained a clear view of the older man's sentiments, a view as clear as seeing a flame in the darkness. Ryūzō tirelessly moved his tongue, spouting thousands of syllables in order merely to conceal a single word: "profit." For the poor to steal was common, but did those not mired in poverty steal as well? Kan'ichi himself had been born into a world of filth, and so it was possible that he would unknowingly be drawn into filthy thoughts or engage in filthy acts. Would he, though, knowing that something was filth, then proceed to befoul himself? Sell a wife in order to gain a diploma! Was this not the greatest act of filth? . . .
> But there was one thing not befouled in a world so filthy. Was there not something about which to rejoice?
> Kan'ichi thought of his beloved Miya.
> His own love (*ai*) for her would stand undaunted even if threatened with death. And what of her love? Could her love ever be changed, even if someone tried to buy it with a matchless diamond that had once adorned a kingly

crown? His love for her and hers for him were like jewels shining in the mud. He would embrace this one spot of purity and forget an entire world of filth. (92–93)

My translation of this passage is purposely awkward to reflect the hyperbolic repetition of "filth" (*kegare*), and yet I have not been able to reproduce in English every instance found in the Japanese text. What should be evident is that the concatenation of "filth" reflects desperate and excessive moral sentiments. For Kan'ichi, the key source of "filth" is "profit." Through this rhetoric, any consideration of financial issues becomes morally condemned. There is no room for the in-between, the mixed, or even a realistic assessment of the financial consequences of personal decisions. To have thought about money is to be befouled. Opposite to "filth" in Kan'ichi's moral structuring is a "love" (*ai*) that shines with an incorruptible purity. As he attempts to make sense of the changes in his situation, Kan'ichi clings to an abstract and extreme view of love as selfless mutual devotion.

It is, of course, his inclination toward bipolar assessments that makes Kan'ichi susceptible to sudden reversals in moral evaluation. The scene at Atami where he kicks Miya after learning of her wish to marry Tomiyama is a direct result of this tendency. A paragon of purity who has sided with filth deserves to be vanquished. Kan'ichi's violence is an inversion of the "love" he had felt so keenly.

But what is this "love" on which Kan'ichi stakes so much? "Love" is by no means a universal or transcendent phenomenon. It is, like all other discursively defined entities, historically and culturally contingent, and this was never more true than in the Japan of the 1890s. Saeki Junko provides one approach to the Meiji coding of love when she traces the gradual displacement of the native concept of *iro* by that of *ai*, which was constructed through a translation of the Western idea of "love."[18] According to Saeki, the Edo-period concept of *iro* had possessed a dominant erotic content, being inseparable from sexual relations and associated with the mores of the licensed prostitution quarters. It assumed a sexual division of labor, allotting reproduction to wives, while assigning the practice of eros to the demimonde. It embraced both male-male relations (the second graph of the character-compound *nanshoku*, the Edo term for male-male sexuality, is the same as the character for *iro*) and the possibility of multiple sexual partners. Saeki is careful to point out that *iro* cannot be reduced to physical desire; there is a strong component of feeling in *iro*, epitomized by longing. There is also a lengthy historical association between *iro* and the development of aesthetic refinement, as well as between *iro* and communion with the gods. The defining difference between *iro* and *ai* was the latter's overwhelming emphasis upon the spiritual or affective link between partners. *Ai* occurred in a domestic context, assumed a mandatory heterosexuality, and held monogamous marriage to be an ideal. It demanded the satisfaction of all romantic and erotic desires with a single partner of the opposite sex. These qualities of *ai* were determined by the fact that its earliest proponents were the Japanese Protestants who gathered around Iwamoto Yoshiharu.[19] This was the very group responsible for introducing to Japan the model of family that was first called the *hōmu* and later translated to *katei*—*ai* was the affective bond behind the conjugal domesticity of the *katei*. These advocates gained cultural supremacy for *ai* by connecting it to civilization and enlightenment while portraying *iro* as a barbaric, purely physical set of relations.[20]

Ozaki Kōyō emerges, in Saeki's argument, as a key figure signaling transformations in the literary discourse on love. She points out that male-female relations in his earlier works invariably unfold within the *iro* paradigm.[21] These relations tend to be located in the demimonde, and they are sexual in nature. *Kyaramakura* (Aloeswood pillow, 1890), for example, follows the life of a prostitute as she enters the licensed quarter at the age of twelve, leaves when her contract is bought out by a patron, and later returns to become a leading courtesan. The protagonist's sexual contacts are, needless to say, numerous and varied. *Sanninzuma* (Three wives, 1892) does not focus on three married women, as its title might imply, but rather upon a nouveau-riche merchant's acquisition and simultaneous liaison with three mistresses.[22] The gender relations in the text are characterized by a sexual division of labor between the merchant's wife and his mistresses, and by the acceptance of all concerned of a well-to-do man's right to have multiple lovers. The success of these works had made Kōyō famous as a writer of the demimonde; he had built his early reputation upon representing prostitution and polygamy. In *Konjiki yasha*, however, he set his story in a respectable household rather than the demimonde, and his heroine was a girl with a bourgeois upbringing rather than a prostitute or a kept woman. While *iro* had appeared as a keyword in prior works, it largely disappears in *Konjiki yasha*, to be replaced, as we have seen, by *ai*. There are also numerous instances in the text when Kan'ichi refers to himself and Miya as *fūfu*, or husband and wife, even though they are only engaged. Saeki thus argues that in *Konjiki yasha* Kōyō has completed the transition from writing about *iro* to representing *fūfu ai*, or conjugal love.

There are parts of the novel that support Saeki's argument about shifting Meiji discourses on male-female relations. Take, for example, the following passage, which comes from Kan'ichi's speech during the scene in Atami where he explodes with wounded and violent rage:

> "Miya, I believed in you as much as I believe in myself. I didn't think that you of all people would have such thoughts, but, if that's the case, your heart too is ruled by greed, by money. That's a disgrace, no matter how you look at it. How can you not be disgusted with yourself?
>
> "You might be pleased with your nice success (*ii shusse*) and with being able to afford such luxury, but put yourself in my place, being jilted and replaced for money. Should I call this frustration or resentment? Don't be shocked—I'd rather stab you to death and die myself. How do you think I feel having to hold this all in and just watch as you're stolen away? How do you think I feel! Don't you care what happens to others as long as you're fine? What is Kan'ichi to you, after all? What do you think I am? I might be an unwelcome guest in the House of Shigizawa, but aren't I your husband (*otto*)? I have no recollection of having become your kept man (*otoko mekake*). You've made Kan'ichi your plaything (*nagusamimono*), haven't you? It stands to reason that I've always thought your behavior was cold. You thought of me as a plaything from the beginning, and there was never any true love (*hontō no aijō*). Not realizing this, I loved you more than I loved myself. I thought of you so much that I hardly had any pleasures aside from you. Miya, are you really going to leave a Kan'ichi who feels so much for you?
>
> "I grant you that, when it comes to the power of money, there's no comparison between Tomiyama and me. He's a rich man, as rich as they come, and I'm just a poor student. But think about this well, Miya—human happiness is one thing money can't buy. Happiness and money are two different things. In human happiness, harmony in the household (*kanai no heiwa*) is what comes first. And what is harmony in the household? It can't be anything else but that a husband and wife love each other deeply (*Fūfu ga tagai ni fukaku aisuru to iu hoka nai*). When it comes to loving you deeply, a hundred like Tomiyama put together can't possibly love you a tenth as much as I do. If Tomiyama boasts of wealth, then I'll fight against him with a love that men like him can't imagine. The happiness of husband and wife depends totally on the power of love. If there is no love there is no husband and wife (*Fūfu no kōfuku wa mattaku aijō no chikara, aijō ga nakereba sude ni fūfu wa nai no da*)." (111–12)

Kan'ichi goes on in this fashion for a dozen pages, and sometimes this reader wonders whether Miya shouldn't just ditch him because of his tiresome self-righteousness. But her later obsession with him shows that to dismiss him as a whining prig would be a serious misreading. We must regard Kan'ichi's speechifying as an action integral to the melodramatic mode. This is a scene where a character states his beliefs without reserve and in no uncertain terms, attempting to install the moral legibility that is the melodrama's aim. Kan'ichi uses "sweeping verbal gestures" to enunciate the moral forces that determine his life.[23]

We see in his vocabulary the reflection of some of the key ideological currents we have already noted. He recognizes that Miya's marriage to Tomiyama might be counted as success in terms of female self-advancement, but he defines it as morally wanting because she has chosen wrong when confronted with the choice between love and money. He repeats the truism that money can't buy love, as he portrays himself as a champion of love whose emotional commitment can't be matched by the moneyed Tomiyama. *Katei* ideology clearly plays a large part in Kan'ichi's views, for he defines happiness as stemming from "harmony in the household." His repeated invocations of *ai* in tandem with *fūfu*—the word used by Christians to refer to a married couple and the term employed by the Meiji Civil Code to designate the partners in a legal marriage—might be read as evidence that Kan'ichi is a believer in conjugal love, so much so that he refers to himself and Miya as "husband and wife" even when they are not legally married.

But something slightly less salubrious also makes its way into this passage. When Kan'ichi rejects the title of "kept man" (and thus suggests that he might appear this way from a certain perspective) or when he insinuates that he might have been used as a "plaything," there is a discursive shiftiness that points away from respectable conjugal love. This is so partially because Kan'ichi is engaging in gender bending; the term that I have translated as "kept man," *otoko mekake*, literally means "male mistress" and the term I have rendered as "plaything," *nagusamimono*, is generally applied to women who are used as objects of male pleasure. Thus Kan'ichi suggests that, by betraying him to improve her own prospects, Miya has placed him in a "female" position, reversing the usual gender hierarchy. This hierarchy is a sexualized one. Women are turned into mistresses or playthings through being subjected to male sexual desire, and, by using these terms to refer to himself, Kan'ichi raises the possibility that he has been used and betrayed by female sexual desire. The presence of such terms suggests that Kan'ichi and Miya's relationship may exceed the boundaries of two affianced young people looking forward to the respectable pleasures of conjugal love.

Although there has been some debate among critics regarding the degree of sexual contact between Miya and Kan'ichi, there should actually be no doubt that the two have been sleeping together. The easy physical intimacy between them—for example, when Kan'ichi, walking beside Miya on the cold night of the novel's opening, burrows in the warmth of her shawl— suggests that there is a history of sexual intimacy. The text, moreover, later goes beyond suggestion and flatly states that Kan'ichi was Miya's "first love to whom she had entrusted her heart and her body" (*kokoro o yurushi had-ami o yuruseshi hatsukoi* [233]). The two protagonists are lovers at the start of the story, and we must also consider the possibility that their sexual union is the defining element in their bond as *fūfu*. Such a union underlies the moral savagery of Kan'ichi's attack upon Miya when he finds out that Tomiyama is also staying at Atami:

> "Looking back on how you avoided me when you left home and how you never sent me any word, I have to conclude that your plan was to rendezvous with Tomiyama. Maybe you even came together. Miya, you're an adulteress (*kanpu*). What you've done is the same as commit adultery."
>
> "That's an awful thing to say, Kan'ichi. It's too cruel, too cruel." Miya lost her composure and dissolved in tears.
>
> She tried to draw near, but Kan'ichi thrust her away, saying, "If you're unfaithful, aren't you an adulteress?"
>
> "When was I unfaithful to you?"
>
> "Your Kan'ichi might be a fool, but he's not fool enough to look on as his wife (*sai*) is unfaithful. Where's the proof that you haven't committed adultery, if you have a rightful husband (*rekki to shita otto*) and you hoodwink that husband to come to a hotsprings with another man?" (107)

Kan'ichi's choice of words shows that he is still thinking of himself and Miya as husband and wife, but the thoroughly sexualized frame of reference makes it hard to fully square his discourse with that of conjugal love as a spiritual and affective bond. Here, to be husband and wife means to be in a monogamous sexual relationship. Reading the passage, it is impossible to deny that Kan'ichi and Miya have a sexual relationship, since this is a precondition for a charge of adultery. The intemperance (Miya is accompanied to Atami by her mother!) and the brutality of Kan'ichi's urge to label Miya an "adulteress" make sense only if we understand his words to be driven by sexual jealousy and the pain of betrayed sexual passion.

Among the varied constituents of "love" in the text, it is not so much conjugal love but rather love inflected as passion that comes to hold the most weight. This is a love deeply invested in the erotic and built upon a prior sexual relationship, yet motivated not by sexual union but by its impossibility, a love limned by separation and painful longing. It is a love that feeds on estrangement. The outlines of such a "love" emerge when we examine Kan'ichi's attitudes toward Miya some years after their separation. By this time, Kan'ichi has proven himself as a moneylender, and he is in a position to afford various pleasures should he want them; yet he experiences no solace whatsoever because what he wants is forever out of reach. A quoted monologue gives voice to Kan'ichi's desperate longing:

> "Even if Miya came crying to me apologizing for her crime and wishing to be husband and wife (*fūfu*), a Miya whose heart has changed and whose body has been befouled (*kegasareta*) can never be the Miya of before, the Miya that had been my treasure. My treasure was the Miya of five years ago. Not even Miya herself can get back that Miya.
>
> "What I long for over and over again is Miya. Even as I sit here, I cannot forget about Miya. But what I long for is not the Miya that is now Tomiyama's wife. Rather, I want the Miya who was a Shigizawa, the Miya of five years ago! Even if I manage to amass a million yen, I can't get back Miya as she was. When you think about it, money is a worthless thing. Oh, if I had only had the money I have now when I followed her to Atami." (206)[24]

We see very clearly what will keep Kan'ichi and Miya from ever becoming a *fūfu* again. When Kan'ichi uses the rhetoric of befoulment, he is making a damning association between filthy lucre and "illicit" sexual contact; money and sexual debasement are largely coextensive in his system of values. In his eyes, Miya has prostituted herself, and this makes her former self irrecoverable. Kan'ichi's binary vision will never allow him to see her in any other way. Yet the bitter irony of his situation is that he yearns all the more for what he cannot have—a Miya purified of her desire for money and her sexual relations with Tomiyama. Kan'ichi's all-consuming "love" is a love predicated upon eternal separation.

What of Miya, then? The irony of her portrayal (and this too is bitter) is that her love for Kan'ichi is multiplied and inflamed the very moment that she makes the decision that divides them forever. Her yearning for what she has lost grows acute even before she has married Tomiyama, and once she becomes his wife, her desire causes her to draw some peculiar distinctions:

> Indeed, after separating from Kan'ichi, Miya became aware for the first time of how much she longed for him. On nights when she found unendurable her longings for a Kan'ichi who had left and would never return, she would

sink deep into thought as she leaned against his desk, she would lose herself in anguish as she breathed in the scent left in his clothes, and she would be filled with yearning as she rubbed his photograph against her cheek. If only he would acknowledge her, she thought, and send her a tender missive, she would abandon her parents and her House (*ie*), and run straight to him. Even on the day of her wedding, the thought hardly occurred to her that she was accepting Tomiyama Tadatsugu as her mate (*tsuma*). But she did not forget that her body was to go to his House. . . .

She thought to herself that she had entrusted her soul to Kan'ichi from the beginning. Circumstances led her to give her body to Tadatsugu. But even if her body were to belong to Tadatsugu, her soul would never forget Kan'ichi.

As she thought this way, Miya knew that her sentiments were immoral. But she also believed that this immorality was her unavoidable fate, and she did not deeply question her own motives. It was thus that Miya became Tadatsugu's wife. (233–34)

Separation transforms a formerly subordinated affection into obsession. Slightly later, the text will use the metaphor of starvation, a craving raised to pain, to describe Miya's emotions for Kan'ichi (235). These emotions cause Miya to reject conventional morality and devise moral principles in keeping with her desires: she conveniently employs the Christian duality of the soul and the body to allow at least a part of herself to cleave to Kan'ichi. That Miya knowingly does what is "immoral" might in the usual melodramatic novel condemn her to the role of villain. But *Konjiki yasha* breaks the mold by making this villainy eventually shine as a kind of virtue.

The "love" that *Konjiki yasha* celebrates, then, veers far away from the moral uprightness of conjugal love. Whatever ideologies of love Kan'ichi may profess, the "love" that he and Miya come to share—the "love" that drives forward the plot of the novel and escalates its hyperbolic emotions— is a dark passion that feeds on separation and embraces its own impossibility. The passion chronicled by *Konjiki yasha* finally draws close to that described by Denis de Rougemont in *Love in the Western World*. The words that de Rougemont uses to portray the bond of Tristan and Iseult, paradigmatic of courtly love, can apply just as well to Kan'ichi and Miya: "Their need of one another is in order to be aflame, and they do not need one another as they are. What they need is not another's presence, but one another's absence. *Thus the partings of the lovers are dictated by passion itself*, and by the love they bestow on their passion rather than on its satisfaction or on its living object."[25] De Rougemont explains that the "love" whose genealogy he traces disdains unions and is "constituted in hostility to marriage" and that it is directed toward death, the ultimate separation.[26]

Concepts of domestic conjugality, propounded by Meiji Christians, were not the only Western ideas on love present in turn-of-the-century Japan. Many of the texts that de Rougemont cites as later manifestations of the myth of dark passion—*Romeo and Juliet, Madame Bovary, Anna Karenina*— were then already in circulation. Although Japanese translations had yet to appear at the time of *Konjiki yasha*, a reader familiar with English, as Kōyō was, had access to this vein of writing either through contact with the original texts or with English translations.

Furthermore, Western ideas of love inflamed by separation would have resonated powerfully with portrayals of erotic obsession in Edo culture, particularly the theatrical genre of *shinjūmono*, or "love-suicide" plays. At least one critic has connected the passions in *Konjiki yasha* to those in the love-suicide plays, which eulogized men and women whose passions erupted in the face of social obstructions and whose ultimate satisfaction lay in mutual annihilation. Nishida Masaru draws a distinction between the concept of *iro*, which he says contains an element of playfulness, and the earlier, more serious idea of *koi*, an erotic vow on which lovers "staked their lives."[27] *Konjiki yasha*, argues Nishida, is a text that enacts a "historic return to the world of *koi*." Such an interpretation is supported by the fact that specific parts of *Konjiki yasha*'s narrative seem to draw on love-suicide plays, most notably the passage describing Kan'ichi's trip to Shiobara, which resembles a *michiyuki*, the indispensable lyrical narration of the doomed lovers' journey to the place of their death.

We have come a long way from Saeki Junko's assertion that *Konjiki yasha* supports a discourse of "love" drawn from nineteenth-century ideas of conjugal domesticity. "Love" in this novel contains elements of the dark passion, antagonistic toward marriage, found in a broad sweep of Western narratives, and it also gestures toward an older strand of Edo writing on self-destructive male-female relations. The text's layered and internally inconsistent construction of "love" complicates the melodramatic structure that Kōyō invokes when he speaks of "love and gold," for a clean binary cannot exist when its elements are themselves fragmented and hybrid. Love is difficult to categorize as virtue if it is not merely conjugal affection or innocent romance but also an obsession predicated upon separation and directed toward death. *Konjiki yasha*'s search for moral certitude is undermined by its embrace of contradictory ideologies of "love."

THE HIGHER SCHOOL BROTHERHOOD

Many critics, starting with those who commented on the novel at the time of its publication, found it difficult to fathom Kan'ichi's decision to become a moneylender. Granted he had been crushed by Miya's betrayal, but why, among all the possible responses, does his reaction to her marriage have to take the particular course that it does? Why not become a social reformer who battles the power of money? Or, if his motive is to acquire the wealth whose lack caused him to be abandoned, why not undertake a more respectable enterprise? My own sense is that these questions are ultimately fruitless as long as they attempt to understand Kan'ichi's actions as a result of his psychology. Melodramatic fiction is an ethical or moral narrative rather than a psychological one. Kan'ichi's actions must be understood through the binary structure of melodramatic morality and the melodrama's preference for sudden peripeties. Once Kan'ichi is denied the sweet virtues of love, his innocence destroyed, he must descend all the way to the other pole and immerse himself in the bitterness of vice. This movement between the poles is confirmed by Kan'ichi's own later judgments on moneylending: "More than a dishonest trade, it's an evil undertaking (*akuji*). I did not discover this today. I degraded myself (*mi o otoshita*) knowing this because I suffered a disappointment so bitter that at the time I wanted to kill the other person and then die myself" (139). It would be hard to state more clearly the effects of a binary morality. Engaging in moneylending had been the moral equivalent of an act of violence. Once Kan'ichi had lost his love, ultimate degradation became his goal.

When we more closely investigate what lies at the opposite pole from "love," however, we run into further contradictions, for we quickly learn that the text undercuts Kōyō's assertion about the power of money being "MOMENTARY" in contrast to the eternity of love. Indeed, the story will provide ample evidence that money, which it figures as filth, is the necessary currency of human relations. No one in the novel is ever free of financial considerations. To refer to the economy of human relations in *Konjiki yasha* is not merely to speak metaphorically, for the demands and flows of money shape love, friendships, and families. There is no outside to the power of money, and this makes it increasingly difficult for any binary to be supported. Encircled by money, love can only exist in a form twisted and compromised.

In this section and the next, I focus upon the economies of fictive families. Like the other works I study, *Konjiki yasha* generates multiple models of family. The work can be read as a frenzied effort to produce one set of family relations after another for its orphaned protagonist. We have already seen, in the frustrated plan to make Kan'ichi an adopted son-in-law, an unsuccessful effort to integrate him into a family through legally sanctioned means. Other forms of family proliferate. The first we encounter is the brotherhood of Kan'ichi's higher school classmates, a brotherhood constructed, as we will see, through a distinctive imbrication of ideas on family, gender, and status. After he leaves this group to become a moneylender, Kan'ichi will go on to form fictive families with Wanibuchi, the loan shark who gives him a start in the trade, and later with Sayama and Oshizu, the young couple he saves from the brink of a love suicide. All of these relationships are enmeshed in the cash nexus.

In examining Kan'ichi's relationship with his schoolmates, an appropriate point to start is the text's observation that Kan'ichi "had regarded as an older brother" (*keiji suru* [120]) a fellow student called Arao Jōsuke. For his part, Arao will say, following Kan'ichi's disappearance into the life of a money-lender, that he "truly mourns Hazama's absence more than the death of my brother" (125). This talk of brotherhood is significant because, as Donald Roden points out, the First Higher School, which Kan'ichi attended, was conceived as an "utopian family of men" in which faculty played the part of fathers and classmates were to be brothers.[28] In the outlook of its early leaders, the school needed to operate as a surrogate family because the family in the Meiji era, weakened by social upheaval, no longer provided students with proper training in morality and social propriety. The familial emphasis within the school, then, was prompted by a perception of moral crisis without.

The view of the First Higher School as a besieged outpost for morality was forcefully articulated in a speech given to his students by Kinoshita Hiroji, the headmaster in the 1890s who played a key role in formulating the ethos of the institution:

> For you students to lead a moral life by cultivating your spirit correctly, while living in a society that reeks of bad manners and obscenity, is a formidable task. I understand your distressing situation, but I believe it essential that you be resolute. In particular, I hope you will realize that when you take just one step off the campus, everyone is an enemy—that the higher school is, in effect, a castle under siege.[29]

It is hard to miss the melodramatic tone of these assertions: the school is a threatened haven for virtue while vice lurks without. The early leaders of the higher schools were convinced that, in the outer world, capitalism and modernization had harmed the social order, unleashing unrestrained competition and material desire.[30] These sentiments were intimately connected to issues of social hierarchy: higher school leaders believed that the abolition of samurai status had deprived Japan of a group devoted to moral leadership. The resulting moral disorder even presented a danger to the cloistered world of the higher schools, because the schools were being infiltrated, in the words of one headmaster, by "the customs of lower-class students."[31] In Kan'ichi's time, the majority of students at the First Higher School were of former samurai origin, but there was a sea change in the offing.[32] By the end of the Meiji period, nearly three quarters of the students would be former commoners. The bigger problem, however, was that students of all backgrounds were products of Meiji class and status fluidity. Even those of samurai background were aware, like Kan'ichi, that status needed to be earned anew by each individual within a social order that was itself in flux; whatever his origins, a student who had grown up with the ideology of self-advancement and had gained his current place through taking entrance examinations would not completely identify with the eternal moral verities of a hereditary elite. The task the higher schools set for themselves was to weld students of various backgrounds into an elite status group aware of its moral duty.

Foremost among the dangers lurking outside the school was money. In the 1890s, there was an acute public awareness of wealth as a source of power and corruption. The growth of industrial capitalism spurred by the Sino-Japanese War of 1894–95 had given increased visibility to business and wealth, and the subsequent years saw a public fascination with stock speculation and get-rich-quick schemes. Japan was now a "world of money" (*kane no yononaka*), where wealth was both desired and detested.[33] Earl H. Kinmonth observes that, during these years, social advancement, which had earlier been defined in terms of bureaucratic or political careers, came to be increasingly seen in monetary terms. To illustrate the tenor of the times, he quotes a sardonic observation made in 1897 by Uchimura Kanzō:

> Get money; get it by all means, for it alone is power in this generation. Wish you to be patriotic? Then get money, for you cannot better serve your country than by getting money for you and it. Be loyal? Then get money, and add wealth to your Master's land. Be filial to your father and mother? You cannot be so without getting money. The strength of your nation, the fear of your name—all come from money. Morality ever for the sake of money. Honesty is the best *policy* for—getting money.[34]

Money was becoming the measure of all things, and moralists were left calling for "diligence and economy" (*kinken*) as an antidote for a money-crazed
society.[35] School officials responded to these challenges by exhorting the higher
school student to be above the stain of money and the temptations of personal gain, anything that might "soil his heart."[36] One headmaster encapsu-
lated this goal by saying, "When standing between heaven and earth, [the
higher school graduate] never feels ashamed nor allows a speck of filth or
ignobility to affect his disposition."[37] We have already seen this rhetoric of
"filth" in Kan'ichi's views on Shigizawa Ryūzō's financial motives. It is only
to be expected that Kōyō, who was himself a First Higher School graduate,
would invest a student of that institution with its moral vocabulary.

Given its leaders' definition of its mission, the First Higher School
evolved into a hothouse for moral training achieved through the formation of group identity and group loyalty. Leaders at the school collapsed
notions of samurai rectitude, Confucian paragons of virtue, and *shinshi* or
zentoruman (the idea of the Victorian gentleman transplanted to Japan)
in defining the social elite they hoped to produce.[38] Socialization toward
such goals involved a peculiar combination of curricular and extracurricular
components. The school emphasized the liberal arts—Chinese and Japanese literature, pure (as opposed to applied) sciences, and literary English
and German.[39] The aim was to produce alumni who shared a common ap-
preciation for Culture rather than to teach the utilitarian vocational skills
emphasized in lesser secondary schools. The extracurricular life of the school
revolved around strenuous participation in sports clubs and spirited engagement in male-bonding rituals epitomized by the institutionalized dormitory
riots called "storms." The particularly lyrical ritual of "dorm rain" called for
students to simultaneously urinate out of dormitory windows while singing
school anthems at the top of their lungs.[40] The sum total of this program
of cultivation, hyper-masculinization, and group formation was to produce
a shared sense of social superiority. An alumnus, speaking in 1909 at a ceremony commemorating the founding of the school, described the results of
such a process in the following way: "I came to this conclusion. We were the
aristocracy (*kizoku*) of Japan. But this was not a matter of status (*mibun*).
And it was not a matter of wealth. We were an aristocracy of the spirit."[41]
Such a statement reveals that the graduates of the First Higher School came
to share a status identity constructed in the face of deeply perceived status
inconsistencies. There were Japanese with actual wealth, and there was a

legally designated aristocracy. The creation of the "aristocracy of the spirit" mediates the self-perception of a group that has neither wealth nor titles, but still sees itself as morally superior. The rhetorical displacement of the actual aristocracy voices the anxious importance of this band of brothers, forced to redefine aristocratic status to locate themselves in the social hierarchies of Meiji Japan.

Most studies of *Konjiki yasha* do not make much of Kan'ichi's school affiliations (perhaps because Japanese critics take their implications for granted). But it needs to be recognized that Kan'ichi's sense of identity depends upon belonging to the higher school brotherhood. This is made obvious when Kan'ichi comes home drunk after a party and speaks to Miya about how his classmates regard their engagement. While toasting his future union, Kan'ichi's friends had made it clear to him that failure would reflect beyond the individual.

> "I knew they were teasing me, but I took on their toasts one after the other, because I was amused at the way they said: If you're a man, you need to go one step further and really make her your wife. To be with her for ten years and then to have her stolen away by someone at this late date—that would be a disgrace not only for Hazama Kan'ichi, the individual, but for all of us friends. What's more, it's not only us but the entire Higher Middle School whose name would be sullied. . . . That's pretty staggering. I hope you'll do me the favor of cooperating."
>
> "Oh Kan'ichi, that's silly."
>
> "Now that all my friends know, my manhood will be in doubt (*otoko ga tatanai*) if we're not properly united as man and wife." (74)[42]

Despite the playful tone of this interchange, it is not hard to see that Kan'ichi's sense of masculine worth depends upon membership in a male alliance. Like a family, this group sanctions private behavior and in turn holds its members accountable. To the band of brothers who grant him his social identity, Kan'ichi will be, after the loss of Miya, at best an object of pity and perhaps an object of derision. His turn to moneylending must be seen, at least partially, as a response to expectations of expulsion from the brotherhood of higher school students.

Konjiki yasha's portrayal of the moral worth of First Higher School graduates is complicated. At times, members of the group appear to occupy the moral high ground appropriate to their education. At other times, however, the text deliberately compromises their moral stature by revealing their unsavory connections to the money economy. We begin to see this side of Kan'ichi's classmates when they appear in the novel four years after his departure from their midst. In the interim, all of these young men have proceeded on the fast track of self-advancement, graduating from the Imperial University and taking their places in government bureaus and other proper institutions. But we also learn that many of them are up to their necks in debt. Kan'ichi's former friends are not aristocrats of the spirit but rather men who live in the grime of financial considerations.

That these considerations can sometimes lead to brutish behavior is apparent in a scene where two classmates, Kamada Tetsuya and Kazahaya Kuranosuke, run into Kan'ichi at the house of their friend, Yusa Ryōkitsu. Kan'ichi, who by this time is the right-hand man of the notorious loan shark Wanibuchi, has visited Yusa in order to collect a loan. At first, Kamada offers a humorous, tongue-in-cheek evaluation of the relationship of moneylenders and "gentlemen," the term by which First Higher School graduates often thought of themselves:

> "If a gentleman were to loan shark, that would affect his reputation, but to borrow money at high interest, that's worthy of being counted an honor, especially in comparison to borrowing money at low interest or no interest. To be a gentleman doesn't mean you never have money troubles. You have these troubles and so you borrow. No one is saying that you borrow without returning. So there's no reason at all for your reputation to be harmed." (178)

Kamada speaks here as someone who is in considerable debt himself, and he draws some moral distinctions between lending and borrowing money. But what cannot be ignored is that, far from maintaining a haughty transcendence, a self-styled gentleman like Kamada is enmeshed in the moneylender's economy.

The veneer of this gentleman is peeled back none too attractively as Kamada confronts Kan'ichi on Yusa's behalf and asks him to show lenience in recognition of their former friendship. When Kan'ichi refuses to rescind his demands, Kamada, who has had training in "Kanō school" judo, leaps on Kan'ichi, grasps him in a choke hold, and proceeds to squeeze the breath out of him. Kamada explains his reliance on violence using the rhetoric of a budding militarist:

> "When it comes to things of this sort, brute force means more than the power of money. . . . In matters of national interest and national power, international law is actually no more use than the skin off a gourd; what's needed is military strength. If no mighty lord stands astride the world of

nations, whose hand will decide fairly and fully the battle between right and wrong? There exists only one instrument capable of rendering judgment, namely war! . . . I've never heard of a powerful nation being shamed, and thus my diplomacy relies on the Kanō school." (195)

Kamada chillingly collapses the personal into the national as he playfully engages in overblown rhetoric. His statements reveal connections in the sentiments defining internal and international hierarchies for an imperialist Japan. Kamada believes that might makes right both in international and personal relations; the action in which he engages as he spouts his philosophy shows how easily power and morality can become conflated in the self-righteous use of violence. The gentleman has been unmasked to reveal a bully. This melodrama raises the self-subverting suggestion that standards of value may be set by force rather than morality.[43]

The reliance upon hierarchies limned by violence is further emphasized when Kamada, speaking in a different register, refers to moneylenders as "animals who can count money" (zeni kanjō no dekiru kedamono) and Kan'ichi in particular as a "beast" (chikushō). A similar rhetoric of beastliness was frequently used to describe the burakumin, the outcaste group considered subhuman and treated with extreme social discrimination. That Kamada's words should not be taken lightly is indicated by his, in turn, referring to himself and other higher school students as "honest-to-goodness humans" (maningen). In the binary structure that Kamada rhetorically constructs, Kan'ichi is deprived of his humanity. Although existing within the same money economy as his higher school classmates, he is doubly abjected as both animal and untouchable. The status inconsistency felt by an "aristocrat of the spirit" beholden to a moneylender leads to the radical degradation of the latter, a degradation that makes Kan'ichi a dehumanized object of violence.

The moral hierarchies upheld by the elite subculture of higher school graduates receive their clearest exposition in the statements of Arao Jōsuke, the schoolmate whom his peers respect for his "seniority, the depth of his thinking, and his sincerity" (120). Unlike Kamada, whose moral enunciations are undercut by his comic portrayal, Arao's judgments are made with high seriousness and with the ringing tones of the male Meiji moralist. Thus it is easy to see his pronouncements as an articulation of the "moral occult" of the text. In fact, many male Meiji readers were enamored of Arao as a character and were willing to accept his statements at face value.[44] However,

FIGURE 2.1   A newspaper advertisement announcing the serialization of *Konjiki yasha* emphasizes the binary of the human and the inhuman in Kan'ichi, the moneylender. The caption engages in hyperbolic rhetoric: "At night in the slums, he drinks human blood and gnaws on human bones. Viewing a loan shark, the world truly regards him as a demon—treacherous, deceitful, cruel, and immoral. Now Kōyō draws the truth, using his taut and burnished prose to project the loan shark into a masterful plot of twists and turns. The demon breathes flames and the storms reek of blood; the beauty cries without her heart, and the moon and the blossoms go into hiding. Ink splatters and the brush flies as the sharpened arrowhead pierces the loan shark's innermost thoughts. Covered in scarlet, evil spirits scream in the dark. . . ." This advertisement ran nine times on the front page of the *Yomiuri shinbun* between December 20 and 31, 1896. Source: *Yomiuri shinbun*, December 20, 1896.

Arao's moral judgments need to be read in the context of the peripeties that he suffers in the plot, as well as the powerful homosocial ties that bind him to Kan'ichi. These require some explanation. Arao disappears from the text for some time after he is shown on the road to success as an Imperial University graduate and a rising bureaucrat in the Interior Ministry. Approximately two years pass before he makes his way back into the plot, jobless, drunk, and dressed in rags. We later learn that he had been dismissed from his position for falling into debt to loan sharks. This had happened because he had cosigned a high-interest loan taken out by a former benefactor. The latter had used the money to fund an unsuccessful election campaign, which had left him broke and Arao responsible for a huge loan he had no hope of repaying. Arao's troubles had led to dismissal from his appointment, after which he had returned to Tokyo, where he continued to be pursued by loan sharks as he eked out a living doing piecework translations.

What we have, then, is the phenomenon of some of the novel's most categorical moral statements being made by a man on the skids who has every reason to be bitter toward moneylenders. There are two ways to evaluate this situation. One is to view Arao as someone who speaks with the purity and knowledge of a victim; his suffering at the hands of moneylenders can be interpreted as a sign of virtue. The other is to take full account of the ideological failure that results from ceding the moral high ground to a deadbeat. One thing Arao's situation shows is that even the most upright and respected of men finds it impossible to sustain the kind of financial indifference envisioned by the leaders of the First Higher School.[45]

When Arao visits Kan'ichi after a long separation in an effort to steer him away from moneylending and toward a morally upright life, the powerful sentiments that course between the two men are evident as soon as Arao begins to speak: "Your *lover* may have betrayed you, but your *friend* never betrayed you. Isn't that so? Why then did you abandon that *friend*? I'm the one who was thus abandoned, but I want you to know that I've come to see you like this because I have yet to abandon you" (325). In constructing the contrast between the faithless lover and the faithful friend, Arao implies that these two relationships are connected in the realm of sentiment. This implication is strengthened by the use of the English words "lover" and "friend," which are inserted using the transliterated glosses known as *rubi*. I will later argue that the text uses linguistic emphasis to mark moments of heightened emotion; in this instance, the pairing of "lover" and "friend" is a sign of the homoerotic undercurrent running through this male relation-

ship. Arao, then, makes moral pronouncements from a particular positionality; he speaks as a spurned "friend" who thinks that Kan'ichi has betrayed
the ethics of a student elite and as a man entangled in the moneylender's
circulation of currency and obligations:

> "Hazama, why do you try to gain wealth? Did you become preoccupied
> with *money* because a great source of pleasure was taken from you and
> you sought something to take its place? That may be acceptable; let it be
> for now. But is there any need to engage in immorality and injustice for
> financial gain? Aren't you now suffering because of the actions of another?
> I would think, then, that you'd avoid causing suffering at all costs. Yet, not
> only do you cause suffering, your business rests on taking advantage of
> those in trouble and squeezing their lifeblood from them. Are you gain-
> ing any solace now from making money by means akin to robbery? *Money*
> may be the source of all power, but someone who's a human being can't
> rest at ease even for a moment when he's committing evil. Or are you hap-
> pily enjoying it? Are you collecting debts and attaching property feeling as
> though you're going flower viewing on a balmy day? Well, Hazama, how
> about it?" (326)

Transliterations of the English word "money" appear at a moment of excess
sentiment. In Arao's melodramatic moral judgment, moneylending is inhuman and evil, a form of persecution visited upon those already in misery.

Given this kind of evaluation, it is not surprising that the discourse of
beastliness crops up in the conversation between Arao and Kan'ichi. Kan'ichi
brings it up when he repeats a term he had first used on the beach at Atami
and refers to Miya as a "beast" (*chikushō*). Arao immediately replies: "But
you're a beast too the way you are now. A loan shark doesn't possess the
heart of a human being. Without a person's heart, you're a beast" (328). Like
Kamada, Arao regards moneylenders as beasts, but his use of "too" in his
response indicates that he would also include unfaithful women among the
abjected. This is consistent with his particular take on heterosexual love and
money, which regards both as sources of suffering:

> "If I were to name the things that destroy capable men in these times, they
> would be desire and loan sharks. . . . Although you may suffer because you've
> lost in *love*, and others suffer because of *money*, there's no difference when
> it comes to the fact of suffering. I am in these dire straits, and so I sin-
> cerely want a true companion with whom I can share my troubles. I've never
> stopped hoping for a *friend* like Hazama Kan'ichi used to be. How happy I
> would be if such a *friend* were to show concern and tell me he would lend

me a hand so that I could go out into society and apply myself fully. In this world, what brings the most happiness is a *friend*; what is most hateful is a moneylender. Because I know how hateful moneylenders are, I think all the more of my *friend*. That *friend* from the past is today a moneylender—a hateful moneylender! It's unspeakable." (333–34)

No other passage illustrates quite like this one the combination of sentiments—the oscillation between an abstract morality and the deeply personal—that lie behind Arao's moral disgust. When he places hetero-sexual love and money on the negative pole of the moral scale, he does so because he assigns the positive pole to homosocial relations marked by shared moral values (again emphatically represented by the echoing of the transliterated term *friend*).[46] His own destitute place in the economy of moneylenders makes him long for a special companion, but that true companion has become a moneylender himself. The cruel irony of Arao's situation is that Kan'ichi has the capacity to lend him a hand precisely because he is a usurer—which makes it impossible for Arao to accept any help. What we hear behind Arao's hyperbolic self-righteousness is the frus-trated desire of a man who needs friendship and money, but who cannot accept any solace or help because of the positions that he and Kan'ichi hold in the money economy.

When this frustrated man runs into Miya, he expresses a spectacular misogyny. The rhetoric of violence intrudes when he verbally defines her transgressions: "But no matter how mistaken Hazama was in choosing his course, your crime is still your crime. Not only that, when you take into account that he became so degraded because you deserted him, you did far more than transgress against female chastity. You also stabbed your husband to death" (306). This rhetoric is especially evident when Arao tells Miya about his reaction, some years ago, when he had first heard that she had decided to marry Tomiyama. He had initially intended, he says, to remon-strate with her in an attempt to change her mind, and if she would not listen he was prepared to conclude that she "could no longer be treated as human" and needed to be "beaten until my anger was satisfied so that you could be made an honest-to-goodness cripple unfit to marry for the rest of your life" (305). But he had not carried out the attack, he says, because "it would have been inexcusable to damage an article for sale (*urimono*) belong-ing to someone else." Amidst the various violent projections that are present in *Konjiki yasha*, this instance is notable for the clarity with which it identifies Miya as an objectified and dehumanized target of violence. Despite his refusal to equate monetary and moral value, Arao has no problem seeing a woman as a commodity.

As this scene progresses, Miya pours out her heart, stating her desire to meet Kan'ichi again and apologize for her actions. Although Arao is not unmoved by her fervent expressions of contrition, his male moralism finally conditions his response, and he refuses to aid Miya in any expression of regret. He couches his refusal in words that reveal a surprising extension of the male alliance:

> "I approve of the sense of remorse that makes you say you want to apologize to Hazama even if it means being killed by him, but in that case you'd be recognizing the existence of Hazama while ignoring your husband. What will you do about your husband? Doesn't this go against the path of moral duty toward your husband? In effect, you began by betraying Hazama for Tomiyama, and now you betray Tomiyama for Hazama. You're betraying not only one person but two. . . . Seeing where your thoughts are going, I can't help feeling sorry for Tomiyama. I have to feel pity for the misfortune of a Tomiyama, married to a woman like you, a wife both unfaithful and immoral. Yes, I truly feel pity. I sympathize much more with Tomiyama than with you. You're the one deserving of hatred." (310)

With this statement it becomes impossible to regard Arao as a man driven by his loyalty to Kan'ichi. Although his allegiance to the latter is clearly important, it lies alongside a no less powerful sense of duty to males in general. Arao has every reason to hate Tomiyama for having stolen Miya—except that he is another male charged with the responsibility of controlling female desire. This is enough to make him feel sympathy for the capitalist who had used money to gain what he wanted. Arao's male alliances may start with the brotherhood that he feels for his First Higher School classmate, but they extend toward other males whose interests lie in the enforcement of female fidelity. His sense of fraternity reveals itself as a commitment to patriarchy. Part of *Konjiki yasha*'s ideological contradiction is that it allows to emerge, behind the surface binary of "money versus love," the picture of male alliances driven by discourses of brotherhood, shaped by economies of need, and directed toward the subjugation of females and others it considers less than human. This male alliance may speak the language of morality, but its ultimate aim is power. The rhetoric of violence erupts when the exercise of power is figured as morality.

FICTIVE FAMILIES AND THE
MONEYLENDER'S ECONOMY

Aside from the brotherhood of higher school students, *Konjiki yasha* features another type of fictive family, formed through an unofficial adoption. The first of this type involves the moneylender, Wanibuchi Tadayuki. Kan'ichi's relationship with Wanibuchi begins as a purely economic affiliation when he signs on as a clerk to the moneylender following his departure from the Shigizawa household. But this relationship soon becomes something more when Wanibuchi begins to notice certain qualities in Kan'ichi. Status-based values lie behind this development. In another instance of the novel's emphasis upon Meiji social fluidity, Wanibuchi is portrayed as an ex-samurai who has grown rich lending out the money of his former lord, now a viscount. Despite his current profession, he still appreciates idealized attributes associated with his former status:

> He [Kan'ichi] did not gain Wanibuchi's trust only by working hard as a clerk or by being wise as an advisor. Wanibuchi secretly admired him as a rare youth who, despite his age, kept lust at a distance, refrained from drink, spent sparingly, engaged in no indolence, always did his duty, disdained affectation, treated others with respect, observed decorum and what was more, possessed more than a little moral backbone. (145)

Kan'ichi, it turns out, is a thoroughly upright loan shark who has to take to his bed after particularly difficult collections! The plot will need to eventually resolve the status inconsistency of a moneylender possessing the ethical bearing of a young samurai. Wanibuchi admires the decorous and upstanding young man so much that he "thought of Kan'ichi as his own child" (*waga ko to omoeru Kan'ichi* [217]). He and his wife take Kan'ichi into their own home, treat him like a member of the family (*uchi no hito to onaji* [150]), and plan to eventually set him up in a business of his own. After Wanibuchi and his wife are burned to death, Kan'ichi ends up inheriting the loan shark's wealth and business. So that we do not miss the point that a form of filiation has taken place, the narrator tells us that Kan'ichi then becomes "Wanibuchi the second" (*nidai no Wanibuchi*).

The novel foregrounds adoption as a solution to problems of family continuity by giving Wanibuchi a son by birth. This son, Tadamichi, is also an admirably upright young man, but his standard of ethics makes him think of moneylending as a "filthy family enterprise" (*kegareta kagyō* [222]).

Unwilling to benefit from tainted money, Tadamichi has moved out of his father's house and makes his own living as a teacher. Whenever he visits, he begs his father forcefully and repetitively to get out of his trade. These remonstrations call forth Wanibuchi's strongest defense of what he does:

> "You say that once a person has made enough money to meet his needs there's no sense in wanting more. I say that's the thinking of a scholar. If people stop what they're doing because they're happy just meeting their needs, then our nation will be destroyed right away. Our enterprises will stop developing, and our country will be filled with young retirees. What will you do then? Desire without limits is the lifeblood of our nation's citizens." (227)

Although Wanibuchi is being deliberately provocative, there is seriousness in his voice. His declarations make clear the novel's recognition of the ties between economic aggrandizement and nationalism. In an age when industrial capitalism and military might were ideologically joined in the national slogan of *fukoku kyōhei* (prosperous nation, powerful military), Wanibuchi feels justified in thinking of moneylending as a patriotic contribution. A condition of modernity erupts here as a threat to filiation. Tadamichi makes it clear that he will not accept any inheritance from his father. "I'm your only child," he says, "and you can't leave a single *sen* of your fortune to me" (226).

While legal *ie* continuity may not be in danger (Tadamichi could conceivably succeed to the house headship while renouncing succession to property), the moral conflicts in Wanibuchi's House have deprived it of any successor to the family trade. The selection of Kan'ichi, then, shows that a quasi-adoption can secure a successor when a birth child proves to be unsuitable or unwilling. The adoption benefits both Wanibuchi and Kan'ichi: the Wanibuchis get permanent help for the family business and would have had a source of support in their old age, had they lived, while Kan'ichi gains a trade, a new identity, and a family. Affiliation is once again figured as filiation. What we cannot miss is that the formation of this fictive family contradicts Kan'ichi's ideology, expressed in his reaction to Shigizawa Ryūzō, that a family must stand apart from the "filth" of financial calculation. The alternative family, it turns out, can be rooted in the moneylender's economy and confer continuity on a family trade coded as vice.

Kan'ichi finds his next fictive family in Shiobara, where he goes in order to escape his own desolation and vulnerability following the death of the Wanibuchis. His journey to the hotspring village of Hataori constitutes one of the most famous passages in Meiji literature. The lyrical narrative here uses the sinified diction that filtered in from Chinese poetry as well as the rhythmic parallel constructions of the Sino-Japanese known as *kanbun* to paint a verbal inkwash of rock and water: "From here onward, wherever there was a road there was water, and wherever there was water there was always a bridge, of which there were thirty in the gorge. Where there were mountains there were cliffs, and where there were cliffs there were always falls, of which there were seventy in the range" (398). The *kanbun*-influenced prose narrates a sequentially unfolding landscape represented rhetorically rather than descriptively. The heightened language constructs a liminal topography that signals a major shift in the melodrama. Occult forces seem to pressure events, for Kan'ichi is struck with a stunning sense of déjà vu; he recognizes the landscape he traverses as that of the bloody dream in which he had stabbed Miya to death.

The reader is left expecting a denouement, and this is provided through the trope of the fictive family. At his inn, Kan'ichi overhears a heartrending conversation between a geisha and her lover. Driven to the brink by entangled problems of money and family, the two plan to commit suicide together rather than be separated. The geisha, Oshizu, is being pushed into the arms of a wealthy man by her stepmother, a woman who raised and trained her, and who now looks to profit handsomely through an advantageous alliance. Her lover, Sayama, a clerk at a wholesaling firm, has spent a considerable sum of his shop's money patronizing Oshizu. The proprietor of the shop has offered to forgive the embezzlement as long as Sayama marries his niece. The two lovers, then, are in a situation to both satisfy the demands of constructed families and respond to financial realities if only they will give each other up. But this they refuse to do, and so they have decided to pursue a desperate and final course.

The decision of these two young people to die together initially suggests that their "love" too lies in the realm of dark passion. But a closer examination of the discourses at work shows that their relationship is a reversed re-narration of what had taken place between Kan'ichi and Miya. The latter relationship had initially seemed devoted to conjugal love but had revealed its true nature as passion; the bond between Sayama and Oshizu starts out looking like passion but turns out to be thoroughly domesticated. The first sign of this appears in the prominence of mutual fidelity in their relationship. Sayama had rejected the easy way out of marrying his boss's niece because this would have betrayed his love for Oshizu. His geisha lover is even more of a paragon. Her rich suitor (who, coincidentally turns out to be

Miya's philandering husband, Tomiyama) had tried to tempt Oshizu with wealth. "He mentioned money, money," she says, "in every other word. He seemed to think that others would be overjoyed as long as he spoke of money" (440). But such blandishments had disgusted her, and she had held firm to her love for Sayama. Oshizu is seemingly capable of standing above the filth of money. What is more, she is a rare creature, a chaste geisha. When Kan'ichi asks her whether Tomiyama is her patron (*danna*), implying sexual patronage, she recoils at the very idea and declares, "I can't do that sort of thing. To this day, I have never once been with a customer" (439). Although Oshizu is here conveniently forgetting that Sayama was once a customer, the implications are still clear. Despite being a woman of the demimonde, Oshizu is a one-man woman. She is Miya's opposite in resisting the promise of wealth and being true to her man. This principled devotion to monogamy will soon make her ideal material for the forging of a domesticated wife.

When Kan'ichi hears of Oshizu's fidelity and imperviousness to money, he is overcome with emotion in a moment of melodramatic excess: "Could Kan'ichi be crying? He had been brought to tears by this lowly woman who sold her charms, but yet had decided—who could have taught her this?— that she would hold fast to a difficult principle even unto death, that she would defend a fidelity so difficult to defend, and finally gain something that could not be stolen" (440). Having discovered an infinitely faithful woman of the sort that he had wished for and failed to find in Miya, Kan'ichi immediately decides to become the protector of Oshizu's love. The text makes clear that this protection involves money; we are repeatedly told that Sayama must repay the 3,000 yen that he embezzled and that Oshizu needs 800 yen to buy out her geisha contract. Ironically, protecting a love that rejects money will require the infusion of a huge sum of cash. This Kan'ichi gladly provides. He then takes the young couple into his own house.

The fictive family that results had already been suggested when, in the process of stopping the young lovers' suicide, Kan'ichi had used a parental metaphor to represent himself as a protector of their lives (*inochi no oya* [432]). Once Oshizu and Sayama are duly ensconced in his house, it becomes clear that Kan'ichi has assumed a paternal role. The quasi-familial atmosphere becomes overwhelming: Kan'ichi sits back and plays the wise and generous patriarch, while Oshizu bustles about drawing his bath, laying out his clothes, and serving him beer. Gone are all the flirtatious gestures of a geisha; Oshizu has become a domesticated quasi-daughter-in-law who throws herself into being the woman of the house. A happy Kan'ichi confirms the contours of his relationship with the younger couple: "When you think about it, human beings are unpredictable creatures. The two of you were absolute strangers to me, and we'd had no ties whatsoever. Yet you've come to my house. Sayama turns out to be an upright person, and you take care of me with such kindness. I could never think of you as strangers" (458).

It seems clear that these three characters now constitute a kind of alternative *ie* with Kan'ichi as the househead (the text calls him the *aruji*, or "master") and with Oshizu and Sayama in the role of *fūfu yōshi*, a married couple adopted together into a family. As in *Hototogisu*, an alternative *ie* reconstructs family ties, institutes new hierarchies, and assigns new social identities. While the Meiji state's *ie* ideology contributes to the formation of Kan'ichi's new family—the adoption of a married couple, for example, is a practice sanctioned by the Meiji Civil Code[47]—there has also been a significant reinscription of that ideology. Kan'ichi's unofficial adoption of the couple has nothing to do with *ie* ideology's concern with family continuity; he is not interested in handing down the family name or preserving family lineage. Unlike the househead within the *ie* system, who had the power to approve marriages, Kan'ichi achieves his patriarchal status by becoming the protector of a love that the young couple have established for themselves. The hegemonic ideology has been adapted and transformed to meet the requirements of a character's sentiments. Such an adjustment may perhaps not qualify as an act of resistance, but, like other alternative families in Meiji fiction, this iteration of the *ie* shows that the family can be continuously re-narrated. The spinning out of alternatives shows that the state's model of the family is not the only one possible.

Although *Konjiki yasha* was left unfinished at the time of Ozaki Kōyō's death in 1903, the emergence of this final fictive family appears directed toward providing a solution to the moral predicaments laid out in the plot. If "love" has been rendered out of reach for Kan'ichi himself, he can still attest to its value through his actions as a protector of "love." The "love" that he works to uphold, moreover, has been stripped of its destructive energies and returned to the safer form of domesticated monogamy; the bond between Oshizu and Sayama can be more easily figured as virtue than anything that occurs between Kan'ichi and Miya. In his new position as the generous guardian of conjugal love, then, Kan'ichi escapes from the villain's role and manages to reclaim the positive side of the novel's moral binary. By doing so, he recovers the humanity denied to bloodsucking moneylenders. He also manages a partial restoration of his status. His role as the househead revered by Oshizu and Sayama allows an erstwhile higher school student to achieve a male dignity more appropriate to his age and background. The figuring of the adopted couple as consisting of a geisha and a clerk, moreover, permits a reinstitution of a status hierarchy wherein a former samurai stands above commoners. The novel thus turns to a patriarchal alternative family to repair the status inconsistency of an educated man of samurai birth working as a moneylender.

But this resolution only ends up magnifying the work's ideological contradictions. Kan'ichi's support of the love between Oshizu and Sayama undercuts the binary opposition of love against money, for his support is essentially monetary. The young lovers have been saved by funds amassed through Kan'ichi's usury; here money serves the interests of love, and a loan shark's filthy lucre constitutes the milk of human kindness. Like the other fictive families in *Konjiki yasha*, this final family ends up testifying to the all-pervasive and enduring power of money. Disentangling the filth of economy from other areas of human interconnection—love, friendships, family—proves impossible. Far from being "MOMENTARY," money turns out to be the eternal and necessary ingredient of the human relations the novel seeks to encompass.

After taking in the young couple, Kan'ichi becomes a much less interesting character. Comforted by Oshizu's ministrations, he is no longer the desperate antihero, driven by dark, inchoate passions. The plot comes to a stop, having lost what had been its motor—Kan'ichi's tortured struggle to blunt his pain through perverse acts of moral inversion. Kan'ichi is now a fat cat, happy in the family that money can buy; his self-satisfaction as he contentedly sips the beer that Oshizu pours for him is, more than anything else, reminiscent of the self-absorption shown by his former antagonist, Tomiyama. Our final image of Kan'ichi is that of a turncoat against love as passion; he has chosen flabby survival rather than consuming obsession.

In contrast to this outcome, Miya gradually develops a strange, mad integrity. With ferocious intensity, she clings to her sentiments, which are only renewed by Kan'ichi's repeated rejections of her. The woman who had once betrayed domestic love now sacrifices herself on the altar of passion. To express emotions that she cannot convey directly to Kan'ichi, she turns to writing lengthy letters to him, letters that he immediately throws away. It is in writing and in language that we must seek the role that "love" comes to play within this novel's compromised moral landscape.

THE LANGUAGE(S) OF MELODRAMA

Konjiki yasha is a wonderland of language.[48] A heteroglot narrative space, it brims with the specialized languages of students and moneylenders, with the gendered speech of men and women, with literary styles that draw from *kanbun* and from classical literature. The linguistic variety within the text was recognized early on. Yasuda Kōami, the moderator of the 1903 panel where Kōyō laid out his opposition between love and money, had the following to say about the novel's language:

> Its prose was surely one way in which *Konjiki yasha* showed its different colors in a literary world then leaning toward *genbun itchi*. In the way Kōyō changes styles and takes up varying modes one after the other, I see his usual attitude of being faithful to his prose and not neglecting his brush even for a moment.[49]

This is a revealing comment on the historical conditions for the linguistic production of *Konjiki yasha*. A few years hence, with the vernacular-based written language of *genbun itchi* triumphant and the autobiographical works of the Naturalist writers accorded the highest prestige, being faithful to one's prose would mean cultivating a single, identifiable "voice" that stamped a text with an author's verbal markings. Although Yasuda is aware of the coming wave, he is still speaking (and Kōyō was still writing) in a literary environment where being faithful to one's prose could mean engaging in the virtuoso performance of numerous different languages. In the discussion that follows, I comment on the consequences of this heteroglot narration for melodrama. The phenomenon of multivocality—found both in the narrator and in the characters—undermines the melodrama's effort to install moral certitude by emphasizing the mixed and contested discursive space of the novel. In particular, the rhetorical power of Miya's letters to Kan'ichi, strikingly written in the stylized epistolary language of *mairase sōrōbun*, resists easy ideological closure. In Meiji melodramatic fiction the *melos* of heightened language marks moments of high emotion; it pulls at the heartstrings, tells us when to be most attentive, and provides clues to the interpretation of the semantic content. Listening to its dynamics must be part of understanding the ideological effects of the text.

The primary level of linguistic difference in *Konjiki yasha* is that between the narrator, who uses classical Japanese grammar, and the characters, who speak in various vernaculars. This linguistic division of labor, inherited from Edo-period fiction, was common in Meiji prose literature until the onslaught of *genbun itchi* texts, which employed vernacular-based languages for both narration and dialogue. But this first level of difference only provides the framework for a further explosion of languages, since both narration and dialogue in *Konjiki yasha* contain numerous linguistic strains. To take dialogue first, the speech of characters is strongly differentiated to note gender and status, regional backgrounds, generations, and educational or professional identifications. Thus we have Arao peppering his speech with English and the sinified compounds appropriate for a man educated at the First Higher School, Wanibuchi speaking in a vaguely provincial dialect that makes him sound both vulgar and sharp, and Oshizu mixing working-class Tokyo speech with usages from the licensed prostitution quarters. Kan'ichi and Miya are distinguished by the way their speech reflects their changing situations. Kan'ichi can go from the righteous rhetoric of the wronged believer in domestic love to the specialized vocabulary of the moneylender. There are also occasions when he uses the argot of the higher school student or the decorous tones of a young man of samurai background. Miya can sound like the willful young bourgeois girl that she is, but once married she can speak in the refined language of a woman of means.

This cacophony of voices surrounds the narrator, who in turn speaks in many tongues. Although he (his language makes clear his gender) holds to the general framework of classical grammar, he can employ metaphors clearly borrowed from Western literature and diction taken from modern juridical language. He sometimes uses a style, probably derived from translations of Western texts, that metronomically inserts grammatical subjects in a way unusual for Japanese. He also frequently and noticeably slips into a style that shows the influence of *kanbun*, the tradition of reading classical Chinese texts in Japanese, and he occasionally employs prose that consciously echoes female writing from the Heian period (794–1185).[50] It is these last two styles that I first examine for their impact upon a melodramatic narration.

The prominence of *kanbun*-derived prose in *Konjiki yasha* was recognized very early on; Yasuda, for example, commented in the 1903 panel discussion that the work was "rich in the structure and the diction of *kanbun*." Because *kanbun* was a fundamental part of elite, male education for centuries, it was inevitable that its peculiar locutions, as well as sinified vocabulary and Chinese rhetorical structures, would appear in the writing of Japanese prose. This is what happens in *Konjiki yasha*, where very little is written in *kanbun* per se, but where the prose in certain sections shows the heavy presence of this already hybrid language. The concentration of *kanbun*-influenced prose is connected to the social groups represented in the work. *Kanbun* had remained a part of male secondary curriculum after the Meiji Restoration. It was taught at the First Higher School as part of courses on the Chinese classics, whose readings included heavy doses of Confucian texts and Tang poetry; pedagogically, then, *kanbun* was a language associated with ethical discourse and with high lyricism. *Kanbun* also filtered outside of the classroom. During the 1880s and 1890s the status fashion for higher school students called for the liberal use of *kanbun* in speech. Thus the presence of *kanbun* elements was to be expected in a work depicting First Higher School students and graduates. *Kanbun* shows up in the dialogue of the former students portrayed in the novel: a drunken Arao, for example, intones a Sino-Japanese poem in the recitation style known as *shigin*. It is *kanbun*'s place in the narration, however, that is important for our purposes, for heavy doses of the language adhere to the portrayal of Kan'ichi, particularly during moments of high sentiment or ethical crisis. We have already seen the use of *kanbun*-derived prose in the lyricism of the famous sequence narrating Kan'ichi's liminal voyage to the resort of Hataori. Another moment of hyperbolic emotion presented through *kanbun*-influenced language occurs as Kan'ichi looks out over the still-warm ashes of the house where Wanibuchi and his wife have died:

> When he looked at his tormented life, it seemed no different from their cruel death. The only contrast was between staying and departing. Should his pained life be comforted by their death, or should their pitiful death be mourned by his life? His vitals had been cut, and his soul torn; their flesh had been scorched, and their bones crushed. (289)

Although I can only reproduce the incessant parallelism gained from Chinese rhetoric, these sentences are also filled with sinified diction and the locutions common to *kanbun*.[51] This passage is a narrated monologue, where the narrator is the speaker but where the language of the character intrudes.[52] I am forced to use the third person by the requirements of English, but the original occasionally shades into the first person (*waga*). The implication is that at a moment of high emotion, where Kan'ichi compares the pain of his life with the violent deaths of Wanibuchi and his wife, his thoughts coalesce in a male language tied to ethical discourse. *Kanbun* is a language associated with Kan'ichi.

But it is hardly his only language. There are other passages conveying

Kan'ichi's thoughts that are devoid of *kanbun*. When his thoughts are narrated directly in the form of a quoted monologue, rather than in the narrated form as above, the language of his interior is presented in the vernacular. For example, there is the passage that shows his refusal to open the letters Miya sends him one after the other:

> "She's probably asking me to forgive her. . . . What good does it do to repent or to forgive? What effect is it going to have on the Kan'ichi and Miya of today? Is the wound on her chastity going to heal because she repents? Or can we go back to a past before Tomiyama because I forgive her? In this matter, I'm absolutely the Kan'ichi of ten years ago. Miya, you're befouled for the rest of your life." (350)

Although this monologue occurs at a charged moment revealing Kan'ichi's continued belief in an ideology of sexual purity, there is hardly any sign of *kanbun*. What are we to do with these contrasting representations of Kan'ichi's inner language? Should we decide that the vernacular is Kan'ichi's "real" language and that *kanbun* belongs to the erudite narrator? There is something to this explanation, since *kanbun* occurs principally in narrated passages. But it does not explain why *kanbun* flows out specifically when what is at stake is Kan'ichi's perspective or his feelings, or why passages redolent with *kanbun* would occasionally use the first person. My conclusion is that *kanbun*, too, is a "real" language for Kan'ichi's inner self, but it is a language that needs to be spoken for him by the narrator. This is because it is not a vernacular but the language of an ethical or philosophical framework that has been learned in the terms of that language. Thus, when a tortured Kan'ichi ponders the proximity of life and death, *kanbun* is the proper language given his gender and education. However, when he considers issues of chastity and purity, influenced by the domestic thought of Meiji Christians, the ethical register is different and better articulated through the modern vernacular.

The linguistic variety of *Konjiki yasha* is shared by many other melodramatic texts, though not in such a bravura performance, and so we can reasonably expand the points that I have been making to some general observations about the narration of Meiji melodrama. First, in relation to the narrator, we must recognize the capacity to move in and out of various languages and voices. Rather than a coherent and unified narrator, we have a linguistically variegated narrator who constructs a hybrid narration out of contrasting threads of language. Second, in relation to characters, we must note that they too are capable of speaking and thinking in more than one voice. Rather than being whole and smooth, their subjectivities are filled with contending languages. These languages appear depending upon the situation or the ideological contexts being invoked; they are also expressive of gender and shifting social positionalities. Finally, we might observe that no language is unmarked in a narrative like *Konjiki yasha*. Given that the narrator's language is itself hybrid, there is no neutral voice for those more colored to emerge against. The language of Meiji melodrama is a language of difference, where shifting linguistic modes help sustain a series of hyperbolic moments. The *melos* of this form of melodrama, then, quotes melodies, phrases, and rhythms from numerous sources. What is important here is not the exposition and the development of a single theme, but the way repeated contrasts and juxtapositions produce succeeding crescendos.

Some further observations regarding the linguistic marking of gender become available through examining the traces of Heian writing present in the portrayal of Miya. Take for example a passage that describes Miya's state of mind when she suddenly spots Kan'ichi after not seeing him for many years following their separation: "For four long years, her thoughts, day and night, had constantly been of love and longing more hopeless than writing figures upon moving waters" (161). This bit of psychonarration contains a direct allusion to a poem that appears in both the tenth-century imperial poetry collection *Kokinshū* and the slightly earlier poetic tale *Ise monogatari*: "More hopeless / than writing figures / upon moving waters / to feel for one / who does not feel for you."[53] Although this poem is listed anonymously in the *Kokinshū*, in the *Ise monogatari* it is attributed to a woman protesting to an unresponsive lover. There is thus an attempt to associate Miya's sentiments with the female experience in Heian texts, where "love" is a matter of fleeting consummations amidst expanses of longing.

Another evocation of Heian literature occurs in a description of Miya writing the letters that will next become our focus. This is a situation that invites reference to a prior paradigm, because aristocratic Heian heroines, shut away in their houses in a polygamous society, constantly resorted to correspondence, particularly poetic exchanges, in order to express their feelings. In this passage, there is no direct allusion, but the language forcefully evokes Heian predecessors:

> Ever since she had seen him at the Tazumi mansion a few years ago (*saitsu-toshi*), she had, in distress at having no way of expressing the unendurable appeals of her heart, taken up her brush merely as a means of momentary re-

lease, and yet she had managed to write well and long about those things she would have found hard to say; but sadly, though she was at one point determined to send him what she had written and tell him about the sorrow that she now knew all too well, she reconsidered when she wondered whether the letter would reach Kan'ichi's hands and be seen by his eyes. (321)

This very long sentence, reminiscent of the cascading flow of courtly prose, relies heavily on native diction and grammatical structures from the Heian period. Sinified compounds are few. Perhaps the clearest indication of the linguistic choices being made occurs in the term translated as "a few years ago," which is written with the character compound usually pronounced *ōnen*, but which here receives a *rubi* gloss indicating that it should be read as *saitsutoshi*. The former is a compound of Chinese origin that occurs frequently in *kanbun*, but the gloss steers the reading toward a term firmly rooted in the language of native, classical lyricism.

Taken together with the *kanbun*-influenced prose that occurs around Kan'ichi, the courtly Japanese used in Miya's vicinity allows us to form some further conclusions about the language in Meiji melodramatic fiction. Linguistic differences often function to reinforce gender differences. The contrast between *kanbun*-derived and courtly Japanese languages emphasizes the gulf between maleness and femaleness. This linguistic divide signals differences in sentiment. Kan'ichi tries to encapsulate his feelings in philosophical and ethical discourse, while Miya abandons herself to the flow of feeling. A linguistically expressed gender division of this sort occurs in other examples of melodramatic fiction. In *Hototogisu*, for example, prose redolent with Heian images, diction, and style coalesce around Namiko, while Takeo's actions in the battle of the Yellow Sea are narrated in prose that resonates with *kanbun* rhythms. There is a strong *kanbun* element in *Gubijinsō's* portrayal of its male heroes, Munechika and Kōno, while Fujio is depicted in consciously elegant *bibun*, language that attempts to drape her in a mantle of feminized evil.

While it is thus tempting to simply conclude that the linguistic divide upholds a gender binary, the multiple languages of *Konjiki yasha* complicate the situation. Just as *kanbun* alone does not serve to articulate Kan'ichi's feelings, Heian-inflected classical Japanese is not the only language used in Miya's portrayal. In some instances, quoted internal monologues appear in classical grammar, but with modern diction uncolored by Heian vocabulary (237). When the topic at hand is Miya's calculating desire for social and economic advancement, the narration can resort to sentences methodically furnished with subjects, in an echo of a style developed for translating Western languages (70).[54] As we will soon see, in her writing Miya expertly uses the premodern epistolary style of *sōrōbun*. Like Kan'ichi, Miya is a character endowed with multiple languages. Gender, then, while a crucial division, is marked in the melodramatic novel by layered and hybrid languages derived from the discursive mélange of Meiji Japan. Rather than articulating a fixed gender binary, language offers shifting and contested visions of gender by situationally employing a fluid stylistic array.

This brings us to what may be the most forceful application of language in a linguistically extravagant work: the use of the *sōrōbun* epistolary style in Miya's passionate and desperate letters to Kan'ichi. We should begin by locating the letters within the plot, for, while the letters themselves only appear at the end, considerable foreshadowing leads the reader to expect that Miya's writing will come to play a central role. Near the midpoint of the novel we read that Miya has been considering writing "a long, long letter that would reveal everything within her heart" (236). The wish to reveal all grows out of the utter desolation of Miya's marriage and the passion for Kan'ichi that it breeds. As a trophy wife, Miya is treated indulgently, but there can be no serious emotional engagement in her marriage: the expectations for her are to be a domestic ornament—"a talking flower or a warm jewel" (231)—and to provide sexual service. The latter is suggested explicitly in one scene where Tomiyama thrusts his cold hand, without warning or provocation, into the bosom of Miya's kimono. The misery of these circumstances turns her imagination toward what has been lost: "She found unendurable the tiresome expressions of love that entangled her, and she discovered the secret delights of longing for the love of her past, now as ephemeral as a fleeing shadow" (241).

The text makes clear the corrosive effects of this situation on the various models of family that surround Miya. To begin with, the loveless marriage with Tomiyama is the antithesis of the *katei*, the conjugal family warmed by a shared emotional commitment. Although Miya now possesses all the accoutrements of the ideal bourgeois marriage, she has none of the contents. She is not unaware of the irony: "She was now enjoying, as if in a dream, the golden moment for a young wife. She could not help sighing, in spite of herself, at the thought that her station in life represented the highest yearnings and desires felt by all young girls" (237). Miya has found that marriage without love is more trap than dream. Having destroyed the happy *katei* that she might have had with Kan'ichi, she keenly feels its absence in her relationship with Tomiyama.

Miya's relationship to the institution of the *ie* is similarly destructive. The key issue here is her childlessness. Miya had become pregnant a few months after her marriage to Tomiyama, and had borne him a son. She had found this "unexpectedly shameful." This shame is connected to the fact that her growing regret makes her view her betrayal of Kan'ichi as an explicitly sexual betrayal, of which a baby is living evidence. Accordingly, Miya seems less saddened by the baby's early death than that he was conceived in the first place. These sentiments make her decide not to get pregnant again: "After the child's death, she had vowed firmly to herself that she would never again bear Tomiyama's child. Strangely enough, she was able to hold to this vow for two years, three years, even four years afterward" (235). Miya unilaterally takes an action to insure that the Tomiyama family line will not endure into the next generation, at least with her physical cooperation. She refuses to reproduce the biological filiation that would perpetuate a model of family conceived as a component of the state.[55]

Miya's letters, then, are cries of passion uttered in the face of hegemonic ideologies. Initially, Miya had been torn about whether or not to send these letters to Kan'ichi—the writing itself was what occupied her. Whenever she found her situation unendurable, she had plunged herself into endlessly revising and recopying her letters. For her, these were sustained moments of hyperbolic emotion:

> Whenever she could not stand her torment, she would take it out and recopy it. And while she did this, she would add to her writing in some places, change her writing in others. It was this act alone that made her feel a pleasure akin to fulfilling the dream of her desires; when she sat before her letter it was as though she were sitting in front of him, sitting in front of him and saying everything so that she had no regrets. (321)

This iterative passage shows that Miya repeatedly undertakes her lapidary process of revision because she enjoys the engagement with language and finds seductive the possibility of "saying everything," a prospect denied her in real life. The letters are Miya's moments of melodramatic enunciation, akin to Kan'ichi's moment on the beach at Atami. The key difference, of course, is that Kan'ichi's speech is uttered directly to Miya, while her letters are written because she is separated from Kan'ichi. Peter Brooks observes that melodramas abound in scenes where "soliloquy has become 'pure

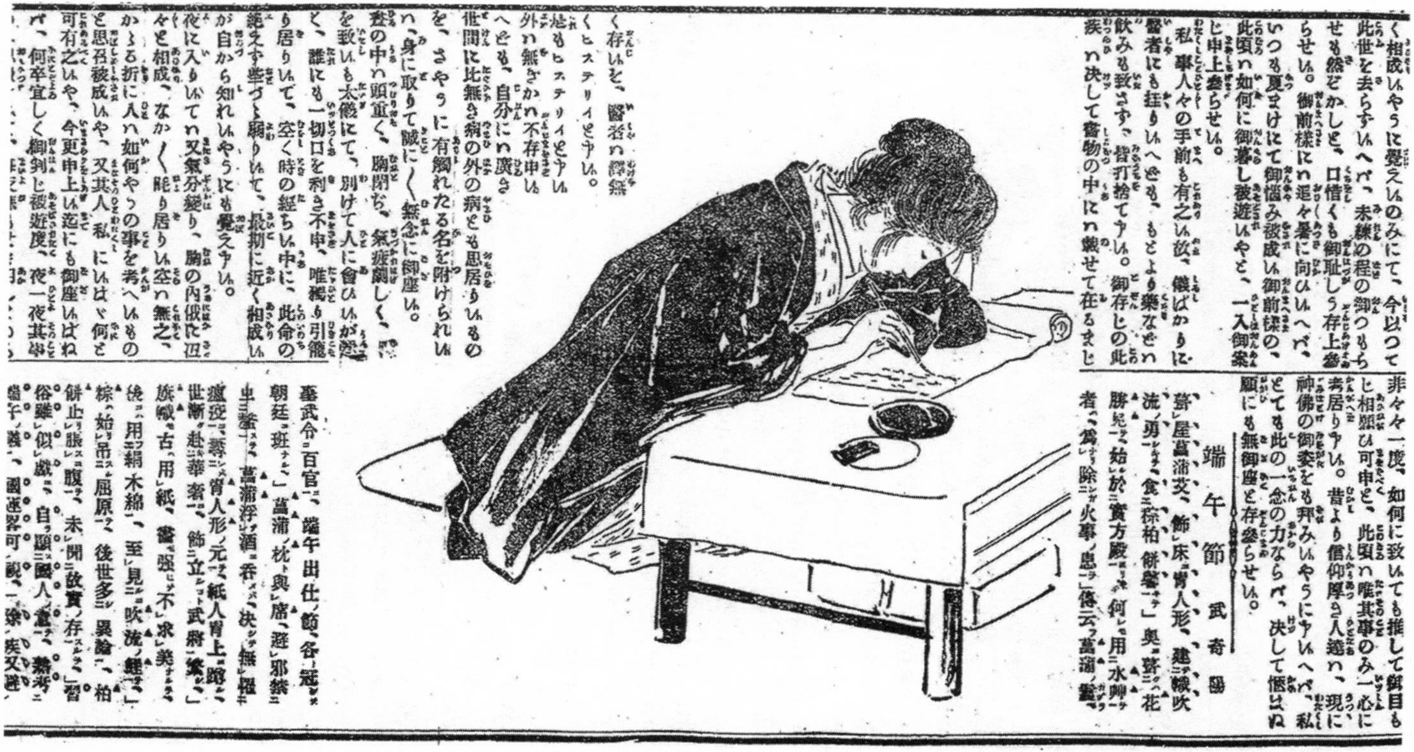

く相成候やうに覺え候のみにて、今以つて此世を去らず候へば、未練の程の御つもらせも然ぞかしと、口惜くも御耻しう存上參らせ候。御前樣には追々暑に向ひ候へば、いつも夏まけにて御惱み被成候御前樣の、此頃は如何に御暮し被遊候やと、一入御案じ申上參らせ候。

私事人々の手前も有之候故、儀ばかりに醫者にも掛り候へども、もとより藥なぞは飲みも致さず、皆打捨て申候。御存じの此疾は決して藥物の中には載せて在るまじく存候を、醫者は[illegible]くヒステリイと申候。是もヒステリイと申候外は無きかは不存申候へども、自分には廣き世間に比無き病の外の病とも思居り候ものを、さやうに有觸れたる名を附けられ候は、身に取りて誠に／＼無念に御座候。晝の中は頭重く、胸閉ぢ、氣疲劇しく、[illegible]を致候も太儀にて、別けて人に會ひ候が懶く、誰にも一切口を利き不申、唯獨り引籠り居り候て、空く時の經ち候中に、此命の絶えず些づゝ弱り候て、最期に近く相成候が自から知れ候やうにも覺え申候。

夜に入り候ては又氣分變り、胸の内俄に冴々と相成、なか／＼眠り居り候空は無之、かゝる折に人は如何やうの事を考へ候ものと思召被成候や、又其人私には候はゞ何と可有之候や、今更申上候迄にも御座候はねど、何卒宜しく御判じ被遊度、夜一夜其事

非々々一度、如何に致候ても推して御目もじ相叶ひ可申と、此頃は唯其事のみ一心に考居り申候。昔より信仰厚き人達は、現に神佛の御姿をも拜み候やうに申候へば、私とても此の一念の力ならば、決して叶はぬ願にも無御座と存參らせ候。

端午節　武奇

菖屋菖蒲艾、飾床冑人形、建幟吹流勇、食粽柏餠馨、奧菖花勝紀、始於實方殿、何用水興者、爲除火事患、傳云菖蒲髪

垂武令百官、端午出仕、飾各冠、朝廷班、菖蒲枕與席、避邪禁中、菖蒲浮酒呑、決無惱瘟疫、壽冑人形元紙人冑上蹈、世漸赴華奢、飾立武尉、旗幟古用紙、當強不求美、後用絹木綿、至見吹流鯉、粽始弔屈原、後世多異論、柏餠止脹腹、未聞故實存、習俗雖似戲、自顯國人意、就端午義、國運翼可祝、一殊疾又避

FIGURE 2.2 Miya absorbed in writing to Kan'ichi, in an illustration used in the newspaper serialization of *Konjiki yasha*. Source: *Yomiuri shinbun*, May 5, 1902.

expression': the venting of what one is and how it feels to be that way, the saying of self through its moral and emotional integers."[56] In a melodramatic novel thematizing a "love" built upon impossibility, Miya's moment of "pure expression" is obtainable only because of Kan'ichi's absence.

Once Miya finally makes the decision to send her letters, they are delivered to Kan'ichi with obsessive repetitiveness. Kan'ichi receives a letter from Miya at least ten times in the novel. He never replies. In fact, he refuses to read the majority of the letters; on all but two occasions he responds to her unopened letters with small acts of violence—he twists them, he tears them to bits, or he consigns them to flames. Miya's letter writing is a one-sided pursuit, an act of communication unwanted by its addressee. It is the expression of a passion fanned not only by absence but by denial. Like the dark passions chronicled by de Rougemont, Miya's passion is merely inflamed by obstacles; it can only end when it has totally consumed itself. The text's strategy of including Miya's long letters verbatim (the longest runs seven pages) ensures the reader will be exposed to the "pure expressions" that Kan'ichi does his best to avoid.

The *sōrōbun* epistolary style, in which Miya writes, is an inauspicious instrument for such expressions. *Sōrōbun* is a thoroughly rule-bound mode of writing, marked by the repetitive use of the polite auxiliary verb *sōrō* and by heavy encrustations of honorific language; it is designed for conveying conventional sentiments. Yet, at the turn of the century, *sōrōbun* was still the accepted form for personal correspondence. A few years hence, in Tayama Katai's *Futon* (The quilt, 1907), the aspiring young writer Yoshiko will write to her lovelorn teacher in "*genbun itchi*, written in a superb, flowing hand," but this phenomenon draws notice precisely because it is new.[57] Miya had little choice but to use *sōrōbun*. The wonder is in how she bends the unpromising style into a powerful rhetorical weapon for the expression of her longings.

Part of the rhetorical force of Miya's *sōrōbun* lies in her choice of a gendered variant. Her prose shows the features of a specific style used only by women called *mairase sōrōbun* (in which the locution *mairase sōrō* is used at major junctures or transitions). Miya, then, foregrounds her gender as she writes. This constant reminder of her femininity works in tandem with her manipulation of honorifics in her writing. The prewar linguist Yamada Yoshio has remarked that "the reason *sōrōbun* presents a special phenomenon comes down, in the end, to the single point that it uses honorific language liberally."[58] Miya's letters reflect this feature of *sōrōbun* faithfully;

nearly every noun or pronoun associated with Kan'ichi (*onme* [your eye], *onmaesama* [you], *onnasake* [your compassion], *onkao* [your face], and so on) as well as many of the verbs denoting his actions or states of being (*onhirakase* [to open], *gohandoku* [to read and interpret], *onkawarinasare* [to have changed]) are preceded by one honorific prefix or another. There is also constant use of passives in their honorific applications. Yamada's explanation for this clustering of honorific language is that, in an epistolary style, "one must use appropriate diction and indirect locutions in order to maintain a tone of respect toward the addressee and to prevent upsetting the addressee's feelings."[59] This is an epistolary requirement that Miya's language beautifully subverts, for, despite its superficial politeness, it is concerned neither with decorum nor with sparing Kan'ichi's feelings.

In fact, it uses the linguistic features of *mairase sōrōbun* to insistently press forth a narrative of defiant self-expression. It does this by employing a key element of the Japanese honorific system—the verbal postulation of a hierarchy, in which the speaker or writer elevates an addressee or a third person, usually at his or her own expense. The concrete effect in the letters is that Kan'ichi's worth as a person is linguistically valorized, while Miya, who constantly refers to her guilt and regret, portrays herself as an undeserving supplicant. This apparent hierarchy is magnified by the gender hierarchy, which the language keeps in view. On the superficial level, Miya is a woman groveling at the feet of a male paragon. But this is an appearance only, for Miya is actually using hierarchy for the purposes of narrating passion, which has the end result of reversing that hierarchy. Miya's manipulation of language works by emphasizing Kan'ichi's superiority, which makes him a fitting object of desire. Yet, the more Miya elevates Kan'ichi and denigrates herself as an unworthy supplicant, the more she portrays herself as a passionate woman, pursuing desire at great cost to herself despite the indifference of her lover. The final impression that Miya leaves is that she has been more faithful to "love" than Kan'ichi, that her desire has only grown while his has been hollowed by hatred. Miya, then, uses the hierarchical features of honorific language to assume the role of a woman who has been morally superior in the realm of "love."

In many ways, Miya's style is the content of her writing. Unfortunately, much of the effect of this style cannot be conveyed through translation, because attempts to reproduce honorific structures in English invariably result in the creation of an exotic orientalized language. Yet it may be possible to suggest the dynamics of her writing as they occur in a letter that Miya writes

after she has managed to penetrate Kan'ichi's guard and meet him, if only
for a moment:

> Recently . . . I beheld your face (*onkao o haishi*), which through the days and
> nights I had resigned myself to never seeing again. Filled with longing that
> made me want to fly to you, with sadness that was beyond words, my tears
> came first, and I could not say any of what I had turned over and over in my
> mind during the last ten years. It is truly a regret of a lifetime that all was
> in vain, even though I had come before you with feelings almost too much
> for a woman to bear—prepared to risk so much and to endure the shame of
> so painful a meeting. My only keepsake from that moment was your image,
> beheld through my tears (*namida no hima ni haishi mairase sōrō onsugata*),
> which still remains before my eyes and which I cannot forget day or night.
> Even the faces of strangers now look like yours, and I spend my days in tears
> with my heart in disorder. (447)

Miya's account valorizes the image of her lover, an image made luminous by
longing. The linguistic markers of hierarchy reinforce this effect by applying
honorific prefixes to nouns referring to Kan'ichi's physical features (*onkao*,
onsugata) and by using a verb for the act of viewing that implies looking at
something or someone with awe or respect (*haisu*). Yet the main thrust of
Miya's writing here is to describe the tangle of hyperbolic emotions that had
siezed her as she gazed at the object of her desire. She is intent on presenting
an image of herself as a woman driven mad by love, a creature possessed by
longing and regret. The message Miya seeks to convey is that, in her own
way, she is the one who has remained truly faithful to the forceful demands
of passion.

Miya's later letters emphasize how she has been consumed by her emotions. While still maintaining the linguistic decorum of *sōrōbun*, she depicts
herself as a woman under unbearable stress, wasting away in the grip of her
obsession.

> I am in torment now so unbearable that I know my illness will be worse
> tomorrow than today. I know that it will be even worse the day after. But as
> long as I can take up my brush, I want to convey to you what is in my breast
> in these moments leading to death, and so I will continue writing, even as
> my hand becomes unsteady. If I pass away, it will be from no other sickness.
> So pity me as one who died of longing for you. There is no untruth to this;
> it is what I firmly believe. (453)

It turns out that Miya's "love" demands self-immolation. Her adherence
to the hierarchies of passion means constant self-denigration; her devotion

calls for the annihilation of everything else but her thoughts of Kan'ichi. The final act of violence in *Konjiki yasha* involves the self-destruction required by a love built on separation and impossibility. The truth that Miya speaks, the truth of her own emotions, ruthlessly complicates the easier morality offered in Kan'ichi's transformation from villainous moneylender to virtuous patriarch of domesticized love. For Miya's uncompromising "love" reveals a realm of excess that lies beyond conventional morality, even beyond survival. This is the most powerful vision of "love" offered in the novel.

When Miya begins writing her letters, the narrator (who has been capable of some harsh evaluations) shows her a surprising sympathy. His narration of Kan'ichi's refusal to read Miya's letters is followed, for example, by an expression of compassion for her fate:

> How sad Miya must have been! Her two missives had been confessions made without heeding the world or her own safety; in them, she had opened her tormented breast and she had expressed the sincere truth (*setsunaru makoto*) within her. If something went wrong, the written evidence here was more than enough to convict her of a crime for which she would be buried alive. (341)

The narrator, then, chooses to underline the pathos of a woman who has gone unheard. His use of the term *makoto* suggests that he values the emotional "truth" within her.

Konjiki yasha thus exhibits ideological contradiction on many levels. It fails to uphold a binary opposition between "MOMENTARY" money and eternal love, because it ends up showing that money is all-pervasive and enduring. It makes it impossible to see "love" as virtue, because it demonstrates that love is eternal only when it is all-consuming. These contradictions are expressed in a multivocal narration that not only highlights the multiple positions possible in the ethical field, but also ends up valorizing the half-crazed declarations of a self-destructive woman. The novel's moral claims are neither comforting nor simple. Although *Konjiki yasha* was left unfinished by Ozaki Kōyō's death, even had he lived he would have found it difficult to devise a conclusion as ideologically tidy as his paratextual statements.

We can conclude this chapter by returning, as Miya does in her last letter, to the fictive family. In the unfinished letter where the novel stopped at the time of Kōyō's death, Miya conveys a family fantasy. She notes, rather unexpectedly, that Tomiyama's mother is a woman of deep compassion who thinks of her as her own daughter. And she muses about the pleasure she might find if she could live together with her mother-in-law and Kan'ichi: "I think longingly all the time for what cannot be; I think how delightful it would be, even if I had to sleep on an earthen floor with a straw mat for my quilt, as long as I could live with this woman as my mother and with you as my husband" (469). Miya's transgressive wish here—to live with her mother-in-law and her lover—is poignant because, being foreclosed, it contrasts so sharply with Kan'ichi's success at attaching himself to various fictive families. As Kan'ichi basks in the domestic warmth provided by a transformed Oshizu, Miya is alone, her only companions her brush, her paper, her passion. This passage might remind us that Namiko in *Hototogisu*, too, had dreamed of an alternate relationship with Takeo, in which a switch in gender would allow her to sail the seas with her husband. Instead, it was Takeo who formed a fictive family with her father, while she made her way toward death. In Meiji melodramatic fiction there is a gendered divide in the capacity of characters to insert themselves into new human relationships. In the novels I analyze, women tend to have one and only one chance to change their place in the world; this occurs at the time of marriage and permanently fixes their family contexts, their social and economic status. Men, on the other hand, have the capacity to continually redefine themselves through joining various alternative models of family. The novel that we will examine next is an exception to this pattern; we will see what happens when a woman sets out to designate a fictive family for herself.

THREE

The Milk You All Drank

Gender and Social Aspiration in *Chikyōdai*

At one point in Kikuchi Yūhō's novel *Chikyōdai* (Raised as sisters, 1903), a girl ecstatically contemplates the vertiginous social ascent that would be hers with a reunion with a long-lost aristocratic father:

> If she were to find the father, how joyful he would be to recognize her as his daughter. She would become a young lady of the aristocracy in one fell swoop. How delightful it would be to wear the latest fashions, to go to plays and flower viewings to her heart's content, to flit here and there to soirées, concerts, charity events, and garden parties. Someone with her looks would be at no disadvantage even were she to make her way into the upper reaches of society. A carriage or a private rickshaw would be hers for the shortest trips, and a maid would be there to do her bidding. Others would dance attendance upon her, saying "your ladyship." . . . Was this not a woman's most cherished dream? Enraptured by these thoughts, she was almost ready to faint.[1]

The problem is that Kimie is dreaming of a father and a position in society that are not hers. But such matters do not stop her: she seeks out a reunion with her "father," pushes her way into an aristocratic *ie*, and scores an astounding social success.

Such a plot immediately brings to mind Freud's almost too famous essay on "Family Romances." It is fashionable now for literary critics to use the term "family romance" in almost any consideration of the psychodynamics of the family. But I would like to return here to the original essay, which posits a narrative plot found in the childhood imaginations "of neurotics and also of all comparatively highly gifted people."[2] A small child, Freud says, at first idolizes his parents, who are "the only authority and the source of all belief." This changes, however, as the child becomes acquainted with other adults and starts to see his parents in relative terms. The onset of sibling rivalries, which cause him to feel he is not receiving the full measure of his parents' love, occurs at the same time. These currents of feeling—the devaluation of once transcendent parental figures and the sense of being slighted—coalesce into the child's fantasy that his parents may not be his own, that he may actually be adopted or a stepchild:

> At about the period I have mentioned, then, the child's imagination becomes engaged in the task of getting free from his parents of whom he now has a low opinion and of replacing them by others, who, as a rule, are of higher social standing. He will make use in this connection of any opportune coincidences from his actual experience, such as becoming acquainted with the Lord of the Manor or some landed proprietor if he lives in the country or with some member of the aristocracy if he lives in town. Chance occurrences of this kind arouse the child's envy, which finds expression in a phantasy in which both his parents are replaced by others of better birth.[3]

This attempt by the child to redefine his own family origins is somewhat modified once he becomes aware of the facts of sexual reproduction. In a subsequent stage of the fantasy, reached after the child is aware of the certainty of maternity as compared to the relative uncertainty of paternity, his imagination focuses upon placing his mother into "situations of secret infidelity and into secret love-affairs" that would explain his own birth. Freud is aware of the transgressive elements of the plot he narrates, a plot that features the rejection of parents or the impugning of a mother's sexual fidelity, for he considers the possibility that his reader might "turn away in horror from this depravity of the childish heart." But he is quick to reassure his reader that "the faithlessness and ingratitude are only apparent." This is because the imagined parents, once examined, turn out to have many qualities in common with the humble parents that a child is seemingly rejecting. "In fact," says Freud, "the child is not getting rid of his father but exalting him. Indeed the whole effort of replacing the real father by a superior one is only an expression of the child's longing for the happy, vanished days when his father seemed to him the noblest and strongest of men and his mother the dearest and loveliest of women."[4]

Freud's plot, then, is fundamentally a reassuring and even conservative one. A child may dream of abandoning his parents and finding new and better ones. But, since these new parents are only projections of the all-powerful parents that the child had initially adored, the plot circles around to a recuperation: "These works of fiction, which seem so full of hostility, are none of them really so badly intended, and . . . they preserve under a light disguise, the child's original affection for his parents."[5] The disappointment, frustration, and anger that give rise to fantasies of origin are finally explained by a child's continuing love for the parents who bore him. In fact, the tone of reaffirmation and reintegration is so strong at the end of Freud's essay that one wonders whether the plot can really be called a *"neurotic's family romance."*

Freud's theorization of childhood fantasy is, of course, specifically situated in the nuclear families of Victorian Europe. Although *Chikyōdai* reflects elements of Victorian sensibility and, as I will later show, rewrites a piece of Victorian popular fiction, my main reason for bringing up "Family Romances" is not to appropriate a culturally specific explanatory schema but rather to acquire a point of leverage for analyzing the Japanese novel. I am interested in using the plot related in "Family Romances" to throw into relief that of Yūhō's novel. Freud himself opens the door for using his plot to consider diverse cultural texts when he says that "these consciously remembered mental impulses of childhood embody the factor which enables us to understand the nature of myths."[6] My focus is not so much on the childhood mental impulse, but on how Freud's particular narrativization of it contrasts with a myth that Yūhō has conjured about an ambitious young woman in Meiji Japan.

Of particular interest to me is that Freud's family romance situates the recognition of family identity in reference to sharp demarcations of status.[7] The kind of envy he describes takes place in a social environment that contains lords of manors, landed proprietors, and aristocrats. A child registers the humble station of his parents because of social and economic divisions that are sanctioned by established social structures and inscribed within established social discourses. The conspicuous presence of such divisions is a precondition for the writing of *Chikyōdai*. For a young woman to fantasize about going to soirées, riding in carriages, and of being called "your lady-ship," there must be a group gifted with such privileges—and those beneath who can only dream of them. Yūhō's story is about the boundless power of social aspiration in a Meiji Japan where hierarchies were extreme but where the ideal of social advancement dominated the popular imagination. His story shows the desire for wealth and status overruling a young woman's moral sense, the capacity of this young woman to re-narrate her origins, and the deadly consequences that follow. This story is directed, as I will show, at a readership who will sympathize with the desire for status, money, and fame.

Freud's gendered perspective is already apparent in his use of the male pronoun for the fantasizing child: his plot narrativizes male social desire. Freud relegates female children to the margins, for they are, by his defini-tion, much less likely to feel the kinds of emotions that motivate a male child's fantasies: "A boy is far more inclined to feel hostile impulses towards his father than towards his mother and has a far more intense desire to get free from *him* than from *her*. In this respect the imagination of girls is apt to show itself much weaker."[8] Female children, lacking the competitive urges that galvanize the father-son dyad, are less likely to imagine the fam-ily romance. This view of the role of gender is precisely what is displaced in *Chikyōdai*, a novel that forcefully narrates the female desire for a new social identity. Although Kimie never voices direct hostility toward her widowed mother, a former wet nurse for a wealthy family, her desire to escape her mother's social station is evident in every fiber of her being: "Kimie was strangely ambitious from the time she was a child, and she knew that she studied various things as a means for fulfilling her ambition" (98). Kimie thus works hard at school and pores over women's magazines to learn the "concerns of female society." Her strivings constitute both a rejection and an affirmation of her mother, Ohama, for the latter had actually nurtured her desires. The mother had supported her daughter's studies because "Kim-ie's cleverness and beauty had stirred Ohama's aspirations," giving rise to an "ambition" to have her marry well (95). The mother, then, had dreamed of social mobility for her daughter, a mobility that would take her daugh-ter away from herself. This problem of a parent's desires actually distanc-ing her from her child is never really confronted in *Chikyōdai* because the mother dies before Kimie's sudden rise in fortunes. But it is significant that once she reaches her new station Kimie never seems to spare a moment of thought for her dead mother. In this model the recuperation of a relation-ship between a birth parent and her child is impossible, for, instead of a remembered aura of all-powerful authority, what this mother instills in her child is an "ambition" that in some degree must be based on her own sense of relative inferiority. The female family romance in *Chikyōdai*, built not so much on competitiveness and hostility as on shared discontent and ambition, launches the daughter into an orbit from which she will never return. Yūhō's emplotment of female social desire, then, offers none of the reassurance available at the end of "Family Romances."

In a key essay on film melodrama, Geoffrey Nowell-Smith has said that "melodrama enacts, often with uncanny literalness, the 'family romance' described by Freud—that is to say, the imaginary scenario played out by children in relation to their paternity, the asking and answering of the question, whose child am I (or would I like to be)?"[9] The many fictive families that we have already encountered attest to the wisdom of Nowell-Smith's observation. Meiji melodramatic fiction is filled with characters, such as Takeo in *Hototogisu* and Kan'ichi in *Konjiki yasha*, who attempt to answer in various and multiple ways the question "whose child would I like to be?" *Chikyōdai* provides us with an opportunity to examine more directly how melodramatic fiction struggles to locate moral value within the family romance. *Ie* ideology is at issue because, in its pursuit of the family romance, the novel negotiates in fascinating and creative ways with the assertion, made by Meiji ideologues, that the *ie* is a "natural" form of family organization. *Chikyōdai* attempts to uphold the idea of "nature" as the constituting force of family and lineage, yet, in a contradiction, also calls into question the validity of "nature."

The plot element mobilized in this ambivalent project is, once again, adoption. *Chikyōdai* contains a superabundance of adoptions, both legal and transgressive. Adoption sets into motion the melodramatic convention of switched identities through which the family romance of the novel is played out. The aristocratic family at the center of the story is continued through adoption. There is even an instance where, through a case of mistaken identity, a character ends up adopting his own blood daughter. *Chikyōdai* applies melodrama's rhetoric of excess to adoption. In the process it engages anxieties attendant upon adoption as a supplement to "nature" and thus a practice with a potential to reveal the fictive character of all families.

In this chapter I examine how the adoptions in *Chikyōdai* refract the Meiji ideology of the *ie*, especially in relation to the complications raised by gender and social hierarchy. I also attend to how the novel reflects generic discourses both from the West and from Japan, and how it posits and recruits its audience. My point of entry will be to examine how *Chikyōdai* presents itself as a *katei shōsetsu*, or "home novel," which is the way it is identified in its subtitle.[10] This subtitle is related to issues of status, gender, and audience, for it signaled something about the work's contents, touted to be appropriate for a respectable home; its targeted readership, which was predominantly female; and its mode of narration, designed to be easily and broadly apprehensible.[11] *Chikyōdai's* author, Kikuchi Yūhō, had established himself as a leading exponent of the *katei shōsetsu* with the enormously popular *Ono ga tsumi* (My sin, 1899–1900); and he clearly intended to follow his earlier success by indicating that his work had been written to meet certain generic conditions. His plan worked: *Chikyōdai* was a hit when it was serialized in the *Osaka mainichi shinbun*, the newspaper for which Yūhō was the fiction editor; it also sold very well when it was published as a book sporting a stylish art-nouveau cover. Its popularity extended even beyond the printed page for it was adapted for the theater in more than seven productions in cities including Osaka, Kyoto, and Tokyo. Eventually, *Chikyōdai* appeared in sixteen movie versions.[12] To understand its appeal, I start by examining its preface, which further reveals how the work and its author attempted to address its audience.

PREFACING CHIKYŌDAI

Nearly every study of *katei shōsetsu* quotes from the preface Yūhō prepared for *Chikyōdai* because it contains a succinct statement on the key elements of the genre.[13] The most often-quoted sentences refer to the aims and restrictions that Yūhō, speaking as both a newspaper editor and a writer, ascribed to *katei shōsetsu* generally and to *Chikyōdai* in particular:

> I wanted us to carry something that was a bit more accessible and a bit less affected than the general run of current novels, yet something that was tasteful and refined. I had been wanting to write something that could be read in the bosom of a happy home (*ikka danran no mushiro no naka de*), be easily understood by everyone, cause no one to blush, contribute to harmony in the home, and assist in nurturing taste. (89)

In what sounds like a recipe for boring, middle-brow fiction, Yūhō defines the *katei shōsetsu* as being both popular and polite, a kind of fiction that could be enjoyed without embarrassment in the home and would also contribute to its happy functioning. Needless to say, such a definition was built upon the prior social currency of *katei* ideology, which saw the home as a valorized site of domestic decency. In specific reference to *Chikyōdai*, we might immediately question the claims to refinement of a story that leads to an enfevered moment when Kimie is stabbed through the heart ("The flash of a blade falling like lightning! The gush of blood!" [235]). But there is even more to be learned by approaching the preface as a paratext. If Yūhō's preface seeks, as all paratexts do, to gain a "more pertinent reading" for the work to which it is attached, it is also itself a text that displays its own patterns of rhetoricity.[14] Rather than flatly accepting Yūhō's statements as a valid definition of the *katei shōsetsu* and as an accurate portrayal of *Chikyōdai*, one might ask what the preface seeks to gain and how it pursues its aims. We will see that the double-edged rhetoric of Yūhō's statement attempts to both conceal and reveal its own ideological agenda. This doubling is required by the cultural and ideological terrain that Yūhō must negotiate. In our examination it will be helpful to keep in mind Louis Althusser's concept of "interpellation," which refers to the "rituals of recognition" through which ideology "transforms" or "recruits" subjects.[15] Ultimately, I am interested in determining what sort of subject Yūhō's rhetoric is designed to recruit.

The first thing to be observed regarding the preface's rhetoric is that the preface is unusual in its formal characteristics. Rather than taking the most common approach for an author's preface—in which the author writes a statement addressed to the reader—Yūhō chooses to quote at length from a lecture on *Chikyōdai* that he was "requested" to give before "a certain gathering of ladies (*aru kifujingata no shūkai*)." This idiosyncratic choice foregrounds certain characteristics of the narratee as she is constructed in the lecture and in the novel, as well as some related issues of language. Yūhō's strategy is deeply enmeshed in the matrix of gender and status, for it functions to clearly mark his reader as female, but a female of a specific type: a genteel woman with the social standing that would earn her the appellation of *kifujin*.[16] In accordance with this designation, Yūhō's language is respectful, with sentence endings taking the relatively polite *desu* and *masu* forms. Yet this respect is clearly not aimed at the intellect or experience of his audience, for his conversational style and diction consistently avoids anything that might sound too difficult or literary. The lady to whom he speaks is hardly well read. We should also note that quoting from a lecture he was "requested" to give allows Yūhō to construct his narratee as someone who already knows about *Chikyōdai* and is interested in learning more about it. To put this a bit differently, Yūhō's rhetorical strategy allows him to present his own book as being socially current and popular.

This aim was clearly important, for Yūhō spends the first third of the preface tooting his own horn. The anecdotes he conveys about the popularity of *Chikyōdai*, however, have the effect of complicating his representations regarding his readers, for it quickly becomes clear that his novel was popular well beyond the "ladies" to whom he addresses his lecture/preface. Yūhō says, for example, that a member of the *Osaka mainichi*'s marketing department had recently returned from a visit to the islands of Shikoku and Kyushu with the news that "in places with a thousand families or so, subscribers anxious to read *Chikyōdai* gathered at the distributors when the paper arrived, thus reducing the need for delivery" (89). He also notes that "there were many teahouses in the South and North licensed prostitution districts where they waited awake for morning editions carrying this novel to be delivered around three in the morning" (89). While the definition of who or what constitutes a *kifujin* can be broad, it would generally not include most female residents of provincial towns and would certainly not apply to women who worked in teahouses. This brings us to the observation that textual narratees are not necessarily the same as actual readers; Yūhō's comments suggest that, despite (or perhaps because of) his choice of narratee, his novel appealed to a broad range of readers, representing differing regional, class, and occupational demographics.

Having established the popularity of his work, Yūhō spends much of the rest of his preface explaining what lies behind its favorable reception. As he sees it, there are three primary factors: (1) the presence of a female protagonist, Fusae, who "attracted a great measure of sympathy from readers"; (2) the fact that the work is a *katei shōsetsu*; and (3) the use of an "extremely easy and polite" version of the vernacular-based language of *genbun itchi*.

Leaving behind for now the matter of the female protagonist, to which we will return at some length, let us briefly take up the issues of genre and language. In reference to *katei shōsetsu*, Yūhō's key statement is the passage already quoted in which he defines the genre as being both accessible yet tasteful. A few comments are in order here, however, regarding the contexts the preface provides for this statement. It occurs, as we have noted, in a discussion of the reasons for *Chikyōdai*'s popularity, a phenomenon that Yūhō has underlined by referring to the concrete practices of newspaper distribution. This indicates that any consideration of the salient characteristics of the *katei shōsetsu* cannot be separated from the commercial goal of attracting readers. *Chikyōdai* appeared at a point in Japanese newspaper history when circulations soared as publishers competed mightily to add new subscribers.[17] To appeal to broader segments of the population, newspapers reduced the space devoted to political editorials and essays, and added more news coverage, features, service articles, and fiction.[18] Women constituted a large segment of potential readers targeted by the newspapers. As Kathryn Ragsdale points out in her highly informative article on the *katei shōsetsu*, the *Osaka mainichi* had, in 1898, become the first newspaper to carry a regular column for women, called "Katei no shiori" (Handbook for the home); the paper's decision to publish *katei shōsetsu* was another step along the same marketing trajectory.[19]

What comes immediately before and after the statement on the essential characteristics of *katei shōsetsu* also requires some attention. Most commentators who quote from Yūhō's preface have slid over the fact that the writer begins his discussion of *katei shōsetsu* by saying that he wanted the *Osaka mainichi* to "gradually stop carrying *kōdan*, and in order to do this there needed to be an appropriate replacement" (89). Yūhō's comments here are being made from his position as the *Mainichi*'s fiction editor, that is, as a cultural gatekeeper, and they work to establish a difference between his new type of newspaper fiction and transcriptions of *kōdan*, an oral narrative form that had matured in the Edo period.[20] Unlike *rakugo*, its humorous and generally briefer cousin, *kōdan* consisted of long narrations treating serious or dramatic themes.[21] The importance of the contrast that Yūhō seeks to draw with the *katei shōsetsu* lies in the fact that *kōdan* was a plebeian narrative art. During the Edo period, *kōdan* had been primarily patronized by commoners—by merchants and artisans, and their wives and children, in major cities as well as in the smaller towns served by traveling raconteurs. Not only did *kōdan* retain this audience in the early Meiji period, it had gained even more fans through the invention of Japanese shorthand, a new technology of reproduction that made oral narratives available to a mass print audience beyond the theater. In the 1890s and the early years of the twentieth century, *kōdan* narratives were a mainstay of newspaper fiction. Although Yūhō makes it sound as though replacing the *kōdan* with *katei shōsetsu* was an easy progression, this was not at all the case. In 1903, *kōdan* still had a devoted readership, and it could not be easily dismissed by a newspaper concerned with circulation. The *Osaka mainichi* had, in fact, also carried *kōdan* during nearly the entire serialization of Yūhō's work.[22] What is more, the *kōdan* had pride of place as far as fiction was concerned. *Kōdan* transcriptions were usually carried on page four, just after the world and national news and before the business coverage. *Chikyōdai* was generally buried on page eight, among what we would think of as "lifestyle articles." While there were certainly gender politics at work in this arrangement, with women's fiction being pushed to the back, the important point is that the *kōdan* was not so easily supplanted. Yūhō was seeking to open a cultural site in a space already occupied by an older, popular form. And he was attempting to do this with something designated as a type of *shōsetsu* (novel or fiction). He was trying to elevate and modernize the fiction carried in his newspaper by moving it closer to newer, higher-brow writing. It is in this sense that we must understand his statement that he wanted the *Osaka mainichi* to carry "something that was tasteful and refined."

These instincts were very much connected to Yūhō's knowledge of Western fiction, for, after describing his vision of fiction that would nurture sensibility and contribute to harmony in the home, the writer gets down to specifics by mentioning a Western writer.

> While reading various foreign novels with this in mind, I came upon a short piece written by a woman called Bertha Clay, with a somewhat amusing plot. It came to me that I might succeed at writing something to replace the *kōdan* if I used a theme like this as the foundation and made up something a bit more complex. This was the beginning of my taking up my pen to write *Chikyōdai*, and thus this novel owes a great deal to Bertha Clay. (89)

The name Bertha Clay will not mean much to the current reader of fiction in English, and it probably did not mean much to most of the readers of the *Osaka mainichi* beyond that it belonged to a female and a Westerner. But in the early twentieth century "Bertha Clay" was a literary brand name attached to hundreds of novels.[23] These novels were not all written by the same person. Initially, Bertha Clay was a pseudonym for Charlotte Mary Brame (1836–84), a popular British writer of "sensational fiction" and "mushy love stories for the English lower classes" who serialized dozens of domestic novels in such publications as the *Family Story Teller*.[24] In their British versions, these stories were often published without an author's name, but they were republished in America under the name Bertha Clay after they were acquired by Street and Smith, the preeminent publishers of dime novels. Street and Smith subsequently instituted a "Bertha Clay Library" and put out over five hundred novels attributed to Clay; these included the Brame works, but also romances written by numerous male authors.[25] As far as I can ascertain, *Dora Thorne*, the work that became the basis for *Chikyōdai*, was one of the "original" Clay works written by Charlotte Brame. That a domestic novel written by a popular writer such as Clay/Brame became the "foundation" for a *katei shōsetsu* shows something of the mixed motives behind Yūhō's wish to write "something to replace the *kōdan*." On the one hand, Clay/Brame did write "novels," her fiction was directed at women, and she advocated the cult of domesticity that influenced the Japanese ideology of the *katei*. She was an appropriate source to mine if one's purpose was to produce a *shōsetsu* that could be edifying to women. On the other hand, Clay was unmistakably linked to commodity fiction. Replacing the *kōdan* clearly did not mean entirely foregoing its low-brow audience. What had caught Yūhō's attention about the Clay novel was "a somewhat amusing plot"; he was keenly aware of the entertainment quotient of the work he was adapting. Yūhō's mission was to offer a veneer of refinement and cultivation, while serving an audience that included not only "ladies," but provincial women and those who worked in teahouses as well.

On the issue of language, Yūhō's decision to write in "extremely easy and polite *genbun itchi*" was made in the midst of a transformation in fictional prose. In 1903, when Yūhō wrote *Chikyōdai*, genuine options remained between writing in classical Japanese and using the vernacular-based language of *genbun itchi*. Both *Hototogisu*, serialized from 1898 to 1899, and *Konjiki yasha*, serialized between 1897 and 1903, had used classical grammar and syntax in their narrations. These works, particularly the latter, had exploited the rich linguistic textures of classical prose to turn language into the *melos* of Meiji melodramatic fiction. Although Yūhō does not mention it in his preface, he had, in fact, written *Ono ga tsumi*, the career-making novel that he serialized in 1899–1900, using the classical language. Thus he was departing from a proven formula and sacrificing the stylistic potentials of classical Japanese by choosing *genbun itchi*. At the same time, by 1903 the vernacular was clearly in ascendance. By this time, the efforts of the Meiji state to promote *genbun itchi* as a more-easily-learned, utilitarian language had intersected with the attempts of avant-garde writers to produce a literary language closer to modern speech. Yamamoto Masahide, the dean of *genbun itchi* studies, has compiled some telling figures: he says that *genbun itchi* pieces constituted 24 percent of published fiction in 1896, 57 percent in 1899, 78 percent in 1904, and 100 percent in 1908.[26] These are stunning statistics. They show that, in the realm of fiction, vernacular-based writing overwhelmed classical styles in a little over a decade. Yūhō, then, was casting his lot with the majority when he decided to write his second major *katei shōsetsu* in a vernacular style.[27]

His further statements in the preface reveal that some ambivalence remained over his choice, especially regarding the objective of being both accessible and refined. In commenting upon the broad comprehensibility of his language, Yūhō assumes a tone of ingratiating humility: "As I have said before, I have made my style as explicit as possible, in order to make it extremely accessible and easy, and so I cannot help thinking that it has become utterly devoid of suggestiveness" (90). Here, the writer gestures toward the utilitarian and mass market orientation of his prose; he has deliberately chosen to write plainly in order to appeal to his broadly based audience, knowing full well that he has abandoned what he considers to be artful and elegant. At the same time, however, Yūhō cannot abandon the posture of writing for a genteel audience, and this side of things comes out in his discussion of the politeness of his prose:

> Moreover, I had felt from before a discomfort with using rough language . . . in the narration of a piece designed as reading matter for the home. I felt as though I would be committing a breach of etiquette against the ladies and gentlemen who were my readers. And so I used polite diction as the basis for my narration. Fortunately, this too was greatly welcomed. My feeling is that, from now on, when I write things for the home, this is the kind of prose I want to use. (90)

Yūhō is anxious to defend the rhetorical position of a writer writing for "ladies" (he has now even added "gentlemen" to his fictive audience), who will be reading his novel in the bosom of a *katei*. God forbid that any "rough language" (*zonzai na kotoba*) should enter such refined premises. Yet we must remember that Yūhō's discussion is keyed upon the broad popularity of his novel, and that he has already explicitly acknowledged tailoring his prose to meet some rather low common denominators.

Having briefly examined some of the linguistic politics coursing through Yūhō's preface and novel, we can now return to the issue of the *kōdan*. We have already observed that the choice of Bertha Clay as an alternative to the *kōdan* did not necessarily mean a rejection of the latter's popular appeal. A consideration of the relations of the *kōdan* to issues of language reinforces our reading of this equivocality. For the *kōdan*, in the transcribed form carried in the newspapers, was a broadly disseminated example of vernacular prose fiction. In effect, by turning to *genbun itchi*, Yūhō was seeking to replace one form of vernacular fiction with another. Although Yūhō probably did not directly model the language of *Chikyōdai* on that of the *kōdan*—because by 1903 *genbun itchi* fiction was broadly available—it is worth noting that some of the features of his writing are similar to those of transcribed *kōdan*. This is true of Yūhō's decision to write in genteel *genbun itchi* by ending his sentences using the polite auxiliary verbs *desu* or *masu* (and their past tenses *deshita* and *mashita*) rather than the more direct *da* or its past tense *ta*, which were more common in the literary vernacular of the time. While *desu* and *masu* are also found in some examples of literary *genbun itchi*, it so happens that these two auxiliary verbs were the favored sentence endings of *kōdan* narrators, who treated their audiences with verbal respect. Another feature of Yūhō's text, the way he sets off dialogue, is also reminiscent of transcribed *kōdan*. In *Chikyōdai*, each passage of dialogue is marked at its beginning with a graph taken from the speaker's name.[28] This kind of marking is rare in *genbun itchi* fiction, but it is the rule in *rakugo* and *kōdan* transcriptions, where speaker identification is repeated in metronomic fashion, although in actual performances all the parts are being performed by a single narrator.[29] There is, then, evidence to suggest that Yūhō was writing in ways that would be friendly to the audience of transcribed oral literature. Replacing the *kōdan* did not mean rejecting it, but rather repeating some of its key features.

The issue of repetition brings us back to the form of the preface itself. We have already noted that the strategy of quoting from his speech allowed Yūhō to engage in a transparent rhetoric that constructed his readers as "ladies." Considering Yūhō's mixed attitudes toward *kōdan* leads us to see another level of ambivalence in the preface's narrative structure, for his use of the extended quotation replicates the narrating situation of transcribed *kōdan*. In effect, Yūhō presents a "transcribed" version of his own oral performance. He prefaces his novel in a way that privileges the illusion of the spoken voice. All the while that he is speaking to his "ladies," Yūhō is narrating in a way familiar to the plebeian readers of *kōdan*.

What can we make of an address to a popular audience barely veiled by pretenses to gentility? We can glimpse here a large part of the appeal of the *katei shōsetsu* specifically, and of the idea of *katei* more generally. Such cultural constructs were being directed at—and were, in effect, also fanning—certain cultural aspirations related to gender and status. *Katei* ideology engaged impulses that both yearned upward and penetrated broadly.

It resonated with the desire for modernity and respectability, yet it had a fundamentally egalitarian appeal in that all could aspire to have a *katei*.[30] When Yūhō referred to the gendered role of the "lady," he was gesturing not toward a restricted aristocratic audience but in a more general sense toward women associated with any female who desired respectability. Yūhō was writing not only toward the educated new middle class of teachers, bureaucrats, and professionals, who were the most ardent proponents of the *katei*, but also toward the old middle class of merchants and even toward those lower on the social scale.[31] This broad swath of society coincided to a large extent with the literate consumers that mass-market newspapers such as the *Osaka mainichi* sought in an era of rapidly expanding circulations. It would not be mistaken to say that Yūhō's preface seeks to interpellate, through its rhetoric of concealment and revelation, an emergent bourgeois audience, an audience who would engage with an ideology of respectability and domesticity coded in ways that were both popular and upmarket. The bourgeois subject Yūhō seeks to recruit is both genteel and plebeian, respectable and ambitious. It is the effort to interpellate such a subject that shapes the family romance and melodrama in *Chikyōdai*.

MELODRAMA AND THE FEMININE IDEAL

We have left until last the one thematic element mentioned in the preface as a reason for *Chikyōdai*'s popularity—that the novel featured a protagonist who "attracted a great measure of sympathy from readers." In making this statement, Yūhō is engaging in his most pronounced act of concealment, for *Chikyōdai* actually has two protagonists, Fusae and Kimie, who cleanly divide into the "good sister" and the "bad sister." In his preface, Yūhō chooses to put the spotlight on the more upright sister, whose virtues he enumerates at length and in hyperbolic terms:

> On the one hand, there is Fusae, who has ended up, in the contexts of Japanese women, as an ideal female, possessing the noblest of spirits and the deepest capacity for sympathy. I made her into a woman whose sum total might be considered perfection: a woman demanded most urgently by Japanese society today, who has both reason and passion, whose sensibilities extend to both nature and human affairs, and who is in no way lacking in the qualities of a lady. I have my doubts whether I accomplished my goal in the end. But, fortunately, you have poured your deepest sympathies upon

Fusae. Seeing this, I think it is clear that a woman like Fusae was your ideal as well. (90)

The virtues of one of the sisters have been exaggerated beyond all relation to reality: Fusae has been created to embody "perfection." In Yūhō's analysis, Fusae's very status as an abstraction has led to her popularity and that of the book in which she appears. Fusae is the kind of "lady" that the "ladies" in his audience hold in their aspirations. Her portrayal even has implications for the nation, for she is the kind of woman needed "most urgently by Japanese society today."

About his other protagonist, Yūhō is considerably less loquacious and more anxious:

On the other hand, the one thing that worried me was that, in contrast to Fusae, Kimie was all too bold, all too extraordinary. Although I thought that she might be reviled as a female Ten'ichi, I have yet to hear any such criticisms, and for this I am secretly grateful. (90)

In these terse and somewhat cryptic remarks, Yūhō leaves Kimie out of any direct discussion of his novel's popularity. One might draw the conclusion that she is simply not as important as the female paragon that attracted readers to the work. We can also gather that Yūhō feared that she was drawn too unrealistically, although it is hard to think what could be more "extraordinary" than "perfection."

The reference to Ten'ichi requires some explanation. Ten'ichibō was an early-eighteenth-century *yamabushi* priest who had been put to death for falsely claiming to be the shogun's bastard son. His story had inspired one of the most famous of late-Edo *kōdan* and had provided the plot for numerous kabuki plays that continued to be produced during the Meiji period.[32] This, then, is another of the preface's ambivalent references. When he says that he is glad that one of the protagonists of his *katei shōsetsu* has not been identified with Ten'ichi, Yūhō is obliquely gesturing toward the plebeian oral narrative that his work was supposed to replace. What we should not miss here is that Yūhō expects the "ladies" in his audience to recognize a character from the *kōdan*; he is addressing readers familiar with the earlier narrative form. Moreover, the Ten'ichibō story belongs to a large group of kabuki and *kōdan* plots known as *oiemono* or *oiesōdōmono*, which thematize the endangerment of a noble *ie* by succession struggles or other threats to its continuation and integrity.[33] It is not farfetched to view *Chikyōdai* as an *oiemono* in modern dress and to connect Kimie with Ten'ichi, for she too is a character who is killed after falsely assuming a noble identity. Once again, in a seemingly offhand remark, Yūhō has revealed how his narrative cannot ignore the discursive pressure exerted by the *kōdan*.

Yūhō's polarized characterization of his two protagonists is, to a point, correct. His novel is ruled by the duality between the paragon and the transgressor. At every opportunity, the narrative, which delights in belaboring the obvious, contrasts the good "sister" with the bad. Fusae is compassionate, calm, self-sacrificing, honest, idealistic, religious (she becomes a Christian early in the novel), and is possessed of a luminous beauty that reflects her inner goodness, while Kimie is vain, excitable, self-centered, mendacious, materialistic, irreligious, and has a showy beauty that is all surface. A few passages will suffice to illustrate how the text deals in extremes. Fusae is always described in terms that suggest an unearthly goodness:

> Fusae was a truly serene, quiet girl. She was not at all defiled by the foul air of society, nor had she ever been tempted by the demons of vanity and greed. Her pure and unsullied spirit was evident on her beauteous face. Even her most amiable expression had a certain inviolability, so that one might imagine that God dwelled therein. (147)

Fusae is characterized by innocence and virtue taken to their extremes. This is a woman who is never tempted, who never has an unkind thought. The text connects her perfection to a Christianity that demands a certain kind of gendered behavior; this is nowhere more evident than when Fusae goes to work as a governess and instructs her charges in proper behavior. In the following passage, Fusae corrects Ayako, a girl under her care, when the latter finds amusement in someone else's embarrassing slip:

> (Fusa) Ayako, don't you always hear about this at church? Do you remember what the two aims are for you and for us?
> (Aya) Yes I do. First, to become a true Christian, and second, to become a lady.
> Ayako repeated just what she had been regularly taught. Fusae continued to talk to her gently.
> (Fusa) Then, will you tell me the aims of a true lady?
> (Aya) It's to try not to say or do anything that might cause others displeasure.
> This, too, Ayako was repeating as she had been constantly taught.

(Fusa) Well then, do you think that it will please others when you act like a know-it-all in order to advertise someone else's mistake?

(Aya) I don't think so. (Ayako blushed slightly.)

(Fusa) Ayako, there's a difference between knowing something, and being well-mannered. Nothing is more important than modesty for a woman; being knowledgeable isn't that much of a value for us. A true lady may not know much about things, but she has to be deeply caring and considerate about everything. (97)

This conversation is a little chilling to us now, what with Fusae's disciplinary self-righteousness coupled with her young charge's robotic replies. But horror over his heroine's efforts to police behavior was probably not what Yūhō intended. As a young man, Yūhō had been an enthusiastic reader of *Jogaku zasshi* (Journal of female learning),[34] the magazine for women edited by the Christian propagandist Iwamoto Yoshiharu. Along with the *katei* ideology discussed earlier in relation to *Hototogisu*, Iwamoto and others in his circle had propagated in the 1880s a wishful view of women as modest helpmeets to male aspirations, pure creatures who were deserving objects of spiritual love.[35] These lessons are obvious in Yūhō's vision of Fusae, whose portrayal, in turn, reveals a pedagogical urge that reaches beyond the hapless Ayako to strike at the willing reader.

Kimie, too, offers lessons in femininity, but of a negative kind. She is a repository of moral defects that the text locates as counterparts to the feminine virtues exemplified by Fusae. Kimie is self-aggrandizing, superficial, and proud, but the one flaw that the text harps on is her vanity:

> Female vanity nearly dominated Kimie body and soul. Her one and only goal was to satisfy her vanity. In her heart, she believed that her beauty and her accomplishments must surely bring forth a day that would see her vanity satisfied.
>
> To worry about clothing or hair accessories is a woman's nature. Kimie was especially prone to this susceptibility; how her heart was drawn, from the time she was a child, to such things as gold brocade sashes and diamond rings. She knew that the circumstances of her family could not possibly allow her to acquire precious gems and costly fabrics, and so, even in her childish heart, she had come to regard the wealthy with envy and jealousy. She thought that if only she had wealth she could pursue every fashion, buy every pleasure. Without knowing it she had come to acknowledge money as being all-powerful. (99)

The gender ideology displayed here by the obviously male narrator does not require much comment. Suffice it to say that he deals in ready stereotypes and that Kimie, the material girl, is easily corrupted when she has her chance to acquire wealth: "Kimie's vanity finally drove out her conscience and let the devil exalt in victory" (104).

The presence of the devil here and of God's radiance in Fusae's visage confirms that the sisters inhabit a melodramatic world of binary alternatives. *Chikyōdai*'s moral universe exhibits the phenomenon of the "excluded middle" identified by Peter Brooks: "Melodramatic dilemmas and choices are constructed on the either/or in its extreme form as the all-or-nothing. Polarization is both horizontal and vertical: characters represent extremes, and they undergo extremes, passing from heights to depths, or the reverse, almost instantaneously. The middle ground and the middle condition are excluded."[36] The sisters exhibit extremes of self-sacrifice and treachery; they experience flights of pure joy and the deepest anxiety and misery. The plot that brings their duality into view is driven by intense conflicts, radical social ascents and descents, searing choices, and violent denouements.

Chikyōdai is a veritable catalog of the plot elements Brooks associates with melodrama: "masked and mistaken identities; lost and refound parents and children, the operation of the *voix du sang*; dramatic and spectacular apparitions; physical struggle and combat; conversion and redemption; bloody villains and innocent victims; rhetorical antitheses and a pervasive moral polarization of the universe."[37] Most of these elements will appear in one form or another in Yūhō's novel. Fusae, the innocent and virtuous victim, separated from her father and deprived of her true identity before finally being called to his side by the *voix du sang*, is clearly a melodramatic heroine. If we are to follow the paratextual direction given in Yūhō's preface, we might be led to believe that *Chikyōdai* is her story.

The trouble, however, is that, whatever Yūhō may claim, Fusae is not the principal protagonist of *Chikyōdai*. It is the evil sister Kimie who sets the story into motion, who is faced with the most important moral choices, who rides her fortunes to their crest, and suffers a violent end. Although I have only limited confidence in numerically evaluating narrative elements, a quick tally shows that Kimie's story dominates the physical space of the book, occupying fully three times as many pages as does Fusae's.[38] She is the character who drives the plot. There are a number of possible ways to understand this. First, perfection isn't very interesting. A character who is never tempted, who never deviates from the path of virtue, doesn't provide much to build a narrative on, especially if virtue is defined, as it is in Fusae's case, by modesty and passivity. Second, as we see in novels from

Great Expectations to *Kokoro*, the plot of hidden truth and its revelation has powerful narrative potential. The harboring of secrets, the anxiety and hopes attendant upon their exposure, and the final unmasking provide a ready and familiar narrative plot. Kimie's assumption of an identity that is not hers and the extremes of emotion tied to her secret knowledge are the stuff of a good story. But, perhaps what most marks Kimie as the more important protagonist is that, in a family romance immersed in considerations of gender and status, she is the one who forcibly breaches social hierarchies. *Chikyōdai* must negotiate constantly and at length with the fact that it ends up mapping a woman's social aspiration alongside mendacity, villainy, and transgression. Much of the ambivalence in Yūhō's preface—the transparently contradicted construction of the narratees of his *katei shōsetsu* as "ladies" and the wish to write in a *genbun itchi* that is both broadly accessible and polite—relates fundamentally to issues of social stratification. We might ask, then, how a *katei shōsetsu*—a novel aimed at a bourgeois female audience—functions as a melodrama about class and status.

SOCIAL HIERARCHY, THE MELODRAMA, AND BERTHA CLAY

The intersection of gender, status, and class in Meiji Japan is a subject that needs far more study. Such upheavals in social hierarchy as the abolition of the Edo status system affected everyone, but there were highly gendered components in these transformations. The Meiji rhetoric of egalitarianism, which claimed equality for everyone from ex-samurai to ex-peasants, manifestly did not apply to women. And *risshin shusse*, the pervasive ideology of self-advancement, could not be easily acted upon by women, who were grossly disadvantaged in the arenas of higher education and work, where self-advancement was contested. The social aspirations of women were necessarily channeled through the institution of family. A woman could try to use a son to better her place in the world or she could attempt to marry well, like Miya in *Konjiki yasha*. But such routes to success were indirect and seriously complicated by the patriarchal nature of the *ie*. *Chikyōdai* unfolds in a world where women, too, experience the pull of *risshin shusse*, but where limitations of status and gender create keenly felt contradictions. Kimie is a female character, stirred by the ideal of self-advancement, who is strikingly unwilling to live within the limitations placed on her. She takes things into her own hands, manipulates the institution of the *ie*, and through her treachery scores an astounding rise in class and status. She attacks the *ie* system at the top, for she forces her way into the aristocracy, the segment of society where lineage most clearly produced social status. Her campaign, indeed, is so successful that it tears away the veneer of "nature" as a determinant of social status and of "blood" as a constituent of family. *Chikyōdai* is a fantasy of female *risshin shusse* that thrillingly deconstructs the idea of status based upon *ie* lineage. While it pays lip service to the idea of hereditary status, it celebrates a transgressive and determined female drive to cross social boundaries. When the provincial nursemaid's daughter passes for an aristocrat, she shows that blood isn't everything; talent, beauty, hard work, and gumption count for a whole lot.

The culturally specific elements of this fantasy become evident when *Chikyōdai* is examined against the Bertha Clay novel that Yūhō had so readily claimed as his work's inspiration. *Dora Thorne* is a melodrama that, at every unsubtle turn, pounds away at the dangers of miscegenation between status groups and the miseries faced by men and women who fail to fulfill status-based expectations of gendered behavior. This story, set among the landed aristocracy of nineteenth-century England, is built upon two promises of marriage exchanged in successive generations; the outcomes of these promises attest to the disastrous consequences of love across status lines. The first of these cases involves Ronald Earle, the future heir of Earlescourt, who falls in love with Dora Thorne, the daughter of his father's "lodge-keeper." Ronald is a young aristocrat with egalitarian instincts—"I never had believed in the cruel laws of caste," he declares[39]—who pursues his love over his parents' most dire warnings. His father's words show that miscegenation is precisely the way the older aristocrat views Ronald's association with Dora: "'You see it, Ronald,' he cried. 'Your idea of the "fusion" of races is well enough in theory, but it will not do brought into practice.'"[40] Ronald insists on carrying out his promise to marry a young woman alien to his background; he ends up being banished by his father ("I dismiss you from my presence, unworthy son of a noble race."[41]); and he is forced to leave the country for Florence, where he tries to make a living as a portrait painter. Ronald and Dora are happy together at first, but his parents' warnings soon prove to be accurate. Ronald begins to tire of a girl whose innocence and simplicity had once charmed him. One of the female aristocrats gets at the heart of things: "There is something in Mrs. Thorne that puzzles me—she does not always speak or look like a lady."[42] Status identity, then, is viewed as a durable marker in *Dora Thorne*, and a servant's daughter has great difficulty becoming a "lady." Dora herself is acutely aware of this. Her anxiety over her position causes her to become jealous of her husband's platonic relationship with a beautiful aristocratic woman. Not even the arrival of twin daughters can hold Ronald and Dora together. After a particularly nasty scene in which Dora's groundless jealousies clash with Ronald's now apparent social prejudices ("May I be forgiven for thinking such a woman fit to be my wife!"[43]), the two separate, with Dora going home to England to live with her parents and Ronald departing on an extended trip through foreign lands to nurse his anger and disappointment. With this coda, the initial consequence of the young lovers' folly becomes clear.

In this story the sins of the parents will be visited upon the children, but a number of years pass before the second set of consequences arrives. During this time, the twins, Beatrice and Lillian, grow into young women. Although they are raised in the house of their humble grandparents, they are not without social training, for Ronald's mother, Lady Earle, dispatches a suitable tutor to insure that the girls receive an education. This tutor manages not only to train the girls to eventually take their place in society, but also to auspiciously affect Dora, who after many years begins to acquire the deportment of a lady. The girls both grow up to be lovely, but with sharply contrasting personalities:

> Beautiful, daring and restless, every day running a hundred risks, and loved the better for the dangers she ran, Beatrice was almost worshiped at "the Elms." Nothing ever daunted her, nothing ever made her dull or sad. Lillian was gentle and quiet, with more depth of character, but little power of showing it; somewhat timid and diffident—a more charming ideal of an English girl could not have been found—*spirituelle*, graceful, and refined; so serene and fair that to look at her was a pleasure.[44]

It's Beatrice, of course, who gets herself into trouble. While still living at "the Elms," her grandparents' farm, she meets a dashing ship's captain, Hugh Fernely. Beatrice's adventurous side is intrigued by the captain, who seduces her both with stories about his travels and with flattering protestations of love ("Beatrice found it very pleasant to be worshipped like a queen."[45]). Before he leaves on a long voyage, Fernely has secured Beatrice's promise to marry him when he returns.

Soon afterward, events radically change the girls' lives. Lord Earle dies, leaving Ronald, who had not been replaced as heir despite his banishment, as the new lord of the manor. When Ronald returns from abroad to take up his title and his estate, the girls are removed from their mother, who remains unreconciled with Ronald, and are taken to Earlescourt to assume their place in society. With this melodramatic ascent, the girls blossom in a new world. They have soon charmed the aristocracy not only in neighboring counties but in London as well. This is particularly true of Beatrice, who succeeds in dazzling the richest and most eligible young lord in London. But Lillian doesn't do too badly either; she manages to attract the attentions of the handsome distant relation who is to succeed the sonless Ronald as the lord of Earlescourt. All proceeds brilliantly, and Beatrice is on the verge of marriage to her young lord when Hugh Fernely returns from his voyage and demands the fulfillment of their promise.

Beatrice is caught in a quandary: despite her previous promise, she cannot imagine marrying a sea captain now that she is about to acquire both title and wealth. She agrees to a secret meeting with Fernely in order to explain her situation. Disaster ensues. An argument breaks out when Beatrice meets Fernely by a lake on the Earle estate, and in the midst of a struggle she falls into the water. Fernely makes no effort to save her as she drowns.

When the family learns about Beatrice's death, the moral imagination of the novel makes itself distressingly clear. Beatrice had been available to Fernely because of her father's earlier indiscretion; the two tragedies caused by the crossing of status lines are linked because one is the consequence of the other. The narrator spells this out in his commentary on Ronald as the latter looks down upon the corpse of his daughter:

> He stood face to face at last with the sin of his youth; it had found him out. The willful, wanton disobedience, the marriage that had broken his father's heart and struck Ronald himself from the roll of useful men; the willful cruel neglect of duty; the throwing off of all ties; the indulgence in proud, unforgiving temper, the abandonment of wife and children—all ended there. But for his sins and errors, that white, still figure might now have been radiant with life and beauty.[46]

This melodrama, then, codes evil according to a status-based ideology emphasizing the proper fulfillment of gender roles. Ronald was supposed to take his place among "useful men," obey the dictates of "duty," and be loyal to family ties. By marrying below his station, he has transgressed the morality of his rank, and he reaps the appropriate punishment through the death of a daughter who herself had crossed social lines.

Beatrice's death is a punishment for Dora as well. Having violated status boundaries, she finds that living as a "lady" requires strict self-discipline. She learns some of this discipline during her years of tutelage under her daughters' governess; but it is her mother-in-law, Lady Earle, who most clearly articulates the role demanded of her: "Take the right course Dora; submit to your husband. Believe me, woman's rights are all fancy and nonsense; loving gentle submission is the fairest ornament of woman. Even should Ronald be in the wrong, trample upon all pride and temper, and make the first advances to him."[47] The reference to "woman's rights" comes out of the blue, because Dora has never shown any feminist impulses. But it does help to squarely place this advice from a real lady to an aspiring one in the realm of the politics of gender. If she wants to ever join her husband again, Dora will need to abandon all pride; she must show utter submission to a man who had treated her contemptuously because of her origins. Dora's words when she returns to her husband after Beatrice's death ties her reinstatement both to her recognition of her place as a woman and her awareness that Beatrice's death is connected to her past misdeeds: "'You will forgive me, Ronald,' pleaded the gentle voice, 'for love of my dead child?'"[48]

The melodramatic trajectory of the plot, then, takes Ronald and Dora toward acceptance of status-based imperatives of morality and gender. Once this is accomplished, the text grants them both a measure of redemption. Lillian—the sister whose modesty, innocence, and purity had made her a poster child for femininity—marries the heir to Earlescourt; the young couple move in with the reconciled Ronald and Dora; and, in an epilogue that occurs some years later, the Earles are shown as a happy multigenerational family.[49] Ronald has now become a satisfied paterfamilias, Dora exhibits the "dignity of her character, acquired by long years of stern discipline,"[50] and the younger couple have had a son, who will carry on not only the family line but also doubtlessly the nobility of behavior demanded by his blood.

Dora Thorne and its severe attitudes toward social hierarchy were already well known in Japan when *Chikyōdai* was published because a loose translation by Suematsu Kenchō (1855–1920) called *Tanima no himeyuri* (Lilies of the valley) had appeared, to considerable acclaim, between 1888 and 1890. The translation had even counted the empress among its fans. We know this because an imperial chamberlain had written to Kenchō after the publication of the first volume, saying that "her majesty indicated that *Tanima no himeyuri*, which had been presented to her earlier, had met her pleasure and that she wished to make known her desire to quickly see the later vol-

umes."[51] In a letter that he sent to the empress's steward, Kenchō emphasized that he had translated *Dora Thorne* precisely because he had wanted to
transmit its lessons on status and gender to a Japanese audience:

> My motive for producing *Tanima no himeyuri* was neither to wax poetic nor
> to entertain the eyes of my readers; the history of Seijin and his wife [Seijin
> is the name given to Ronald Earle in the translation] shows that lifelong
> misery is the necessary fate of those who recklessly enter a promise of mar-
> riage despite yawning gulfs between their families as well as between their
> basic values. The differing fortunes of Midori and Ruri [Beatrice and Lillian,
> respectively] may contribute toward forming judgments about maidenly be-
> havior. In fact, all such matters relate to the public morals of society.[52]

These two letters were printed at the front of later volumes of Kenchō's
translations. Needless to say, they serve a powerful paratextual function.
Their inclusion serves to show the reader that *Tanima no himeyuri* had found
favor at the highest reaches of the status and family systems. Kenchō had
used the indication of imperial approval to trumpet the salubrious effect of
his text upon "public morals." It was not mere pleasure that the reader was
to gain from *Tanima no himeyuri*; the work was to be read as a morally significant statement on social miscegenation and feminine deportment.

The ideological thrust of *Dora Thorne* and *Tanima no himeyuri* being
what it is, Kikuchi Yūhō's adaptation was bound to address the intersection of status and gender. *Chikyōdai's* treatment of this problem, however, is
ambivalent and double-edged. In some ways, it shares *Dora Thorne's* belief
in the sanctity of blood and social position. The polarized division it effects
between the self-aggrandizing Kimie and the self-sacrificing Fusae displays
a gender ideology that values a status-based vision of femininity. Yet, at the
same time, *Chikyōdai* shows a fascination for social border-crossings that is
distinct from the unmixed condemnation expressed by *Dora Thorne*. In the
process, it offers a vision of femininity that is active, daring, and enterpris-
ing. These ideological shifts are effected in Yūhō's novel through an auda-
cious transformation of the source text.[53]

A MELODRAMA TRANSFORMED

The key change that Yūhō makes is to turn *Dora Thorne's* twins into "sisters"
joined through a secret adoption. The motif of secret adoption allows Yūhō
to give the girls different origins, and this radically changes the ideological

terrain traversed by his melodrama. Instead of a drama of girls striving for a social position that is theirs by birth, we get the story of Kimie's treacherous ascent to the heights of the aristocracy—we get a family romance.

Given its import, it is no surprise that this change is foregrounded in the most prominent of paratextual elements, the title. *Chikyōdai* is written with the graph for "breast" or "milk" combined with the character compound for sisters (which is usually read *shimai*).[54] The term *chikyōdai* refers to individuals who have developed a sibling relationship as a result of infant fosterage or adoption, individuals who have literally or metaphorically suckled at the same breast. Thus the title puts front and center the fact that the sisters in the text are unrelated by blood. Yet there is a certain playfulness as well, for the term for "milk" is homophonous with that for "blood." Although this second meaning remains hidden by the semantic value of the chosen graph, the capacity for *chi* to mean "blood" resonates in the background, suggesting the potential for blood relations to be conflated with constructed ones.

Yūhō's title indicates one other related change. Whereas the title of the Bertha Clay novel points to Dora, the female character whose presence instigates the conflicts in that novel, the title of *Chikyōdai* emphasizes the sisters in the generation following. This difference is faithful to relative weighting in the two works. *Dora Thorne* spends nearly half of its length detailing Ronald and Dora's unhappy union, and, even when the focus shifts to Beatrice and Lillian, their parents' story remains prominently in the background through the continuing suggestion that the girls' fates have been determined by their parents' errors. By contrast, *Chikyōdai* dispenses with the initial marriage in only a few pages, and there is no indication that what happens later is retribution for a prior transgression of social boundaries.

The brief opening of the novel deserves some discussion, however, because it sets into motion Yūhō's major change and because it establishes *Chikyōdai* as a melodrama of social hierarchy whose values contrast sharply with those of the novel by Bertha Clay. The names of the characters will be initially confusing in the following account, but necessarily so, since naming in the novel is used to underline the fluidity of personal and social identity. *Chikyōdai* opens with the arrival of a beautiful "lady" (*kifujin* is used here) named Mano Kimie, at the home of her former nurse, Ohama, in the rustic, seaside village of Shikama, located in what is now Hyōgo Prefecture. She has brought with her her beloved three-year-old daughter, Kimiko, whom she intends to leave with her old nurse. The story of why this is necessary, and how Kimiko came to be born, is largely told through Kimie's dialogue. The narrative perspective provided by Kimie's own telling of her tale introduces a view of social mixing that differs radically from that of *Dora Thorne*. In Bertha Clay's novel, Ronald and Dora's story is told retrospectively by a narrator who knows about the tragedies that will result and, more importantly, valorizes the order provided by social hierarchy. By contrast, the Kimie who tells her story is a woman still very much in love; she has not suffered any great loss for having crossed status boundaries and thus her story does not have a cautionary edge. Kimie explains to the nurse that her father, a wealthy industrialist, had lost his money through the failure of a mining enterprise. She had subsequently been left an orphan (*minashigo*) by the death of first one parent and then the other. While working as a governess, that stock job for impoverished yet genteel young women, she had met and fallen in love with a navy lieutenant with family ties to the aristocracy. The lieutenant had loved her back, but his family had prevented him from formally marrying her. Kimie explains that the lieutenant, an orphan like herself (*watashi to onnaji minashigo*), had been raised by his uncle, a high aristocrat (*rippa na kazokusama*), who will not permit his charge to marry a commoner's daughter (*heimin no musume*).[55] Unwilling to confront his uncle, the lieutenant marries Kimie in a secret church ceremony. The two are happy together, and Kimie gives birth to her daughter, whom she calls Kimiko. The lieutenant, however, has become gravely ill during one of his voyages and Kimie has been called to a hospital in Taiwan where he is being treated. She has come to Shikama to leave Kimiko with Ohama while she makes the trip to Taiwan. The former nurse gladly accepts this responsibility because she herself has a daughter the same age. In fact, her love for her old charge has led the nurse to name her own daughter "Kimie." The older Kimie remarks on this by saying that "the three Kimis have ended up together here" (93).

When Kimie leaves her daughter in Shikama, she is destined never to see her again, for the ship on which she travels to Taiwan is lost in a storm, taking her down with it. Ohama is left in a quandary; she can't reach the lieutenant, because Kimie, intent on maintaining the secrecy of her marriage, has never told her his name. All Ohama can do is to wait for word from the lieutenant, which never comes. She concludes that he has either abandoned his daughter or that he has himself died in Taiwan (he was after all gravely ill). Either way, Kimiko is an orphan, and Ohama decides that she will raise her as her own daughter. The passage describing this decision and the subsequent decision to rename Kimiko explains how the "milk sisters" of the title come into being:

> Ohama loved Kimiko as though she were her own daughter and treated her no differently from her actual child (*jitsu no ko*). She decided to raise Kimiko as her own. But calling the girls would have been confusing with their names being Kimie and Kimiko. And so she renamed Kimiko, calling her Fusae; this was the name of her former charge's mother—that is, Kimiko's maternal grandmother—and Ohama thus thought that the change would not have displeased the dead Kimie. There was one thing more: Ohama thought that, in bringing up the two children as sisters, it might later raise their suspicions if they were the same age. She thus made Fusae, who had been born slightly later, a full year younger. (95)

A comparison with *Dora Thorne* shows that family and social identity has been made much more slippery in the Japanese novel. The situation is considerably different here from one where the logic of blood and "race" determines status and family membership. The trope of orphanage—applied here to the older Kimie, her lieutenant, and Kimiko/Fusae, and later to the younger Kimie—carries much of the significance we have already observed regarding Kan'ichi in *Konjiki yasha*. The orphaning of these characters is a break in filiation that signals larger discontinuities in social relations. The orphans in *Chikyōdai* are marginal figures and free agents with the capacity to disturb the supposedly universal order of the *ie* system, perhaps even reveal the arbitrary logic of *ie* organization. They also call into question a status system invested in heredity.

The fluid and ambiguous assignment of status identities supports this last agenda. The older Kimie comes from a bourgeois family that has suffered social descent through losing its money, and the lieutenant is technically not himself an aristocrat, being merely a dependant relation in the household of a marquis. (The text later explains that he is the son of the marquis's divorced sister.) Their daughter, Kimiko, is thus only tenuously connected to the aristocracy. Ohama's decision to secretly adopt the orphaned Kimiko/Fusae obscures the child's paternity and already uncertain status identity. It also creates sisters who are unrelated by blood and whose social stations by birth are far apart. Unlike *Dora Thorne*'s characters anchored in status and family, *Chikyōdai*'s characters are purposefully and relentlessly unmoored. They are creatures of a world where status is both murky and unsettled.

The issue of naming and renaming emphasizes the instability of social identities in *Chikyōdai*. The name "Kimie" has migrated down the social scale; in the world of this novel a nursemaid can hope to replicate in the child of her own womb another that she had once attended in the household of a man of means. Kimiko must lose the name that she was given at birth, a name that points to her blood tie with her mother, because a similar name is already being used by a nursemaid's daughter. On the one hand, then, her renaming signifies displacement and social descent. But, on the other hand, the choice of "Fusae," the name of her maternal grandmother, bears further thought. There is a suggestion that maternal lineage—independent of the lineage of men—remains important. When we understand this suggestion in the context that, in the renaming of Kimiko to Fusae, a woman has renamed a girl after another woman, then we see that female agency is important in this work. Despite the gendered ideology of sacrificial femininity manifested in Fusae's near beatification, *Chikyōdai* is also a novel in which women act decisively toward the formation of fictive families and the establishment of social identities.

Once Fusae is adopted to become Ohama's daughter, the novel begins to roughly trace the plot of the second half of *Dora Thorne* and events unfold to reveal the sisters' contrasting personalities. But the signal change that Yūhō has made in kinship relations, as well as the setting of the story in a Meiji world of social aspiration, constantly transforms the significance of experiences and episodes. The education of Kimie and Fusae is a case in point. Instead of being trained in the social graces by a tutor, the girls are sent to public schools and graduate from a girls higher school (*kōtōjogakkō*), generally the highest level of schooling available to young women in the Meiji era.[56] They receive this schooling because the "strong-minded" Ohama is determined to educate Fusae properly in case she is rediscovered and wants her own beautiful daughter to have the same opportunities. Ohama's social position is specifically set to allow her to hold such aspirations for her daughters; the former nursemaid had married a shipowner and "was able to live without lacking anything after his death" (94). Ohama, then, is enough of a bourgeoise to dream of upward mobility for her daughters and to finance a fitting education. A passage that describes the two girls' contrasting responses to their schooling makes clear that Ohama's desires are inherited by Kimie and that these desires are inscribed within the ideology of self-advancement: "Strangely enough, their temperaments differed even as children, and while Fusae loved learning from her very core, Kimie's little brain had been infused with the idea that she would not be able to succeed in life (*shusse ga dekinu*) if she did not pursue learning" (95). Kimie is a young woman who has learned to associate education and getting ahead, a combination enshrined in the Meiji consciousness. When a nursemaid's daughter dreams of using public schooling to push to the front, we are in a world of hopes and ambitions unknown to the aristocrats of Earlescourt.

Different expectations also condition Kimie's relationship with Takahama Isamu, who is *Chikyōdai's* Hugh Fernely. By making Fernely a ship's captain, *Dora Thorne* had portrayed him as a man who, though not an aristocrat, was dashing enough to attract Beatrice with tales of foreign adventures. Fernely had been a man with a profession tied to England's far-flung imperial destiny. Takahama, by contrast, is an immigrant laborer who has briefly returned from the United States, a man whose life is rooted in Japan's export of impoverished excess labor to foreign shores. Takahama's courtship of Kimie makes plain that he is a man driven by economic imperatives; he plies Kimie not so much with stories of adventure abroad but with tales of wealth: "He quickly discerned what kind of story would appeal to Kimie's heart and he fervently began to describe what a rich country America was, how easy it was to acquire riches there" (99). By giving Kimie a diamond ring, he finally secures her promise to marry him after he returns from another sojourn abroad. Kimie's susceptibility to the lure of money is very much in line with historical transformations in the ideology of self-advancement; like Miya in *Konjiki yasha*, Kimie lives in a time when wealth has become the preeminent standard for success. Her fascination with money also indicates that, in contrast to *Dora Thorne*, where status was at the root of the conflict, *Chikyōdai* is concerned with both status and economic class. An immigrant laborer such as Takahama has little to offer in the way of status, but, were he to strike it rich overseas, he could possibly help Kimie move upward in class. The doubled opportunity to enormously improve her status and class is what will eventually prove to be Kimie's fatal temptation.

Yūhō's transformation of his source material becomes most radical in the portion of the story that describes the switching of identities. Needless to say, this is a portion of the novel that has no corresponding element in the source work, for *Dora Thorne's* twins possess the same family and social origins. The sequence of events leading to the trading of places begins when Ohama falls critically ill. Fusae is already working elsewhere as a governess, and so it becomes Kimie's duty to nurse her mother. Just before she dies, Ohama reveals to Kimie the secret she has been carrying within her and instructs Kimie to tell Fusae about her origins. Thus Kimie becomes the first of the sisters to learn about Fusae's background. When Fusae arrives, the girls grieve together over the death of their mother and they mourn being left "orphans in the world" (*kono yo ni minashigo to nokosareta*), but Kimie is also gnawed by the secret she has learned: "When Kimie thought about how Fusae's station in life, so enviable and desirable, was far above hers—that her sister was really a young lady from the upper crust of society (*jōryū shakai no reijō*)—she felt unbearable regret that their situations had not been reversed, that she was instead the birth child of a commoner (*heimin*) like Ohama" (103). Kimie's possession of her mother's secret, then, makes her fantasize a family romance and leads her to the defining moral moment in the melodrama, an "irreconcilable battle between good and evil" (*zen aku himizu no tatakai*) in which evil speaks directly:

> The devil whispered to her—Fusae is totally ignorant about the secret. The only ones who knew were her mother and Fusae's, and now they were no longer of this world. Kimie was the only person to whom the secret had been revealed, and she was now its sole possessor. . . . Who could possibly reveal the truth if she were to change places with Fusae? What good fortune it was that she was the one who possessed the name "Kimie" and that the real Kimiko had been renamed Fusae and had even been made a year younger than her actual age. Fusae was satisfied with her current circumstances, and so it wouldn't be particularly heartless to do this to her—following these murmurings, Kimie finally came to her frightening decision. The desperate battle between her conscience and the devil, waged within her for seven days and seven nights, sadly ended in the utter defeat of her conscience. (104)

The Manichean inner battle has been fought and virtue is the loser: Kimie tells her sister what her mother had revealed, changing only one key detail—she says that she herself is the issue of noble blood adopted by Ohama. With this, the "devil" reigns triumphant and virtue is eclipsed. Kimie's actions simultaneously conceal both her social identity and that of her "sister"; the virtuous Fusae does not even know she has been robbed of her birthright.

A word is in order here about why masked identities play so large a part in the melodramatic plot. Masking is a productive device for melodrama because it gives concrete and personified form to the initial concealment of the moral order, a concealment that intensifies the final revelation. The melodrama "tends to become the dramaturgy of virtue misprized," because temporary misapprehension eventually contributes to the production of "virtue made visible and acknowledged, the drama of a recognition."[57]

This kind of plot is deeply connected to the phenomenon noted earlier

that the villain, Kimie, is on stage far longer than Fusae, the pure and innocent victim. In speaking of the French melodrama proper, Brooks notes that
"in the clash of virtue and villainy, it is the latter that constitutes the active
force and the motor of the plot. . . . Despite the ultimate triumph of virtue, it
was the moment of evil triumphant that fascinated. The villain had the *beau
rôle*, the one played by the famous actors."[58] In *Chikyōdai*, the virtuous heroine Fusae is rendered passive by ignorance—through the course of the novel,
she does not know she has been betrayed and robbed of her birthright, and
she thus takes no actions to recover what is rightfully hers. By contrast, Kimie
faces the most dangerous moral choices and undertakes acts of concealment
and transgression; she is the "motor of the plot" in this melodrama.

After Kimie makes her fateful decision, the novel removes Fusae from
the scene by sending her away to work as a governess in Hokkaido. It then
proceeds to detail the all too easy fulfillment of Kimie's dreams. A short
analepsis describes what had happened to Fusae's father, the lieutenant, after
the death of her mother. It turns out that the lieutenant, who is now por-
tentously identified as one Matsudaira Akisada (Matsudaira is the surname
of a Tokugawa branch family) had not abandoned his daughter. His wife
had not told him where she had left Kimiko/Fusae, and thus after her ship
went down he had lost all contact with his daughter. Once he had recovered
from his grave illness, he had desperately tried to find her, hiring detectives
and advertising in the newspapers, but it had all been to no avail.[59] The
lieutenant had sadly returned to his career in the navy, vowing never to love
anyone but his dead wife.

A dozen years later, however, his fortunes had suddenly changed when circumstances had led him to assume his uncle's title. Akisada's elevation reveals
a side to this novel that views social hierarchy as an arbitrary construction.
The cartoonish tragedy that strikes the Matsudaira family cannot but suggest
that lineage is an irrational fiction and nobility an accidental phenomenon.
The text engineers Akisada's rise by having the old marquis and his two sons,
who had been summering at their villa in Odawara, conveniently swept out
to sea by a tsunami. Since the family had no immediate successors, Akisada
is designated the new Marquis Matsudaira. The former "orphan" and dependant relation becomes the head of a family that had been the hereditary
lords of a feudal province (his servants refer to him as *tonosama*) and takes
up residence in his uncle's mansion in Tokyo. Akisada's assumption of the
headship of his *ie* seems no less arbitrary than Kimie's efforts to become his
daughter. The focus upon the artificiality of the *ie* is amplified, moreover,

when Akisada quickly adopts a son, whom he calls Akinobu, in order to insure the continuity of the family line. Like other adoptions in this book, Akinobu's designation as the heir apparent shows the *ie* to be a social institution whose lifeblood is human agency rather than nature.

At this point the returning analepsis rejoins the story concerning the sisters, and the two accounts begin to merge. With Akinobu's encouragement, the marquis sets out to use his newly acquired wealth to resume the search for his now grown daughter. This time he is successful. Or at least he thinks he is, for his emissaries find Kimie, who is now ready to identify herself as the long-lost daughter of Mano Kimie and a highborn naval officer whose name she does not know. The younger Kimie is brought to the Matsudaira mansion. Belying her upbringing, she stuns everyone with her beauty and the speed with which she acquires the bearing of a young noblewoman. She has soon conquered Tokyo, becoming one of the capital's most celebrated young ladies. Except for occasional pangs of conscience about her betrayal of Fusae and an understandable fear of discovery, Kimie succeeds in her subterfuge beyond her wildest dreams. In this story, a young woman of humble origins chooses a family more in keeping with her wishes and makes the leap to the highest reaches of society. Kimie does not wait for a marriage or any other accepted means of female self-advancement to come her way; she spots her opportunity and, in a show of female agency, grabs it and makes it hers. With one decisive action an "orphan" manipulates an *ie*, lives out her family romance, and bounds over social boundaries.

When we view *Chikyōdai* as a melodrama about social hierarchy, this remarkable ascent presents some discontinuous and contradictory facets. As we have seen in comparison to the rigid world of *Dora Thorne*, the status system in *Chikyōdai* is permeable and fluid. Relations across status boundaries are not condemned, and there are examples of both social descents (Fusae's adoption by Ohama) and vertiginous social ascents (Kimie becoming a Matsudaira daughter). In the case of Akisada, the poor relation become marquis, gaining the peerage owes a lot to accident. The hierarchy here is unsettled. Yet we must also note that the novel has a deeply conservative side. It has labeled as evil the social aspirations of a lowborn young woman who has acted out a family romance; and it has assigned virtue to someone with noble blood flowing in her veins. As much as it depicts a looser status system, *Chikyōdai* also reveals a moral imagination that equates virtue with aristocracy. This is a contradiction that deserves further inquiry through examining the novel's tortured discourse on nature and nurture.

NATURE AND NURTURE

Observing that the French melodramatic theater arose after the Revolution and that it played to an audience that spanned the classes, Peter Brooks argues that the melodrama "represents a democratization of morality and its signs."[60] Appearing in a "post-sacred universe," where the moral assumptions upholding social hierarchy have been sundered, melodrama functions as a "theatre of grandiose and absolute moral entities put within reach of the people, a moral universe made available."[61] This characteristic is apparent within the social dynamics dramatized in melodrama:

> There are other elements as well that define the form's democracy. Villains are remarkably often tyrants and oppressors, those that have power and use it to hurt. Whereas the victims, the innocent and virtuous, most often belong to a democratic universe: whatever their specific class origin, they believe in merit rather than privilege, and the fraternity of the good. Among the repressions broken through by melodramatic rhetoric is that of class domination, suggesting that a poor persecuted girl can confront her powerful oppressor with the truth about their moral conditions. If the social structure of melodrama often appears inherently feudal—landed gentry or bourgeoisie and their faithful yeomanry—it is also remarkably egalitarian, and anyone who insists upon feudal privileges is bound to be a villain.[62]

These observations are obviously problematic in analyzing *Dora Thorne* and *Chikyōdai* as melodramas.[63] Although both texts display key elements of the melodramatic cluster, they display social attitudes that are either deeply conservative (in the former) or deeply conflicted (in the latter). They suggest that melodrama's project of putting an intensified moral universe "within reach of the people" can be directed toward varying uses, depending upon historical circumstances as well as the ideologies of authors and their allies. The issues of class and status are likely to be engaged, given the character of melodrama as a mode concerned with social order that appeals across class lines. But a Bertha Clay, writing in late-nineteenth-century England rather than post-Revolutionary France, could create a melodrama that enforced hierarchy by awarding the most severe punishments to those who would obscure it; and a Kikuchi Yūhō, writing in Meiji Japan to an audience of would-be "ladies," could produce a text whose approach to social hierarchy cuts both ways.

We have noted earlier that, contrary to Yūhō's own assertions, Kimie is the protagonist of *Chikyōdai*. As we have seen, this is connected to a melodramatic plot that employs a lengthy contemplation of evil as a precondition for the later celebration of virtue. But we must also account for the complex role played in such weighting by problems of social hierarchy. For Kimie's evil act involves transgressing class and status lines, an endeavor that the text recounts at length and in loving detail. The process of Kimie's brilliant success and her consequent negotiations with the possibility of discovery are what add dimension to her portrayal. There is clearly an egalitarian side to the work that upholds "merit rather than privilege." In effect, the novel celebrates Kimie's capacity for self-transformation while coding it as evil. The ambivalence of this approach can be illustrated by examining the novel's engagement with the ideas of nature and nurture.

The importance of these ideas becomes apparent the moment Kimie arrives at the Matsudaira mansion. This section of the narrative begins by incorporating the gossip of unnamed servants waiting for the arrival of their lord's newly discovered daughter:

> The maids wondered what kind of young mistress she would be. Some noted that she was supposed to have been raised in a peasant's house in the country and said that upbringing was more important than lineage. She was in all probability a splendid example of a country girl, a rustic with roughness apparent in her every expression. Others said, no, the master had been quite a dashing lord in his youth, and his wife was reputed to have been attractive. Even if their daughter was raised in the country, she would still be a jewel in a dungheap. She must surely be beautiful. (114)

The discovery of a long-lost daughter raised in humble circumstances occasions comments about the impacts of nature and nurture, but Kimie's act of misrepresentation gives an odd spin to the comments. Expectations at the mansion are based upon the mistaken belief that Kimie shares Matsudaira blood; thus her potential shortcomings are attributed to her provincial and plebeian upbringing, while her strengths are seen as evidence of her lineage. Kimie has created a situation in which nature and nurture will be consistently misread.

Chikyōdai does not exploit the comic possibilities inherent in a situation where misrepresentation leads to major misperceptions—it takes itself too seriously for that. But there are seams in the text where comedy, intended or not, seeps out, because Kimie's assumption of her new identity illustrates that characters see what they want to see. One of these occasions occurs when Akisada meets his "daughter" for the first time. His contradictory comments show the marquis desperately trying to understand his daughter's beauty within the context of a discourse on nature.

> (Marquis) Oh, my daughter! Finally I've found you. I've never been happier than this moment. It's as though I'm meeting the Kimie who died. I can finally make some amends to her now that I've found you. Oh, my daughter, you're called "Kimie" too, aren't you? Let me see your face. Umm, you've certainly become beautiful. (As he said this, the marquis appeared to swell with pride.) And you've grown up so refined. One's origins can't be fought. (Gazing rapturously on his daughter's face, the marquis continued.) But whom do you look like? You don't look much like your mother Kimie. You were probably born so beautiful, having inherited the bloodlines of my house rather than those of your mother. Your mother was a charming, gentle beauty, but she was nowhere near as beautiful as you. (116, parentheses in original)

FIGURE 3.1   Kimie is united with her "father" the marquis in this illustration from the newspaper serialization of *Chikyōdai*. Source: *Osaka mainichi shinbun*, September 13, 1903.

Believing that he has found his daughter, the marquis reaches for physical resemblances. He initially thinks that seeing Kimie is like seeing his dead wife. When he is forced to readjust this impression, he merely reaches the satisfying conclusion that her beauty must be the result of his genes. The marquis's bumbling effort to establish a biological connection shows that nature, in this novel, is not necessarily a given but rather a construct dependant upon expectations. In the very confidence with which he states the inevitability of nature, the marquis displays its contingency. *Chikyōdai*, then, contains a strain that subverts the idea that the natural must be connected with the authentic or the essential.

Alongside its ironic take on nature, the novel presents a forceful view of the power of nurture. It stresses what can be achieved through education, self-discipline, and self-cultivation. In fact, much of what is initially mistaken for the work of nature by the marquis and others at the Matsudaira mansion is the result of nurture. We have already seen how Ohama's pride had driven her to give both her daughters the best schooling available for girls. Without this schooling, Kimie would have been immediately dismissed as a provincial boob, her great beauty notwithstanding. The single fact that the Kansai-born Kimie is capable of speaking politely in perfect "standard" Japanese (based on upper-class Tokyo dialect) keeps her from seeming totally alien when she arrives at the mansion.[64]

Once Kimie arrives in Tokyo, the issue of her cultivation is taken up openly and earnestly. A Mrs. Maruki, a widow with experience in society, is hired by the marquis to take charge of Kimie's education and teach her "enlightened manners in such things as social deportment, speech and conversation, and formal protocol" (121). Mrs. Maruki is a one-woman finishing school, and Kimie soaks up her lessons like a sponge:

> Kimie, who was extremely sharp and resourceful, studied assiduously so that she would never in any circumstance embarrass her position as the daughter of the marquis's House. Her progress was rapid. Every single one of her teachers was filled with praise, and this gave the old lord extraordinary satisfaction. The impact of Mrs. Maruki was especially noteworthy. Through her spoken instructions, through gestures, and even just by example, she tutored her charge in the social graces. Within just three months or so, Kimie had been trained to become a woman of such poise that she was never at a disadvantage in any situation. (121)

The novel, then, admiringly recounts the characteristics that actually allow Kimie to succeed in her new environment: her intelligence, resourcefulness, determination, and capacity for hard work. *Chikyōdai's* egalitarian side recognizes that its villain can "pass" in aristocratic society because of her merits. Kimie's successful self-transformation shows that an aristocratic bearing is not an inborn trait but something that can be acquired by a country girl, provided she is smart enough and diligent. This thrust of the novel wrestles with issues of status inconsistency. Beauty and brains do not simply coincide here with aristocratic blood. In Kimie, we have a young woman both immensely beautiful and capable, but of relatively humble birth. The narrative charts the way she brings her social status and her economic position (though definitely not her moral standing) into alignment with her gifts.

Her exertions shape Kimie into an elegant and well-spoken lady. In fact, her self-cultivation is so stunning that she begins to take on the dimensions of a Japanese feminine ideal. The following conversation takes place between the marquis and his adopted son, Akinobu, upon the latter's return from a year abroad. Akinobu's approbation is important to Kimie, both because she has fallen in love with him and because she can truly consolidate her new social position by marrying the adopted heir of the family.

> (Marquis) How about it, Akinobu, what do you think after seeing Kimie? Hasn't she changed a great deal?
> (Akinobu) I could hardly recognize her. Even among the beautiful women in Paris and Rome, I've not seen anyone with her beauty and wit. How is it possible that she could have cultivated herself to that extent? Father, I can only guess at your satisfaction.
> The marquis was so overjoyed that he all but lost his usual dignified mien.
> (Marquis) So you think so too. Does it seem to you that there's no one to equal Kimie even abroad?
> (Akinobu) Absolutely not. And, after all, for Japanese eyes we've got to have a Japanese-style beauty. (125)

This passage resonates interestingly with the preface, where Yūhō calls the other sister, Fusae, "in the Japanese context, an ideal female." It would seem that, at this point in the story, Yūhō's male characters would tend to disagree. Their ideal is the stunning Kimie, whose sly social climbing and self-cultivation has turned her into a national standard. Indeed, this Kimie, who has forged herself into an aristocrat, is a source of national pride, for her equal does not seem to exist outside of Japan.

The ironic view of nature and the celebration of nurture fostered by Kimie's dizzying social ascent become more complicated when Fusae returns to the novel. On the one hand, she is the marquis's blood daughter, and her presence allows the novel to occasionally use the rhetoric of the natural in a straightforward way. On the other hand, because Fusae is not recognized as a daughter by birth, she must enter the Matsudaira family through other means. This happens when the marquis, who believes that Fusae is Ohama's daughter, takes it into his head that he must adopt the girl in order to repay the former nursemaid's kindness in raising his "daughter," Kimie. He writes to Fusae, saying that he wants to "*make her his true daughter*, and spend the remainder of his life being cared for by her and Kimie" (136, emphasis mine). Fusae is initially reluctant to accept the invitation; being modest and plain in her desires, she is content with her life as a governess and views life in an aristocratic household as a burden. Yet she finally relents because the call of blood summons her with its sacred power:

> Fusae had initially declined when she had received a letter from Kimie some-time earlier, and she had had no regrets about the matter. She had forgotten entirely about this problem of being taken into the marquis's House. But the blood lineage of a true parent and child (*shin no oyako*) cannot be fought, and as soon as she saw his letter, the old marquis's wish mysteriously touched the breast of Fusae, his true child (*makoto no ko*), and she began to feel that being admitted into his house was not a personal matter but a command from God. (136)

Read by itself, a passage of this type can only be understood as an affirmation of the sanctity of the bloodline. Lineage is linked to truth and exerts an undeniable and transcendental pull. Indeed, the narrative partially attempts to construct blood lineage as the "moral occult," the hidden source of ethical order whose eventual revelation is the goal of melodrama. At this point, one might expect the plot to follow a melodramatic trajectory toward the unmasking of the evil Kimie and the marquis's acknowledgement of Fusae as his "true child." This would result in one of the classic conclusions of the melodrama, the "recognition of error by those set in the position of judges."[65] But this isn't what happens. The marquis never learns that Fusae is his birth child; he dies still thinking that what he has done is "make her his true daughter." He maintains until the end an adoptive relationship with his biological daughter.

What *Chikyōdai* does, then, is maintain an edgy, sometimes contradictory stance on the discourse of nature and nurture; in this novel, daughters are both born and made (in the case of Fusae, born *and then* made). Adoptions play such an important role because the novel contains an insistent strain that sees major social identities—whether they be connected with family or status—as being constructed through acts of human agency. In some instances, adoption in the novel functions within *ie* ideology, which recognized adoption as a necessary supplement to nature. This is the case with Akisada's adoption of Akinobu, which instantly produces a Matsudaira heir to succeed the unmarried and sonless new marquis. After Kimie blossoms into a feminine ideal, Akisada even decides that he wants his "daughter" to marry his adopted son. This union would fall within the classic *mukoyōshi* pattern, enshrined within the *ie* system because it allowed the simultaneous maintenance of blood lineage (through the daughter) and the acquisition of a male successor. Akisada feels so strongly about this that he makes a manipulative deathbed demand that his adopted son marry Kimie. In doing so, he seems to have forgotten the lessons of his youth, when the former marquis's attempts to control his romantic life had caused him a lifetime of misery. More importantly, because he is being deceived by Kimie, such a marriage would not achieve the desired results and would, in fact, result in a subversion of *ie* lineage. In the befuddled marquis's efforts, then, we see the judgment of a noble househead being held up to question; the suggestion may even be present that there is something arbitrary about lineage. The fragile logic that rationalizes adoption as part of a "natural" lineage system already appears to be coming apart at the seams.

If Akinobu's adoption raises questions about the *ie*, then Fusae's situation shows us, through a rhetoric of excess, how families, identities, and alternate lineages can be constructed outside its assumptions. Fusae's identity is determined by the fact that she is adopted twice: once by Ohama and later by Akisada. In a sense, it is the very success of the initial adoption that makes Kimie's treachery successful. Ohama's parental affection for Fusae had been unequivocal. As we have seen, the text indicates that "Ohama loved Kimiko as though she were her own daughter, and treated her no differently from her actual child." Fusae is so fully Ohama's child that she has no reason to doubt Kimie when the latter says that she is the one who has been adopted. As far as Fusae is concerned, she *is* the daughter of the former nursemaid, and she feels neither disappointment nor desire when told that her sister is actually of aristocratic blood. An adoption motivated by compassion and love and carried out through female agency, an adoption that has nothing to do with the *ie*, proves successful in providing Fusae her family and status identities. When Fusae is later adopted by her biological father, the rhetoric of blood lineage becomes inescapable. But we must also note that the text simultaneously affirms that the adoptive relationship is a sufficient vessel for the expression of parental and filial love. Despite their blood relationship, both Fusae and

Akisada *think* that their relationship is an adoptive one; this does not keep them from feeling the deep mutual affection of father and daughter. Fusae's two adoptions show that families can be constituted through constructed human relationships that confound *ie* expectations. There is an implied dismissal of the notion that the patriarchal *ie*, characterized by the inexorable succession of male heirs, is the essential or only form of Japanese family.

We might also think of Kimie's acting out of her family romance as an "adoption," albeit a transgressive one that contravenes many of the rules of the adoptive relationship. Adoption usually assumes a hierarchy, with the adoptive parent playing the knowing and active role. Kimie, however, takes it upon herself to "adopt" a family and a status that are not hers by birth. She thoroughly infiltrates an *ie* and momentarily becomes part of its future. Her brilliant success—although built upon deception—adds testimony to the effectiveness of family relationships constructed through female agency. *Chikyōdai*, then, repeatedly traces the success of adoptive or fictive family relationships while also sometimes hewing to the notion that nature equals truth.

The scene that best illustrates this contradiction relates directly to the title of the work. It occurs after Fusae, in another example of occult moral forces at work, becomes mesmerized by an oil portrait of the older Kimie, her birth mother, and returns again and again to gaze at the picture of a woman she has seen repeatedly in her dreams. Noting Fusae's attachment to the portrait, the marquis conceives of the idea of "milk lineage":

> (Marquis) The more you look at it the more perfect it looks. It's her living image.
> (Fusae) Yes, when I look at her, I think she's about to step out of the frame. I could look at her all day.
> The marquis could hardly keep from showing how touched he was.
> (Marquis) So, you too find your longings in this portrait. Though she came well before you, she too grew up on your mother's milk, and so her ties with you are stronger than her ties to me.
> Hearing these words, Fusae was drawn to tears by something she could not explain, and she looked downward without speaking. The Marquis spoke to her gently.
> (Marquis) Fusae, your mother's milk nurtured my dead wife, as well as the current Kimie, and yourself. When you consider that all three of you grew up to become ladies far above the norm, it would seem that it's due to the milk you all drank. Isn't that so? It was all because that milk was so good.
> (152–53)

Fusae's fascination with the portrait of her birth mother could have been turned into another opportunity to trumpet the power of blood relations, yet the marquis's interjections take the scene in another direction entirely. His views on the ties formed through milk can possibly be dismissed as the rantings of a man who has been thoroughly misled by Kimie's treachery. But it becomes hard to do this when we recognize that the milk lineage outlined here echoes the idea of milk sisterhood given prominent paratextual expression in the title. Milk is an elemental image of nurture. The marquis acknowledges that a tie exists between his dead wife and his two daughters in that they have all been nurtured by one woman, the nursemaid Ohama. What has made all three "ladies far above the norm" is that they have been raised at the same breast.[66] The marquis, whom we know to be a strong believer in the inevitability of blood, ends up articulating the superior power of nurture over nature, milk over blood. It is striking, here, that the lineage produced by nurture crosses status lines, uniting a nursemaid with the women from various backgrounds she has nursed. What is more, this lineage unfolds in the absence of men. Heterosexual reproduction really has no place in this model, and neither does heterosexual love. Having suckled at the same breast, the marquis says, Fusae's ties with the older Kimie are stronger than his own; the bond of nurturance takes precedence over marriage. This *katei shōsetsu*, a work aimed largely at a female readership, contains the suggestion that the most powerful constituents of identity are those passed from one woman to another. For the moment, the *ie* has been utterly displaced by a fictive female lineage based upon nurture.

To sum up, *Chikyōdai* presents cross-cutting allegiances to nature and nurture. It makes insistent references to the rhetoric of blood, suggesting that lineage determines identity and that powerful hidden forces draw together biological parents and children. These references are, however, often undercut because they are made in inappropriate circumstances by characters who have misperceived the blood tie. At the same time, the novel shows through its protagonist that a woman can resolve her problems of status inconsistency through a great deal of self-cultivation and a bit of treachery. The superabundance of adoptions suggests that human agency—and specifically female agency—constitutes social and family identities. Finally, *Chikyōdai* raises the possibility of a female lineage that exists independently of blood ties and of the *ie*. There is much to be resolved as the story moves toward the completion of its plot.

IDEOLOGICAL FAILURE AND SUCCESS

The trajectory of the story now moves toward the destruction of its villain, Kimie, and the restoration of Fusae to her rightful place. But there are twists and turns along the way that bear on issues of nature and nurture, status and gender, that have been raised in the course of the novel. The most important plot element in the latter stages involves a triangular love relationship. Kimie initially sets her sights on Akinobu, the adopted and anointed heir, because a marriage with him in the *mukoyōshi* pattern would reinforce her position.[67] True to form, she seeks to use the *ie* system for her own purposes. But something happens to her outside her calculations and she soon finds herself falling genuinely in love. Akinobu, however, is inexorably attracted to the gentle and self-effacing Fusae, who returns his affections. Despite her feelings, Fusae eventually decides to step aside so that her sister, whom she believes to be the family's blood daughter, can marry the heir. An inside view into Fusae at a moment of high emotion explains her motives:

> It had been an incomparable stroke of good fortune for a common girl to become a daughter in the marquis's family. No matter how accustomed she had become to her new circumstances, falling in love with the heir to the marquis was still an act of presumption that showed a complete disregard for her own place. Why had she forgotten her usual discretion and allowed herself to become mesmerized by the devil's doings?
>
> It was immediately apparent to one and all that the marquis's intentions lay in having his true child (*makoto no ko*) Kimie marry Akinobu and have her inherit the Takanawa mansion. No matter how careless she had been, why hadn't she realized this until now?
>
> Even if she were so much in love that she was dying of longing, her obligations to the marquis called for her to resign herself to giving up her love. For a lady who was a true Christian, this was the command of God.
>
> Were she without the bonds of sentiment and obligation tying her to the marquis, she would nevertheless know that God would forbid her to love the lover of a sister to whom she owed the deepest obligation. Self-sacrifice for others had been part of her belief until now. And this sacrifice was for those to whom she owed many obligations. How could she be called a woman of belief if she could not now bury her love? (162)

When Fusae faces her heartrending decision, we see the unlikely intersection of various ideologies. Her moral sentiments fuse together elements of Christian self-renunciation with the powerful sense of social obligation known as *giri*; these are both combined with a belief in static social hierarchy that assumes the primacy of blood and nature; and all are supported by a gendered understanding of what it means to be a "lady." A believer in the *ie* system, Fusae also recognizes the moral value of the *mukoyōshi* solution.

Fusae's moment of truth can easily be regarded as an analogue to the earlier melodramatic moment when Kimie faces the choice between truth and deception, good and evil. Where Kimie had chosen social ascent and the fulfillment of personal desire at the cost of truth, Fusae chooses social stability and principled action at the cost of love. When we remember that Fusae is the feminine "ideal," the kind of woman "demanded by today's Japan," it is possible to come to the conclusion that *Chikyōdai*'s ideological thrust is the celebration of female virtue based upon sacrifice, knowing one's place, and upholding the *ie*. To an extent, the plot of the novel supports such a reading, for Kimie's subsequent death allows Fusae to eventually resume her love for Akinobu; in terms of affirming moral principles, the work allows Fusae to have her cake and eat it too.

But such a reading would fail to account for Kimie's continuing and dominant role in the novel, as well as the many plot elements that foreground her experience. To begin with, there is her place in the triangular relationship. Although it would have been easy for the novel to contrast Fusae's genuine love with Kimie's manipulativeness, the narrative insists upon the core of sentiment in the latter's relationship with Akinobu:

> It was true that Kimie had set her mind on becoming Akinobu's wife in order to consolidate her own position, but nevertheless *the natural and irrepressible love that began to well up in her was motivated by purity*, and had no connection with her other calculations. . . . At least regarding this one issue, Kimie had awakened from the vain, cold dreams that had long beset her. (125, emphasis mine)

The love triangle, then, complicates the binary opposition between the female characters; when it comes to love, the virtuous Fusae and the villainous Kimie share a similar purity. This allows Kimie's portrayal in the latter stages of the novel to take on a more sympathetic cast, even as she faces the possibility of being exposed as a pretender. While her treachery renders her beyond redemption, she can now be portrayed not only as a calculating upstart fearing discovery but as a woman protecting her love, a "natural" emotion that can transcend her "vain, cold dreams."

These two sides to Kimie are emphasized in the dream that she has

shortly after Akinobu, in reluctant obedience to his adoptive father's deathbed wish, gives her a diamond ring. (The diamond, needless to say, dwarfs
the one given her by her erstwhile suitor, the immigrant laborer Takahama
Isamu.) In the early part of the dream, where Kimie faces the terrors of
exposure, the focus is upon patriarchal anger over the breach of status and
family lines. An enraged Akinobu appears before her eyes to pass judgment
on behalf of the father: "Kimie, your dreadful plot has come to light! Beyond that I cannot say anymore! (As he said this, Akinobu pulled out the
memorial tablet for the dead marquis.) Acting in place of this tablet, I now
disown you" (228). An adoptive son confronts and casts out a woman who
has "adopted" a family and a status identity. He can even recruit an object
symbolic of *ie* lineage, the ancestral tablet, to express both his moral outrage
and his place in the line of fathers.[68]

As the dream progresses, however, there is a shift of focus to the realm

FIGURE 3.2   Akinobu wields the ancestral tablet, a symbol of family lineage, when
he confronts Kimie in her nightmare. An illustration from the newspaper serialization of
Chikyōdai. Source: *Osaka mainichi shinbun*, December 16, 1903.

of love as the engagement ring supplants the tablet as the primary image. Akinobu maintains a patriarchal stance by using a servant as his agent to retrieve the ring, but Kimie clings to sentiment when she steadfastly refuses to give it up:

> Akinobu turned to the manservant who had followed.
> (Akinobu) Tomura, take back that ring on Kimie's finger! She has no right to it.
> (Tomura) As you say, sir.
> The servant, who hadn't a single teardrop in his entire body, walked straight up to Kimie and tried to rob her of the aforementioned ring, which was dearer to Kimie than her own life. Kimie, so pale she seemed on the verge of fainting, quickly hid the hand with the ring under her right sleeve.
> (Kimie) Please, have some mercy. . . . I . . . I won't part from this ring even if I die!
> (Tomura) That won't do. Hand it over.
> (Kimie) No, at least this . . .
> Just when she felt herself being pushed to the ground in the midst of a struggle, Kimie abruptly awoke from her terrifying dream. (228)

Despite Akinobu's utter rejection of her and the robotic manservant's efforts to take the ring by force, Kimie fights to retain a symbol of love. In the world of her dreams, she is the one who continues to be motivated by love when all have coldly turned against her.

It is finally Kimie's determination—her stubborn refusal to capitulate, confess her crime, and seek some kind of absolution—that keeps her the dominant character in the novel. In the latter stages of the work, her situation looks increasingly hopeless. Takahama Isamu returns from America and begins a stalking campaign to make her live up to her promise to marry him. He pursues Kimie through countless letters and forced meetings, and threatens to expose her using evidence that he possesses regarding her treachery. He vows to kill her if, after all this, she still refuses to fulfill her promise. Despite the assault on her will, Kimie doggedly clings to her new social identity and to her hopes of marrying Akinobu; she bluffs, deceives, and pleads to keep Takahama from revealing her secret. And if all of this does not work, she is prepared to die pursuing her desires:

> But Kimie was a truly remarkable woman. Gaining a certain respite as the moment of crisis approached, there arose unbidden in her bold breast a determination that if it became unavoidable—and if it was at all possible—she would add a final flash of brilliance to the short and eventful history of her life. Since her crime was one that she herself had sought out and committed,

she was prepared to accept its consequences with a smile on her lips. The stubborn Kimie possessed the kind of pride that would make her show the spirit of a victor even in the face of the thing called "death" that human beings fear above all else. (227)

Kimie, then, becomes larger than life as she approaches the resolution of the fiction that she has set in motion. No sniveling second thoughts, no lingering doubts cloud her mind as she faces her fate. She will pursue her dreams of love and social ascendance until the very end. And, if she must reap the consequences of her villainy, she will do so bravely and gracefully. With such steadfast adherence to her own goals, Kimie manages to carry her ruse until the eve of her wedding day. When she is then finally cornered by a murderous, knife-wielding Takahama just short of reaching her dearest goal, she recognizes the inevitable, and "ceasing any resistance, closed her eyes before the knife descended" (235). The evil side of *Chikyōdai's* dualistic equation may be vanquished, but it remains unbowed. The energies of upward aspiration and desire that motivated Kimie may be blocked, but they are yet unspent.

The novel's conclusion renders an ambivalent judgment upon these energies in keeping with the social ambivalence of this melodrama. In the short coda after Kimie's death, Takahama goes to Akinobu and divulges all that he knows about Kimie's treachery. At this point, the truth of blood lineage stands revealed; Fusae and the other members of the family know that she, rather than Kimie, was Akisada's blood daughter. The stage is set for melodrama's climactic moment, when there occurs "a remarkable, public, spectacular homage to virtue, a demonstration of its power and effect."[69] What is called for in the melodramatic formula is a public unmasking of Kimie for the pretender that she was and the installation of Fusae as the daughter whose deportment and principles had always indicated her true identity. Nobility and virtue might have been fused in a dramatic celebration of status consistency. But Fusae herself forecloses such a possibility and argues for the continued conflation of identities:

> (Fusae) Akinobu, please, I beg of you to let Kimie be buried as she was, as my sister. This is the one thing I will ask for in my lifetime. Was it not my father's wish that a nursemaid's child be made a daughter of this noble house? That is the role I've been favored with until now. . . . (240)

Fusae gives identity and patriarchal authority a distinctive reading. She acknowledges that her identity and Kimie's *are* interchangeable, since that is what they have been proven to be. She has been a nursemaid's daughter and now she is the daughter of a marquis. For her, identity is not something fixed or natural, but rather something determined by human agency. Her interpretation of the mandate of patriarchal lineage stands in direct opposition to that expressed in Kimie's dream, where the patriarch (symbolized by his tablet) had cast out deception in favor of true blood lineage. Here, Akisada's wishes are interpreted to support the forging of new family ties and new status identities through adoption. At a moment in the melodrama when blood lineage might have been identified as the moral occult, the emphasis is shifted to virtue that acknowledges fluid status identities and recognizes sisterhood in the absence of blood ties. In the novel's final act of female agency, Fusae upholds the fictive family.

Chikyōdai's opposition of the upwardly mobile villain and the virtuous, victimized aristocrat resolves, rather messily, into a partial restoration of Kimie. This is underscored by the narrator: "Kimie died an untimely death because of crimes she had committed, but through the mercy of others she was buried, with due ceremony, as the daughter of a marquis. She was probably able to enter her eternal sleep without regrets" (240). The narrator goes on to tell us that, sometime later, Fusae was acknowledged as the marquis's "true daughter" (*shin no reijō*) and that she and Akinobu went on to "form the warmest and the most beautiful of homes" (240). The events surrounding these two lovers are so abundant that they "would make a volume of fiction by themselves," but the narrator refrains from going into them because that would be "superfluous." These events are "superfluous," perhaps, because what we have been reading is a story of boundless and indomitable social aspiration, the kind of story that can be appreciated by an audience of provincial "ladies."

What really is the "moral occult" in this family romance told as melodrama? The kind of resolution enacted in Freud's essay—where the son fantasizing about a more exalted family is recuperated as a lonely figure longing for an all-powerful father—is impossible for the ambitious heroine of *Chikyōdai*. She cannot be so easily reintegrated into either patriarchy or her own social origins. Driven by her aspiration for self-advancement, and unwilling to accede to the limitations imposed by gender, family, and status, Kimie is a loose projectile shooting through the social hierarchy. Along her one-way trajectory she reveals the arbitrariness of the state-sanctioned *ie* and subverts its investment in lineage. As much as *Chikyōdai* pays lip service to blood lineage and inherited social order, its confused "moral occult" also embraces female desire and the powerful social aspirations that coursed through Meiji culture. In its own way *Chikyōdai* participates in melodrama's "democraticization of morality and its signs." The contradictory ideological positions it takes may be interpreted as a sign of what Nowell-Smith calls "ideological failure." Such failure may actually indicate success at reflecting the ideological contradictions of an age.

FOUR

I'll Be Doing the Giving

The Traffic in Women and Men in *Gubijinsō*

In a scene in Natsume Sōseki's novel *Gubijinsō* (The poppy, 1907) one of the characters speaks with his stepmother, who asks him to take care of her daughter, his half-sister. Kōno Kingo's father has just died, and, according to the provisions of the Meiji Civil Code enacted in 1898, he is slated to become the head of the *ie* and heir to the family's property. Thus, when the stepmother asks Kōno to care for Fujio, his headstrong sister, she is asking him both to display the familial concern proper to a househead and to fulfill his legal obligation to financially support a dependant. Kōno's response shows his tortured view of the responsibilities he has inherited along with the family headship:

> "But . . . ," Kōno began to say, and then stopped abruptly. His mother waited for him to continue. Kōno uncrossed his arms and bent toward her until his chest almost touched the table. "But, mother," he said, "Fujio has no intention of being looked after by me."
>
> "That's hardly so." This time it was the mother who drew back and leaned against her chair.
>
> Kōno's face was absolutely still. He continued to speak in the same low voice. *"When you look after someone, that person has to have faith—that's a little funny. Using the word 'faith' makes it sound as if we're talking about god."*

Having gotten this far, Kōno stopped for awhile. His mother waited quietly, perhaps sensing that her moment had not yet come.

"In any case," Kōno continued, "there needs to be a kind of trust, where a person willingly wishes to be looked after."

"Well, there's no more to be said, if you've decided to abandon her . . ." This much Kōno's mother managed to get out calmly, but then her tone suddenly became more anxious as she said, "But Fujio is truly to be pitied. Please change your mind, and do something for her."

Kōno put his elbows on the table and pressed his hands against his brow. "But Fujio despises me. If I try to look after her, all we'll do is fight . . ."[1]

Kōno's ambivalence over the use of the word "faith" (*shinkō*) reveals something of the burdens of masculinity in the age of the *ie*. On the one hand, Kōno, who is a rationalist and an Imperial University graduate in philosophy, finds it odd to apply a term connoting religious belief to relations within the family; thus he quickly replaces "faith" with "trust" (*shin'yō*), a word more explicitly based in human interactions. On the other hand, his original choice suggests Kōno's understanding of what the *ie* requires for its proper maintenance. Kōno betrays the perception, unacceptable to his rationalist side, that the *ie* demands an unreasoned and unquestioned belief in the divine will of a male househead. His perception here is clearly connected to *ie* ideology, in which the family is a microcosm of a nation headed by a divine emperor.

Kōno's problem is that he knows he is a fallen god. Neither his stepmother nor his half sister observes his transcendent authority; they have even begun to plot to displace him. Put in other terms, Kōno faces a predicament because of his awareness of female subjectivity and agency. Kōno understands that the *ie* system requires the *willing* subordination of women. The question he confronts is whether or how he can assume the headship of the family when belief in the *ie* hierarchy has been shattered. Can patriarchal rule be restored when the women in the family have ceased to obey? Can moral conviction bring moral order to a family in disarray? Can the legal prescriptions inscribed in the Civil Code enforce moral behavior within the family?

The crisis of filiation faced by this would-be head of a House belongs to a set of interlocking family exigencies detailed in a novel serialized in the Tokyo and Osaka *Asahi shinbun* from June through October of 1907. *Gubijinsō* is famous for being Sōseki's first work of fiction after he took the unprecedented step of resigning a prestigious lectureship in English at Tokyo Imperial University in order to become a house writer for what was then a middle-brow newspaper. It is also famous for having earned its writ-er's disdain: just a few years after its publication, Sōseki refused an offer to translate it into German, saying that he would gladly have the work disap-pear were it not for the royalties it continued to yield.[2]

Although the initial public reception of *Gubijinsō* was enthusiastic, it soon fell into general critical disfavor, reflecting perhaps its author's jaun-diced view. The critical barbs were most often directed at two prominent features of the work. The first was its prose, partially written in a consciously elegant *bibun* style built out of rhythmic parallel repetitions, imagistically striking metaphors and similes, difficult and deliberately literary diction, and frequent allusions to Chinese and English literature. Although the grammar and syntax of this prose were largely drawn from modern rather than classical Japanese, its elaborate rhetoric soon struck readers as fussy and old-fashioned at a time when plainer, vernacular-based *genbun itchi* had al-ready been adopted by the vast majority of writers. The other feature critics attacked was the work's explicit handling of moral issues in a manner that struck many as being overly rigid, even Confucian. This criticism was con-nected to the perception that the novel's characters were cardboard cutouts of moral absolutes rather than credible human beings. The most influen-tial summing up of these two responses belongs to the Naturalist writer and critic Masamune Hakuchō who, in a critique written in 1927, famously crystallized the dominant reaction by saying that the work reminded him of a "modernized Bakin."[3] By alluding to Takizawa Bakin, the eighteenth-century writer of popular *gesaku* fiction, Hakuchō was expressing his con-tempt for both *Gubijinsō*'s prose, which he saw as labored and much too fond of aphoristic judgments, and its moral imagination, which he consid-ered ossified and conventional.[4] Although Hakuchō does not use the term, with his evaluation of the novel's morality he was clearly alluding to Bakin's oft-stated allegiance to the fictional paradigm of *kanzen chōaku*, or "the en-couragement of good and the chastisement of evil." These assessments have stuck, and the dominant critical reaction to the work has been to regard it as a failure, perhaps a result of Sōseki trying too hard to please his audience on his first outing as a professional writer. In this view, *Gubijinsō* embodies a schematic and pandering moral vision that Sōseki needed to get out of his system before achieving the exquisite moral complexity of his later works.

Although there were sporadic attempts to unseat this dismissive view,[5] it was not until the 1990s that there was a sea change in the approach to the work. The critique that brought a new seriousness to the consideration of

Gubijinsō was Mizumura Minae's brilliant essay, which analyzed the work as a site of conflict between a "world of men," a homosocial fictional universe with its roots in Chinese literature, and a "world of men and women," the realm of heterosexual relations that is the locus of the Western novel.[6] Mizumura argues that by attempting to hybridize what was incompatible, the text necessarily created fissures and contradictions that could not be resolved by any fictional logic. What logic could not accomplish needed to be ventured through language. In this regard, the exemplary figure is Fujio, whose only transgression, according to Mizumura, is to want to marry the man she loves. The threat that this desiring female poses to the homosocial order of the "world of men" can only be represented—and simultaneously contained—through the use of the *bibun* style to depict her as a femme fatale.[7]

My argument in this chapter follows Mizumura's in viewing *Gubijinsō* as a text defined by its contradictions. But I find literary antecedents a little bit closer at hand than Chinese fiction or Western novels. I draw connections between *Gubijinsō* and Meiji melodramatic fiction, which I have argued is a form marked by ideological contradiction. The circumstances of the novel's publication suggest the validity of such an approach: It would not have been lost on a canny author starting his professional career that the mega-hit newspaper novels of the previous decade had been melodramas. This possibility was suggested by Masamune Hakuchō, who had observed that "because *Gubijinsō* was Sōseki's first newspaper novel, the writer's frame of mind differed from that shown in his previous fiction written for magazines; his calculation is apparent."[8] Hakuchō had grouped *Gubijinsō* with two other newspaper melodramas—*Hototogisu* and *Konjiki yasha*—by referring to all three as *tsūzoku shōsetsu*, or popular novels.[9]

Hakuchō's categorization is anachronistic; *tsūzoku shōsetsu* is a term that did not achieve currency until the 1920s, when it arose as an antonym to *junbungaku* or "pure literature," a concept that was directly linked to the autobiographical, high-culture fiction known as *shishōsetsu* (personal fiction).[10] As I have argued in the Introduction, Meiji melodramatic novels inhabited a cultural field that preceded the division between high and low fiction, and thus their status as "popular" writing must be understood within their own historical context. Yet, despite Hakuchō's ahistoricism, we cannot but acknowledge that there is a deep connection between *Gubijinsō* and the newspaper melodramas that preceded it. *Gubijinsō* relies upon dramatic emplotment, with characters representing contrasting moral values clashing against each other in a sequence of emotionally extravagant scenes. It focuses on themes rooted in contemporary social morality—in this case the conflict between female desire and patriarchal succession. And it applies a polarized moral vision that drives the "evil" characters toward death, utter submission, or conversion. Like other examples of Meiji melodrama, it engages both male and female characters in a world of moral choices and consequences; women are major characters in this novel because they are regarded—in a way that contrasts sharply with their treatment in some of Sōseki's other work and many pieces of later high-culture fiction—as individuals with moral agency. Mizumura is fundamentally correct in pointing out that there is a conflict in *Gubijinsō* between a "world of men" and a "world of men and women." But this is also a feature of Meiji melodrama in general, which, as I have shown, reveals an oscillating fascination with homosocial alliances and heterosexual relations.[11]

Furthermore, *Gubijinsō* recycles some of the major motifs—among them orphanage and adoption—of earlier melodramas set in the family. It reiterates their key concerns by grappling with ideas about the family laid out in *ie* ideology, particularly the concept of succession, which occasions Kōno's tortured uncertainties in the quotation that opens this chapter. In fact, a lack of consideration of the problems of family succession is a blind spot in Mizumura's argument. By highlighting marriage—more specifically the process of choosing a marriage partner—as the central family conflict in *Gubijinsō*, Mizumura fails to fully account for succession as a point of contestation in the novel and as a key component in the family ideology of the Meiji period. In *Gubijinsō*, we need to think about the connections of marriage *and* succession. We need to recognize as well that *Gubijinsō*'s concern with family succession makes it a modern version of an *oiemono*. Like *Chikyōdai*, *Gubijinsō* is a work about the subterfuges of those who would wrongfully assume control of a family and the virtues of the defenders of lineage.

Keeping this in mind will give us a finer-grained understanding of the text's family dynamics and its gender politics. I will begin my investigation of the connections of marriage and succession in *Gubijinsō* by referring to a kinship chart—prepared by Sōseki before he wrote his novel—illustrating the carefully designed family structures that underlie the work's tensions. The chart makes clear that the characters in the novel were deliberately organized into multi-generational families poised at moments of transition in family headship. It also shows that such transitions are very much bound up with marriage and that marriage in *Gubijinsō* can be fruitfully analyzed according to the paradigm Gayle Rubin has famously called the "traffic in women." Other melodramas—for example, *Hototogisu* and *Konjiki yasha*—suggest that women are transacted to further male bonds, but the structuring of families in *Gubijinsō* makes this obvious. How obvious will become clear when we turn to Lévi-Strauss—the key theoretical lever for Rubin's intervention—to demonstrate how a potential "marriage by exchange" exists in the family structure of the novel. Defining the unconsummated "marriage by exchange" in the starkest terms will provide the basis for analyzing some of the contradictions that come to the fore as the novel attempts to reach ideological closure. One key contradiction involves female subjectivity and desire, which here manipulates the *ie* system's investment in adoption to attempt a coup within the family. Another contradiction concerns status and class differences, which are shown as threats to settled family hierarchies. My argument comes to focus on the central image of the gold watch once owned by Kōno's father, which functions as a multivalent signifier of masculine power, homosocial alliance, status privilege, female objectification, and female desire. The watch's destruction at the end of the novel shows that *Gubijinsō's* irresolvable ideological contradictions could only be ended by an act of violence.

SŌSEKI ON MORAL FICTION

Sōseki expressed his own views on moral fiction in an interview that was published in the literary journal *Bungeikai* in September 1906, that is, less than a year before the serialization of *Gubijinsō*. Although Sōseki ranges widely in the interview, commenting on such topics as the inception of his literary career and the vicissitudes of writing for serialization, he eventually comes to focus on the moral work of fiction. When he does this, he reveals himself to be a moralist who cannot conceive of writing fiction without a moral content.

> If one were to posit the writing of the usual novel, then it would involve depicting something of the web of social and human relations, and thus whatever one writes would need to be concerned with morality. Of course, in a short piece, just writing about the radiance of the moon or the coolness of the wind might allow appreciation of the beauty of the prose, but when it comes to a lengthy novel, one cannot but be concerned with the issue of morals. When a writer starts out to write a novel, he must provide black and white judgments (*kokuhaku no handan*) about the events in the work, and

he must evaluate virtue and vice (*zen'aku no hihyō*) in reference to the work's characters. . . . Literature involves the expression of preferences (*kōo*), and in the case of the usual novel, where these preferences involve morality, the writer's moral preferences must perforce become visible in the work. From this perspective, literature is still engaged in something akin to encouraging good and chastising evil (*bungaku wa yappari isshu no kanzen chōaku de aru*).[12]

We can see here the sensibility that would lead Sōseki to write melodramatic fiction. Not only does he regard the novel as a morally engaged form, he believes that its writer must express "black and white judgments." He shares the melodramatist's urge to provide polarized and binary moral evaluations. What is more, when he speaks of "encouraging good and chastising evil," Sōseki engages in a calculated and iconoclastic reference to the moral fiction of the Edo period. Calculated because, as discussed in the Introduction, *kanzen chōaku* was the credo of Takizawa Bakin, famous for his portrayals of samurai paragons locked in battle against the forces of evil. Sōseki thus gestures toward a well-known body of prior fiction based upon moral dualism. This reference, however, was iconoclastic because *kanzen chōaku* had been seemingly discredited by the time Sōseki began to write. It had been the bête noire of Tsubouchi Shōyō, who had lambasted it in *Shōsetsu shinzui* (Essence of the novel, 1885–86) as an abstract and artificial fictional framework that stood in the way of social observation and the accurate representation of human feelings. As I have observed earlier, Shōyō's view of Bakin's writing was actually quite ambivalent, but it was his dismissal of *kanzen chōaku* that had left a lasting impression. By the early years of the twentieth century, *Shōsetsu shinzui* had come to be widely revered as a foundational text of modern Japanese literature, especially by the Naturalists, sober students of lived experience and actual social conditions who regarded the work as an honored harbinger of their own fictional tenets. Thus, when Sōseki uttered the words *kanzen chōaku* in 1906, the year that witnessed Naturalism pushing to the forefront of the Japanese literary world, he was thumbing his nose at one of the verities of the moment. When he said that literature was still engaged in *kanzen chōaku*, he was deliberately tweaking the sensibilities of those who thought that fiction needed to move beyond the explicit consideration of moral issues. In a sense, Sōseki had preempted the criticism of Masamune Hakuchō, a writer who got his start as a Naturalist and who would twenty years later call him a "modernized Bakin." Sōseki was a believer in moral fiction, who could ironically use an archaic term to point to his own literary sensibilities.

Just how ironic he is becomes apparent as Sōseki presses on to illustrate, in concrete terms, his idiosyncratic views on *kanzen chōaku*:

> Even if an author were to write something that might commonly be called an endorsement of wrongdoing, showing sympathy toward a character who had violated socially accepted morality, this too is the expression of a person's preferences (*kōo*), and from that person's perspective involves encouraging good and chastising evil. For example, a character in a novel commits murder. Murder is generally considered wrong, and thus it would certainly be encouraging good and chastising evil if one were to write so that the reader of the novel concludes that killing is reprehensible. But there may well be a writer who thinks that a given person in a given situation might have no other choice but to commit murder, that it's perfectly fine for him to do this. Such a writer might write about a murder committed under certain circumstances so that a reader would feel no horror, would in fact want to go out and kill someone. This too is fine: for the writer in question this constitutes encouraging good and chastising evil. Another writer might come forward and use his pen to say murder is bad, but there are issues therein that demand sympathy. The crime itself deserves hatred, but the person committing it is to be pitied. I have no objection to this. It, too, encourages good and chastises evil in its own way.
>
> I would be happy taking any of these three approaches. I just want to encourage good and chastise evil in a way that does not embarrass my conscience. I might stand against socially accepted morality in some instances; and there may be times when I indicate that standard morality is morality as it should be. And there may be yet other instances when I write simultaneously that socially accepted morality is correct, but that there is something worthy of admiration in a person who violates it. In short, I want to write in a way that does not betray my perceptions.[13]

It turns out that Sōseki's version of *kanzen chōaku* is considerably different from Bakin's. Sōseki refuses any morality that is transcendent or universal. From the start, he is aware that morality is a matter of "preference"; moral principles are deeply personal, and thus contingent and situational.[14] Sōseki's statement here resonates to a certain extent with Peter Brooks's observation that in melodrama, a mode that arises after epistemic rupture, "mythmaking could now only be individual, personal; and the promulgation of ethical imperatives had to depend on an individual act of self-understanding that would then . . . be offered as the foundation of a general ethics."[15] Sōseki's distinctive approach to melodrama emphasizes the personal nature of morality, while resisting a connection to a general ethics. *Kanzen chōaku* here means only that a writer engages moral issues in a way that honors his conscience. There is room for a writer's morality to oppose "social" or "standard" morality. A text can endorse murder and still epitomize "encouraging good and chastising evil." Moreover, Sōseki's moral vision eschews abstraction or purity. Because his morality is anchored in personal sentiment rather than logic, it can embrace contradiction: a text can simultaneously uphold socially accepted morality and sympathize with those who violate it. As a moralist and a melodramatist, then, Sōseki would not be afraid of a little "ideological failure."

THE FAMILY MELODRAMA

An intriguing set of scribblings found among Sōseki's notes from 1907 suggests that family structure was uppermost in the writer's mind as he began to plan *Gubijinsō*. These scribblings contain a fair facsimile of an anthropologist's kinship chart in which characters are identified by letters of the alphabet (see Figure 4.1). The chart is accompanied by an outline of chapters in which the same letters are used to designate the major characters appearing in each chapter.[16] I will use the chart to illustrate each major character's place in the interdependent family relations portrayed in the novel. And, as I do so, I refer frequently to the Meiji Civil Code, because among the works I discuss *Gubijinsō* most clearly shows families negotiating within and with the state's juridical prescriptions.[17] Before speaking about specifics, however, there are some general observations that can be made on the basis of the chart, which arranges the main characters into three family groups and lays out the most important inter-familial linkages. First, the chart shows the novel's concern with two generations. The strong vertical and horizontal lines that bind these families indicate that the novel will deal with both the inter-generational issues of descent or succession and with the intra-generational issue of marriage. Second, the novel's engagement with gender is made clear by the circling of the letters designating female characters (B = Kōno's stepmother, E = Fujio, H = Sayoko).[18] Finally, there is a repeated pattern of single-parent families in the first generation.[19] The two families on the wings are headed by widowers, and the central family has two deceased members (indicated by the character for "death"), a man and his first wife, leaving only the widowed second wife alive. If the presence of a husband and a wife in each generation is the norm, these families are incomplete or broken. The repetition here indicates an emphasis on families

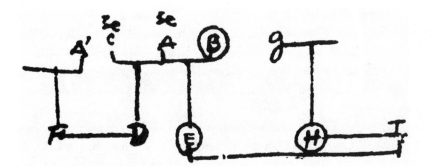

FIGURE 4.1   Kinship chart used in planning *Gubijinsō*, found in Sōseki's notes from 1907. Source: *Sōseki zenshū*, vol. 13 (Tokyo: Iwanami Shoten, 1966), p. 296.

in transition, families at a stage when members of the older generation are being claimed by death and where younger members are being called upon to assume their adult places.

The most complex family structure belongs to the central family in the chart and in the novel, the Kōnos, who are designated by the initials A through E. The chart shows that this family contains two separate lines of descent because the father in the family had married twice, producing a son by his dead first wife and a daughter by his second. The Kōnos are an upper-class family, who had been headed by a senior foreign service officer posted abroad.[20] The very recent death of the father, designated as "A" in the kinship chart, is clearly of great significance. The novel begins just after his death (the family is still waiting for his belongings to be sent back to Japan), and his demise sends his introspective son, Kōno Kingo, into gloomy and obsessive musings about the role of death as the single certain determinant that overwhelms all human desires ("Death is the only truth," he says [22]). The father's death—more precisely, the loss of the paternal authority that would support untroubled filiation—lies behind the complications that will ensue as the family confronts the issues of succession and marriage that form the foundation for the novel's plot.

Succession has arisen as a problem because Kōno has refused to assume the responsibilities of the new head of the family. Kōno (shown as "D" on the chart) is the child of the senior Kōno and his first wife (C); as the firstborn son, he is required, under the provisions of the Meiji Civil Code, to assume the headship of the family, inherit its wealth, and care for its dependents. As we have seen, however, this filiative destiny is challenged by his stepmother (B) and his half-sister, Fujio (E), who question his authority and have designs of their own upon the family fortune. Because he is intelligent enough to know that the *ie* institution is built upon faith and belief—as well as too sensitive to think of the *ie* as being organized by brute exercises of power—Kōno finds himself immobilized when he runs into the opposition mounted by his stepmother and his sister.

Marriage is an issue because Fujio refuses to marry the partner her father has picked for her. Although the marriage "promise" made by her father was set forth in the most ambiguous terms imaginable (we will return later to the specifics of this ambiguity), her brother expects her to honor her father's wish. Fujio, however, wants to be the one to choose the man that she marries. The product of a bourgeois upbringing, she wants to marry someone who will understand her need for romance and "poetry" in her life. A headstrong young woman, she also wants a husband who will be acquiescent to her wishes. The provisions of the Civil Code impinge upon her decision in a number of ways. Although this is only implied in the novel, the Civil Code required that members of an *ie* gain the consent of its head before entering into marriage; thus Fujio needs to have her brother's permission in order to marry. The economic implications of the Civil Code's provisions are much more directly addressed. The Code famously established male primogeniture as the ruling principle for family inheritance. This means that upon his father's death all of the family's wealth passed into Kōno's hands. (The narrator provides an inside view showing the stepmother's keen awareness of this reality: "One problem was the family property. Now, four months after her husband's death, it had naturally fallen into Kingo's possession" [224].) As the household, Kōno is legally obligated to support Fujio as long as she is a member of his *ie*. But once she marries and joins another *ie* this obligation ceases; Kōno will no longer be required to offer any further support, although he can if he so wishes. This is the context for the mother's plea that Kōno "do something" for Fujio. Her wish is that, instead of cutting Fujio off entirely, Kōno provide assistance to allow Fujio to maintain her accustomed standard of living.

The mother's plea also has a strong component of self-interest. A believer in the primacy of blood and therefore a woman obsessively aware that Kōno is not her birth child, she has never had close ties to her stepson. The Civil Code's provisions on inheritance mean that she, too, along with Fujio, has no direct access to the family wealth; she is in a situation where she must now depend on her distant stepson for economic support. How much better it would be, she thinks, if Kōno would settle a substantial amount of money on Fujio and she could go to live with her biological daughter instead.

Kōno's reluctance to formally assume the headship, in fact, opens the doors to an even more attractive, though problematic, proposal. The Civil Code, which contained numerous provisions to secure *ie* continuity, prohibited any *ie* from being headless, and, if Kingo were to truly abandon the headship, the opportunity would arise to adopt a male successor who would marry Fujio according to the *mukoyōshi* pattern (the legal term used for such adoptions in the Civil Code is *nyūfu*). This possibility illustrates how intimately marriage and succession are connected in the Civil Code and the family dynamics of *Gubijinsō*. These two crucial elements of family continuity are intertwined, and this means that the consequences of marriage upon succession, as well as the reverse, must always be carefully gauged. With the right calculations, the potential exists for the mother to choose a fitting husband for Fujio, acquire a son-in-law more manageable than her moody stepson, and secure the family wealth. The *ie* would, under this scenario, be effectively continued along a maternal line, with a consequent effect upon family power dynamics. Only one real problem constrains Kōno's stepmother—a woman concerned about appearances, she does not want to risk the social disapproval that would ensue if she were to push out the *ie*'s rightful heir. The biggest puzzle she faces is how to displace Kōno without obviously having had a hand in it.

This problem is made all the more difficult because of the Kōnos' ties with the Munechikas, who are distant paternal relatives and longtime family friends. If Kōno is to be replaced, this needs to be justified to the Munechikas. The son in the family, Munechika Hajime, is Kōno Kingo's best friend and can be expected to leap to his defense. A further complication is that Munechika is the man to whom Fujio has been "promised." Fujio, however, dislikes the plain-spoken and morally righteous Munechika, whom she finds stupid, loutish, and totally lacking in the "poetic" sensibilities she desires in a husband. The proposed union, then, is already problematic, but it also raises difficulties for any plan to change the line of succession in the Kōno family; if Fujio is married to Munechika (who is his family's only son and heir) she becomes a member of his *ie*, and thus unavailable to participate in any modification of succession in her own natal family.

The way the Munechikas are presented on the kinship chart raises some important questions. First, the senior Munechika is marked as "A[1]," repeating the designation used for Kōno's father (A) with the addition of a superscripted numeral. The semiotic doubling here is suggestive in several ways. "A" is the first letter in the alphabet and speaks to the primacy of these fathers. There is at least an implication of confident patriarchies, where alpha males exercise (or exercised) proper authority. We might also infer a reference to temporal order, in the sense that these fathers were founders of their families in the Meiji historical context, where families needed to be (re)established amidst social transformations. Finally, there is an implication of some sort of association or overlapping—either in terms of intimate friendship, or shared values and social roles. Perhaps it is not going too far to see the senior Munechika (A^1) as a stand-in for the confident father-figure missing from the Kōno family.

It is significant, moreover, that the semiotic doubling does not cross generational boundaries. In other circumstances, it might be tempting for a maker of a kinship chart to repeat designations within a given family—for instance, to show the filiative link between a father and his successor son. Here, however, the powerful associations are intra-generational. This is not only true for the fathers, but for the sons as well. Critics have puzzled over the fact that Munechika (F) and Kōno (D) are the only male pair joined by a horizontal line, which elsewhere designates actual or potential marriages. Ochi Haruo even goes so far as to consider the possibility that "F" refers to Oito, Munechika's sister who eventually emerges as Kōno's future marriage partner.[21] But such speculations are foreclosed by the fact that "F" is uncircled, and by the chapter outline, in which the letter is listed in chapters where Munechika has a major role. The conclusion is inescapable that the horizontal line signifies a powerful homosocial relationship. Although the confident and decisive Munechika is temperamentally the opposite of the anguished and immobilized Kōno, they share a mutual affection, a common discourse based on status and education, a sense of sympathy, and finally (after some initial doubts on Kōno's part) a bond of trust. Theirs is a friendship, a moral alliance, of rare intimacy; the horizontal line uniting them is an indication of the strength of this male bond. The chart reveals that, in this novel, a homosocial bond stands alongside marriage as a determining intra-generational tie.

What then to make of the place of Oito in the story and her absence from the chart? She is by no means a minor character, and the fact that she is missing leads to some interesting speculations. She was apparently conceived at a later stage in the planning for the novel, and it seems, on the evidence of her qualities as a character, that she was constructed as a feminine counterpart to her hypermasculine brother. Oito is an image of female domesticity (true to her name, which literally means "thread," she is often shown with sewing in her hands) who shares with her brother a genuine devotion to Kōno. Although Oito hardly speaks with Kōno and does not have the university education that allows her brother and Kōno to share the same language, she is depicted as possessing an intuitive understanding exceeding her brother's knowledge of his friend. There is a scene in the novel where Munechika complains to his sister that his friend is stupid to even consider renouncing his fortune and the headship of his House (*jibun no zaisan o sutete waga ie o deru nan te bakagete iru* [346]). Oito immediately defends Kōno, saying that he is ready to step down because, by his nature, he desires neither wealth nor the authority of family headship. At this point, Munechika, struck by a revelation, says: "Oito, you're Kōno's true friend. You're a truer friend than me. I didn't know you had so much faith in him" (*sore hodo shinkō shite iru to wa omowanakatta* [348]). Munechika defines his sister's faith in his friend here by using the word *shinkō*, the very term that had given Kōno pause when he spoke of the necessary ingredients for the successful functioning of an *ie*. Oito, then, is someone who has faith in Kōno, someone who could accept him as a househead and thus provide the emotional logic for his succession. Munechika picks up on this immediately and goes off on a mission to persuade his friend to marry his sister. I will later comment further on the structure of kinship implied by a situation in which a man offers his sister to a friend or kinsmen, whose sister he in turn hopes to marry. What I wish to note now is another instance where marriage is entwined with succession.

The final family group in the kinship chart ties together Inoue Kodō (g), his daughter Sayoko (H), and Ono Seizō (I). Kodō is the only character on this chart represented by a lower-case letter; this designation is used, perhaps, because he is a diminished father, caught in a social and economic decline. Although he had once been a man of consequence and a teacher (presumably of the Chinese classics, given his sensibilities), he is now retired and barely managing to make ends meet. A thin wraith of a man afflicted with a persistent cough, he is constantly portrayed amidst shadows and darkness. This darkness afflicts, as well, his daughter Sayoko (whose name literally means "night"), a woman who, while sweet and devoted, seems too wan and retiring to survive in the glare of the Meiji present.

Ono's place on the chart reflects the destabilizing role that he plays in the novel. An orphan and a person of uncertain parentage, he is located on the margins, the only member of the second generation not tied to a line of descent. Ono is a kind of free agent, someone not fully integrated into the networks of responsibilities and obligations attendant upon *ie* membership. This relative freedom has played a role in Ono's past relationship with Kodō. In an arrangement that resembles Shigizawa Ryūzō's support of the young Kan'ichi in *Konjiki yasha*, Kodō had taken the smart but needy young man into his home and had helped him gain an education. As a result of this affiliation, an understanding had grown between Kodō and Ono that the latter would eventually marry Sayoko and help support the older man; this understanding is reflected in the horizontal line connecting Sayoko with Ono. By the time of the novel, Ono has completed his education, graduating from the Imperial University, and Kodō has moved from Kyoto to Tokyo expecting that the earlier expectations will now be fulfilled.

The lowest horizontal line on the chart, connecting Fujio and Ono, shows the threat he presents to well-ordered plans for marriage and succession. This long horizontal line, connecting a daughter of the family at the center with an individual at the margins, parallels another line that already exists and has to skirt Sayoko along the way; there is more than a suggestion of the illicit and of overreaching. Many of the same qualities that make Ono attractive as an addition to the family of Kodō and Sayoko make him attractive to Fujio and her mother (especially because they are unaware of his previous understanding with Sayoko). As an unattached man, he is someone who can marry Fujio and be adopted to replace Kōno and succeed to the family headship. As a university graduate, and one who has received the silver watch presented by the emperor to the best students in the graduating class, Ono is a man of clear ability who has risen in the status hierarchy; as a scholar of literature, he is someone who comprehends the "poetry" that Fujio desires. His combination of ambition and ethical malleability means that he can be recruited to play a part in a female plot to undermine a legally prescribed pattern of male succession.

THE EXCHANGE OF WOMEN

A slight detour into Claude Lévi-Strauss's theories on kinship will help to clarify the structures of family threatened by Ono's presence. Various critics have suggested that the marriage arrangements attempted in *Gubijinsō* constitute transactions in women carried out by men.[22] But no one I know of has credited the concept of the "exchange of women" to Claude Lévi-Strauss, who makes it the lynchpin in his analysis of kinship; I make this connection explicit because Lévi-Strauss's ideas hold implications for thinking about the ideologies and hierarchies set forth in the novel.[23] In Lévi-Strauss's formulation, the prohibition against incest (which he equates with mandatory exogamy) is "the fundamental step because of which, by which, but above all in which, the transition from nature to culture is accomplished."[24] This is so because reciprocal gift giving is the underlying motor for social organization, and because women, when they are made available to others through the incest taboo, are the most valuable commodity that can be exchanged. Such an analysis leads to a view of marriage as an "exchange of women," a view neatly summarized in an often-quoted passage:

> The total relationship of exchange which constitutes marriage is not established between a man and a woman, where each owes and receives something, but between two groups of men, and the woman figures only as one of the objects in the exchange, not as one of the partners between whom the exchange takes place. This remains true even when the girl's feelings are taken into consideration, as, moreover, is usually the case. In acquiescing to the proposed union, she precipitates or allows the exchange to take place; she cannot alter its nature. This view must be kept in all strictness, even with regard to our own society, where marriage appears to be a contract between persons.[25]

In this view, the key organizing force in kinship is the relationship forged between men through the exchange of women. As the last sentence in the passage indicates, Lévi-Strauss intends his analysis to go beyond "primitive peoples" and extend to all societies. Wherever the incest prohibition makes women available beyond a given group, male social bonds are being constructed through the exchange of women.

A number of observations become possible when we return, with these ideas in mind, to *Gubijinsō*, a novel in which potential marriages are frequently designed to seal male relationships.[26] When Kodō pursues a marriage between Ono and his daughter, he is not only looking out for her future but also insuring a permanent connection between himself and his most gifted pupil. A marriage between Munechika and Fujio would reinforce the male friendships between both the fathers and the sons in the two families. Lévi-Strauss's theories, however, are most specifically helpful in understanding the late introduction of Oito into the family schema depicted in Sōseki's kinship chart. While Lévi-Strauss is clear that a relationship of exchange exists even when women are made available to an "ever-open collectivity," Oito's presence makes possible the most paradigmatic of his examples, that of "marriage by exchange," where there is explicit reciprocity in the trading of one woman for another. The structuring of the Munechikas and the Kōnos as each having a male and a female in the second generation establishes an ideal situation where Fujio can be exchanged for Oito, sealing the affection between the fathers and strengthening the bond between Kōno and Munechika, who would become brothers-in-law doubly counted.[27] Oito, then, comes into being as a female object to deepen homosocial ties. Her presence in the novel signals the potential for a perfect exchange that is wrecked by Fujio's rebellion.

Lévi-Strauss's theoretical thrust can sometimes take on what Eve Sedgwick has called a "celebratory" tone;[28] he can be read to say that the exchange of female objects is the necessary precondition for all cultures. In an incisive feminist intervention, however, Gayle Rubin uses his formulations as a springboard for theorizing and critiquing the implications of a society built around the "traffic in women." Her key ideas, working off of Lévi-Strauss, are summarized in the observation that "at the general level, the social organization of sex rests upon gender, obligatory heterosexuality, and the constraint of female sexuality."[29] These implications can be logically drawn. If kinship systems (and social organization) are based upon the exchange of women, then gender must function to divide those who do the exchanging and those who are exchanged. Rubin observes that, whatever their objective differences, men and women do not constitute binary opposites: "From the standpoint of nature, men and women are closer to each other than either is to anything else—for instance, mountains, kangaroos, or coconut palms."[30] The social construction of men and women into mutually exclusive categories responds to the hierarchies inherent in the system of exchange. The second requirement, obligatory heterosexuality, underlies Lévi-Strauss's kinship system for obvious reasons: same-sex sexuality, either male or female, disrupts the smooth union of men and women in marriage. The requirement of heterosexual exogamy prohibits other kinds of sexual contact, including those between members of the same sex. Finally, the requirements of a system of marital exchange controlled by men favor a passive, pliant female sexuality:

> It would be in the interest of such a system if the woman in question did not have too many ideas of her own about whom she might want to sleep with. From the standpoint of the system, the preferred female sexuality would be

one which responded to the desire of others, rather than one which actively desired and sought response.[31]

Rubins's extrapolations from Lévi-Strauss resonate with the world of *Gubijinsō*. First, like so many Meiji melodramas, *Gubijinsō* builds its plot upon an exaggerated division of genders.[32] At key points in the work, individual characters resolve either into a "man" or a "woman," emphasizing how clearly they reflect masculine or feminine essences. This is what happens, for instance, when the narrator provides a gloss on a conversational give-and-take between an incisive Fujio and an embattled Ono:

> A woman of twenty-four is the equal of a man of thirty. She knows neither right nor wrong; much less does she know why the world turns and why it comes to rest. From the start, she has no idea where she stands and what role she will play in the infinite stretch of the grand stage of history. Only her tongue is clever. A woman cannot stand up before the realm, nor can she deal with the nation, nor take action with a crowd before her eyes. A woman is only equipped with the skill to deal with just one person. When the battle is one on one, it is always the woman who wins. The man always loses. A woman flutters about happily trapped in the cage of materiality and eating the seeds of the tangible. Anyone who tries to out-sing her in the tiny world of the cage is sure to fail. Ono was a poet. And because he was a poet, he had his head half stuck in the cage. When he tried to sing, he was a splendid failure. (32)

For the narrator of *Gubijinsō*, Fujio is a character whose qualities are overdetermined by her femaleness. A "woman" is here described as being essentially immoral and irrational, unaware of her historical positionality. She is unequipped to function in any public setting, but her glibness and philistinism make her a fierce canary in the private confines of the home. Although mountains, kangaroos, and coconut palms are not addressed here, a woman is clearly closer to a canary than to a man. The metaphor of the bird at the end of the passage suggests she is meant to be owned and caged by a higher species. We should not miss that this other species is being defined, by contrast, as moral, rational, historically conscious, and prepared to engage the outer world. Through its language and rhetoric *Gubijinsō* produces a gender system built upon polar opposition.

Gubijinsō also forcefully reflects Rubin's second point regarding obligatory heterosexuality, principally in the way it depicts the male friendship between Munechika and Kōno. Although there is no overt sexual contact between these two men, theirs is the most intimate human relationship in the novel. Built upon affection, mutual sympathy, and a shared ideology, their alliance allows for the frank discussion of issues both public (foreign relations, for instance) and private (mutual marriage opportunities). At the beginning of the novel, they are portrayed as traveling companions who go everywhere together, eat the same food, and sleep in the same room. That they are represented as a couple on the kinship chart is no accident. One way to understand the late introduction of Oito is to observe that she allows for this preeminent relationship to evolve in a heterosexual framework. When Munechika offers Oito to Kōno as a "true friend," he presents a female extension of himself and thus allows for a proper triangulation of close male relations. In Sōseki's other novels there is a tendency to view strong male-male ties as a dangerous developmental stage on the way toward an inevitable heterosexuality. The love triangles found in *Sorekara*, *Mon*, and *Kokoro*—in which close friends end up betraying each other over a woman—can be understood as expressions of the powerful and treacherous currents of feeling that run through this transition. Munechika's capacity to offer his sister in place of himself allows the gentle shepherding of his friend into an obligatory heterosexual relationship while keeping the homosocial tie intact. His affection for Kōno can now continue, nicely mediated through the exchange of the sister-wife.

Rubin's third point—that the exchange of women requires the constraint of female sexuality—is readily demonstrated by comparing Fujio with Oito and Sayoko. The latter two, presented as models of feminine deportment, show little in the way of sexual desire or agency. Oito's loyalty and fresh-faced domesticity qualify her to be a future *ryōsai kenbo* or "good wife and wise mother," but there is nothing seductive about her. Sayoko is beautiful, but her beauty is consistently associated with images of cold and darkness. Both women are ready to marry men approved by their male relations. When Munechika is in the process of offering Oito to Kōno and suggests to his father that they might do well to inquire what she thinks, the father simply replies, "There's no need to ask her" (336). Although Munechika does eventually consult his sister, this does not change the fact that she is a woman who can be readily traded by men. Fujio, however, is another matter. She is aware of her effect on men, and she brings all of her considerable resources to bear on Ono. She is the active partner in expressions of desire: "Love's object is a plaything, a sacred plaything. A regular toy exists only to be played with. But the rule for playthings in love is that each plays with the other. Fujio played with men. But not for a bit would she allow herself to be played with. Fujio was the queen of love" (211). Fujio, then, is not an object to be toyed with or exchanged; she expects to be the agent of her own desires. The constraint of this woman's sexuality consumes much of the plot of *Gubijinsō*.

MORAL POLARITIES

Rubin's intervention helps clarify *Gubijinsō*'s melodramatic qualities, for she helps us see that the novel employs moral polarity to narrate the "traffic in women." Put simply, the work tries to judge as virtuous those who observe gender roles and sexualities supporting a "traffic in women"; those who do not are condemned as evil. It is this dynamic that explains the text's heavy-handed and exaggerated effort to pass judgment upon Fujio. In her article on *Gubijinsō*, Mizumura points out that compared to the typical *dokufu* or femme fatale—who lies, cheats, steals, seduces and kills in order to satisfy

FIGURE 4.2   Decorative image from the newspaper serialization of *Gubijinsō*. Although the figure here does not directly represent any character, the partially nude woman resting in a poppy—depicted in an art-nouveau-like style—suggests Fujio's exotic, intoxicating, and morally disorienting seductiveness. Source: *Asahi shinbun*, Tokyo edition, October 22, 1907.

her desires—Fujio's transgressions seem nearly nonexistent. Fujio's "only crime is to choose a man who will do what she wants."[33] Yet the text insists on associating her with the image of the snake, with a spider waiting in its web, with Cleopatra, and with Circe ready to turn men into willing beasts. Mizumura locates the portrayal of Fujio as evil—a portrayal wrought in the elegant language of *bibun*—in the text's own anxiety about having brought together two incompatible fictional worlds. My own inquiries take me in the direction of asking what happens when the kinship structure adumbrated by Lévi-Strauss intersects with the moral dualism of melodrama.

By flouting the constraint of sexuality, Fujio, whom the narrator frequently calls a "willful woman" (*ga no onna*), makes herself an unwilling object of exchange. Her refusal to cooperate with the smooth circulation of goods and good will jeopardizes the future relationship of the Munechikas and the Kōnos. It also threatens family continuity by preventing the formation of a married couple to succeed Munechika's father and deceased mother and undertake the reproduction of children for future generations. In her own natal family, Fujio's eagerness to choose a husband upsets the order of succession and threatens to install a weak parvenu as an alternate head of the family. By refusing to be exchanged, Fujio seeks, along with her mother, to establish female power as the source of authority within the family. If we accept Lévi-Strauss's hypothesis that the giving of live female gifts stands at the point of origin of culture and social organization, then female power and agency, especially female power expressed as sexual agency, stands against order, institutions, families, and morality. Is this not, then, a kind of "evil"?

It is entirely consistent with the moral polarities of the text that Fujio's mother, too, is judged to be evil, perhaps even more so than Fujio herself because she calculates more explicitly. Instead of leaving her daughter to be properly exchanged by men, the mother encourages Fujio's pursuit of Ono in order to serve her own ends. When Kōno doodles as he speaks to his stepmother, he draws a pattern of interlocking scales, the iconographic representation of a snake. Since the value of the snake in the Japanese symbolic universe is not merely that of deviousness, but deviousness in the service of female sexual desire,[34] we see Kōno judging his mother as a source of female vice.

It is also consistent that women who are willing objects of exchange are portrayed as sources of virtue. Sayoko, who cleaves to the idea of marrying Ono—the man chosen by her father—despite every indication that he has grown away from her, receives staunchly sympathetic treatment from the narrator. She also gets her man in the end. The woman who shines the brightest as the novel proceeds, however, is Oito. She is a character whose virtue determines her value as an object of exchange. This is most clearly articulated by her brother, the male prepared to exchange her. Munechika gives his sister the following extravagant evaluation when he races over to Kōno's house to convince him to make Oito his wife:

> "Oito is your true friend. Even if your mother or Fujio misunderstand you, even if I misjudge you, even if all of Japan were to persecute you, you can be assured about her. Oito is neither schooled nor talented, but she understands your worth. She knows what is in your heart. Oito may be my sister, but there's no denying that she's a remarkable woman. She is a precious woman. There's no chance of her becoming degraded, even if she's left without money. —Kōno, please take Oito for your wife. You can leave your house if you want. You can go into the mountains. It doesn't matter where you go or how you wander. Whatever the case, just please take Oito with you. —I've made a serious promise to her. If you don't listen to me, I won't be able to face my sister again. I'll have killed my only sister. Oito is a precious woman, a woman with truth in her. She's honest. She'll do anything for you. It would be a waste to kill her." (378)

In a moment of exorbitant emotion and hyperbolic expression, Munechika speaks in the voice of male love, achingly crying out its desire through proposing a transaction in female virtue. For this transaction to have meaning, the woman exchanged must be invaluable, she must be truly precious (*tattoi*). And she is so because she is a woman who gladly places her future in her brother's hands, a woman prepared to believe in Kōno no matter what.

The reference at the end of the paragraph to killing will puzzle those who read it out of context. It can also puzzle readers of the novel, for nowhere does the dependable Oito speak a word about dying if she cannot marry Kōno. The hyperbole is understandable only if we remember that a similar overheated rhetoric is at work throughout the text. When Kōno contemplates the effect of Fujio on a woman like Sayoko he says: "When a Fujio appears, she kills five women like the one we saw last night" (248). And when Kodō hears Ono's excuse that he cannot marry Sayoko because he is too busy working on his dissertation, the question he poses is whether Ono "intends to gain a doctorate even if it means killing another person" (385). There is a lot of killing of virtuous women being contemplated. All of this killing must be placed in the context of the moral dualism of the melodrama. Within this world of exaggerated sentiments, the frustration of virtue is metaphorically construed as murder. Such a logic requires hyperbolic acts of retribution against "evil"; it justifies a violent trajectory that leads to the actual killing of Fujio.

Among the men, it is Munechika who stands for virtue. He is the one who articulates and lives by the manly code of *majime*. This might be translated as "honesty," but the text's understanding of the term is broader, implying a state of being where a man is in touch with the Truth and thus capable of acting with sincerity and moral conviction. The certitude with which Munechika discourses upon *majime* makes Ono eventually think of him as someone who reveals the "true character of men" (*danshi no honryō* [253]). This male paragon is the ideal trafficker of women. Not only does Munechika display a relentless masculinity, he is able to maintain a resolute heterosexuality, thanks to the triangulation of desire allowed by his sister. As a counterpart to the ideal female with a pliant or passive sexuality, he is active in making known his desire for Fujio. He approaches his friend Kōno on a number of occasions to declare that he wants the marriage promise to be fulfilled. In conversation with his father, he voices his determination to use his own resources to implement the "marriage by exchange" that the prior generation had left ambiguous. He finally backs up his words with action, masterminding the entirety of the dramatic conclusion of the novel, in which Oito is united with Kōno and an unrepentant Fujio is driven to death. Munechika, then, proves his moral worth by ensuring that the exchange of women takes place insofar as the situation allows, by causing the destruction of "evil" and setting the world aright.

The two other male characters in *Gubijinsō* prove somewhat problematic to analyze according to standards of male virtue derived from trafficking in women. Although the trajectory of the novel encourages us to view both Kōno and Ono as temporarily lost men reintegrated into the homosocial order through Munechika's moral influence, elements of their portrayals make such an interpretation too reductive. Both possess qualities that make them sites of ideological contradiction. To take Kōno first, we can understand some of the complications implicit in his portrayal by noting that he plays the key melodramatic role of "virtue misprized" and victimized.[35] The text carefully grooms Kōno to fulfill this role: Although Kōno's inability to exercise the powers of a househead stems from a sensitive man's paralyzing awareness of the opposition offered by his half-sister and his stepmother, the latter succeeds in presenting his paralysis as a kind of mental illness. Even Munechika had believed that Kōno was ill; he had agreed to go on the trip to Kyoto as a means of giving his friend a change of scenery. Through most of the novel, then, the man who most clearly sees the moral decay in his family—and suffers as a result—is thought by most of the others around him to be on the verge of madness. Virtue misprized finally declares itself in a moment of revelation when Kōno shows his real self to his best friend:

> "I'm superior to my mother. I'm wiser. More understanding. And I'm a better person than my mother."
>
> Munechika was silent. Kōno continued to speak.
>
> "When my mother asks me to remain in the House, what she really means is that she wants me to get out. When she tells me to accept my inheritance, what she means is for me to hand it over. When she says that she wants me to take care of her, she means that she loathes the idea. —That's why I'm going to go against her stated wishes, and actually give her what she wants. —You just wait. After I've left my House, she'll say that I left because of my shortcomings, and everyone will believe it. —I'm taking the step of sacrificing myself, and going along with their scheme."
>
> Munechika suddenly rose from his chair. He walked to the corner of the desk, rested his weight on an elbow, and peered downward into Kōno's face.
>
> "Have you gone mad?" he said.
>
> "I know I'm mad. —Behind my back, they've been calling me stupid and mad all this time."
>
> At that moment, tears fell from Munechika's large round eyes onto the volume of Leopardi open on the desk.
>
> "Why did you stay silent? All you had to do was send them packing." (376)

Here again is the urge to express all. Kōno declares his moral superiority in no uncertain terms—"I'm a better person," he says—and explicitly defines his own status as a previously silenced victim. The plot now only waits for his action-oriented friend to turn moral superiority into a victory for morality. The victim-hero whose virtue has been misrecognized will eventually be delivered from the clutches of female vice.

Munechika's response that Kōno should have sent his stepmother and his sister packing, however, points to a clear difference between Kōno and the poor, powerless victims often found in melodramas both in Japan and the West.[36] It says a great deal about *Gubijinsō's* class and gender values that the work assigns the role of "virtue misprized" to a male occupying a privileged social position. Kōno's own awareness of his advantages colors the summation he delivers when he berates his beaten stepmother after Fujio's death:

> "You wanted to give Fujio both the House and our property, didn't you? And so I offered them to you. But it was your failing that you always held me in suspicion and never trusted me. You weren't very pleased that I was in the House. And so I said that I would leave. But you wrongly thought I was saying this out of spite or something of the sort. You wanted to have Ono become Fujio's adopted husband, didn't you? You thought I would object, and so you sent me off to Kyoto and made sure that their relationship grew steadily closer in my absence. It's that kind of plotting that's wrong. Even when it came to the trip to Kyoto, you said both to me and to others that you were sending me off in order to help cure my illness. It's that kind of lying that's wrong. —If you'll just rethink such behavior then there's no particular reason for me to leave the House. I'm happy to take care of you for the rest of your days." (427)

The machinations of his stepmother and Fujio had been transparent to Kōno. While he may have seen the conflict in his household as a moral one, he was also very much aware of stratagems, of moves and countermoves. He reveals, in his tone and his final magnanimity, that he has had the upper hand in these struggles—and it is here that we see the consequences of having a male rather than a female play the role of "virtue misprized." Kōno may have moral force on his side, but he also possesses the juridical and economic advantages granted to him as a male householder. In the passage above, he indicates that he has at various times offered the *ie* and the family property to his stepmother and Fujio. It bears remembering that Kōno must first possess what he offers and that this fact of possession gives him enormous power no matter how beleaguered he seems at times. In another conversation with his stepmother, Kōno had explicitly said, "I have inherited the House. I am legally the successor" (314). According to the provisions of the Civil Code, this means that he has control of the family property and that he has right of approval over all marriages and adoptions undertaken by those in the *ie*.[37] The efforts of the stepmother and Fujio to disrupt the traffic in women, then, must unfold in a situation where Kōno has legal authority over them. Their plot can succeed only if Kōno *allows* it to succeed. Moreover, even if the stepmother had managed to pressure Kōno into giving up the headship, the Civil Code included a provision that permitted the relatives of a deposed householder to petition for his reinstatement.[38] The entire structure of homosocial alliances, represented in the novel by the

Munechikas, would likely have been brought to bear on the stepmother had she managed to proceed with her plans. *Gubijinsō*, then, is a novel in which relatively powerless forces of "evil" maneuver in a futile effort to gain some kind of advantage against the entrenched power of a househead and his allies. *Gubijinsō*'s privileged victim-hero creates the possibility for an ideological contradiction in which male social and economic power can be conflated with moral force.

ONO AND THE TRAFFIC IN MEN

The case of Ono Seizō requires extended consideration because he is the male character with the most complicated relationship to a morality built around the "traffic in women." If Kōno's portrayal muddles the moral framework of *Gubijinsō*, then the portrayal of Ono subverts it by laying bare the exigencies faced—in the name of morality—by a marginalized individual. This has a lasting impact because Ono stands at the center of the ethical contestations in the text. His availability and malleability allow Fujio and her mother to plot against a morality upheld by homosocial alliances. His conversion by Munechika foils the plot and brings on its disastrous end. As the one character who switches alliances over the course of the story, he represents the novel's most sustained engagement with the issue of moral agency. The ideological dualism of the text could have been left more distinct and unambiguous had this character been presented in strictly moral terms—as a man who makes the transition from evil to good. But, as Mizumura observes, Ono is never designated as "evil" in the same way that Fujio is. Although he is shown as weak and easily tempted, he is not turned through baroque rhetoric into a creature of malice, nor is he imagistically associated with snakes and spiders. Instead, his portrayal, the most detailed in the text, focuses upon his background and the traits it fostered. The narration of his origins is supplemented by the longest and most particularized inside views in the novel; the reader is provided with intimate access to the textures of experience of a man whose insecurity stems from his positionality.[39] In sum, the novel's approach to Ono is social as much as it is moral.[40] The former works to subvert the latter because it often shows that Ono's responses, if less than admirable, are also perfectly understandable; the contradictions between these two modes of understanding lead to ideological failure.

Let us begin, then, by examining how Ono appears in the first extended passage describing his background. The passage is a long one, and it requires analysis in stages:

> Ono was born in a dark place. Some people even say that he was illegitimate (*shiseiji*). Friends started to taunt him when he went off to school wearing a child's kimono. Dogs barked at him wherever he went. Then his father died. Ono, who was mistreated whenever he went out, no longer had a house (*ie*) to which to return. He had no choice but to depend on the kindness of others.
>
> A waterweed in the depths drifts in the darkness and knows nothing of the sunlight striking the shore, where the white sails pass close by. Whether it moves to the right, or whether it drifts to the left, it is at the mercy of the waves. The simplest thing is not to resist the waves. With time, one hardly notices them. There is no chance to ponder what the waves are made of. The question of why the waves single one out for a beating never arises. Even if it did, nothing could be changed. Fate is all there is, commanding one to stay in a dark place. And so one stays. Fate is all there is, telling one to drift morning and night. And so one drifts. Ono was a waterweed growing in the depths. (64–65)

In this account calculated ambiguity functions to render Ono doubly fatherless. The suggestion of his illegitimate birth is immediately tied to the social ostracism experienced by a bastard. The subsequent mention of his father's death is thus certainly odd, but it works to bring the father briefly into the picture only to remove him. It is clearly important to the narrative to overdetermine Ono's fatherlessness. There is also an implication that Ono grew up without a mother. That he is left homeless upon the death of the father means the woman who bore him is no longer in the picture. Ono, then, is perhaps a bastard by birth, but certainly an orphan by some point in his childhood. The text makes clear that he was victimized for his origins and faced grave material deprivation. A failure of filiation defines his place in the world.

The precise terms used to address illegitimacy and orphancy here deserve attention. *Shiseiji*, used interchangeably with the related term *shiseishi*, is a word of Meiji coinage written with characters that literally mean "self-born child."[41] These terms have legal implications. The Meiji Civil Code employs *shiseishi* to refer specifically to a child born out of wedlock who is not acknowledged by his or her father.[42] Thus, when the narrative uses *shiseiji* in reference to Ono, it emphasizes his lack of a legal paternity (whatever the reality may be about the presence of a father in his life). When the term *ie* occurs in the discussion of Ono's deprivations, the primary reference is to physical domicile. But the juridical sense of the word is at work as well, since the passage emphasizes Ono's social and familial placelessness. Although the Meiji Civil Code provided that a *shiseiji* could eventually enter the mother's *ie*,[43] Ono's mother is, as we have seen, purposely elided. He is presumably one of those unfortunate orphans who comprises an *ie* of his own.

Aside from the terms in which it discusses Ono's birth, the passage is also noteworthy for the way it employs images of darkness and drift. Although Mizumura is correct to point out that the prose used to represent Ono, written in vernacular-inspired *genbun itchi*, differs markedly from the baroque rhetoric used to conjure a deadly Fujio,[44] the language here is not without rhetorical flourish. Metaphor, image, concatenating diction, and repeated sentence structure emphasize the deprivations of an orphan's life and the passivity they have encouraged. Being a waterweed consigns Ono to a dark world of oscillating temporal stasis where all one can do is "drift morning and night." Human agency is erased in a world where the orphan is buffeted by necessity and bullied by fate. Even the capacity to examine the social bases for one's circumstances is lost: "The question of why the waves single one out for a beating never arises."

The passage we have been examining continues chronologically and describes the changes in Ono's circumstances as he makes his way to Kyoto, where Kodō takes him in, and subsequently to Tokyo, where his talents are rewarded:

> In Kyoto, he came under Kodō-sensei's care. From Kodō-sensei, he received a *kasuri* pattern kimono, his tuition of twenty yen a year, and occasional lessons on various books. He learned how to circumambulate under the cherry trees of Gion. He gazed up in awe at the emperor's calligraphy hung high at the Chion'in temple. And he started to eat a full portion of rice. The waterweed from the depths left the mud and finally started to float.
>
> Tokyo is a dazzling place. A person so blessed as to grow to be a hundred in the Genroku past actually has a shorter life than someone who lives for three days in the world of Meiji. Elsewhere, people walk on their heels. In Tokyo, they walk on their toes. They stand on their heads. They dart sideways. And the impatient ones come skipping along. In Tokyo, Ono spun around and around.
>
> When he opened his eyes after he was done spinning, his world had changed. He rubbed his eyes, but the changes were still there. Only when changes are for the worse does one think them strange. Ono proceeded without thinking. His friends said he was brilliant. His professors said his future was bright. At his lodgings, they called him Mr. Ono. Ono proceeded

without thinking. When he proceeded he received a silver watch from the emperor. The waterweed that had floated upward gained a white blossom on the surface. To the fact that it had no roots it was insensible. (65)

Ono's passage out of darkness occurs under the tutelage of Kodō, who clothes and feeds him, provides for his education, and even personally instructs him; in essence Kodō provides an affiliative family for the orphan. Under the older man's protection, Ono is initiated into national aesthetics (cherry-blossom viewing) and begins to function as an imperial subject (gazing in awe at the emperor's calligraphy). He also starts on a life of full consumption (by eating an adult's portion of rice). It is no wonder Ono agrees to eventually marry Sayoko, for this would gain juridical sanction for his fictive family.

In Kyoto and Tokyo, the stasis of Ono's childhood is replaced by gradually increasing movement and by temporal acceleration. But his continued lack of agency or intent is emphasized by the repeated circling of his movements (circumambulation, spinning). By noting the dazzling speed of time in Tokyo and the odd movements of its citizens, the narrator associates Ono's predicament with urban modernity's rootlessness and hyperstimulation. He calls attention to Ono's bewildered obedience to his circumstances by repeating twice that Ono proceeds "without thinking." The irony is that this unconscious forging ahead leads to the recognition of Ono's brilliance and the gift of the silver watch that the emperor annually awarded to Tokyo Imperial University's best graduates. Ono has come to possess a key symbol of *risshin shusse* without a real consideration of intent. The implication is that obliviousness is actually a key component to his success. Not thinking too much has allowed him to be academically superior and to be swept along by the quickening tides of his times.

The narrator's ironic tone and the final judgment that he delivers on Ono's insensibility certainly indicate that Ono embodies something less than virtue. Yet, if he is not virtuous, neither is he ruled by vice. He is a man whose weakness can be traced to his peculiar social background. Although gifted, he will be haunted by memories of an orphan's deprivations. Although ambitious, his moral sense will remain that of a creature whose life has been ruled by "fate."

These qualities dictate Ono's desires and preferences. His academic field is literature, and the narrator makes much of the fact that Ono is a "poet." In the world of this novel, the lyrical sensibility is associated with romantic yearning and a longing for sensual pleasure. The latter is given concrete expression in Ono's love for small luxuries. The desk in his boarding house is covered with a green cashmere throw, and upon it he has placed a bud vase of colored glass with a single red camellia. Ono is something of an aesthete, but even more he is a man seduced by bourgeois consumption and its promise of social status gained through the possession of material objects. He is partial to sharply cut suits and starched white cuffs. His accoutrements repeat what may be his favorite color; he wears gold-rimmed glasses and smokes gold-tipped Egyptian cigarettes. The narrator's account of Ono's fantasies clearly shows how these sensibilities mix with his yearning for Fujio and his wish for academic advancement; it also indicates how much these desires are edged by desperation:

> You would have to ask someone with a doctorate whether you become a doctor because you've written a thesis or whether you write a thesis in order to become a doctor. But, in any case, Ono had to write a thesis. An ordinary thesis wouldn't do; it had to be a doctoral thesis. Doctors were, among academics, the ones who boasted the most brilliant colors. Whenever Ono looked through his peephole to the future, the word "Doctor" blazed before his eyes in gold. Next to the word "Doctor," a gold watch hung from the heavens. And beneath the watch there swayed a garnet watchfob, a red flame that pierced his heart. Beside that stood a dark-eyed Fujio beckoning to him with her slender arms. It was all a beautiful painting. The poet's ideal was to become a person in this painting.
>
> Long ago, there was someone called Tantalus. Written accounts say that he was cruelly punished for some evil deed. He was made to stand in water that came up to his neck. Above his head delicious-looking fruits hung heavily from the branches. Tantalus's throat would become parched. But when he tried to drink, the water would recede. His stomach would become empty. But when he tried to eat the fruit, it would run away from him. If his mouth moved a foot, the fruit would move away a foot. If he moved forward two feet, then the fruit would shift two feet. Three feet, four feet, even a thousand miles—no matter how far he went his stomach stayed empty and his throat remained parched. As far as we can tell, Tantalus is still chasing after water and fruit. —Whenever he looked through his peephole to the future, Ono felt like one of Tantalus's protégés. That wasn't all. There were times when Fujio seemed indifferent to him. There were other times when she glared at him, with her eyebrows pushed together. On occasion the garnet would burst afire, and the female figure would be engulfed in flames before fading from sight. There were times when the word "Doctor" would grow dimmer and slowly vanish in the darkness. Or the watch would fall from the sky like a meteor and break against the ground with a sharp crack. Because Ono was a poet, he pictured various versions of the future. (67–68)

In Ono's fantasies, the erotic is joined with the desire for material wealth and position. The gold pocket watch with the red garnet fob is a central image that reveals the inseparability of these desires; a marker of male status, the watch also speaks to Ono's love of luxury. As I will explain later, it is moreover an object so powerfully associated with Fujio that it ends up testifying to the forces seeking to objectify her.

When the passage switches registers to digress upon Tantalus, we see the hunger and frustration that underlie Ono's desires. The excursion into mythology shows, through calling up an image of cruel denial, the connections between Ono's yearning for luxury and his earlier life as an orphan. As one of "Tantalus's protégés," Ono is someone achingly near, but ultimately denied, fulfillment.[45] Given his talents, everything he wants would have been his had he been born into the same social stratum and the same familial security as Kōno and Munechika. Yet being an orphan means that what he wants will always be out of reach. The woman bursting into flames, the fading title, and the falling watch are surreal foreshadowings of his future.

The role that money—or perhaps more accurately, his relative poverty—plays in Ono's life explains some of the specific contours of his desires. Ono is the only major male character in the novel who must work for a living. Although he, Kōno, and Munechika had graduated from the Imperial University at the same time, two years before the beginning of the novel, the latter two have been leading lives of relative leisure: Kōno has been nursing his angst and Munechika has been taking (and repeatedly failing) the entrance examination for the foreign service. The wealth of the Kōnos and the Munechikas allows these two young scions to enjoy a postgraduate holiday without financial worry. They can draw upon their family fortunes to enjoy expensive extras, like the lengthy trip to Kyoto that begins the novel. By contrast, Ono supports his dissertation research through working as a tutor. He does not teach English to Fujio merely out of kindness or infatuation; at one point, Fujio's mother comments that she has been giving Ono a "considerable gratuity" (229). From the first, Ono is engaged in a fee-for-service relationship with Fujio and her mother. His work brings Ono a monthly income of 60 yen.[46] This income strikes Kodō, his impoverished former mentor, as plenty enough to support a household; but Ono feels that his earnings are "only a little" and "just barely enough for one" (283). The difference in opinion here stems from Ono's expensive preference for snappy suits and Egyptian cigarettes. But what must be kept in mind is that Ono's clothes are an orphan's means of making himself acceptable, of distancing himself from the dark depths from which he has come. The difference between Ono's neediness and the financial ease enjoyed by families like the Kōnos and Munechikas is nowhere more apparent than when it is revealed that Munechika *père* has spent 25 yen on a single bonsai plant. Munechika's father is able to throw away on a potted plant what amounts to almost half of Ono's monthly income.

This kind of economic hierarchy is never far from Ono's mind when he dreams of marrying Fujio. Although he finds Fujio attractive—he is stunned by her beauty and undone by her confident presence—he is also very much drawn by her family's money. Whenever he sees Kōno's study—a bourgeois Meiji interior in the Western style, with its French windows, heavy roll-top desk, and shelves of books with gilt-stamped spines—he is filled with an unavoidable envy: "He thought it would be paradise to be in a study like this, to read books he liked whenever he wanted, and, when he grew tired of that, to be able to talk to people he liked about topics he enjoyed. He'd be able to finish his doctoral thesis in no time. After he wrote his thesis, he'd get to work on a magnum opus that future generations would hold in awe" (291). The very same study where Kōno groans guiltily under the heavy stare of his father's portrait signifies freedom and luxury for Ono. The text, then, acknowledges the gulf between a young scion of the upper class and a covetous orphan by conveying in palpable terms the yearnings of a gifted young man who has to do his writing in a cheap boardinghouse where neighbors constantly shout through the walls.

Ono's portrayal makes him a creature riven by status inconsistency. He stands in stark contrast to such men as Kōno and Munechika, who display a consistent alignment of privileged status defined by birth and educational attainment, upper-class membership guaranteed by inherited wealth, and moral superiority supported by a sense of entitlement. As an orphan, Ono has inherited neither status nor money. His university education and the emperor's silver watch mean that he has made good according to the standards of the Meiji period. But the status derived from education does not fully repair the disadvantage of his birth and it certainly does not give him a superior class position based upon wealth. Ono, then, has achieved a limited social mobility; his success means he can be admitted into the Kōno residence. Yet he enters there as a tutor, a paid employee, who develops a burning desire for Kōno's study and Kōno's sister. Ono's moral vulnerability is underpinned by the gap between his academic achievement and his continuing awareness of his own orphanage and limited income.

While the narrator is not without understanding in his portrait of Ono,
he also maintains an ironic and critical distance from a placeless man striving mightily to gain some kind of familial, social, and economic security.
He draws a portrait of an Ono, enmeshed in the material, who for all his
passivity is also calculating in his marriage choices:

> There is no business that earns less money than being a poet. At the same
> time, no business requires more money than being a poet. In this civilized
> age, a poet must write his poetry and lead an aesthete's life using someone
> else's money. It was only natural that Ono would want to pin his hopes on
> Fujio, who so comprehended his specialty. The Kōnos were supposed to have
> more than a middling fortune. That mother wouldn't allow Kōno to send his
> half-sister out to be married with only a dresser full of clothes to her name.
> What's more, Kōno was sickly. The mother might even intend to get a hus-
> band for her daughter and depend on them for her future. (201–2)

As this passage gradually moves from the narrator's ironic voice to a narrated monologue reflecting Ono's own language and concerns, it reveals
the scheming present in his thoughts. He is thoroughly aware of the Kōno
family's wealth and he surmises that Fujio's mother will not let her daughter
go unprovided for. His guess is dead on; as we have seen, Fujio's mother
is relentless in pleading her daughter's case before Kōno. The mention of
Kōno's frail constitution shows that Ono is also aware of an even more appealing possibility. He might end up being adopted as a *mukoyōshi* into the
Kōno family. There is a juridically sanctioned means for him to gain access
to the family's status and wealth.

In considering the possibility of an adoption, Ono is again prescient, for
Fujio's mother has been weighing just such a scenario. A believer in the ideology of self-advancement, who thinks that "education is a tool for success"
(*gakumon wa risshin shusse no dōgu de aru* [222–23]), Fujio's mother recognizes Ono as a man endowed with numerous fitting qualities. A narrated
monologue shows us her evaluations:

> Everyone said that Ono was a truly gifted scholar. They said that he had re-
> ceived a watch from the emperor. He was supposed to get a doctorate soon.
> Not only that, he was personable and kind. He was refined and pleasant.
> There wouldn't be any embarrassment in having him as Fujio's husband. It
> would probably be pleasant to be in his care.
> Ono was a worthy son-in-law. His only flaw was that he had no money.
> But, it was also true that one could never have much clout being supported
> by a son-in-law's wealth, no matter how fond one was of the man. It would

be to Fujio's advantage and to hers as well to bring into the family someone without a penny to his name and have him obediently care for his wife and his mother-in-law. The one problem that remained was the family money. At this point, four months after her husband's death in a foreign land, it had naturally become Kingo's possession. Her designs started here. (224)

The mother, then, sees Ono as a suitable replacement for Kōno. Ono's silver watch and his imminent doctorate, combined with an accommodating personality, make for a perfect son-in-law. Even Ono's poverty is a blessing of sorts, because it makes him more yielding.

Reviewing the mother's motives, we quickly see that the concept of a "traffic in women" can hardly accommodate the scenario she envisions. In contrast to men exchanging women to build male relationships, she seeks to instigate a marriage that benefits herself and her daughter. The instrument that allows them to hold such hopes is, ironically, the *mukoyōshi* system protected by the Meiji Civil Code. The institution of the adopted son-in-law meant, in effect, that there was a "traffic in men" that paralleled the "traffic in women." Just as women went in marriage from one family to another, men were being exchanged between families. Marriage and adoption functioned as parallel strategies for the consolidation and continuation of *ie*. The exchange of a male object would also normally function to build ties between men; in the common case of a second or third son sent to be the successor of another family, the two fathers would enjoy a transaction similar to that involving a daughter. Even a second or third son was a precious commodity, especially if he could insure family continuity, and his transaction would seal an important bond. *Gubijinsō*, however, shows the potential for the "traffic in men" to be used for female ends. Fujio and her mother want to recruit a penniless outsider without family connections of his own because such a man would be more tractable. Through the *mukoyōshi* solution, Fujio and her mother seek to acquire a man who will give them control of the *ie*.

As an orphan, Ono is in a position to respond directly to the transactions being proposed by the Kōno women; instead of being exchanged by a househead, he is in a position to traffic himself. He can take his assets—his educational attainment and his prospects—and use them to marry upward, gaining family, social status, and wealth in one swoop. His status inconsistency resolved to his satisfaction, he can legitimately come to occupy Kōno's study.

What we have in *Gubijinsō*, then, is a situation where the "traffic in women" is challenged by the possibility of a man being an object of exchange. Ono's presence stands in the way of the "marriage by exchange" that might have developed between the Kōnos and the Munechikas. And it threatens to become an instrument for the establishment of female dominance in the Kōno house. When we remember that the "traffic in women" underlies the novel's polarized morality, we know that a melodramatic resolution will struggle toward its enforcement. Exploring the moral consequences of the potential exchanges in *Gubijinsō* will now take us to an examination of the gold watch that functions as the paradigmatic object of exchange in the plot of this novel.

THE TRAFFIC IN WATCHES

When *Gubijinsō* designates a pocket watch as an object of contestation, it employs an artifact saturated with specific cultural and historical associations. An instrument of rational timekeeping designed (and at this time still largely manufactured) in the West, the watch was a device that linked its wearer to a bureaucratic and capitalist modernity. Bringing Japan into synchrony with the West had been a key preparatory step in the Meiji state's modernization project.[47] When it switched from the lunar to the Gregorian calendar on January 1, 1873, the state was making a structural change that supported diplomacy and trade between Japan and the West. The government also simultaneously brought timekeeping into alignment with Western standards. The system in place during the Edo period had broken the day into twelve segments whose durations were linked to changes in sunrise and sunset, and thus varied over the course of the year. Adopting the twenty-four-hour day and the sixty-minute hour reorganized time into precise and homogenous units, transcendent in their abstraction, that ticked irreversibly toward the future.

The transformation of time spurred the demand for Western clocks to display the newly regularized hours: in 1873, the number of wall clocks imported to Japan rose to 39,090 units compared to only 7,511 units the year before.[48] By 1890, when domestic clock manufacturing began to get off the ground, Japan was importing more than 100,000 wall and mantle clocks per year from the United States.[49] Such numbers meant that clocks became visible features on the walls of government bureaus, army barracks, schools, train stations, factories, shops, and, increasingly, private homes. The social penetration of the object that Lewis Mumford called the "key-machine of the modern industrial age"[50] meant that trains could run on a schedule, that children attended school for regular hours, that government and factory workers went to work at the prescribed moment and labored for a premeasured temporal span. The change in timekeeping subjected the Japanese to a new chronological discipline and allowed the creation of a capitalist nation-state.

In comparison to clocks, which leapt into public spaces as symbols of institutional timekeeping, pocket watches, which allowed private access to the larger march of time, spread at a slower rate. Uchida Hoshimi, in his history of the Japanese watchmaking industry, estimates that in 1879 only 0.3 percent of the population owned pocket watches; the watch was then still the possession of an extremely restricted, well-to-do elite.[51] Through much of the Meiji period, the pocket watch remained the province of those most invested in a rationalized model of time: men who ran government bureaus, represented Japan in diplomatic relations, commanded regiments, or operated banks and factories. Its symbolic value was enhanced by the fact that it was a possession carried on one's person; slipping out a pocket watch and leaning back ostentatiously to check the time signaled a personal connection to the institutional power of regularized timekeeping. The pocket watch, moreover, retained a strong symbolic connection to the West. While domestic clocks quickly overtook imports, watches remained largely a product imported from either the United States or Switzerland. It was not until 1909 that the Seiko corporation succeeded in producing a pocket watch with mostly Japanese content, which it proudly called the "Empire."[52] Until the end of the Meiji era, holding a pocket watch meant having a physical product of the West in one's hands.

Watch ownership increased gradually: Uchida estimates that in 1897 one in twenty Japanese possessed pocket watches. By 1907, the year of publication of *Gubijinsō*, one in ten owned pocket watches, which had become "nearly a necessity for adult males of the middle class and above."[53] There are a number of observations to be made about this trend. An object that had once been the exclusive province of government leaders and captains of industry had become available to the aspiring classes. It had become an attainable object of bourgeois desire; yet it was still out of reach for most. Moreover, women were left out of watch ownership entirely; the Meiji imports and early domestic products were all large timepieces specifically meant for men.[54]

This background is pertinent to *Gubijinsō*, where a pocket watch becomes a trophy in power struggles involving gender and class, and where, as I will later show, the narrative divides time into an accelerating progression of ever more precise and measurable segments. There are actually two watches that play important roles in the novel: the silver watch awarded by the emperor to Ono and the gold one that once belonged to Kōno and Fujio's father. The symbolic value of the former—typically a Waltham with "Presented by His Majesty" (*onshi*) engraved prominently on the back—cannot be overstated. The silver presentation piece signified more than academic prowess. It also showed imperial approval and validation. The specific symbolic value of the silver watch—as opposed to some other ceremonial object, say a medal or a cup—is worth pondering. When the emperor presented a watch, the suggestion was that the subject thus honored had used his time well and was expected to continue to be industrious. It confirmed that the subject stood at the vanguard of an imperial modernity and contributed to the national project of modernization. Meant to be carried on one's person through the course of the day, the watch signified the merit attached to the bearer's quotidian activities. The silver watch, then, is a powerful symbol of worth and potential. It is thus no surprise that it looms large, as we have seen, in Fujio's mother's consciousness when she considers Ono as a possible son-in-law. The watch's value as social capital is also apparent in Ono's interactions with his friend Asai:

> "What time is it? Can you check your watch?" [the speaker is Asai]
> "It's twelve sixteen." [the speaker is Ono]
> "Twelve sixteen? —Is that the watch from the emperor?"
> "Well, yes."
> "You've made out well. I should have gotten one too. When you have something like that the world treats you differently."
> "I doubt that's so."
> "No, it's true. There's no doubt because, after all, you've received the emperor's guarantee" (*tennō heika ga hoshō shite kudasatta*). (79)

Although the shallow and mercenary Asai is more responsive than most to outward symbols of success, the social significance of the silver watch is beyond question. The silver watch is an imperial stamp of approval. At a point later in the novel, Ono thinks that "His Majesty's watch measures not only time, but the quality of one's brains. It measured future advancement and success in academia" (292). Clearly, the watch has special meaning for a former orphan. Ono has gone from being a homeless waif dependant on the kindness of others to being a young man with a "guarantee" from the emperor. The silver watch is a stunning sign of *risshin shusse*. Using this watch, Ono measures time to the minute: "It's twelve sixteen." Always in a hurry, he is constantly checking his watch. He is a man for whom chronological precision is important, because he knows that time is the commodity with which he must buy his future success.

The other pocket watch, the gold one, has an even greater significance in the novel. In fact, the plot of *Gubijinsō* turns upon its fate. The watch in question was bought many years ago in London by Kōno's father. Its large hammered gold case makes it unquestionably a man's watch and the watch of a man of means (first acquired, we should note, when pocket watches were a rare item possessed only by members of the Meiji elite). But the imagistic value of the watch cannot be so simply dismissed because there is something unsettlingly hybrid, even hermaphroditic, about it. Attached to the watch is a golden chain tipped with a fob fashioned from a red garnet. In Fujio's hands, the chain undulates suggestively: "When she gripped the rounded head of the slender snake in her palm, and swung the strand of gold into the air, a bright flash of crimson blazed from its tail" (371). The chain resonates with associations, both Japanese and Western, that connect the serpent with sexual desire; its sinuous line and sensual colors render it disturbingly "female." The watch then is an odd, purposely unstable image: it simultaneously signals wealth and masculinity, sensuality and femininity.

The ambivalent gendering of the watch is relevant to the roles it plays in the novel. We first hear about it when it comes up in a discussion between Kōno and Munechika as being among the senior Kōno's effects shipped back from his last post abroad. Here, its qualities as a masculine object predominate; yet there is the insinuation of something more:

> "I wonder what's happened to that watch." [the speaker is Munechika]
> "Well, well. That's the famous watch he bought in London. It'll probably come back to us. Ever since she was small, Fujio liked playing with it. She'd never let it go when she got her hands on it. The red garnet on the end of its chain really appealed to her." [the speaker is Kōno]
> "It's an old watch, when you think about it."
> "That's so. My father bought it on his first trip to the West."
> "Would you give it to me as a memento of your father?"
> "I'm intending to do that."
> "When your father went abroad this time, he left promising that he'd give it to me as a graduation gift when he returned."
> "I remember that too. —But, Fujio might have taken it by now and she might be playing with it as usual. . . ."
> "So, Fujio and the watch are inseparable. Ah, ha, ha, that doesn't matter. I'll still take it." (63–64)

The watch is meant to seal two overlapping male bonds. As a gift from Kōno to Munechika, it would mark the special affinity between these two friends. As a memento or a graduation present from Kōno's father, it is a kind of torch being passed from a senior diplomat to an aspiring one. The watch will continue to measure the time for another man serving the nation in a mission abroad.

A dissonance foreshadowing conflict enters the transaction between men, however, with the information that the watch has also been a favorite toy of Fujio's. Ever since she was a child, she has wanted to take control of an object associated with male power and prestige. In fact, she and the watch are so inseparable that she has become identified with it. We see here the reason for the hermaphroditic figuring of the watch. On the one hand it is a masculine possession; on the other it stands for a woman, a woman who wants to be her own mistress. The stage is set, then, for a contestation over both the watch itself and Fujio, the woman metaphorically rendered as a watch.

The connection between Fujio and the watch needs to be examined at some length, because it becomes evident that the marriage "promise" her father had made had been articulated wholly in reference to the timepiece. We first learn about this in a conversation between Fujio and her mother. Fujio asks explicitly whether she has been promised to Munechika. Her mother denies it, but she does say that when her husband promised his watch to Munechika he had, in fact, mentioned Fujio in the same breath: "He said this half jokingly in front of everyone—There's a deep connection between Fujio and this watch, but I'll give it to you. But I won't do it now. I'll do so when you graduate. But Fujio might want it and come along with it. How would that be?" (132). This lighthearted reference was apparently the *only* paternal comment regarding Fujio's marriage; but the other men present—presumably Kōno, Munechika, and Munechika *père*—construed it as an explicit promise of marriage. We know Munechika remains convinced that he has been offered Fujio; when Oito later tries to point out that Fujio doesn't seem to like him very much, he confidently replies by referring to the object associated with her: "Oito, I've been promised his gold watch. . . . Don't worry. I talked this over with Kōno, too, while we were in Kyoto" (181). For his part, Kōno also believes that his sister has been pledged to his friend. He makes this evident to his stepmother in a conversation that once again brings up the watch:

"Wasn't there a promise of some sort?" [the speaker is Kōno]
"There wasn't anything that amounted to a promise." [the speaker is his stepmother]

"I recall that Father once said that he'd give him his watch, or something of the sort."

"The watch?" The mother cocked her head quizzically.

"Father's watch. The one with the garnet."

"You're right, you're right. There was something like that," the mother said, as though she had just remembered.

"Hajime is still counting on it."

The mother only said, "Is that so," quite without concern.

"If a promise has been made, we've got to deliver. We'd be shirking our obligations."

"Fujio has the watch now. I'll explain that to her carefully."

"The watch is an issue, too, but mainly I'm talking about Fujio."

"But there's absolutely no promise about giving them Fujio."

"Is that so. —Well, then, that's that." (315–16)

What we have here is a collision between a man who thoroughly identifies his sister with a pocket watch and his stepmother who pretends not to grasp the implications. Kōno's understanding, like that of Munechika, totally conflates an object and a person, and, for him, the failure to transfer ownership of either means the failure to fulfill a male obligation.

The repeated male urge to reduce Fujio to a pocket watch has several consequences. To begin with, it emphasizes how this novel constructs marriage as a "traffic in women." When a woman is repeatedly figured as a watch, she is unmistakably turned into what Lévi-Strauss would call "one of the objects of exchange." She is no different from her father's gold watch in being an object trafficked in order to build social bonds between men. The conflation of Fujio and the gold watch shows the extent to which the world of male friendships, alliances, and obligations occupies the ideological center of this melodrama. But there is another, ultimately subversive, level to the novel's discourse on woman as watch. When a woman is so baldly and thoroughly objectified, it cannot but problematize the very objectification of that woman. When a woman is being passed from one man to another along with a pocket watch, the question has to arise whether she might have something to say about this. The overdetermined figure of the woman as watch, then, carries its own potential for ideological contradiction. This is especially so because the text makes clear that when Fujio's father "promised" her to Munechika he did so half in jest. We are made aware that the men in this novel believe with deadly seriousness that the fate of a woman can be decided by mere banter.

The problematical nature of figuring a woman as a watch becomes apparent when Fujio herself begins to use the gold watch to express her determination to decide her own future. Much as Kōno had expected, Fujio immediately commandeers the watch when it arrives home along with her father's other belongings. It remains in her possession until the climax of the novel. Fujio initially uses the pocket watch as an instrument for seducing Ono. She leaves it partially hidden where Ono is likely to see the glint of gold—his favorite color. And then she flaunts it before his eyes:

> She held out her right hand, jingling the shining object she held. Just then, its chain slid from her palm, seemingly heading toward the tatami mat before being brought up short as it extended a foot in length. The force remaining in the chain sent it swaying sideways, and it swung along its length two or three times together with the garnet ornament waving at its end. On its first swing, the crimson ball struck the woman's alabaster arm. On its second swing, it traced a swirl and lightly brushed her sleeve. When the third swing was just about to still, the woman suddenly stood up. (43)

In this passage, baroque language, much like that used to describe Fujio herself, turns the watch into a visually arresting image of femininity. Needless to say, Ono cannot take his eyes off of the watch or Fujio. We see here a consequence of the watch's ambivalent gendering; its femininity can be used to ensnare male desire. When it swings in Fujio's hands it becomes an extension of her—active, colorful, and alluring. It becomes an expression of female will.

Fujio understands the male urge to treat her like a pocket watch, and she challenges the men in her family by making the watch an instrument of her own agency. This intent receives its clearest expression when Fujio uses the watch's symbolic significance to declare her wish to marry the man that she chooses. When her mother questions her about why she insists on hanging onto a man's watch she cannot possibly wear, Fujio responds: "I hope you won't mind if I give the watch to Ono" (133). And in the most direct confrontation with her brother, Fujio insists on her right to dispose of the watch as *she* sees fit:

> "Kingo." [the speaker is Fujio]
> "What is it?" he said, looking down at her.
> "I won't give that pocket watch to you."
> "If you don't give it to me, whom do you intend to give it to?"
> "I'm going to hold onto it for awhile."
> "Hold onto it? I suppose that's alright. But I've promised to give it to Munechika . . ."
> "When it's time to give it to Munechika, I'll do it."

"You'll do it?" said the brother slightly tilting his head and lowering his eyes toward his sister.

"Yes, me—I'll be doing the giving—to someone." (219)

Both Fujio and her brother are aware that they are talking about more than a watch. Fujio states her intention to determine whom she marries, and she does so in no uncertain terms. When a woman asserts her right to traffic in a watch, knowing its symbolic significance, she repudiates the "traffic in women." Late in the novel, Fujio places the watch on Ono's vest, this time in the full view of her brother and Munechika. Kōno recoils in shock and tries to hustle his friend away from the scene. For the reaction it evokes, Fujio might as well be sticking her tongue down Ono's throat.

To understand the full measure of Fujio's rebellion, we must note that, in this novel, the emperor and the father determine the ownership of watches. When a woman seeks to give a watch, she stands against the entire edifice of imperial power and male moral authority constructed through *ie* ideology. Fujio's use of the watch, however, already contains contradictions that foreshadow her eventual defeat. Although she manages to express her own agency, she also ends up cooperating with her own objectification when she repeats the male discourse equating her with a timepiece.[55] A pocket watch is a thing meant to be possessed by men. Unfeeling and unthinking, made to be given and held, it does not participate in the minute negotiations of consent that constitute human engagement. When Fujio identifies herself with a watch, she forecloses the possibility of figuring her relationship with men in a way that will acknowledge her future spirit and independence. As long as she remains an object, Fujio will be, once she has given herself, a thing whose disposal remains the purview of men.

MASTERS OF TIME

As the novel moves towards its resolution two other timepieces come into play. Neither of these—a desk clock in Kōno's study and Munechika's pocket watch—is described explicitly: it is precisely their physical invisibility that is significant. In this novel, watches whose ownership is problematical—such as those controlled by a woman or possessed by someone morally suspect or of uncertain origins—receive conspicuous attention. These watches are made visible because there is something contested or incongruous in their ownership; they are markers of status inconsistency. Ono's watch emblematizes his advancement beyond his social and moral limitations; the gold pocket watch shows Fujio's effort to gain an agency improper for her sex. Other timepieces are rendered less explicitly, but measure time with a fierce regularity because they are owned by upper-class males who are the proper masters of time. These watches are naturalized indicators of time that serves homosocial interests. Kōno's desk clock appears only briefly at a crucial moment in the alliance between Kōno and Munechika. After Fujio has placed the gold watch on Ono's vest, Kōno and Munechika repair back to Kōno's study, where they lock the doors. Within this sealed male space, Kōno will declare his own moral superiority and Munechika will offer him his sister Oito as a "true friend." As Munechika renounces the gold watch and what it implies, another timepiece is heard in the background.

> There was a sharp peal of female laughter, which resounded as though she had her mouth right against the door. Running footsteps receded toward the Japanese-style room. The two men looked each other in the face.
> "It's Fujio," Kōno said.
> "Is that so," Munechika replied.
> Afterwards, all was quiet. *The clock on the desk ticked noticeably.*
> "Forget about the gold watch."
> "All right. I'll forget about it."
> Kōno kept on staring at the wall, and Munechika still had his arms crossed—*the clock continued to tick.* Off in the Japanese room, a large group of people laughed at once.
> "Munechika," Kingo said, turning his face toward him again. "Fujio dislikes you. It's better for you not to say anything more."
> "Yes, I won't pursue it."
> "Fujio can't understand character of the sort you've got. She's a shallow twit. Give her to Ono." (373, emphasis mine)

The ticking of the clock in the background emphasizes the stillness of a room filled with tense male emotions. But that it is heard precisely when Munechika abandons any hope of gaining the gold watch seems to indicate something more. There is a suggestion here that time itself is larger than the gold watch, that there are other timepieces measuring increments of value, the passage of time, and the progress of the plot.[56] Fujio may have commandeered the watch but that does not mean she controls the future. Munechika's renunciation of the watch testifies to his moral superiority, and the plot can be heard ticking toward his ultimate victory.

Fujio's fate, it turns out, will be measured on Munechika's watch. Examining how this happens requires a slight digression to discuss *Gubijinsō's* temporal structure, which, like that of *Hototogisu*, is designed as a series of returning analepses. The earlier novel, it will be recalled, deploys analepses to create a sense of "simultaneity" that embraces and unifies distant points in the Japanese empire. *Gubijinsō*, too, portrays actions occurring simultaneously in separate locales, but the effects it achieves are different. The temporal pattern of this novel is produced through the progressive reduction of the overlapping units of time.[57] The scenes in the early chapters, which show roughly concurrent events in Kyoto and Tokyo, take place over an unspecified period of perhaps a week. In the middle chapters, parallel events in different areas of Tokyo unfold over a few days, and in the later chapters, a single specific day. On the fateful afternoon of Fujio's death, events in three different locations are chronologically laid on the same hour. Time becomes concentrated as the novel progresses. Events trip on each others' heels, and they begin to accumulate on increasingly precise moments. Each hour, each minute, each second gains in significance because there is more at stake in any given temporal unit. This is accompanied by a pattern of geographical contraction, as the setting moves from the cities of Kyoto and Tokyo, to a few houses in the latter city, and finally to Kōno's study. The chronotope of this novel is of temporal and geographical compression.

I want to illustrate this feature of the novel by focusing upon the events of the final afternoon, when Munechika manages to force his moral vision upon the rest of the characters. In this sequence, Munechika becomes the agent of the convergences marking the climax of the novel; he plans and directs the synchronous events that will result in Fujio's death. After hearing Asai's account of how Ono intends to end his relationship with Sayoko and marry Fujio, Munechika sends out three rickshaws from his house in quick succession. One carries his father, who goes to Kodō's house to prevent the latter and Sayoko from doing anything rash. Another goes to Kōno's house, carrying Oito, who will lend moral support to her future husband as he confronts his stepmother. The third rickshaw, with Munechika in it, heads to Ono's boarding house, where, at this very moment, Ono is readying himself to meet Fujio at the train station in order to go to Ōmori for what is probably a sexual assignation.

The scene that transpires at the boarding house is bracketed by the mention of two different watches. The first is Ono's silver watch, which marks the acceleration of time as the moment nears for his rendezvous with Fujio:

> The watch from the emperor urged him to fulfill his promise with each passing second. It was as though he had placed his enervated body on a sled. If

he crossed his arms and waited, he would just naturally slide into the pit of his promise. Nothing slid as precisely as the sled called "time." (391)

Through the wildly mixed metaphors—perhaps a reflection of the mental state of an agitated poet—we learn what time has come to mean for Ono. In its relentless forward movement, palpably ticking by in seconds, time is a component of fate. Ono no longer uses time to his advantage; rather, he is overmastered by it, rendered passive to its insistent demands.

When Munechika arrives just in the nick of time, he uses a moral argument to convert Ono, but be does so while manipulating status-based rhetoric. Anticipating that Ono might think he has come to exact revenge for the loss of Fujio, Munechika states that he is not "so vulgar a person" and that taking retaliatory action would be "against the customs of my House" (394). Anyone who uses such terms must, unlike an orphan, possess a confident place in social hierarchy and family lineage. After thus establishing his superiority, Munechika leverages his own social self-assurance to offer provisional equality to Ono; he does this by addressing him as "an educated man who will respond to reason" and "a person of equal standing" (*taitō no ningen* [394]). Munechika's appeal based on "reason" involves the ideology of *majime* or "honesty," which he claims will offer salvation to an anxious Ono:

> Munechika drew his face even closer. He pulled himself up on one knee, put his elbow on it and leaned forward, supporting his chin with his hand. He then began speaking.
> "You're a better scholar than I am. You've got a better head. I admire you. It's because of this admiration that I've come to save you."
> "To save me . . ." When Ono raised his face, Munechika was right there in front of his nose. Munechika pushed forward some more, so that his face was almost right up against Ono, and spoke again.
> "You'll be anxious for the rest of your days if you fail, at a crucial point like this, to beat yourself into shape and change your nature. . . . This is the place, Ono, for you to become honest (*majime*). . . . All will be lost if you miss this chance. You'll die without knowing what honesty tastes like. Always anxious, you'll wander around like a shaggy dog until you die. The more these occasions for honesty accumulate the more a human being becomes complete. You begin to feel like a human being. . . . The reason I'm more assured than you isn't because of education, or study, or anything else. It's because every now and then I become honest. . . . Honesty, my friend, means a fight with drawn swords. It means crushing your opponents; it means being unable to stop yourself from crushing them. It means that the whole human being springs into action. A clever mouth or nimble fingers isn't honesty, no matter how well they work. You only begin to feel honest

when you've taken the inside of your head and thrown it against the world with nothing held back." (396–97)

The ideology of *majime* connects to this melodrama's "moral occult." *Majime* involves tearing away pretense and recognizing virtue. It means acting decisively according to one's moral sense and achieving true selfhood. *Majime* is a transcendent value, and thus Munechika can represent himself here as altruistic. An admirer of Ono's academic brilliance, he holds out *majime* as an ideal that will allow them both to stand together on the common ground of the human. We should not miss, however, that this purported egalitarianism is built on hierarchy. At the root here is the notion that humanness is something achieved rather than imparted to all. This assumption allows Munechika to portray himself as human in contrast to Ono, the shaggy dog, and to argue that the latter must accept his moral standards in order to qualify as human. By substituting a moral hierarchy for a social one, Munechika dangles equality before an orphan while reserving for himself the superior position of one who has already achieved moral and human completion, a completion, we might add, built upon his social assurance.

When Munechika forces Ono to declare a concrete content for *majime*, it becomes clear that the moral and the social cannot be separated. Ono says: "The honest solution is for me to marry Sayoko as quickly as possible. It would be inexcusable for me to abandon Sayoko. I would be behaving inexcusably toward Kodō-sensei" (399). The honest solution—clearly the only one Munechika will accept—turns out to be one that observes the established social order. By returning to Sayoko, the orphan will respect the boundaries of an upper-class family, and rebellious females will be prevented from using him as a means of gaining control. Ono will need to abandon all that the gold watch represents—Fujio, but also wealth and social position—to fulfill the dictates of *majime*. In order to be recognized as human, he must give up the desires rooted in his background. To put it differently, ideological contradiction results from the urge to make the preservation of social hierarchy a moral value even if this runs counter to the earlier sympathetic portrayal of Ono's social positionality.

Another contradiction is present in Munechika's reference to a "fight with drawn swords" (*shinken shōbu*) where the virtuous are impelled to crush (*yattsukeru*) their enemies. This rhetoric is part of what makes *Gubijinsō* a melodrama: the moral struggle is conceived as a battle to the death between dualities. But we must also recognize the violence that courses through this hypermasculine language. Munechika's morality is not far from brute force; it seeks validation in the subjugation of others. There is a possibility here of might being confused with right. As part of the plan to dramatize *majime*, Munechika demands that Ono drag Sayoko before Fujio and declare before the latter's eyes that Sayoko is his future wife. Ono recognizes that this course of action is designed to hurt and humiliate: "It's too spiteful—I'd much rather do it peaceably." Munechika, however, insists that his way is the only way: "I don't like acting spitefully, but it can't be helped because our aim is to rescue Fujio. A personality like that can't be set right with ordinary means" (400). Again we see self-righteousness, and perhaps even malice, masquerading as altruism. Part of the ideological contradiction of this novel lies in assigning virtue to a moral bully.

It is when Ono finally agrees to Munechika's plan for crushing Fujio that Munechika's otherwise undescribed watch comes out of his pocket. This happens just after Ono has confessed to his three o'clock rendezvous with Fujio:

> "Three o'clock, you say—I wonder what the time is now?" There was the sound of something clicking open near the center of Munechika's vest. "It's already two o'clock. I doubt you'll go."
>
> "I'm not going."
>
> "There's absolutely no chance of Fujio going off to Ōmori by herself. She'll head home if we just ignore her. Once three o'clock passes."
>
> "We don't have to worry about her waiting. If I'm late by even a minute, she'll head home right away."
>
> "That'll suit us just fine." (401–2)

Ono's observation about the unlikelihood of Fujio waiting for even a minute shows that she is a woman who expects men to hew to her schedule. She wants to be in control of time. Yet what is clear in this passage is that time is now being regulated by Munechika's pocket watch.[58] He not only knows the current time, he can predict what will happen an hour hence. It is no wonder that Munechika had struck Ono as a "hero in charge of the future" (393).

In planning events that converge at a single moment and at a single place, Munechika is a master of precision timing.[59] He sends for Sayoko, who has been with his father, and arrives at the Kōno house with her and Ono just as Oito reaches an impasse in her verbal combat with Kōno's stepmother. All the players are present now except for Fujio, and the stage is set for the kind of grand finale common in kabuki plays. Although the theatricality of this last sequence has long been counted among *Gubijinsō*'s defects, the point I wish to emphasize is that the characters here are not brought together by accident or coincidence, as so often happens in kabuki plays, but through the kind of synchronization possible only with modern chronometry. As all wait for Fujio to return, Munechika's watch again makes an appearance: "Munechika clicked something open in front of his vest. 'Three-twenty.' . . . 'Twenty-five.' Even before he had finished speaking, an avatar of anger stood in the center of the study like a humiliated queen" (418–19). It is Munechika's watch that marks off the progress of his plot and the plot of the novel. A watch that is deliberately undescribed, a watch that is an unquestioned possession of a male sure of his social position, has been measuring a woman's fate.

Fujio had taken her father's gold watch to the train station—she may even have looked at it at three o'clock—but by then time had slipped from her control. When she brings out the gold watch now, it falls victim to the potential for violence that Munechika had exhibited all along. The scene unfolds exactly as Munechika has planned. He introduces Sayoko as Ono's bride to be, and Ono expresses contrition, sounding like a brainwashed automaton: "Everything that Munechika says is true. This is without question my future wife. —Fujio, I was a frivolous human being until today. I owe apologies to you. I owe apologies to Sayoko. I owe apologies to Munechika-san. I will change from today. I will become an honest human being" (421). The price for becoming an honest human being, it seems, is to become a broken one. What happens next, when Fujio reacts in shock to Ono's change of mind, is even more disturbing because its violence, meant to show ideological assurance, also reveals something else:

> Her hysterical laughter rang out, piercing through the rain outside the window. At the very same moment, she suddenly pushed her clenched fist into the folds of her sash and quickly drew out a long, slithering length of chain. Its crimson tail shone with a strange luminosity and wavered to the left and to the right.
> "Then you won't be needing this. That's fine—Munechika, let me give it to you. Here."
> She reached out, baring her white arm. The watch fell securely into Munechika's ruddy palm. Munechika took one large step toward the fireplace. With a shout, he made his fist dance in the air. The watch shattered against the corner of the marble mantle.
> "Fujio, I didn't go to the trouble of interfering just because I wanted a watch. Ono, I didn't pull these stunts because I wanted a woman desired by someone else. My spirit should be clear to you if I destroy it like this. This is an action based on first principles, isn't it Kōno?"
> "Yes it is."

Fujio stood there stunned. The flesh on her face was frozen. Her arms stiffened. Her legs stiffened. Upending a chair, she fell on the floor, like a stone statue that has fallen off balance. (422)

Such is the victory of virtue in *Gubijinsō*. A hero denies self-interest and acts upon "first principles" (a term derived from Buddhist discourse used by both Munechika and Kōno to indicate essential values that transcend secondary distractions). The vanquished villain of the story falls to the floor dead. Morality is served. This is precisely the kind of sensational vindication, a decisive affirmation of the moral order, that makes *Gubijinsō* a melodrama. It is also what makes Masamune Hakuchō dismiss *Gubijinsō* as a modernized version of Bakin's moral imagination.

But what are we to do with the gold watch's unsettling end? Fujio's hysterical laughter, her dramatic gesture of pulling out the watch chain to its full length, and her bold, even contemptuous, words invite us to understand the conclusion differently. When Fujio holds out the watch, she shows both despair and defiance. She knows she has lost in her struggle to satisfy her own desires, control her own fate, and assume power in her own family. Yet she still attempts to be, as she said to her brother, the "one doing the giving." Her gesture is a scornful acceptance of defeat. Understanding this allows us to appreciate the disturbing implications of Munechika's violence. When he dashes the gold watch against the fireplace, he deliberately destroys an object that Fujio had accepted as a symbol for herself. He is figuratively smashing Fujio against the marble fireplace. His action is not so much a show of disinterested moral resolve but a ferocious act of vengeance that symbolically murders a woman who had stood against the homosocial "traffic in women," a woman who had been unyielding to the end. His action is directed, as well, at the already chastised Ono; the broken watch and the dead woman serve as a final lesson on the repercussions of crossing class and status lines. Converting Ono is not enough for Munechika; he must destroy Ono's objects of desire before his very eyes. The final confrontation reveals that *Gubijinsō*'s moral exemplar is also a brute, its villains also victims. Order is reinstated in the world of this novel not because virtue itself is so powerful, but because those who espouse it are so dangerous. The *ie* is restored not through "faith" but force. *Gubijinsō*'s ideological failure lies in acknowledging that virtue is defined by those with the power to enforce it.

In Place of a Conclusion
Kokoro and the Age of Melodrama

To uncover the moral extravagance and the emotional intensity hidden beneath the commonplace, to probe the ethical implications of new social identities and the modern social environment, to write into being fictive families providing alternative models of human association—this was the project of Meiji melodramatic fiction. Melodrama's charged moral vision trained itself on the relations of the personal to the national, the possibility of love in a mercenary age, the contestations of gendered power, and the ethics of aspiration in a world of status inconsistency. The fictive family functioned as a key trope for addressing all of these issues. Orphans and adoptions, and affiliations refigured as filiations, offered powerful ways of thinking through social problems. But the prevalence of the fictive family was not merely a matter of instrumentality. The repeated re-narrations of the family suggest that institutionally recognized models of family were insufficient for meeting the needs of men and women caught in the maelstrom of modernity. Melodrama's fictive families question blood lineage, subvert male power, and bring together strangers. Through their number and variability they relativize the *ie*, the Meiji state's specified model, and celebrate the dynamism of "family." Although they reach for moral certitude, the very proliferation of fictive families shows why they so often end up revealing contradictions.

I have discussed only four of the scores of melodramatic novels that were produced at the turn of the twentieth century, and there are a few more that I wish I could have taken up.[1] But limitations of space, and the prospect of diminishing returns, convince me that I have done enough. A mere handful of melodramatic novels continue to be remembered in our current literary histories. Most have been forgotten. But the sensibility of these works continues to live on. The melodramatic imagination was inherited by the *taishū shōsetsu*, the popular fiction that became a huge publishing phenomenon in the 1920s, after commercial, mass-market writing gained a separate identity. Yoshiya Nobuko's portraits of female virtue and villainy spelled out gender ideals for the early part of the Showa period (1926–89). And Yoshikawa Eiji's historical novels, despite their ostensible setting in the samurai past, employed a dualistic morality to address issues of ethical and ideological import for a modern culture. Melodrama's polarized moral sensibility and hyperbolic sentimentality have continued to pulse in Japanese popular culture ever since, whether in *shinpa* theater, movies, television, or even newer forms of cultural production.

What may be less obvious is that the melodramatic mode also persisted in the very texts that are thought to have sent it into eclipse. When the Japanese Naturalists came to dominate the literary scene in the first decade of the twentieth century they inaugurated the writing of self-consciously serious art fiction by eschewing the moral and emotional extravagances, the unrestrained plotting, and the lavish prose of the texts discussed here. It would be fair to say that, taking its cue from Naturalism, high-culture fiction through much of the twentieth century defined itself through the abjection of the most obvious markers of melodramatic writing. But, like so much that is abjected, the melodramatic imagination could not be entirely eliminated. Only a little consideration reveals that Naturalism's founding works, which were actually written during the heyday of melodramatic fiction, drew more than a little from the melodramatic mode. Tayama Katai's *Futon* (The quilt, 1907) centers on the dualistic struggle between its protagonist Tokio's ethical impulses and his overwhelming physical desire for his young charge Yoshiko. The infamous closing scene of the novella, in which a weeping Tokio buries his face in Yoshiko's quilts and inhales the sweet fragrance of his departed obsession, is nothing if not hyperbolic. Shimazaki Tōson's

Hakai (Broken commandment, 1906) actually has much in common with *Chikyōdai*, written three years earlier. The suffering of Ushimatsu, an *eta* outcaste passing in mainstream society, parallels the torments of Kimie, a common girl passing as an aristocrat. Although opposite moral evaluations are applied to these characters, with Ushimatsu being virtuous and Kimie villainous, there is still a shared concern with the validity of status distinctions when talented outsiders can so convincingly cross social boundaries. The problem of status inconsistency is being addressed in both. The climax of the novel, where Ushimatsu gets down on his knees before his students and both confesses his origins and insists upon his identity as a good Japanese, is a moment of exorbitant moral revelation. *Hakai* finally shares in melodrama's ideological contradiction by overdetermining Ushimatsu's *eta* identity all the while showing that he is equal to (and in most cases better than) the "normal" Japanese around him. Beyond Naturalism, it is even possible to see the melodramatic imagination at work in Shiga Naoya's *An'ya kōro* (A dark night's passing, 1921–28), where Tokitō Kensaku grapples with the good and evil within his own being and struggles with the truth of his own dark origins.

The melodramatic imagination in Japan thus has a life well beyond the texts and the period that I have discussed, and there is no convenient point of closure. But, perhaps, in place of an ending, I can suggest the ways a novel at the center of the current canon, Natsume Sōseki's *Kokoro* (1914), wrestles with the melodramatic mode. My argument here is not that *Kokoro* should be grouped with turn-of-the-century fiction, but rather that this work—produced seven years later by an author who had clearly endeavored to write a melodramatic novel in *Gubijinsō*—embodies an attempt to conduct a dialogue with the melodramatic imagination. Set partially in the age of melodrama, but narrated from a point beyond it, *Kokoro* invokes melodrama in order to examine it as a historically indispensable mode for understanding human experience. In this sense, *Kokoro* is different from melodramatic texts, which insist on the primacy of their own worldview. It presents the melodramatic imagination as one possible and powerful vision, perhaps to be approached with understanding and sympathy, but not as the singular and prevailing mode of perception. Still, the melodramatic imagination lies heavily over the work; the dialogue is not just one of sympathy but also of struggle. And this struggle ensues because the melodramatic mode continues to exert its power, to hold forth the promise of a coherent moral interpretation of the messy stuff of human sentiment.

It should be clear that *Kokoro* shares many of the concerns and tropes of Meiji melodramatic fiction. The initial narrator's attraction to Sensei in this novel reproduces the pattern in which affiliation leads to the forming of an alternative family. This portrayal reflects, to borrow Brooks's words once again, a "concern with authority, legitimacy, the conflict of generations and the transmission of wisdom."[2] The relationship of the narrator to Sensei is hardly the only example of a fictive family in the novel. As I will later show, Sensei's path through his earlier life is figured as an orphan's serial path through constructed families. All of the fictive families in *Kokoro* are formed under the pressure of modern social exigencies. Both of the subnarratives that constitute the novel focus upon the vicissitudes of students from the countryside living in Tokyo: this is quintessentially a modern experience, for which the preconditions include the existence of a modern educational system crowned at its pinnacle by the Imperial University; the pervasiveness of mobility both geographical and social; and the expansion of urbanization that brings into close interaction people originally from different areas. The fictive families in *Kokoro* form in the absence of birth families of the countryside and in answer to the various needs of male students in Tokyo: the need for food and shelter provided by a boarding house, the demand to find mates outside of rural family connections, the desire to affiliate with others possessing a similar educational background. The world of *Kokoro* is, in fact, built upon the possibility of what Yanagita Kunio had called "domicide," the possibility of urban migration doing murderous damage to rural *ie*.

As we explore the fictive families of *Kokoro*, a key question concerns whether the dynamics of these families are stated as moral dynamics. Do the portrayals of these families display the dualistic morality characteristic of the melodramatic mode? Does the reference to a polarized ethics contribute to a heightening of sentiment in the work?

MORAL DUALISM IN SENSEI'S TESTAMENT

My discussion of how *Kokoro* engages the melodramatic mode builds upon an approach, pioneered by Komori Yōichi and by now extensively employed by others, that views the work as a text in dialogue with itself.[3] This approach prioritizes the divided narrative structure of the work and attempts to read the contested meanings produced by the novel's two narrators, its two temporal settings, and its two narrating instances. Komori's method contrasts markedly with prior critical interpretations of the novel as a single, organically unified whole. The focus now is on how the novel's two separate narratives interact—reinforcing each other and continuously acknowledging their interdependence, but also disagreeing with and relativizing the assertions made in the other. Meaning exists, in such a reading, not *in* either narrative but *between* them.

With this in mind, I would like to look first at "Sensei's Testament," which appears last in the structure of *Kokoro*, but which largely covers events occurring before those described in the initial narrator's sections. "Sensei's Testament" is also narrated some years before the rest of the text; the initial narrator has read and thought at length about the contents of Sensei's letter before setting down his own account.

The letter that Sensei writes to his younger friend is an exorbitantly moral document explaining how he gained a painful and crippling knowledge of his own moral worth. The ethical preoccupations of the man who writes this letter are made clear near its beginning:

> I will not hesitate to throw upon you the dark shadows of life. But you should not be afraid. You should gaze intently at the darkness, and grasp from within it anything that will be of use to you. When I speak of darkness, I am speaking of moral darkness. I was born a moral man. And I was raised a moral man. My moral perceptions may differ considerably from those who are young now. But whatever the difference, they belong to me. (153)[4]

The deliberate and repeated incantation of "moral" here leaves no doubt about the mode of understanding that will be applied to the experience to be related. The heightened rhetoric is also inescapable; the image of darkness, which will run through Sensei's testament and be later recycled in the younger man's narrative, is a leitmotif that resonates throughout melodrama because of its implied binary pairing with the image of light. We should not miss, however, that Sensei pointedly declines to claim universal status for his moral vision. For him, morality is something either generationally determined or privately owned. This refusal to extend one's moral perceptions to others lays the groundwork for the moral dialogue that will ensue.

Sensei's account of his moral self-discovery begins with his earliest contacts with ethically loaded behavior. This is an account narrated wholly in terms of family. Sensei was born as the only son to a rural landholder, a "thoroughly honest man who sought to carefully guard the inheritance from his ancestors"; he is, then, the successor to an *ie*. When his parents die just as he is about to enter higher school, his affairs are placed in the charge of his uncle, his father's far more worldly younger brother who is a business-man in a nearby town. This relationship is depicted as the first of Sensei's fictive families: his uncle becomes someone "necessary for my existence" (159). Sensei's trust is betrayed, however, when the uncle appropriates his in-heritance and attempts to permanently and officially link Sensei to his own family by having him marry his daughter. In his letter to his younger friend, Sensei defines his disillusionment with his uncle as an encounter with evil:

> You will still remember that I once said to you that there was no such thing in this world as a made-to-order evil person. I said to you that one could never let down one's guard because many good people suddenly turn evil when push comes to shove. At the time, you cautioned me, saying that I seemed overly excited. And you asked me under what circumstances a good person turns evil. You looked dissatisfied when I simply answered, "money." I still remember that look of dissatisfaction on your face. I will reveal to you now that, at the time, I was thinking of this uncle. With hatred, I was thinking of this uncle as an example of how an ordinary person becomes evil at the sight of money, as an example of how nothing existed in this world that merited trust. My brief answer may not have been enough for someone like you determined to push through to the bottom of philosophical ques-tions; it may have seemed trite. But for me that answer was alive. Was I not, indeed, excited. It is my belief that there is far more life in a commonplace observation stated with a heated tongue than a new interpretation made with a cold head. This is because the body is moved by the power of blood. Words do not only vibrate in the air; they work much more powerfully on something far stronger. (168)

For Sensei, the family has been the crucible of moral action and moral education. And the lesson he has learned is that no one can be trusted to be principled in the face of temptation. That the specific temptation here involves money is very much in tune with melodramatic fiction's concern with modernity's mercenary impulses. The conclusions Sensei draws from his experience are thoroughly locked in a binary worldview: people are either good or evil depending on the situation. Despite the mention of ordinary people, there is really no in-between in this paradigm where human beings swing between the moral poles. This dualistic view is a consistent part of Sensei's perceptions; it was there when he judged his uncle and it is still in place as he writes his testament. We should also note Sensei's assertion that sentiment validates his belief in dualism. The moral view is authenticated by an excitement felt in the blood.

After the betrayal by his uncle, Sensei will move away from his homeland forever. He will gradually enter into a fictive family with the war widow and her daughter with whom he comes to board. This process accelerates with the addition of Sensei's friend, K, a young man whose prior experience, too, involves passage through a non-natal family. His record includes an unsuccessful adoption: the second son of a Buddhist priest, he had been legally adopted by a childless doctor, who had paid for his education in the mistaken belief that K was receiving training in medicine. In other words, K was someone being groomed to become an eventual successor within the *ie* system. When the truth comes out that he has been studying far less utilitarian subjects, he is disowned and forced to support himself as he completes university. Moved by K's poverty, but also troubled by his own complicity in K's deception of his adoptive family, Sensei persuades a reluctant K to move in with him. Although K and Sensei are nominally boarders, Sensei's desire is clearly to make K a part of his fictive family. At one point, Sensei says that it was his wish that K become "a member of this *katei*" (193). His intent is forcefully expressed in symbolic terms through his acquisition of a quotidian object identified with family life:

> It was eventually time for all of us to see each other at the dinner table. When I first arrived as a boarder, I had been treated as a guest in all respects, and the maid had brought all of my meals to my room on a tray. But this had gradually given way, and it had become the custom for me to be called over to join Okusan and Ojōsan at mealtimes. When K moved in, I made a point of having him treated the same way. In return, I gave Okusan a flimsy dining table made of a thin board equipped with folding legs. *Every household seems to use one of these now, but at the time there were hardly any families that ate their meals ranged around a table of this sort.* I went to the trouble of going to a furniture maker in Ochanomizu and having him make this up to my specifications. (213–14, emphasis mine)

The passage is one of many instances in Sensei's testament when we are made to feel the temporal gap between his narrating instance, which is 1912, and the time of events near the turn of the century. By the end of the Meiji period, the low dining table (*shokutaku*) was becoming more commonplace, but earlier, in an era when family members often ate from individual trays, the dining table had been a powerful new symbol of family togetherness associated with *katei* ideology.[5] When Sensei provides a dining table for his meals with K, Okusan, and Ojōsan, he endeavors to use the bonding powers of commensality to construct a fictive family enfolding both K and himself.

This is a goal, of course, that will be doomed by the desire that K and Sensei come to feel for Ojōsan. In an alternative family unregulated by the incest taboo, K and Sensei become involved in a triangular relationship that will add urgency to Sensei's desire for Ojōsan and reveal something to both men about their moral capacities. The course of this entire struggle is colored by the fact that K possesses melodramatic impulses as powerful as Sensei's own. K is a man who hopelessly yearns for his own perfectibility. He reads about the lives of saints and speaks repeatedly of the need for "spiritual discipline" (shōjin) and his desire to follow the "way" (michi). His adherence to a binary view is apparent in the formulation with which he judges Sensei: "Someone without spiritual aspiration is a fool" (seishinteki ni kōjōshin no nai mono wa baka da). K lives in a world whose inhabitants are split into fools and aspiring saints, with nothing in between. It is precisely this quality that Sensei exploits when a wavering K—torn between his love for Ojōsan and his long-held belief in spiritual discipline—turns to him for advice. Instead of seriously considering his friend's internal conflicts, Sensei takes a path of personal convenience. He responds to his tormented friend by throwing K's own words back in his face: "Someone without spiritual aspiration is a fool." Sensei, then, plays upon K's dualistic mindset in order to make him give up Ojōsan and return to his prior course. Sensei's own belief in polarities is apparent throughout his narration of this encounter. K is depicted as a pure soul unaware of Sensei's calculations: "K was much too honest to admonish me. He was much too innocent. His character was much too virtuous" (251). In keeping with the dualistic framework, Sensei must place himself at the opposite pole. This he does when he says that he acted like "a wolf looking for an opportunity to sink his teeth into a lamb's throat" (252). In Sensei's representation rival males become engaged in a hyperbolic morality play, and he must finally understand himself as a beast who went for the jugular.

The morality play reaches its climax at the moment when Sensei discovers K's body:

The moment my eyes glanced into K's room, they lost their capacity for movement, as though they were made out of glass. I stood paralyzed. When that had passed like a sudden wind, the thought came to my mind that all was lost. A black light that told me that now nothing could be reversed penetrated into my future and in one terrifying moment illuminated what lay before me. And then I began to shake. (267)

The understandable shock of discovering a suicide's body notwithstanding, there is something hyperbolic about Sensei's reaction and the way it is conveyed. The paralysis, the fantastic image of "black light" (*kuroi hikari*) that combines both elements of a classic duality, and the conviction of a transformed future contribute to the staging of a moment of moral crisis charged with extravagant sentiment.

The impact of this dramatic moment causes a moral revelation of the sort that is the stock in trade of melodrama. When he was cheated by his uncle, Sensei had recognized the ordinary face of evil while conveniently excluding himself from its workings. His smug moral superiority is forever shattered by his involvement with K:

> When I was betrayed by my uncle, I was totally convinced of the untrustworthiness of others. But as much as I understood others to be wicked, I still felt sure about myself. Somewhere there was the conviction that, no matter the state of the rest of the world, I myself was a fine person. This had been totally destroyed by K. I felt faint when I realized that I was a person just like my uncle. I, who had lost faith in others, became paralyzed when I lost faith in myself. (278)

In directing his moral disgust at himself, Sensei reveals the potential for peripety within the binary paradigm. Since a person is either at one end of the moral hierarchy or the other, a slip means descending to the realm of the abject. Sensei has discovered a realm of moral exorbitance that will forever exact its punishment, a realm where moral self-knowledge is a matter of life and death. His narration has been throughout what Brooks calls a "melodrama of consciousness," in which the moral conflict is played out internally within characters and "excitement derives from the characters' own dramatized apprehension of clashing moral forces."[6]

If the contents of Sensei's narration are melodramatic, so too are the terms through which it refers to its own narrating situation. As is well known, the imagery of blood suffuses Sensei's narration. Sometimes the blood is real, like the blood from K's carotid artery against the sliding doors, a sanguinary reminder of the violence that erupts in melodramatic novels at moments of unsupportable emotional pressure. At other times, it is figurative, as in the famous passage where Sensei speaks of the transmission of knowledge through narration as a transmission of blood:

> You pressed me to unfurl my past before you as though it were a picture scroll. Within my heart, I respected you then for the very first time. This was

because you showed the will to boldly reach within me and take something that was alive. You sought to split open my heart and drink my warm, flowing blood. I was still alive at that point and did not want to die. And so I put off your demands, promising to respond to you another day. I am now prepared to rip open my own heart and bathe your face with my blood. I will be satisfied if, when my heart stops, a new life pulses within your breast. (154)

The extravagance of figuring knowledge or information as blood emphasizes the intensity of the extraordinary encounter between Sensei and his younger friend. The violent, sacrificial transmission that occurs here gives a new twist to the image of blood, which is identified by Brooks as a major melodramatic sign that "renders the world expressive of moral sentiments."[7] For Brooks, the "celebrated topos of the *voix du sang*" enacts "the secret impulse by which parents and children and siblings are irresistibly drawn to one another despite mistaken and lost identities."[8] In *Kokoro* the *voix du sang* speaks out not to identify lost relations but to create new ones. The novel attempts a redefinition of blood relations.

VERSIONS OF FICTIVE FAMILY

The nature of these new relations bears investigation. A convenient point of departure is Komori's interpretation of this issue, which insists on a fundamental difference between the relations formed, on the one hand, among Sensei, K, Okusan, and Ojōsan, and, on the other hand, between Sensei and the initial narrator. Komori's argument begins by recognizing that Sensei seeks to construct a "quasi-family" with K and with the women with whom he boards. This urge to reproduce the family is viewed as being reactionary and ultimately destructive:

> It has heretofore been overlooked that a major factor in the "tragedy" that occurs in the relations with K exists in the halfway nature of Sensei's separation from the logic of "blood," that is, the logic of "family." Sensei, who has abandoned his homeland, finally cannot live without constructing a quasi-familial relationship with Okusan and Ojōsan. And it is because he presupposes this kind of relationship that he is tormented by "suspicions." Moreover, by trying to financially play the parental role vis-à-vis K, who has been trying on his own to proceed down the "way" of autonomy, he ends up pulling K into the quasi-family that he has himself manufactured.
>   Unable to separate himself from the logic of "family," Sensei has stolen K's solitude from him. This is, at first glance, disguised as something done

for K's benefit, but it was actually nothing else but a means of easing the "loneliness" of his own solitude. The prohibition of solitude, the prohibition of each person possessing time and space for himself—from the standpoint of the "family," this is a taboo that has a binding power similar to the taboo against incest. [9]

Komori's judgments on Sensei's efforts are founded on his view that the "logic of 'family'" is ultimately prescriptive and restrictive, forcing people into naturalized roles that prevent the realization of truer connections anchored in the recognition of ultimate human aloneness. In this analysis, Sensei's partial restoration of family can only be seen as a form of foreclosure that stunts the human possibilities contained within both K and himself.

In Komori's argument, the initial narrator is placed at the opposing pole. Unlike Sensei, who must resort to an institutionalized prior form to relate to others, the narrator engages Sensei with his "heart" and with his "breast." What he is able to do is to live out a "new 'logic' and morality of 'blood'" that has nothing to do with the family.[10] This logic allows the initial narrator to encounter Sensei directly, letting the latter's "blood"—in the form of language and memory—course through his person. Because it strips away the coercive union of family, it permits him to embrace the essential separateness of each individual and aspire toward truer forms of human interaction. Komori's valorization of non-familial relationships between autonomous individuals ultimately leads him toward the controversial argument that the initial narrator will seek out Sensei's widow and establish a new kind of relationship with her. His vision of what will occur between these two characters is the clearest statement of his conception of the new consciousness that the narrator embodies. The narrator's life with the widow, Komori says, will be

> to live out a free association between one person and another, which a person can enter through an act of choice and leave also from an act of choice—a relationship that can never consist of becoming a member of the realm of family, a relationship that cannot be categorized within familial models such as parent and child, sister and brother, husband and wife, and "Sensei" and disciple.[11]

Komori, then, constructs the narrator as a heroic autonomous individual, an antithesis to the weak, family-bound Sensei.

There is considerable overreaching here in positing the nature of a relationship that occurs totally outside the novel's plot. But what I would like to point out is the striking binarism that makes Komori's speculations resonate with melodramatic structures of feeling. Komori attempts to establish a hierarchy of value between two opposing positions and grants the imprimatur of true sentiment to the valorized pole. A melodramatic analysis of this type cannot capture the qualities of the initial narrator, whose inclination is to negotiate with Sensei's beliefs and assumptions rather than negate them. The binarism of either/or and the structure of the excluded middle is precisely what the initial narrator refuses.

I will eventually return to the issue of melodrama, but we must first deal with the model of family that occupies the degraded pole in Komori's argument. We must interrogate the "logic of 'blood,'" which Komori describes as follows:

> The logic of "blood" joined parents and children, siblings, and relatives. It upheld an unquestioned, almost transcendent, sense of physical connection and identity of one person with others in the form of kinship. A silent, almost unconditional "trust"—the notion that somehow all was well if there was a connection of "blood"—was assumed, and the "morality" surrounding human relationships was fed by the logic of "blood." In premodern society this logic operated as a "naturalized" system, and, in Japan in particular, a set of "ethical principles," . . . in the form of a "moral" network modeled upon quasi-filial relations, enfolded everything from the nation to private relations.[12]

Komori will go on to argue that in the Meiji period the trust engendered by the logic of "blood" was undermined by the forces of capitalism, which commodified human beings and treated human relations in terms of use value. This is what lies behind Sensei's betrayal by his uncle. Despite this, however, Sensei remains nostalgic for the certitude offered by the logic of "blood" and tries to reinstate it, albeit unsuccessfully, first in his relations with Okusan and Ojōsan, and later in his attempt to pull K into the household.

This is an argument with a certain persuasiveness; and Komori must be credited with recognizing Sensei's familial aspirations. But the view of Sensei as a retrograde adherent to an older ideology of family misses some key distinctions. Komori's concept of the "logic of 'blood'" appears to point to *ie* ideology, though with the difference that he views his version of the "traditional" family as a premodern phenomenon destroyed by modernity. Not every family, however, is an *ie*. What Komori's approach fails to grasp is the gulf between *ie* ideology and the alternative families envisioned by Sensei. To begin with, the "logic of 'blood'" does not operate within the fictive family consisting of Okusan, Ojōsan, Sensei, and K. There is no blood

lineage, except between Okusan and Ojōsan, and there is no evidence that
Sensei seeks "an unquestioned, almost transcendent, sense of physical connection and identity of one person with others in the form of kinship" in
his relations with the two women. In fact, Sensei is constantly aware of
his difference from Ojōsan and Okusan, initially keeping his distance from
them because of the suspicions bred by his history with his uncle. Sensei departs most radically from the logic of "blood" in trying to make K a part of
his alternative family. Here, an attempt is made to bring an unrelated male
into the fictive family. Although part of the motive is to offer financial assistance, there is little evidence that Sensei seeks to play a parental role over
K, whom in many ways he regards as being superior to himself. Sensei operates out of both a sense of responsibility, having encouraged K's deception
of his adoptive family, and a sense of sympathy for the pressures K faces as a
person on his own. Instead of being a failed or partial attempt to reinstitute
a prior logic of family, Sensei's efforts to construct an alternative family constitute a departure—an endeavor to create human bonds that can respond
to the needs of women deprived of a husband and a father by a modern war,
the needs of two young men torn from their childhoods in the country.

Put somewhat differently, Komori's argument fails to take account of the
full dialectic of Said's notion of affiliation. Said, we will recall, noted that
affiliative associations have a tendency to reproduce the forms of filiative
relationships, but they do so in the process of rejecting biological filiation
under the "pressure to produce new and different ways of conceiving human
relationships."[13] In a dialectic that *re-presents* the forms of family, affiliation
both transforms and recycles the family. Komori stresses the latter without
fully acknowledging the transformations.

Where, then, does the initial narrator stand on the ideology of the family? Does he truly leave the family behind and achieve the kind of true
autonomy prized by Komori? One place to prosecute this question is in a
passage where the narrator partially repeats Sensei's rhetoric of blood:

> I compared my own father and Sensei within my heart. From the point of
> view of the larger society, both men were so modest in accomplishment that
> it hardly mattered whether they were dead or alive. In terms of gaining rec-
> ognition, neither had anything to show. Yet my father, with his taste for the
> game of *go*, seemed lacking to me, even as a partner for a bit of recreation.
> Sensei, whom I never visited just for entertainment, had affected my mind
> far more than anyone I had approached in search of enjoyment. To say that
> he affected my mind sounds too cold, so I should correct myself by saying

that he touched my heart. *At that time, it seemed to me no exaggeration at all to say that Sensei's strength had become part of my flesh, that his life ran in my blood.* When I deliberately laid out before my eyes the self-evident fact that my father was indeed my real father, and that Sensei was totally unrelated to me, I felt as surprised as if I had discovered some major truth for the first time. (64, emphasis mine)

In this passage, the initial narrator reveals that the heated and sanguinary rhetoric of Sensei's letter—which, given the chrono-logic of the narration he has already read—now flows through his prose. And he shows that he too contemplates a radical reconfiguration of "blood relations." The terms of the discussion here do not allow us to conclude, as Komori does, that the narrator seeks or achieves a non-familial and autonomous relationship with Sensei that stands apart from the logic of blood or family. Rather, it reveals that the narrator, like Sensei before him, is a man who seeks to understand the new human connections of modernity using the discourse of reconstructed family, a man who thinks about affiliation through the terms of filiation. The narrator's act of comparison draws a parallel as much as it constructs an opposition. When he yokes together his father and Sensei, he reveals that the two men both occupy a paternal position in his imagination. Such comparisons simultaneously recognizing similarity and difference become a recurring feature of the narrator's account. He becomes acutely aware of this propensity as he spends time with his dying father: "As I repeatedly encountered my father's forlorn attitudes and words, I again thought of Sensei, who did not answer my letters. In the sense that they gave me entirely the opposite impression, Sensei and my father often arose in my head together, both by way of contrast and association" (122).

These kinds of comparisons most assuredly do not show the narrator's attachment to a conventional and rigid ideology of family. Nor do they indicate that Sensei has become a "second father" for him in any deterministic sense in which filiation fixes identity or sensibility. But they do show that the narrator thinks about his relationships with these two men as contiguous phenomena, that the figure of fatherhood and family remain important to him as he attempts to define his new relationship. Like Sensei before him, he is a man who thinks about human ties through the trope of the alternative family.

There is evidence in the text that this approach has been directly suggested to the narrator by Sensei, who more than once points to the family as a means for understanding their relationship. Sensei's most telling comment in this vein occurs when the younger man becomes involved in a discussion between Sensei and Okusan regarding their childlessness:

> Sensei's household consisted only of him, his wife, and a maid. It was usually quiet whenever I went there. Never once did I hear peals of laughter. Sometimes it felt as though Sensei and I were the only ones in the house.
> "It would be better if we had children," Okusan once said turning to me. I replied, "That's true." But no sympathy rose in my heart. I had not had children then, and I only thought of children as a source of annoyance.
> "What if I adopt one for you?" Sensei said.
> "But an adopted child. What do you think?" Okusan asked, turning toward me again.
> "No matter how long we wait, we'll never have children," Sensei said.
> Okusan was silent. When I took her place and asked "Why is that so?" Sensei simply replied, "Divine retribution," and laughed loudly. (25)

When Sensei mentions "divine retribution" he is speaking of the specific guilt that weighs on his consciousness, but the portrayal of his childless marriage also resonates with numerous depictions in nineteenth- and early-twentieth-century fiction, pointed out by Said, in which "the failure of the generative impulse" stands in for broader epistemic and social ruptures.[14] To the extent that *Kokoro* locates Sensei's predicament in the mistrust, the loss of moral verities, and the cutthroat competition loosed by modern social and economic conditions, his childlessness too can be said to represent a more general social malaise. The solution to childlessness that Sensei proposes here, albeit jokingly, is adoption. Since this proposition is pointedly made before a worshipful young man, there is an inescapable suggestion of the latter's candidacy. Sensei has exposed his young friend to the idea that an affiliative relationship responding to modern conditions of social isolation and atomization can be figured as filiation. After this conversation, even Okusan begins to operate within a familial framework, doing the young man's washing and sewing. The text pointedly notes that these actions form something of a compensatory mechanism: "Okusan, who didn't have children, said that helping me with such things helped her pass the time and was actually good for her" (57). As Komori notes, Okusan also begins to call her own husband "Sensei," copying the narrator and mirroring the way Japanese mothers frequently call their spouses "Father" to accord with the form of address used by their children. All of this underlines that much has transpired to give the narrator cause to think of Sensei within the framework of an alternative family.

KOKORO'S NARRATOR AND
MELODRAMATIC MORALITY

If this is the case, then, and the narrator understands his experiences through the trope of the fictive family—at least partly suggested to him by Sensei— does he also inherit the melodramatic sensibility that so deeply colors the older man's understanding? Does he see his world in terms of moral binaries? Does a polarized vision generate extravagant sentiments within his narrative?

There is much to tempt the reader into concluding that the initial narrator shares Sensei's view of the world. In many scenes, he speaks to Sensei using a voice filled with ethically charged homosocial hyperemotionalism. One such scene occurs in response to Sensei's declaration that good men or ordinary men "suddenly turn evil when push comes to shove" (77). Finding this assertion too abstract to be convincing, the narrator later aggressively presses Sensei to reveal the experience that lies behind it:

> Sensei stared at my face, as though taken aback. His hand, in which he held a cigarette, was trembling slightly.
> "You're awfully bold," he said.
> "I'm simply sincere. I sincerely want to learn from life."
> "Is that so, even if it means exposing my past?"
> The word "expose" had a frightening ring to it. I felt as though the man before me was not the Sensei I habitually respected, but a criminal of some kind. Sensei's face was pale.
> "Are you really sincere in what you say?" he said, as if to make sure. "I distrust others as a consequence of my past. To be honest, I distrust you too. But I don't want to suspect you. You seem too straightforward to suspect. I want to go to my death having trusted at least one person. Can you become that one person? Will you? Are you sincere from the bottom of your soul?"
> My voice trembling, I said: "If my life is sincere, then what I've just said is sincere."
> "I understand," Sensei said. "I will tell you. I will tell you everything about my past." (86)

This moment of emotional male communion eventually produces the letter constituting the last part of the novel. The narrator's potential for evaluating human value as binaries is revealed by the momentary illumination of his respected friend as perhaps a "criminal." His own declaration of his worthiness to be taken into his friend's confidence is enunciated using the moral discourse of "sincerity." The trembling voice and the assertion of sincerity seem to echo the high-toned sentimentality of melodrama.

It goes without saying, moreover, that the narrator's repeated comparisons of his father and Sensei has a melodramatic component. The holding up of two men one against the other and seeing them as polar opposites reveal a binary mindset; the narrator's use of the rhetoric of blood displays the investment of sentiment in duality. The idea of the narrator as someone forced to make a binary choice between his father and Sensei is most clearly set forth in the account of his father's last days. Here the narrator's perception of his father's accelerating deterioration is paralleled by his growing concern for what Sensei may be encountering in Tokyo. The association of these two men in the narrator's mind makes the emotional demands of attending to one generate a longing for the other. The anxieties caused by his dual loyalties crest when the narrator receives Sensei's suicide note as his father lies in a coma on the verge of death. When the narrator leaves his dying father to jump on the train bound for Tokyo, he appears to have made a choice between two difficult alternatives. But the reader is actually left with that convention of serialized melodrama—the cliffhanger. We do not know the consequences of the narrator's actions. We do not know what he finds when he arrives in Tokyo, nor do we, in any direct terms, find out what his actions do to his relationship with his parents.

This unresolved cliffhanger is emblematic of *Kokoro*'s relationship to melodrama. On the one hand, through the portrayal of an emotionally pressured choice between binary alternatives there is a clear reference to melodrama both as a narrative form and as a form of imagination. On the other hand, there is a deliberate refusal to answer the questions that melodrama raises. Any reader attuned to the trajectory of melodrama and expecting an outcome enunciating moral certitude will feel frustration over the narrator's termination of his own account. How can the moral or ethical content of the narrator's choice be judged if we do not know the outcome? In effect, *Kokoro* juxtaposes a narrative that gestures toward melodrama yet adamantly resists melodramatic closure against Sensei's testament, which uses suicide to narrate the ultimate consequence of moral failure within a binary framework. This juxtaposition destabilizes the assumptions of melodrama—for it suggests that the moral value of actions may not always be made clear, as it is in Sensei's case, in a spectacular moment of revelation. For those who continue to live beyond moments of moral choice, the value of their choice may be forever contingent, requiring strategies of suspension rather than closure.

The narrator's account, then, suggests that the melodramatic imagination exemplified by Sensei is *one* way of interpreting experience rather than the only way. The ideological effect here is momentous, for a melodramatic morality robbed of its primacy becomes merely a perspective rather than a singular, overwhelming paradigm for understanding human actions. If we examine the narrator's comments about Sensei with this in mind, we arrive at a closer view of the dialogue that the narrator conducts with Sensei's dualism. For clarity, it makes sense to divide our inquiry here into examinations of the younger man's attitudes toward Sensei at the time of the story and his later feelings about him at the time of narration. To deal first with the former, Sensei's clearest statements on his binary morality both fascinate the younger man and raise questions in his mind. There is no immediate acceptance of the validity of melodramatic judgments. When Sensei makes his famous statement, based upon his experience, that "love is guilt," the younger man feels that "the meaning of the 'guilt,' of which Sensei spoke, seemed vague and difficult to comprehend" (38). Made unhappy by Sensei's mystifying statements, the young man demands clarification: "Sensei, please explain more clearly what you mean by 'guilt.' If not, please don't speak any more about this problem. At least until I understand the meaning of 'guilt'" (38). The young man is at this stage, then, an interrogator of the melodramatic spirit rather than an adherent. A similar reaction occurs after Sensei's declaration about the evil found in ordinary men. Instead of immediate assent, Sensei's observations cause the narrator to demand more meaningful knowledge:

> Among the things that Sensei had said, there was one thing that I wanted to get to the bottom of. This was the meaning of his words when he said that anyone could become evil when push comes to shove. It was not that I could not understand this on the level of words. But I wanted to know more about the phrase. (79)

It is, then, none other than Sensei's dualistic moral view that calls forth the younger man's curiosity, the rapacious need to know fueled by a homosocial ardor. This inquisitiveness, which prompts Sensei to promise that he will one day reveal his past, is fueled precisely by the fact that the younger man stands outside of the circle defined by melodramatic morality.

We might expect that the younger man becomes inscribed within this circle once he has read Sensei's letter and especially after he has established his own reasons for feeling guilt by abandoning his dying father. In narratological terms, we might expect that the narrator, who has been subjected to the full onslaught of Sensei's melodramatic rhetoric through the letter, would reveal, at the time of narration, a stronger sympathy for the melodramatic imagination. In a sense he does, but not in any way that shows agreement with melodramatic judgments. Rather, he exhibits a sympathy laced with understanding and affection that at the same time maintains a palpable distance from Sensei's values. This stance appears in the way he contravenes Sensei's expectations of what will happen when his past is revealed. The older man's secrecy about his past had been fueled not only by his sense of guilt but by a belief that others would naturally condemn him were his secret to be exposed. He warns the inquisitive younger man away with the suggestion that the latter might not like what he finds: "In any case, you shouldn't trust me too much. You'll regret it soon enough. And in return for having been fooled, men have been known to engage in brutal revenge" (41). A binary value system that castigates moral weakness lies behind such a statement. But the narrator, who already knows Sensei's story as he narrates, does not express disappointment over being fooled, nor does he engage in brutal revenge. Instead, he writes with compassion about a man consumed with self-hatred: "How sad it is that Sensei had been warning those that drew near him to stay away because he was not worth approaching. Sensei, who did not respond to the affection of others, felt contempt for himself long before he felt contempt for others" (13). What is present here is not moral condemnation, but a recognition of the pathos of unforgiving moral judgment. A similar tone characterizes the conclusions the narrator reaches regarding Sensei's behavior toward him: "A man who was capable of loving others, a man who could not keep from loving, yet a man who could not hold his arms wide and embrace someone who sought to draw near him— such a man was Sensei" (18). The narrator writes, then, with an affection laced with regret—regret over Sensei's recrimination of himself, regret over the unfulfilled nature of his own relationship with Sensei. Eschewing the discourse of "good and evil" and "morality," he writes in an ethical register that contrasts significantly from that of the older man. The narrator understands the dualistic moral vision that drove Sensei to suicide, yet his own stance is outside of the melodramatic binary. Rather than demanding that Sensei's predicament yield some kind of polarized moral clarity, he turns to embrace the imperfection of an all too human friend.

The narrator's acceptance of moral complexity also extends to his view of himself. Were he a man operating under the exacting requirements of a binary morality, we might expect that he would blame himself for abandoning his dying father. Because the unresolved cliffhanger prevents any direct account of the aftermath of the young man's actions, we must look for his judgments on himself in the tone with which he speaks at the time of narration. What is striking here is the total lack of bitterness or self-recrimination. Unlike Sensei, whose regret ultimately leads him to suicide, the narrator is a man who has accepted his decisions. He is still "proud and pleased by the intuition" (18) that led him to approach Sensei and he counts his drawing close to Sensei, without overly analyzing him, as "one of the things that ought to be valued in my life" (21). There is no regret here about what happened as a result of the narrator's meeting with Sensei; rather there is pride and self-affirmation.

This is not the pride of someone who has made the right choice between binary alternatives. The section of the novel entitled "My Parents and I" contains one of the more moving accounts of parent-child relations to be found in Japanese fiction. The portrait of the dying father is unsparing yet tender and deeply affectionate. The narrator's depiction of himself, though tempered by the lessons learned along the way, offers a quiet understanding toward his younger self. The scene exemplifying this combination of qualities is the one regarding the young narrator's changing responses toward his father's delight over his graduation, a delight that initially strikes him as vulgar and unsophisticated:

> I had been thinking of my graduation from school as a matter of course for any normal person, and so I was embarrassed when my father was much more pleased than I had expected.
> "It's really fine that you've graduated."
> My father repeated these words many times. Within my own heart (*kokoro*), I compared my father's pleasure with Sensei's expression when he had said "congratulations" to me over the dining table at his house on the night of my graduation. To me, Sensei, who congratulated me with his words but was disparaging within, looked far more refined than my father, who was so pleased with something neither rare nor special. In the end, I began to feel disgust for the rusticity that flowed from my father's ignorance.
> "There's nothing particularly fine about graduating from university. There are hundreds of graduates every year." I finally began to speak in this manner.
> There was a strange expression on my father's face. "I'm not saying that it's

fine just because you've graduated. Of course, it's fine to have you graduate, but when I say this, there's a bit more to it. If only you'd understand this . . ."

I tried to get my father to tell me the rest. He seemed not to want to go on, but he finally said: "When you get down to it, the fact is that it's fine for me. As you know, I'm ill. When I saw you last winter, I thought that I might only have three or four months left. But through some kind of luck, I'm still here today. I'm still here and I have no trouble getting around. And now you've graduated. That's why I'm happy. Don't you think, for a parent, it's a lot better to have a cherished son finish school while you're well, rather than to have him graduate after you're gone? It's probably unpleasant for someone like you, with big hopes for the future, to repeatedly hear that it's a fine thing when all you've done is graduate from university. But look at it from my side. The view's a little different. In other words, your graduation is a fine thing for me rather than for you. Do you understand?"

I had no reply. Even more than being apologetic, I hung my head in shame. My father, it seemed, had calmly accepted his own death. Not only that, he had thought he would die before I graduated. I had been stupid not to realize how my graduation would reverberate in my father's heart. I took out my diploma from my bag and carefully showed it to my father and my mother. Squashed by something, the diploma had lost its original shape. My father straightened it out carefully. (102–4)

This finely modulated scene relates a moment of epiphany. At the beginning, the narrator engages in a binary comparison that disparages his father for viewing his accomplishments without the requisite irony. But as the scene proceeds he learns a great deal that turns out to be of continuing significance—he learns that he was deeply loved as a child, that his father possessed a bravery and an assurance missing in Sensei. By including this episode in his narration, he testifies to the importance of his father in his memory. Scenes of this sort resist a binary imperative in a number of ways. When his initial belief is complicated by evidence of his father's love for him, the young man knows that it is possible to feel multiple loyalties and to understand others in more ways than one. The narrator, in effect, reflects this knowledge in the organization of his account: by choosing to include his father in a narrative that had begun as a story of his relationship with Sensei, he is affirming the importance of both men in his life. Offered a binary choice between his father and Sensei, the narrator, in his act of narrating, chooses both. The binary view is also rejected in the narrator's view of himself. Although this is a scene in which the narrator discovers a painful personal shortcoming, there is no moral condemnation for his initial disparagement of his father. He does not resort to a binary of good and evil, nor does he engage in a hyperbolic rhetoric of ethical judgment. What is there instead is a quiet acceptance of a blinding youthful enthusiasm and an acknowledgement of the need to learn from error. While the narrator writes, then, about a world filled with melodramatic choices, he does so in an unmelodramatic tone. He writes in dialogue, but not in accordance, with a melodramatic understanding of family.

KOKORO, THE IE, AND THE MEIJI MELODRAMATIC NOVEL

Let me summarize my argument thus far by saying that *Kokoro* consists of two narratives that put forth fictive families: Sensei's testament hews to the melodramatic mode, describing his path through serial families as a confrontation with evil, while the younger man's narrative engages but stands outside of melodrama as it recounts his youthful enthusiasm with forgiveness and understanding. The combined effect of these two narratives is to repeatedly return to the fictive family while refusing to enshrine melodrama as the single, authoritative mode for moral thinking about the family. In a sense, *Kokoro* has made explicit in its formal division of narratives the ideological contradiction implicit in Meiji melodrama's search for certitude. It shows us that the melodramatic quest for moral assurance can be relativized by approaches that refuse to yoke morality to restrictive dualities.

Taking account of these features allows us to more accurately gauge *Kokoro*'s position vis-à-vis *ie* ideology. Here, it will be especially useful to refer back to Yanagita Kunio's fears for the future of the *ie*, discussed in the Introduction. Yanagita had constructed, in 1906, a melodramatic narrative in which the blissful pastoral continuity enjoyed by generations of farm families was endangered by migration to urban areas. When members of an *ie* were uprooted, Yanagita had argued, they lost touch with the narratives and practices of their ancestors and this ultimately would lead to the destruction of *ie*. Since all Japanese *ie* had served the imperial institution for generations, its loss would weaken the nation and threaten the Japanese sense of identity. The dangers of urban migration were so great that Yanagita had coined, in a distinctly melodramatic move, the neologism "domicide" to drive home the evil of allowing an *ie* to expire.

Setting *Kokoro* against Yanagita's statements quickly makes apparent that the novel recounts the process of "domicide" in a number of families. Sensei, the only child of his parents and the inheritor of his family's headship, had left the countryside after being betrayed by his uncle and had never returned, even to visit his parents' graves (171). Although his separation from his roots had effectively ended Sensei's *ie*, this termination has been made final by Sensei's failure to have children. His death means the end of his *ie*. Okusan's *ie*, too, had ended with the marriage of its only daughter. There are signs that the initial narrator's *ie* will also likely meet with "domicide." The narrator's older brother, the presumptive heir, left the countryside first to pursue an education and later to take up a job in another prefecture. When asked about coming back to take up a househead's responsibility, he brushes off the possibility by saying, "How can I do such a thing?" (141). He even suggests that the narrator might want to live in the country and take his place. But the latter, too, is determined to make his career elsewhere, in his case in Tokyo, where he has gone to university and where he has formed his bond with Sensei. The most explicit comment on the future of the narrator's *ie* is voiced by his father shortly before the latter's death:

> My father appeared to be thinking about what would happen after his death. At the very least, he seemed to be imagining his own *ie* after he was gone.
>
> "Educating your children is both good and bad," he said. "If you take the trouble to educate them, they never come home. This is practically like supporting their schooling in order to separate parents and children."
>
> As a result of having studied, my brother was now far away. The consequence of my education was that I was firmly determined to live in Tokyo. Having raised such children, my father's complaints were not unreasonable. My father's thoughts must have been unbearably lonely when he pictured my mother being left alone in the country house where they had lived so long.
>
> My father thoroughly believed that his *ie* was something that could not be moved. He also believed that my mother, who lived within it, could not be moved as long as she was alive. It was a source of terrible anxiety for him that after his death my lonely mother would be left by herself in an empty house. Despite this, he wanted to urge me forward, saying that I should find a good position in Tokyo. There was a contradiction in my father's thinking. At the same time that I found it funny, I was also delighted I could go back to Tokyo thanks to this contradiction. (118–19)

The contradiction being lived out by the father is a version of a conflict we have seen in other forms: the clash between the powerful ideologies of *rishin shusse* and of the *ie*. The father believes in professional advancement for his son, but advancement and the geographical mobility it requires threaten the *ie*. With two sons who will not return to the countryside, his *ie* faces the fate Yanagita had warned against in such dire terms.

The attitudes of *Kokoro* to the extinction of *ie*, however, differ markedly. *Kokoro* does not share Yanagita's melodramatic view of the tragic consequences. Although it acknowledges the sadness of *ie* left to die—the empty houses and lonely parents—it emphasizes the alternative families that arise in its place. These alternatives, to put it mildly, are not necessarily happy ones, but they testify to the powerful drive to form affiliations, and, in the case of Sensei and the narrator, the potential for trust, intimacy, and the transmission of knowledge. When Sensei speaks about his knowledge in the language of property, he makes his letter to the younger man a kind of inheritance: "My past was experienced only by me, and so it would not be mistaken to say that it is my property. . . . Among the millions of Japanese, it is only to you that I want to relate my past" (153). This figuring of a narrative as inheritance echoes in fascinating ways Yanagita's contention that "family legends" are among the things passed down in an *ie*. When the initial narrator writes about Sensei with a generous and sympathetic understanding of the life related in his letter, we see the possibility of knowledge being passed down between people that official ideology viewed as strangers. This knowledge continues to exert force upon someone living in the present. The relationship between Sensei and the narrator affirms, finally, the possibility of memory in the fictive family. *Kokoro* shows the dead living on in affiliations constructed and reconstructed amidst the exigencies of modernity.

The novel, then, resists the relentless drive of official ideology to prescribe the *ie* as the locus for the most meaningful bonds. It insists on the potential to remake the family in response to chance meetings that occur in a modern world. Yet, like the turn-of-the-century novels that simultaneously struggle against and accept elements of state ideology, *Kokoro* is an ideologically ambivalent text. At the same time that it articulates potential alternatives, it upholds certain hegemonic interests. To begin with, despite its undermining of rigid notions of *ie*, *Kokoro* also emphasizes the connection of personal to national experience. Much of this emphasis is located in the temporal structure of the novel, which places the end point of its two narratives (as well as the time of the narration of "Sensei's Testament") in 1912, the year of the deaths of the Meiji emperor and of Nogi Maresuke, the general who followed his emperor to the grave by committing a modern version of *junshi*, the feudal act of following one's lord in death. The endings in this novel are made to deliberately resonate with events that produced a "sense of an ending" throughout the nation. When Sensei says that he intends to "commit *junshi* to the spirit of the Meiji era" (286), we are invited to read his experience not only as the record of one tortured individual but as an expression of an era that cannot be separated from the emperor who shared its name and the modern nation-state that arose during his reign. This goes beyond insisting on the historicity of an individual life and suggests the indissoluble ties of person to nation. However *Kokoro* may present alternatives to the Meiji state's family ideology, it ultimately seals the individual within a national framework.

When the temporal structure of the two narratives allows the deaths of Sensei and the narrator's father to be more or less simultaneous to the deaths of the Emperor Meiji and Nogi, it creates, as many critics have pointed out, a moment marked by the deaths of fathers and father-figures. This fixation upon fathers is characteristic of a text that insistently claims that the most significant relationships are those between men. The affiliations and transmissions of knowledge in the text, despite their departures from official prescriptions, work toward the reproduction of patriarchy. This goes hand in hand with the homosocial thrust of a text that views heterosexual desire as arising out of intense, triangulated male relations. The male-centered nature of the novel is most apparent in Sensei's insistence that his wife be excluded, in the name of preserving her purity, from any knowledge of his past. If knowledge is the substance of inheritance in the novel, Okusan is to be left with nothing. Her part in the drama that transpired between Sensei and K is reduced to that of a contested yet ignorant object. When we view Okusan's fate as one of moral exclusion, a clear contrast emerges between *Kokoro* and turn-of-the-century melodramas in their approaches to female moral capacity. Although the earlier works, too, had unfolded in a patriarchal world, they had portrayed women as being subject to the same exorbitant moral claims as men. Called to respond to modern discourses of love and marriage, individuality, and social advancement, yet exposed to the contradictions of gendered hierarchies, women in Meiji melodramas had confronted ineluctable ethical choices. They had taken decisive action and they had suffered extravagantly as a consequence. *Kokoro* mostly works to remove women from moral relevance.[15]

If *Kokoro* rejects an engagement with female moral agency, it also avoids Meiji melodrama's preoccupation with status and class. Taking an approach that seems too obvious to be less than deliberate, the novel gives its two main protagonists nearly identical social backgrounds. Both Sensei and the initial narrator are the sons of substantial rural landowners and they share similar paths by attending higher school and Tokyo Imperial University. This has the effect of naturalizing the movement of rural elites into the metropolitan intelligentsia and of eliding a consideration of status inconsistency, which makes its clearest appearances when characters from different social backgrounds collide. In Sensei and the narrator, relative economic ease, high educational attainment, and the capacity to engage in male moral discourse occur in a consistent cluster. The emphasis upon the social similarity of Sensei and the young narrator is, moreover, enhanced by the work's failure to identify the precise regions from which they come. Because these two characters are defined as the offspring of rural landowners from unspecified (although different) regions, the contrasting regional identifications of men from, say, Tōhoku and Kyushu, are obscured in favor of stressing their similarities. The inconsistencies and the conflicts that arise out of social and geographical mobility are thus abstracted into broadly generalized oppositions—for example, the country and the city—without ever evoking the edgy discomfort that resides in complex, multi-layered identities.

Kokoro, then, mutes or elides the consideration of social and gender differences that had animated Meiji melodramatic fiction. Its posture of telling a story of national significance goes hand in hand with the portrayal of a less contested social space. These features may very well have contributed to the novel's canonization. Yet it is also worth remembering that *Kokoro*'s place in the canon has enshrined a text that argues the need to understand melodrama as a pivotal mode of moral enunciation and the fictive family as a powerful form for modern human affiliations. As long as *Kokoro* draws the attention of critics, lines bookstore shelves, and appears on reading lists, the charged morality and the fictive families of the age of melodrama will continue to ripple through Japanese culture. If the thrust of *ie* ideology was to attempt to fix and homogenize the Japanese family for the moral good of the nation, *Kokoro* and the Meiji melodramas that preceded it seek the moral value of the family within its protean adaptability.

Notes

Notes to Introduction

1. Ozaki Kōyō, *Konjiki yasha*, in *Ozaki Kōyō shū*, vol. 5 of *Nihon kindai bungaku taikei* (Tokyo: Kadokawa Shoten, 1971), pp. 114–17.

2. The concept of melodrama may see more frequent use by Japanese critics now that Peter Brooks's *The Melodramatic Imagination* has been translated into Japanese by Yomota Inuhiko and Kimura Keiko as *Merodoramateki sōzōryoku* (Tokyo: Sangyō Tosho, 2002).

3. In applying concepts of melodrama to Meiji fiction, I am preceded by Richard Torrance, who has called the period from 1895 to 1905 the "golden age of Japanese melodrama." Torrance has also used the ideas of Peter Brooks, but his discussion retains the pejorative view, because he considers the melodramatic fiction written by his subject, Tokuda Shūsei, as mere preparation for the more serious writing that followed. See *The Fiction of Tokuda Shūsei and the Emergence of Japan's New Middle Class* (Seattle: University of Washington Press, 1994), pp. 36–42. Concepts of melodrama have also been used by M. Cody Poulton in analyzing the dramatic works of Izumi Kyōka. See *Spirits of Another Sort: The Plays of Izumi Kyōka* (Ann Arbor: University of Michigan Center for Japanese Studies, 2001), pp. 17–51. Keiko McDonald discusses the film adaptation of Meiji melodramatic fiction in *From Book to Screen: Modern Japanese Literature in Film* (Armonk, NY: M. E. Sharpe, 2000), pp. 3–16. More recently, Jonathan Zwicker has argued for the continuity of Japanese print culture from the Edo to the Meiji periods, using the melodramatic mode as a key point of reference. See *Practices of the Sentimental Imagination: Melodrama, the Novel, and the Social Imaginary in Nineteenth-Century Japan* (New York: Columbia University Press, 2006).

4. Peter Brooks, *The Melodramatic Imagination: Balzac, Henry James, Melodrama, and the Mode of Excess* (New Haven, CT: Yale University Press, 1976).

5. Ibid., pp. 20–21.

6. Ibid., p. ix.

7. Linda Williams, *Playing the Race Card: Melodramas of Black and White from Uncle Tom to O. J. Simpson* (Princeton, NJ: Princeton University Press), p. 19.

8. Ben Singer, *Melodrama and Modernity: Early Sensational Cinema and Its Contexts* (New York: Columbia University Press, 2001), pp. 48–99.

9. Ibid., p. 44.

10. Brooks, *Melodramatic Imagination*, p. 22.

11. Ibid., p. 15.

12. Ibid., p. 43.

13. Marsha Kinder, *Blood Cinema: The Reconstruction of National Identity in Spain* (Berkeley: University of California Press, 1993).

14. Williams, *Playing the Race Card*.

15. Brooks, *Melodramatic Imagination*, p. 21.

16. Thomas Elsaesser, "Tales of Sound and Fury: Observations on the Family Melodrama," in *Movies and Methods*, vol. 2, ed. Bill Nichols (Berkeley: University of California Press, 1985), p. 169.

17. Christine Gledhill comments on these tendencies in "The Melodramatic Field: An Investigation," in *Home Is Where the Heart Is: Studies in the Melodrama and the Woman's Film*, ed. Christine Gledhill (London: BFI Books, 1987), pp. 8–9.

18. Laura Mulvey, "Notes on Sirk and Melodrama," in *Home Is Where the Heart Is: Studies in Melodrama and the Woman's Film*, ed. Christine Gledhill (London: BFI Books, 1987), pp. 75–76.

19. Geoffrey Nowell-Smith, "Minnelli and Melodrama," in *Movies and Methods*, vol. 2, ed. Bill Nichols (Berkeley: University of California Press, 1985), p. 194.

20. Elsaesser, "Tales of Sound and Fury," p. 167.

21. Ibid., pp. 167–68.

22. Martha Vicinus, "'Helpless and Unfriended': Nineteenth-Century Domestic Melodrama," *New Literary History* 13.1 (1981–82): 128.

23. Carol Gluck's study, *Japan's Modern Myths: Ideology in the Late Meiji Period* (Princeton, NJ: Princeton University Press, 1985), is the standard source on the ideological currents of this period.

24. Ibid., p. 20.

25. Ibid., pp. 21–35.

26. Ibid., p. 28.

27. Singer, *Melodrama and Modernity*, pp. 10–11.

28. Vicinus, "Helpless and Unfriended," p. 128.

29. Pitrim A. Sorokin, *Social and Cultural Mobility* (New York: Free Press, 1959).

30. Lewis Mumford, *Technics and Civilization* (New York: Harcourt, Brace, 1934), p. 14.

31. Along with "vertical mobility" on a social axis, "horizontal mobility" across a geographic axis is a measure of modernity for Sorokin. See *Social and Cultural Mobility*, pp. 381–89.

32. For a discussion of the Neo-Confucian thought of an important late-Tokugawa leader, see Herman Ooms, *Charismatic Bureaucrat: A Political Biography of Matsudaira Sadanobu, 1758–1829* (Chicago: University of Chicago Press, 1975), pp. 23–48.

33. James Legge, trans., *The Ch'un Ts'ew with The Tso Chuen, The Chinese Classics*, vol. 5 (Taipei: SMC Publishing, 2000), p. 385.

34. See Hamada Keisuke, "Kanzen chōaku," in *Nihon koten bungaku daijiten*, vol. 2 (Tokyo: Iwanami Shoten, 1984), p. 74.

35. Susan Burns's *Before the Nation: Kokugaku and the Imagining of Community in Early Modern Japan* (Durham, NC: Duke University Press, 2003) provides a useful summary of late-Tokugawa social and ideological contexts. See esp. pp. 16–34.

36. Hamada, "Kanzen chōaku," p. 74.

37. Noguchi Takehiko emphasizes the ideological struggle that Bakin undertook to construct a fictional world ruled by *kanzen chōaku*. He argues that Neo-Confucianism, of which Bakin was a self-declared adherent, defines "evil" as the absence of "virtue." In order to make "evil" present—and thus complete a dualistic moral universe—Bakin needed to draw from Buddhism and native animism, and employ a "metaphysics of naming" in which nomination determined essential character. Bakin's desire to dramatize Confucian dualism forced him to undertake a syncretic effort. His Edo-period attempt to generate a dualistic moral structure, it seems, involved contradictions (though of a different sort) no less pressing than those I delineate in Meiji examples. Noguchi's interpretations of Bakin are built on his view that late Edo belongs not to a self-contained "premodern" of fixed values, but rather to a "pre-modern" ruled by contingency. See *Edo to aku—"Hakkenden" to Bakin no sekai* (Tokyo: Kadokawa Shoten, 1991).

38. The *ninjōbon* is what Jonathan Zwicker has in mind when he argues the continuity of the melodramatic mode from the Edo to the Meiji periods. See *Practices of the Sentimental Imagination*, esp. pp. 71–124.

39. For an incisive revision of standard approaches to *Shōsetsu shinzui*, see Atsuko Ueda, *Concealment of Politics, Politics of Concealment: The Production of "Literature" in Japan* (Stanford, CA: Stanford University Press, 2007).

40. Tsubouchi Shōyō, *Shōsetsu shinzui*, in *Tsubouchi Shōyō shū*, vol. 3 of *Nihon kindai bungaku taikei*, p. 70.

41. Ibid., p. 71.

42. Ibid., p. 68.

43. The other two key terms are also deeply rooted in past discourse. *Setai*, whose Japanese use dates back as far as the fifteenth century, carries the sense of the prevailing state of the world and does not align with the English concept of "society," which began to be translated with the now ubiquitous *shakai* in the early Meiji period. Yanabu Akira traces the torturous route through which *shakai* became established as a translation for "society" and concludes that, although there were prior Chinese usages, the modern use of the term in Japan was close to a neologism produced expressly for the purpose of translation. See *Hon'yakugo seiritsu jijō* (Tokyo: Iwanami Shoten, 1982), pp. 3–22. *Fūzoku* was used as early as the ninth century to mean customs and manners; Bakin used the term in the title of his *Fūzoku kingyo den* (Goldfish tales for our ways, 1829–32), where *fūzoku* indicated the adaptation of a Chinese story to suit Japanese customs and manners.

44. Tsubouchi, *Shōsetsu shinzui*, p. 90.

45. Maeda Ai, "Kindai bungaku to Bakin," in *Nihon kindai bungaku daijiten*, vol. 4, ed. Nihon Kindai Bungakkan (Tokyo: Kōdansha, 1977), p. 108.

46. Tsubouchi, *Shōsetsu shinzui*, p. 41.

47. "Shakai shōsetsu shuppan yokoku," *Kokumin no tomo*, October 1896, quoted in Ino Kenji, *Meiji bungaku shi*, vol. 2 (Tokyo: Kōdansha, 1985), p. 62.

48. "Nihon kindai bungaku to Dickens," *Nihon kindai bungaku daijiten*, vol. 4, p. 353.

49. "Meredith no fu," in *Sōseki zenshū*, vol. 16 (Tokyo: Iwanami Shoten, 1967), pp. 664–68.

50. "Nihon kindai bungaku to Meredith," *Nihon kindai bungaku daijiten*, vol. 4, pp. 384–85. Elaine Hadley discusses Meredith's use of the melodramatic mode in *Diana of the Crossways*. See idem, *Melodramatic Tactics: Theatricalized Dissent in the English Marketplace, 1800-1885* (Stanford, CA: Stanford University Press, 1995), pp. 180–222.

51. "*Konjiki yasha* no ranpon—Bertha M. Clay o megutte," *Bungaku* 1.6 (Nov.–Dec. 2000): 188–232. Establishing connections between *Konjiki yasha* and preceding works has been something of a preoccupation for Japanese critics; Kōyō's novel has been variously linked with two works by Bertha M. Clay (a penname used in the U.S. editions of some of the works of Charlotte M. Brame [1836–84]), *Dora Thorne* and *When the Bell Is Ringing*, with *Wuthering Heights*, with Futabatei Shimei's *Ukigumo*, with *Hamlet*, with the *ninjōbon Musume setsuyō*, and with the verse of the Sung poet, Lu You. This critical history suggests that Kōyō marshaled multiple sources as he created his novel. Kitani Kimie offers a useful summary of this stream of critical writing on *Konjiki yasha* in her *Ozaki Kōyō no kenkyū* (Tokyo: Sōbunsha, 1995), pp. 132–46.

52. Vicinus, "Helpless and Unfriended," p. 128.

53. See James L. Huffman's interesting discussion of newspapers and the reading public during this period in *Creating a Public: People and Press in Meiji Japan* (Honolulu: University of Hawai'i Press), pp. 224–70.

54. Ibid., pp. 199–223, 271–309.

55. Ibid., pp. 224–70.

56. Ibid., pp. 386–87.

57. Tamai Kansuke, "Shinbun shōsetsu," in *Nihon kindai bungaku daijiten*, vol. 4, p. 242.

58. Huffman, *Creating a Public*, p. 181.

59. Takagi Takeo, *Shinbun shōsetsu shi—Meiji hen* (Tokyo: Kokusho Kankōkai, 1974), pp. 269–70.

60. Ino, *Meiji bungaku shi*, vol. 2, p. 73.

61. Yanagida Izumi, Katsumoto Sei'ichirō, Ino Kenji, eds., *Zadankai—Meiji bungaku shi* (Tokyo: Iwanami Shoten, 1961), p. 478.

62. Izumi Kyōka, "Waga Ozaki Kōyō-kan," in *Ozaki Kōyō, Uchida Roan, Hirotsu Ryūrō, Saitō Ryoku'u shū*, vol. 3 of *Gendai Nihon bungaku taikei* (Tokyo: Chikuma Shobō, 1970), p. 391. Originally published in 1927.

63. Seki Hajime, "*Konjiki yasha* no juyō to mejia mikkusu," in Komori Yōichi, Kōno Kensuke, and Takahashi Osamu, eds., *Mejia, hyōshō, ideorogii—Meiji sanjūnendai no bunka kenkyū* (Tokyo: Ozawa Shoten, 1997), p. 159.

64. Quoted in Williams, *Playing the Race Card*, p. 45.

65. Seki, "*Konjiki yasha* no juyō," pp. 158–94.

66. This characterization of *shinpa* is taken from M. Cody Poulton's study of Izumi Kyōka's theatrical melodramas, *Spirits of Another Sort*, pp. 17–24.

67. These pictorial narratives included Kaburaki Kiyokata's lavish "*Konjiki yasha*" *emaki* (Tokyo: Shun'yōdō, 1912), from which the cover illustration of this book is taken, and a fascinating team effort by a group of artists led by Ōta Samurō, "*Konjiki yasha*" *gafu* (Tokyo: Seibidō, 1911).

68. Seki, "*Konjiki yasha* no juyō," p. 186.

69. McDonald, *From Book to Screen*, p. 9.

70. Martha Vicinus, for example, notes that "the focus on the family and its emotional conflicts gives melodrama its archetypal power." See her "Helpless and Unfriended," p. 129. See also Nowell-Smith, "Minnelli and Melodrama."

71. I have followed Muta Kazue here in noting both a general and more specific sense of crisis as the background for Meiji family ideology. See *Senryaku to shite no kazoku: kindai Nihon no kokuminkokka keisei to josei* (Tokyo: Shin'yōsha, 1996), pp. 81–82.

72. Yanagita Kunio, "Inaka tai tokai no mondai," *Jidai to nōsei*, in vol. 16 of *Teihon Yanagita Kunio shū* (Tokyo: Chikuma Shobō, 1962), pp. 28–50. See also Irokawa Daikichi, *The Culture of the Meiji Period* (Princeton, NJ: Princeton University Press, 1985), pp. 287–293.

73. Hozumi Yatsuka (1860–1912), a constitutional scholar, and Inoue Tetsujirō (1856–1944), a philosopher, were key conservative intellectuals aligned with the Meiji state. Both had studied in Germany in the 1880s and had returned to take up bully pulpits in Japanese academia. Hozumi became a professor of law at Tokyo Imperial University in 1889 and served as chairman of the College of Law from 1897 to 1911. He was an important theorist of the *kokutai*, the concept of the national polity headed by a divine emperor, which he connected with the *kazoku kokka*. Inoue, professor of philosophy at Tokyo Imperial University from 1890 until his retirement in 1923, was invited by the Ministry of Education to write the quasi-official commentary on the Imperial Rescript on Education. He is also known for his opposition to Christianity, which he saw as harmful to national morality. On Hozumi Yatsuka, see Richard H. Minear, *Japanese Tradition and Western Law: Emperor, State, and the Law in the Thought of Hozumi Yatsuka* (Cambridge, MA: Harvard University Press, 1970).

74. The word *ie* has a long history in the Japanese language dating to the eighth century. In a way somewhat resembling the English "house," the term has been applied both to physical places of residence and to groupings of people. The former usage indicates a dwelling, as well as sometimes its immediately surrounding spaces. The latter usage can be broad, referring to cohabiting persons generally; to those bound by kinship relations, regardless of domicile; and to a family group together with its retainers and servants. In the most specific sense, the term *ie* was historically applied to family groups that were characterized by a diachronic consciousness

of lineage or surname. It is this last sense that the Meiji state utilized and embroidered in its ideological and juridical projects.

75. In an important essay, Kathleen Uno has called attention to the disjuncture between the range of family structures in Japan during the Edo and Meiji periods and the restricted way such structures have been characterized in Japanese ideological discourse and Western scholarship. See "Questioning Patrilineality: On Western Studies of the Japanese *Ie*," *Positions* 4.3 (Winter 1996): 569–93.

76. Kawashima Takeyoshi, *Ideorogii to shite no kazoku seido* (Tokyo: Iwanami Shoten, 1957), pp. 33–34.

77. Ibid., p. 33.

78. "Minpō idete, chūkō horobu," in *Meiji shisō shū* 2, vol. 31 of *Kindai Nihon shisō taikei*, ed. Matsumoto Sannosuke (Tokyo: Chikuma Shobō, 1977), p. 17. Originally published in *Hōgaku shinpō*, August 1891.

79. "Sosenkyō wa kōhō no minamoto nari," quoted in Matsumoto Sannosuke, "Kaisetsu," in *Meiji shisō shū* 2, p. 417.

80. Kawashima, *Ideorogii*, p. 34.

81. Itō Mikiharu discusses this tendency in the works of Yanagita Kunio, Kawashima Takeyoshi, and Nakane Chie. See *Kazoku kokka kan no jinruigaku* (Tokyo: Mineruba Shobō, 1982), pp. 46–57. Itō's very useful book, whose argument merits consideration for its own sake, also functions effectively as a guide to prior scholarship on the *ie*.

82. Ibid., pp. 11–12, 42, 58.

83. Kawashima, *Ideorogii*, p. 8. The samurai—who provided the model for the Meiji version of the *ie*—had constituted only 3 percent of the total population of Edo-period Japan; together with their families, they may have made up 10 percent of the population. See Ueno Chizuko, *Kindai kazoku no seiritsu to shūen* (Tokyo: Iwanami Shoten, 1994), p. 69.

84. Kawashima, *Ideorogii*, pp. 8–9.

85. Muta, *Senryaku*, pp. 15–18.

86. Ueno, *Kindai kazoku*, pp. 76–77.

87. For much of the following discussion, I have relied upon Matsumoto Sannosuke, "Kazoku kokka kan no kōzō to tokushitsu," in vol. 8 of *Kōza kazoku* (Tokyo: Kōbundō, 1974), pp. 55–78. Takashi Fujitani has also discussed the dynamics of the *kazoku kokka* in *Splendid Monarchy: Power and Pageantry in Modern Japan* (Berkeley: University of California Press, 1996), pp. 190–91.

88. See Gluck, *Japan's Modern Myths*, pp. 35–37.

89. Ibid., pp. 120–27.

90. Inoue Tetsujirō, *Chokugo engi* (1891), in *Kyōiku no taikei*, vol. 6 of *Meiji shisō taikei*, ed. Yamazumi Masami (Tokyo: Iwanami Shoten, 1990), p. 416.

91. *Shūshin kyōkasho* (1890), quoted in Kawashima, *Ideorogii*, p. 43.

92. Ibid., p. 43, emphasis mine.

93. Anne McClintock, *Imperial Leather: Race, Gender, and Sexuality in the Colonial Context* (New York: Routledge, 1995), p. 357.

94. Sekiguchi Yūko et al., *Nihon kazoku shi* (Tokyo: Kazusa Shuppansha, 1989), pp. 199–219.

95. Irokawa, *Culture of the Meiji Period*, pp. 281–82.

96. Ishida Takeshi, *Meiji seijishisōshi kenkyū* (Tokyo: Miraisha, 1954, reprinted 1992), p. 113.

97. Kawashima, *Ideorogii*, p. 350.

98. Itō, *Kazoku kokka kan*, pp. 196–99.

99. Edward Said, *The World, the Text, and the Critic* (Cambridge, MA: Harvard University Press, 1983), p. 16.

100. Ibid., p. 17.

101. Ibid., p. 19.

102. There are elements of Said's argument that I find problematic, especially when he attempts to extend his pattern beyond families in fiction to the cultural or social positionality of actual authors. When Said argues that the transition from filiation to affiliation occurs in Erich Auerbach's shifting relations with European literature or in T. S. Eliot's conversion from Protestantism to Catholicism, the argument is stretched beyond its breaking point. A critic's or an author's relationship to culture can never be filial in the biological sense. Cultural positioning always involves an engagement with alternatives that biological descent does not. As a European Jew, Auerbach presumably had various Europes at his disposal, including a Jewish one. The Protestant America that Eliot rejected was a culture variously inflected by race, class, and region. The hybridity of culture and its function as a realm of contestation means that a person's connection to culture can never be "natal" or "natural." Cultural identity always involves affiliation.

103. Ibid., p. 23.

104. Peter Brooks, *Reading for the Plot: Design and Intention in Narrative* (Cambridge, MA: Harvard University Press, 1984), p. 63.

105. Ibid., pp 63–64.

106. *The Civil Code of Japan*, trans. W. J. Sebald (Kobe: J. L. Thompson, 1934), Article 727, p. 164.

107. Ibid., Article 874, p. 201.

108. For example, ibid., Article 788, p. 180. "A wife enters her husband's house by marriage. A *nyūfu* or *muko-yōshi* enters his wife's house." See also Articles 736, 769, 786, 813, 866, 964, 988, 989.

109. Nobushige Hozumi, *Lectures on the New Japanese Civil Code—As Material for Comparative Jurisprudence* (Tokyo: Maruzen Kabushiki-kaisha, 1912), p. 116.

110. Basil Hall Chamberlain, *Japanese Things: Being Notes on Various Subjects Connected to Japan* (Rutland, VT: Tuttle, 1971, reprint of 1905 edition), p. 17.

111. Kawashima studies fictive kinships of the *iemoto* variety present in artistic lineages. See *Ideorogii*, pp. 321–69.

112. The advantages of a good marriage were well advertised in the popular discourse of the Meiji period. Newspapers lionized geisha who had become the wives of government luminaries or wealthy businessmen; in a locution common to the

time, such women were said to have hitched a ride in a "jeweled palanquin" (*tama no koshi*).

113. Although Miya is still alive at the end of *Konjiki yasha*, which is incomplete, I place importance on Kan'ichi's dream, where she kills herself in spectacular fashion.

114. Iida Yūko notes the male-centric nature of late-Meiji canonical novels in comparison to earlier *katei shōsetsu*, or "home novels." See *Karera no monogatari: Nihon kindai bungaku to jendaa* (Nagoya: Nagoya Daigaku Shuppankai, 1998).

115. The Meiji fever for *risshin shusse* has been aptly described by Earl H. Kinmonth in *The Self-Made Man in Meiji Japanese Thought: From Samurai to Salary Man* (Berkeley: University of California Press, 1981). In Japanese, see Takeuchi Yō, *Risshin shusse shugi: kindai Nihon no roman to yokubō* (Tokyo: NHK Shuppan, 1997).

116. In Meiji melodramatic fiction, the educational backgrounds of characters are typically described with considerable precision.

117. Michael McKeon, "Generic Transformation and Social Change: Rethinking the Rise of the Novel," in *Theory of the Novel: A Historical Approach*, ed. Michael McKeon (Baltimore: Johns Hopkins University Press, 2000), pp. 389–97. See also, Michael McKeon, *The Origins of the English Novel: 1600–1740* (Baltimore: Johns Hopkins University Press, 1987), pp. 131–75.

118. McKeon, "Generic Transformation," p. 390.

119. "Rule by status" is a formulation originated by John W. Hall. See "Rule by Status in the Tokugawa Period," *Journal of Japanese Studies* 1.1 (Autumn 1974): 39–49.

120. David Howell, *Geographies of Identity in Nineteenth-Century Japan* (Berkeley: University of California Press, 2005), p. 17.

121. Douglas Howland, "Samurai Status, Class, and Bureaucracy: A Historiographical Essay," *Journal of Asian Studies* 60.2 (May 2001): 355–56. Howland's article is a useful synthesis of Japanese and American scholarship on class and status during the Edo period.

122. This consistency pertained primarily to ideology. Recent work by historians has stressed the incongruities that arose in practice, as well as the considerable contestation over the status system. David Howell has emphasized the widening gap between occupation, understood as status-specific work, and livelihood, as a means of subsistence, especially as the Edo period moved forward. And Douglas Howland points out that by the 1800s lower-ranking samurai were worse off than the majority of commoners. Some merchants, theoretically members of the lowest estate according to Confucian ideology, were financially powerful enough to be managing the affairs of daimyo. See Howell, *Geographies of Identity*, pp. 57–59, and Howland, "Samurai Status, Class, and Bureaucracy," p. 362.

123. Max Weber writes: "In contrast to the purely economically determined 'class situation' we wish to designate as 'status situation' every typical component of the life fate of men that is determined by a specific, positive or negative, social estimation of *honor*." *From Max Weber: Essays in Sociology*, ed. H. H. Gerth and C. Wright Mills (New York: Oxford University Press, 1946), pp. 186–87.

124. Howell, *Geographies of Identity,* p. 46.

125. *Kōtōgakkō,* or higher schools, were public preparatory academies for the Imperial Universities. They functioned as the prime state-run institution for male elite socialization in prewar Japan. See Donald Roden, *Schooldays in Imperial Japan: A Study in the Culture of a Student Elite* (Berkeley: University of California Press, 1980). In Chapter 2, I discuss how *Konjiki yasha* both trades on and subverts the moral pretensions of the higher school.

126. Wylie Sypher, "Aesthetic of Revolution: The Marxist Melodrama," in *Tragedy: Vision and Form,* 2nd ed., ed. Robert W. Corrigan (New York: Harper and Row, 1981), p. 219.

127. Ibid.

128. Inoue, *Chokugo engi,* p. 433.

129. For example, see Robert Heilman, *Tragedy and Melodrama: Versions of Experience* (Seattle: University of Washington Press, 1968), pp. 79–87.

130. Hozumi, "Minpō idete chūkō horobu," p. 18.

131. Yanagita, "Inaka tai tokai no mondai," pp. 38–39. Quoted in Irokawa, *The Culture of the Meiji Period,* p. 288. I have expanded Carol Gluck's translation of this passage. Yanagita's remarks were contained in an address to the Greater Japan Agricultural Association in September 1906.

Notes to Chapter I

1. George Mosse, *Nationalism and Sexuality* (Madison: University of Wisconsin Press, 1985), p. 9.

2. Timothy Brennan, "The National Longing for Form," in *Nation and Narration,* ed. Homi K. Bhabha (London: Routledge, 1990), p. 49.

3. Benedict Anderson, *Imagined Communities: Reflections on the Origin and Spread of Nationalism* (London: Verso, 1991).

4. Ino Kenji, *Meiji bungaku shi,* vol. 2 (Tokyo: Kōdansha, 1985), p. 73.

5. Quoted in Nakano Yasuo, *Roka Tokutomi Kenjirō* (Tokyo: Chikuma Shobō, 1972), p. 374.

6. Takakura Teru, "Nihon kokuminbungaku no kakuritsu," *Shisō* 171 (August 1936): 77–79.

7. Mizoguchi Hakuyō wrote a poetic adaptation of the novel, *Katei shinshi: "Hototogisu" no uta* (Tokyo: Tōkyōdō, 1905), which went through twenty-nine printings within two years of its publication. There were a number of different stage adaptations. The first, by Namiki Heisui, was performed at the Osaka Asahiza in February 1901 and at the Hongōza in Tokyo in May 1903. In September 1904, the Tokyōza presented an adaptation by one of its house writers, Takeshiba Shinkichi. The Hongōza put on yet another version, this one by Yanagawa Shun'yō, in April 1908. See entry for "Hototogisu" in *Engeki hyakka daijiten,* vol. 5, ed. Waseda Daigaku Engeki Hakubutsukan (Heibonsha, 1961), pp. 188–89. As for movies, *Nihon eiga sakuhin jiten, senzen hen,* vol. 3, ed. Nihon Eigashi Kenkyūkai (Kagaku

Shoin, 1996) lists more than fifteen films based on Roka's novel made between the years 1909 and 1932.

8. On *Hototogisu*'s reception, see Fujii Hidesada, *"Hototogisu" no jidai* (Nagoya: Nagoya Daigaku Shuppankai, 1990), esp. pp. 56–59. Fujii points out that *Hototogisu* benefited from thematizing the Sino-Japanese War and tuberculosis, two issues that were prominent in the popular consciousness at the time of its publication.

9. This line has been left out of the English translation by Isaac Goldberg, *The Heart of Nami-San* (Boston: Stratford, 1918). William Johnston is probably correct that the translator despaired that the passage would not make sense to an audience unused to the notion of reincarnation.

10. Linda Williams, *Playing the Race Card: Melodramas of Black and White from Uncle Tom to O. J. Simpson* (Princeton, NJ: Princeton University Press, 2001), p. 21.

11. *Roka Tokutomi Kenjirō* (Tokyo: Chikuma Shobō, 1972), p. 379.

12. Hiraoka Toshio, *Nichirosengobungaku no kenkyū*, vol. 2 (Tokyo: Yūseidō, 1985), p. 173.

13. Gérard Genette, "Introduction to the Paratext," *New Literary History* 22.2 (Spring 1991): 261.

14. Quoted in Kōno Toshirō, *"Hototogisu* shūhen," *Nihon bungaku* 6.11 (November 1957): 822.

15. When Sakai wrote this review, he was more a liberal than a socialist. His thinking was to take a sharp turn leftward when he became acquainted with Kōtoku Shūsui after the turn of the century. Sakai's magazine for the home, *Katei zasshi*, founded in 1903, featured a progressive ideal of the family. It advocated flexible divisions of household labor, encouraged female participation in the larger society, and saw the family as an institution that could be opened outward as an agent of social change. See Kinoshita Hiromi, "Kindai fujin-katei ron no tenkai—Sakai Toshihiko o chūshin ni," *Rekishi hyōron* 446 (June 1987): 78–88.

16. Sakai Toshihiko, *"Hototogisu* o yomu," in vol. 1 of *Sakai Toshihiko zenshū* (Tokyo: Chūōkōronsha, 1933), pp. 86–87.

17. Senuma Shigeki locates both *Hototogisu* and *Konjiki yasha* as precursors to the *katei shōsetsu* proper in his "Katei shōsetsu no tenkai," in *Meiji katei shōsetsu shū*, ed. Senuma Shigeki, vol. 93 of *Meiji bungaku zenshū* (Tokyo: Chikuma Shobō, 1969), pp. 423–25.

18. Kathryn Ragsdale has effectively discussed the ideological and the commercial parameters of the *katei shōsetsu* in her article, "Marriage, the Newspaper Business, and the Nation State: Ideology in the Late Meiji Serialized *Katei Shōsetsu*," *Journal of Japanese Studies* 24.2 (Summer 1998): 229–55.

19. My following discussion of the idea of *hōmu* is heavily indebted to Inuzuka Miyako's article, "Meiji chūki no 'hōmu' ron," *Ochanomizu Joshi Daigaku jinbun kagaku kiyō* 42 (March 1989): 49–61.

20. These qualities are enumerated by Barbara Welter in "The Cult of True Womanhood: 1820–1860," *American Quarterly* 18.2 (Summer 1966): 151–74. For this citation, I am indebted to Sharon Nolte and Sally Ann Hastings, "The Meiji State's

Policy Toward Women, 1890–1910," in *Recreating Japanese Women, 1600–1945*, ed. Gail Lee Bernstein (Berkeley: University of California Press, 1991), p. 172.

21. Inuzuka, "Meiji chūki," pp. 52–53.

22. Ibid., p. 55.

23. "Kazokunai no kaiwa," no author listed, *Jogaku zasshi* 338 (2/18/1893), quoted in Inuzuka, "Meiji chūki," p. 53.

24. Yamaoka Kunisaburō, "Saikun no shokumu," *Jogaku zasshi* 114 (6/16/1888), quoted in Inuzuka, "Meiji chūki," p. 56.

25. On Iwamoto Yoshiharu and *Jogaku zasshi*, see Rebecca Copeland's *Lost Leaves: Women Writers of Meiji Japan* (Honolulu: University of Hawai'i Press, 2000), esp. pp. 7–51. Copeland's discussion makes clear that encouragement of *hōmu*-building was only one aspect of *Jogaku zasshi*'s agenda; within the proper boundaries of domesticity, the magazine also advocated women's education and improving the social, cultural, and political status of women.

26. Inuzuka, "Meiji chūki," p. 50

27. The best discussion of *katei* ideology in English occurs in Jordan Sand's *House and Home in Modern Japan: Architecture, Domestic Space, and Bourgeois Culture, 1880–1930* (Cambridge, MA: Harvard University Asia Center, 2003), esp. pp. 21–54.

The character compound for *katei* had been used in pre-Meiji times, but to denote a garden attached to a house or more generally to the physical locus of family life, meanings that are closer to the original Chinese. The term *katei* entered general usage as it gained an identification with *hōmu*. See *Meiji Taishō shingo zokugo jiten*, ed. Kabashima Tadao et al. (Tokyo: Tōkyōdō Shuppan, 1984), p. 75.

28. Muta Kazue skillfully analyzes the content and dissemination of *katei* ideology in Meiji journalism. See *Senryaku to shite no kazoku: kindai Nihon no kokuminkokka keisei to josei* (Tokyo: Shin'yōsha, 1996), esp. pp. 51–77.

29. One scholar counts the publication of eleven major women's magazines between 1887 and 1906. See Horie Shun'ichi, "Meiji makki kara Taishōki no 'kindai kazokuzō'—fujin zasshi kara mita 'yamanote seikatsu' no kenkyū," *Nihon minzokugaku* 186 (May 1991): 39–73.

30. Muta, *Senryaku*, pp. 56–57.

31. Sachi Jitsunen, "Katei seikatsu no risō," *Rokugō zasshi* 327 (1908), quoted in ibid., p. 56.

32. Muta, *Senryaku*, p. 58.

33. Ishii Terumi, "Waga kazoku dōtoku o ronzu," *Rokugō zasshi* 249 (1901), quoted in ibid., p. 17.

34. Anonymous writer, "Katei no shinsei to fūfu no dōjō," *Rokugō zasshi* 215 (1898), quoted in Muta, *Senryaku*, p. 18.

35. Muta, *Senryaku*, pp. 67–68.

36. The collection of ideas that found a home under the rubric of "commonerism" cannot be easily summarized, but in an instructive article Peter Duus tells us that *himinshugi* advocated "a society in which the interests of the 'common man,' rather than those of an entrenched privileged elite, were dominant." The goal of the

Min'yūsha was "basically an idealized version of liberal bourgeois society, gleaned from the self-congratulatory works of mid-Victorian Englishmen." Specifically, the Min'yūsha advocated parliamentary politics, a capitalist economy, egalitarian social policies, and a pacifist foreign policy. Sohō and the Min'yūsha were to move rightward over the course of the 1890s, with Sohō coming to advocate patriotism at home and expansionism abroad. The new nationalist identity of the group and its leader were confirmed in 1897 when Sohō joined the oligarchy by accepting a high government post. See "Whig History, Japanese Style: The Min'yūsha Historians and the Meiji Restoration," *Journal of Asian Studies* 33.3 (May 1974): 421.

37. Tokutomi Sohō, "Kazokuteki sensei," *Kokumin no tomo* (6/23/1893). Translated and quoted in John D. Pierson, *Tokutomi Sohō, 1863–1957: A Journalist for Modern Japan* (Princeton, NJ: Princeton University Press, 1980), p. 208. For Sohō's attitudes toward family I have relied on Pierson, pp. 208–9, and Kenneth B. Pyle, *The New Generation in Meiji Japan: Problems of Cultural Identity, 1885–1895* (Stanford, CA: Stanford University Press, 1969), pp. 134–36.

38. These five points are included in "Kazokuteki sensei." Discussed in Pierson, *Tokutomi Sohō*, p. 209, and Pyle, *New Generation*, p. 135.

39. Quoted in Honda Hiroshi, entry for *Katei zasshi*, vol. 5 of *Nihon kindai bungaku daijiten*, ed. Nihon Kindai Bungakkan (Tokyo: Kōdansha, 1977), p. 53.

40. At the back of the 1900 edition of *Hototogisu*, the advertisement for the "Home Library" is followed by those for the "Commoner's Library" (*Heimin sōsho*) and the "Citizen's Library" (*Kokumin sōsho*). The paratextual implications of these advertisements are also considerable, suggesting that the target audience for the book included males interested in issues of social status and nationalism. The Citizen's Library included a volume penned by Sohō himself entitled *Katei shōkun*, or *A Short Lesson on the Home*. The *katei*, it seems, was not something relegated to its own series but was also deemed proper for discussion within the context of the nation.

41. No author is listed on the cover or in the front matter of this volume, where the only attribution is to the Min'yūsha. Since Tokutomi Sohō was a dominating presence in the company, it would be safe to assume that the volume passed his inspection. The original publication date is 1894. I have examined this work in a reprinted edition, vol. 2 of *Katei kyōiku bunken sōsho*, ed. Ishikawa Matsutarō (Tokyo: Kuresu Shuppan, 1990).

42. Ibid., p. 10.

43. Although the narrator deliberately refuses to name his hero and his heroine in the opening pages of the novel, the young man does refer to his wife as "Nami-san" when he speaks to her in these passages.

44. This opening resembles a typical first scene in nineteenth-century French theatrical melodrama, which, as Brooks has observed, tends to begin in a "space of innocence" where virtue is shown "taking pleasure in itself." The import of such a scene is to present "virtue *as* innocence," which, in the course of the drama, will be threatened, misconstrued, or eclipsed. See Peter Brooks, *The Melodramatic Imagination: Balzac, Henry James, Melodrama, and the Mode of Excess* (New Haven, CT: Yale University Press, 1976), p. 29.

NOTES TO CHAPTER I 275

45. All quotations from the text are taken from *Hototogisu*, in *Kitamura Tōkoku/Tokutomi Roka shū*, vol. 9 of *Nihon kindai bungaku taikei* (Tokyo: Kadokawa Shoten, 1972), pp. 224–418. Further page references to *Hototogisu* in this chapter will be shown in parentheses. I have benefited from Satō Masaru's thoughtful annotations to this edition.

46. Robert Bechtold Heilman, *Tragedy and Melodrama: Versions of Experience* (Seattle: University of Washington Press, 1968), p. 90. Heilman argues that this kind of characterization connects to melodrama's tendency toward what he calls "monopathy," the effort to evoke a singleness of feeling. "In melodrama . . . character is viewed as essentially undivided; whether intentionally or unknowingly, a part is taken for the whole, and it does duty for the whole; the complicating elements are eliminated or made ineffectual; there is an impression of unity of being and singleness of direction. In structure of feeling, the form is what I have called 'monopathic'" (p. 89).

47. Quoted in Kōno, "*Hototogisu* shūhen," p. 829.

48. In actuality, the text rarely calls this character by her proper name, choosing to refer to her situationally using such terms as *mibōjin* (widow), *haha* (mother), or *shūto* (mother-in-law). When the given name does appear, the text uses either "Keiko" or "Okei." I have chosen to refer to the character by her proper given name for stylistic convenience.

49. *Chokugo engi*, in *Kyōiku no taikei*, vol. 6 of *Meiji shisō taikei*, ed. Yamazumi Masami (Tokyo: Iwanami Shoten, 1990), p. 416.

50. *Shūshin kyōkasho* (1890), quoted in Kawashima Takeyoshi, *Ideorogii to shite no kazoku seido* (Tokyo: Iwanami Shoten, 1957), p. 42.

51. Quoted in Kōno, "*Hototogisu* shūhen," p. 825.

52. Other examples of this character type include Honda Noboru, the unctuous brownnose in Futabatei Shimei's *Ukigumo*, and Ono Seizō, the ethically challenged but gifted young scholar in Natsume Sōseki's *Gubijinsō*.

53. The application of a discourse of "filth" to morally questionable behavior is an indicator of Meiji melodrama's investment in moral clarity. In *Konjiki yasha*, this discourse will be repeatedly used to pass judgment on mercenary desires.

54. Takie Sugiyama Lebra discusses the history and the composition of the *shinkazoku* in *Above the Clouds: Status Culture of the Modern Japanese Nobility* (Berkeley: University of California Press, 1993), pp. 53–56.

55. Nagatani Ken, "Kindai Nihon ni okeru jōryū kaikyū imeeji no hen'yō—Meiji kōki kara Taishōki ni okeru zasshi mejia no bunseki," *Shisō* 812 (February 1992): 193–210.

56. Ibid., p. 201.

57. Theirs is literally a *Sat-Chō* marriage, uniting partners from Satsuma and Chōshū, two domains whose samurai led the overthrow of the Tokugawa *bakufu* and later became prominent in the Meiji government.

58. In the character compound *kafū*, meaning the customs followed in the house, the first character is that used for *ie*. Namiko is thus literally attempting to learn the practices of Takeo's *ie*.

59. See William Johnston, *The Modern Epidemic: A History of Tuberculosis in Japan* (Cambridge, MA: Harvard Council on East Asian Studies, 1995); Fukuda Mahito, *Kekkaku no bunkashi* (Nagoya: Nagoya Daigaku Shuppankai, 1995); and Fujii, *"Hototogisu" no jidai*. See also Karatani Kōjin's thought-provoking comments in his *Origins of Japanese Literature*, ed. Brett de Bary (Durham, NC: Duke University Press, 1993), pp. 97–113.

60. On the epidemiology of the disease in late-nineteenth-century Japan, see Johnston's excellent discussion in *The Modern Epidemic*, pp. 59–67. Fukuda Mahito traces the romanticization of the disease; see his *Kekkaku no bunkashi*, pp. 100–176.

61. See Susan Sontag, *Illness as Metaphor* (New York: Vintage Books, 1979), esp. pp. 26–35. Keats's death from tuberculosis was especially well known in Japan because his final "heartbreaking" (Sontag's term) letters from Italy to Fanny Brawne had been translated into Japanese in 1894 and published in *Bungakkai*, the organ of the Meiji Romantic movement. See "Nihon kindai bungaku to Keats," in *Nihon kindai bungaku daijiten*, vol. 4, ed. Nihon Kindai Bungakkan, p. 333.

62. I am indebted to William Johnston for his concise discussion of the current understanding of the etiology of tuberculosis. See *The Modern Epidemic*, pp. 23–35.

63. Brooks, *Melodramatic Imagination*, p. 36.

64. This sentence is just as awkward in the Japanese: "Saredo waga haha wa waga na ni yotte kare o ribetsu shi, kare ga chichi wa kare ni kawatte kare o hikitorinu." Because the narrative is focalized through Takeo at this point, the first person possessive pronoun *waga* ("my" or "our"), which I have rendered in the third person as "his," refers to Takeo. It is also clear, in the original, that *kare* refers to Namiko, because it is written with the character compound usually pronounced *kanojo* ("she" or "her"). There is a *rubi* gloss, however, that indicates that the compound should be read as *kare*.

65. In this formulation, I have drawn on Linda Williams, who has written that, in melodrama, "visible suffering transmutes into proof of virtue." See *Playing the Race Card*, p. 29.

66. I sometimes imagine an alternate plot, in which Takeo abandons his mother and goes AWOL from his ship in order to be with Namiko. He is caught and imprisoned for desertion, while Namiko dies alone, unable to face her father, the general. It is doubtful that my version of the novel would have garnered the critical praise and popularity that *Hototogisu* did.

67. M. M. Bakhtin, "Forms of Time and of the Chronotope in the Novel: Notes toward a Historical Poetics," in *The Dialogic Imagination*, ed. Michael Holquist (Austin: University of Texas Press, 1981), p. 84. Bakhtin uses the term "chronotope" to denote the characteristic configuration of time and space in a literary epoch. I am taking liberties in applying the concept to a single text.

68. See Anderson, *Imagined Communities*, pp. 22–36.

69. Roka's autobiographical novel, *Fuji*, was published in four volumes between 1925 and 1928. *Hototogisu* is mentioned by name in this work.

70. Tokutomi Roka, *Fuji*, in *Roka zenshū*, vol. 17 (Tokyo: Shinchōsha, 1929), p. 203.

71. Williams, *Playing the Race Card*, p. 25.

72. Tokutomi Roka, *Fuji*, pp. 214–15.

73. In formulating my closing arguments here, I have benefited from reading Eve Sedgwick's *Between Men: English Literature and Male Homosocial Desire* (New York: Columbia University Press, 1985).

Notes to Chapter 2

1. Takeuchi Keishū's illustration of this scene, from the first edition of *Konjiki yasha*, can be found on the frontispiece of my book.

2. Ozaki Kōyō, *Konjiki yasha*, in *Ozaki Kōyō shū*, vol. 5 of *Nihon kindai bungaku taikei* (Tokyo: Kadokawa Shoten, 1971), pp. 388–89. Further page references to *Konjiki yasha* in this chapter will be shown within parentheses.

3. In this and other works of Meiji melodramatic fiction, dreams and outbursts of violence occur in functionally similar situations. They erupt into the text when quotidian experience cannot contain the emotional excess produced by the moral collisions in the plot. When violence occurs in a dream, as in the passage quoted above, there is a doubled marking of emotions too intense to bear.

4. Yasuda Kōami et al., "*Konjiki yasha* jōchūgehen gappyō," *Geibun* (August 1902): 137–38.

5. The Ministry of Agriculture and Trade was created out of the Ministry of Home Affairs in 1881. See Ozaki, *Konjiki yasha*, p. 65n7.

6. This figure comes from *Nedan no Meiji Taishō Shōwa fūzokushi—jō*, ed. Shūkan Asahi (Tokyo: Asahi Shinbun Sha, 1987), p. 583.

7. Aside from Chijiwa in *Hototogisu* and Kan'ichi in *Konjiki yasha*, the orphans in the novels I study include Fusae in *Chikyōdai* and Ono in *Gubijinsō*. Another notable orphan in Meiji melodramatic fiction is Hayase Chikara in Izumi Kyōka's *Onna keizu* (A female lineage, 1907).

8. In fact, Article 968 of the Meiji Civil Code says that "for purposes of succession to a house a child in the womb is regarded as already born." *The Civil Code of Japan*, trans. W. J. Sebald (Kobe: J. L. Thompson, 1934), p. 226.

9. In the period of the novel, male students on the elite track would attend three years of higher school after five years of middle school. The age range of students at the higher school was thus near that of current college students. See Donald Roden, *Schooldays in Imperial Japan: A Study in the Culture of a Student Elite* (Berkeley: University of California Press, 1980), p. 39. Kan'ichi, who is "twenty-four or -five" and in his last year of higher school when the novel begins, appears to be a little older than the norm.

10. See Takeuchi Yoh, *Risshin shusse shugi: kindai Nihon no roman to yokubō* (Tokyo: NHK Shuppan, 1997), pp. 13–139.

11. Roden, *Schooldays in Imperial Japan*, p. 7.

12. Near the turn of the twentieth century, there emerged a "new middle class" comprising civil servants, educators, managers, and professionals, whose status depended upon manipulating newly constituted "social knowledge." See David

Ambaras's informative article, "Social Knowledge, Cultural Capital, and the New Middle Class in Japan, 1895–1912," *Journal of Japanese Studies* 24.1 (Winter 1998): 1–33.

13. My reading of the gendering of success in this novel has been affected by Takada Chinami's incisive argument in "'Ryōsai kenbo' e no hairei—*Konjiki yasha* no heroin o yomu," *Nihon bungaku* 36.10 (October 1987): 21–22. Rebecca Copeland has commented on female *risshin shusse* in her study of Miyake Kaho's *Yabu no uguisu*. See *Lost Leaves: Female Writers in Meiji Japan* (Honolulu, University of Hawai'i Press, 2000), esp. pp. 82–85.

14. Though the use of the term "jeweled palanquin" (*tama no koshi*) to refer to a woman's rise in the world through sexual alliance with a higher-status male originates in the Edo period, it appears prominently in Meiji texts such as Higuchi Ichiyō's "Nigorie" (Troubled waters, 1895) and Kosugi Tengai's *Hatsusugata* (New Year's finery, 1900).

15. More than the diamond signals Tomiyama's defining characteristic: the characters for his name can be read semantically as "Mountain of Wealth."

16. Yasuda et al., "*Konjiki yasha* jōchūgehen gappyō," pp. 137–38. "POWER" and "MOMENTARY" appear in capitalized English in the original.

17. This formulation juxtaposing the momentary power of money against the eternal significance of love probably owes something to the thinking of the Christian Romantic poet Kitamura Tōkoku. In "Saigo no shōrisha wa darezo" (Who will be the final victor, 1892), Tōkoku had written that "the management of the world as an economic problem is momentary; the rule of Christ is eternal." Although, in this statement, the opposite of economics is Christ, Tōkoku was best known in the 1890s for his apotheosizing of love. He had famously begun "Ensei shika to josei" (The world-weary poet and women, 1892) by asserting: "Love (*ren'ai*) holds the secret key to life; life exists only after there is love; what color is there to life after love is removed?" Kōyō's formulation, then, could very well have been pieced together from components of Tōkoku's thinking. For Tōkoku, marriage ends up being hostile to love, because "marriage controls and vulgarizes people" through miring them in social obligations. Tōkoku's poet is thus fated to be disillusioned by love's fulfillment, finding love's true meaning in its existence as a "castle of the ideal." *Konjiki yasha*'s approach to love could be a refraction of this aspect of Tōkoku's thinking. For a discussion of Tōkoku's ideas, see Janet Walker, *The Japanese Novel and the Ideal of Individualism* (Princeton, NJ: Princeton University Press, 1979), pp. 62–92.

18. Saeki Junko, *Iro to ai no hikakubunkashi* (Tokyo: Iwanami Shoten, 1998).

19. Although my discussion here and Saeki's book from which I draw focus upon modern uses of *ai*, the term and the concept have a more complicated history. *Ai* as a term dates as far back as the eighth c. *Man'yōshū*, where it designated feelings of affection or tenderness between parent and child or between siblings. During the medieval period, *ai* took on a negative coloring when it was seen in Buddhist belief as a form of attachment standing in the way of salvation. The word's Edo-period usages included the sense of caring that one might feel toward a child and the charm exuded by a pretty face or a beguiling manner, as well as the attachment that one

might feel toward a favorite object. The modern history of *ai* starts with its use as a translation for the English "love," a term that spans the impossible semantic range from the erotic to the spiritual, from the physical to the transcendent. The association between *ai* and the spiritual was reinforced through the use of *ai* for "love" in Japanese translations of the Bible. Still, there was discomfort with the semantic range of *ai* as a translation for the English "love," for the related term *ren'ai* was developed to refer specifically to heterosexual romantic love. *Ai* continues to be used broadly in Japan, with *ren'ai* still designating a specific premarital heterosexual attraction.

20. The Christian-led campaign for *ai* was enmeshed with other elements in their modernizing program of social and cultural reform, such as the movements to abolish prostitution and enforce monogamous marriage.

21. Saeki, *Iro to ai*, pp. 40–58.

22. In choosing the title *Sanninzuma*, Kōyō employs premodern usage, where *tsuma* could refer to a man or a woman in either a marriage or a less formal relationship. The modern use of *tsuma* to refer only to a wife in a legal marriage gained strength with the Meiji Civil Code, which was promulgated the year after Kōyō began the serialization of *Konjiki yasha*. See, for example, *The Civil Code of Japan*, Article 788, page 180: "A wife enters her husband's house by marriage. A *nyūfu* or *muko-yōshi* enters his wife's house" (*Tsuma wa kon'in ni yorite otto no ie ni hairu. Nyūfu oyobi mukoyōshi wa tsuma no ie ni hairu*).

23. Brooks writes: "The action of Balzac's novels tends to resolve itself, in moments of crisis, into tableaux of confrontation, where the actors stand at center stage and say their states of being, using a vocabulary that defines their positions and the sense of their lives, that sums up all they are in relation to one another in sweeping verbal gestures." *The Melodramatic Imagination: Balzac, Henry James, Melodrama, and the Mode of Excess* (New Haven, CT: Yale University Press, 1976), p. 110.

24. The last lines of this passage highlight the contradictions contained in Kan'ichi's wish to separate money from love. Despite seeing money as "worthless," he still feels that he might have bought Miya's affection had he been wealthy enough at the time of their confrontation in Atami. He has trouble disentangling love from the "filth" of the cash nexus. This fact presages the additional contradictions that will arise when Kan'ichi attempts to valorize "love" by paying off the debts owed by Sayama and Oshizu.

25. Denis de Rougemont, *Love in the Western World* (Princeton, NJ: Princeton University Press, 1983), pp. 41–42.

26. Ibid., p. 396.

27. Nishida Masaru, "Soshite 'iro' kara 'koi' e—*Konjiki yasha* no egaita mono," *Shizuoka kindai bungaku* (August 1990). Quoted in Kitani Kimie, "*Konjiki yasha* no sekai," in *Ozaki Kōyō no kenkyū* (Tokyo: Sōbunsha, 1995), pp. 112–13.

28. Roden, *Schooldays in Imperial Japan*, pp. 57–58. The rhetoric of family was absorbed by at least one famous alumnus of the First Higher School. Natsume Sōseki wrote in a postgraduation essay that: "When attending the higher middle school, my classroom became a home and my classmates became members of a family" (58).

29. Quoted in ibid., p. 56.

30. Ibid., p. 45.

31. Quoted in ibid.

32. See Takeuchi, *Risshin shusse shugi*, pp. 83 and 85. The statistics included here show that in 1887 the student body at the First Higher School was 60 percent former samurai and 39.7 percent commoners. By 1910, these figures had more than reversed, with 27.1 percent of the students being of former samurai background and 71.8 percent being commoners.

33. Sekikawa Natsuo, "Nisshin sensōgo no 'kane no yo,'" *Bungakkai* 48.1 (January 1994): 170.

34. Uchimura Kanzō, "The Voice of Kishiu," quoted in Earl H. Kinmonth, *The Self-Made Man in Meiji Japanese Thought: From Samurai to Salaryman* (Berkeley: University of California Press, 1981), p. 157.

35. Nagatani Ken, "Kindai Nihon ni okeru jōryū kaikyū imeeji no hen'yō—Meiji kōki kara Taishōki ni okeru zasshi mejia no bunseki," *Shisō* 812 (February 1992): 203.

36. Roden, *Schooldays in Imperial Japan*, p. 46.

37. Yoshimura Toratarō, the first headmaster of the Second Higher School, quoted in ibid.

38. Ibid.

39. Ibid., p. 50.

40. Roden sketches these practices and memorably defines them as "rituals of intensification." See ibid., pp. 95–132.

41. Yoshida Kumaji, quoted in Takeuchi, *Risshin shusse shugi*, p.89.

42. Kan'ichi refers here to the "Higher Middle School" because the official name of the school he attends was the First Higher Middle School until 1894, when it was renamed the First Higher School.

43. In my reading, a similar problem is raised in Natsume Sōseki's *Gubijinsō*, a novel I analyze later in this study.

44. For example, at the panel discussion published in *Geibun* where Kōyō made his pronouncements on love and money, the sinologist Yoda Gakkai had the following to say: "Among the characters who have already appeared, the one who is most deserving of admiration is the friend of Kan'ichi's called Arao Jōsuke. Of the many characters, he is the only one with whom we can rightly sympathize." Yasuda et al., "*Konjiki yasha* jōchūgehen gappyō," p. 125.

45. We must also not miss the way Arao's experience ties the moneylender's economy to Meiji modernity. When a university graduate is being held responsible for election debts, we have come a long way from the Edo-period usury pictured by Ihara Saikaku, in which the borrowers were invariably townsmen needing living expenses or money to repay debts incurred in the licensed prostitution quarters. The modernity of the moneylending depicted in the novel is underscored, moreover, in the depiction of the loan industry as supported by a modern juridical system. For example, when the text uses the term *rentaisha* to refer to Arao, it employs a term derived from *rentai saimu*, a translation for the Western concept of joint and

several obligation, which was enshrined in the Meiji Civil Code. The loan sharks in the novel also make use of notarized documents (*kōsei shōsho*), resort to attachment of collateral (*sashi osae*), and refer to their debtors as obligors (*saimusha*). This discourse indicates that loan sharking in this text is not some atavistic remnant of Edo financial customs but rather a business embedded in the fabric of Meiji life and institutions.

46. Arao significantly redefines the melodramatic binary of love and money proposed by Kōyō at the panel discussion. This is another indication of the ideological contradiction in the text.

47. See *The Civil Code of Japan*, Articles 841 and 876, pp. 193, 202.

48. In applying the term "wonderland" to *Konjiki yasha*, I am preceded by Ishikura Michiko, "'Jō' no wandaarando—Ozaki Kōyō *Konjiki yasha* kō," in *Zoku Kōyō sakuhin no shosō*, ed. Senshū Daigaku Daigakuin Bungaku Kenkyūka Hata Kenkyūshitsu (Kawasaki: Senshū Daigaku, 1993), pp. 68-81. As indicated in her title, however, Ishikura locates the "wonder" of the work in its intense sentiments.

49. Yasuda et al., "*Konjiki yasha* jōchūgehen gappyō," p. 87.

50. For a concise discussion of *kanbun*, see Roy Andrew Miller, *The Japanese Language* (Chicago: University of Chicago Press, 1967), pp. 112–20.

51. Take for example the first part of this passage: "Waga hanmon no katsu o miru ni, karera ga santan no shi to aionaji karazaru nashi, tada koto ni suru tokoro wa saru to todomaru to nomi." The choice of *katsu* ("life"), a character pronounced with the *on* or sinified reading, rather than a word of Japanese origin such as *inochi*, strengthens the *kanbun* flavor of the passage. Both the double negative in *aionaji karazaru nashi* ("not, not same" thus, in my translation "no different") and the reinforced limiter *tada . . . nomi* ("only") are characteristic of *kanbun* locutions.

52. In employing the terms "narrated monologue," "psychonarration," and "quoted monologue," I am using the typology developed by Dorrit Cohn, *Transparent Minds: Narrative Modes for Presenting Consciousness in Fiction* (Princeton, NJ: Princeton University Press, 1978).

53. *Kokinshū* 522, *Ise monogatari* 50. "Yuku mizu ni / kazu kaku yori mo / hakanaki wa / omowanu hito o / omou narikeri." The sentence in *Konjiki yasha* starts: "Yuku mizu ni kazu kaku yorimo hakanaki koishisa to natsukashisa to no asayū . . ." (161). I am indebted to Oka Yasuo's annotation for pointing out this allusion. *Konjiki yasha*, p. 161n12.

54. My translation of this passage is on pages 95–96.

55. In a stimulating feminist study, Takada Chinami has argued that Miya's use of birth control challenges the gender ideology of the "good wife, wise mother" propounded by the state. Takada is correct to point this out, but it is also necessary to note that the ideology of the "good wife, wise mother" worked hand in glove with *ie* ideology and that it is the latter that Miya's decision not to have Tomiyama's children directly attacks. See "'Ryōsai kenbo' e no hairei," p. 24.

56. Brooks, *Melodramatic Imagination*, p. 38.

57. *Futon*, in *Tayama Katai shū*, vol. 19 of *Nihon kindai bungaku taikei* (Tokyo: Kadokawa Shoten, 1971), p. 140.

58. Yamada Yoshio, *Keigohō no kenkyū* (Tokyo: Hōbunkan, 1931), p. 186.
59. Ibid., p. 185.

Notes to Chapter 3

1. Kikuchi Yūhō, *Chikyōdai*, in *Meiji katei shōsetsu shū*, vol. 93 of *Meiji bungaku zenshū*, ed. Senuma Shigeki (Tokyo: Chikuma Shobō, 1969), p. 103. Further page references to *Chikyōdai* in this chapter will be shown within parentheses.

2. Sigmund Freud, "Family Romances," *The Freud Reader*, ed. Peter Gay (New York: W. W. Norton, 1989), p. 299.

3. Ibid., p. 299.

4. Ibid., p. 300.

5. Ibid.

6. Ibid., p. 298.

7. The importance of social hierarchy in Freud's essay has been pointed out by Dana Heller: "An emphasis on class structure underscores Freud's insistence that psychological tensions be understood always in relation to cultural tensions, one of the more salient of which, in Freud's instance, was class difference." See her *Family Plots: The De-Oedipalization of Popular Culture* (Philadelphia: University of Pennsylvania Press, 1995), pp. 22–37. This issue has also been discussed by Richard de Cordova, who is less convinced that Freud actually addresses the problem of class: "In Freud class appears simply as a prop for the child's Oedipal desires in these fantasies." See "A Case of Mistaken Legitimacy: Class and Generational Difference in Three Family Melodramas," in *Home Is Where the Heart Is: Studies in Melodrama and the Woman's Film*, ed. Christine Gledhill (London: BFI Books, 1987), pp. 255–67.

8. Freud, "Family Romances," p. 298.

9. Geoffrey Nowell-Smith, "Minnelli and Melodrama," in *Movies and Methods*, vol. 2, ed. Bill Nichols (Berkeley: University of California Press, 1985), p. 193.

10. The term *katei shōsetsu* appears in the form of a *tsunogaki*, a subtitle usually consisting of two lines of smaller type appearing above the main title (hence *tsuno* or "horns").

11. On the *katei shōsetsu*, see Kathryn Ragsdale, "Marriage, the Newspaper Business, and the Nation-State: Ideology in the Late Meiji Serialized *Katei Shōsetsu*," *Journal of Japanese Studies* 24.2 (1998): 229–55.

12. Keiko I. McDonald, *From Book to Screen: Modern Japanese Literature in Film* (Armonk, NY: M. E. Sharpe, 2000), p. 11. The first chapter of this study covers the adaptation of Meiji melodramas to the screen.

13. Yūhō attached this preface to the book version of the novel, published in two volumes by Shun'yōdō in 1904.

14. Gérard Genette, "Introduction to the Paratext," *New Literary History* 22.2 (Spring 1991), p. 262.

15. Louis Althusser, "Ideology and Ideological State Apparatuses," in *Cultural*

Theory and Popular Culture: A Reader, 2nd ed., ed. John Storey (Athens: University of Georgia Press, 1998), p. 162.

16. The term *kifujin*, written by combining a graph meaning "noble" or "exalted" with the compound for "woman," refers to a female of significant social standing. During the Meiji period, the term was used as a translation for the English word "lady," with which it shared both a specific aristocratic reference and a more generalized application, where it was used for women deemed worthy of social esteem.

17. The *Osaka mainichi*'s circulation in 1903, the year of *Chikyōdai*'s serialization, was 92,355, the third largest in Japan. This contrasted with 68,475 in 1895. By 1907, the newspaper's circulation would be 289,699. These figures are from James L. Huffman, *Creating a Public: People and Press in Meiji Japan* (Honolulu: University of Hawai'i Press, 1997), pp. 386–87.

18. Ibid., pp. 228–29.

19. Ragsdale, "Marriage, the Newspaper Business, and the Nation-State," p. 244.

20. See the entries for *kōdan* in *Engeki hyakka daijiten*, vol. 2, ed. Waseda Daigaku Engeki Hakubutsukan (Tokyo: Heibonsha, 1960), pp. 444–45, and *Nihon kindai bungaku daijiten*, ed. Nihon Kindai Bungakkan, vol. 4 (Tokyo: Kōdansha, 1977), p. 145.

21. The form had its beginnings in the oral recitation of incidents from the fourteenth-century martial tale, the *Taiheiki*, and other stories of samurai life. Narrations about succession struggles in the great clans, known as *oiesōdōmono*, were particularly numerous. *Kōdan* also developed a side that dealt with the lives of commoners, *sewa kōdan*, which included stories about criminals and thwarted lovers, vendettas and ghosts. In the Meiji period, *kōdan* raconteurs began to find subjects for their narrations in current events, even fashioning stories out of the Satsuma Rebellion. With the development of Japanese shorthand in the 1880s, transcribed *kōdan* gained enormous popularity. The *Yamato shinbun* became the first newspaper to serialize these transcribed stories in 1886, and thereafter *kōdan* became a regular feature of many newspapers.

22. *Chikyōdai*'s run in the *Osaka mainichi shinbun* largely overlapped with the serialization of *Kōdan: Date Hyōjō* by Koganei Bakin. I am grateful to the libraries of Ritsumeikan University and Dōshisha University for allowing me to view microfilm and, in the case of the latter, actual copies of the *Osaka mainichi* for the period of *Chikyōdai*'s serialization.

23. For information on Bertha Clay and Charlotte Brame, I have relied on Arlene Moore, "Searching for Bertha Clay: Problems in Researching the Topic and Areas for Further Study," *Dime Novel Roundup* 60.1 (February 1998): 10–14; Nakano Kii, "*Konjiki yasha* no hikaku bungakuteki ichikōsatsu: Bertha Clay to kanren shite," *Eibungaku to eigogaku* 24 (1987): 5–20; and "Suematsu Kenchō," in vol. 20 of *Kindai bungaku kenkyū sōsho*, ed. Shōwa Joshidaigaku Kindai Bungaku Kenkyūshitsu (Tokyo: Showa Joshi Daigaku, 1963), pp. 40–49.

24. The descriptions of Brame's writing are quoted in Moore, "Searching for Bertha Clay," p. 11.

25. Ibid.

26. These figures appear in "Genbun itchi," in vol. 4 of *Nihon kindai bungaku daijiten*, p. 141, and *Kindai buntai hassei no shiteki kenkyū* (Tokyo: Iwanami Shoten, 1965), p. 51.

27. We should also note that Yūhō was serializing his novel in a newspaper that had made decisive steps toward using *genbun itchi*. Hara Kei, the president of the *Osaka mainichi* from 1898 to 1899 and an ardent supporter of the vernacular-based style, used *genbun itchi* in editorials on language reform. It would have been odd for Yūhō, the fiction editor of the newspaper, not to have felt the pressure toward linguistic conversion. See Takagi Takeo, *Shinbun shōsetsu shi—Meiji hen* (Tokyo: Kokusho Kankōkai, 1974), pp. 230–31.

28. Each instance of Kimie's dialogue, for example, is preceded by the character for "Kimi" placed in parentheses.

29. This kind of speaker identification is also common in late-Edo and early-Meiji *gesaku* fiction.

30. An indication of the broad appeal of the concept of *katei* can be found in the large number of homemaker's magazines that began publication around the turn of the century. See Horie Shun'ichi, "Meiji makki kara Taishōki no 'kindai kazokuzō'—fujin zasshi kara mita 'yamanote seikatsu' no kenkyū," *Nihon minzokugaku* 186 (1991): 39–73.

31. David R. Ambaras discusses the new middle class's investment in the *katei* in "Social Knowledge, Cultural Capital, and the New Middle Class in Japan, 1895–1912," *Journal of Japanese Studies*, 24.1 (Winter 1998): 1–34.

32. See the entry for "Ten'ichibō mono" in vol. 4 of *Engeki hyakka daijiten*, pp. 89–90. The most famous of the late-Edo raconteurs, Kanda Hakuzan (d. 1873), built his career around his version of the Ten'ichi story, *Ōoka seidan Ten'ichibō*.

33. See the entry for "Oiesōdōmono" in vol. 1 of *Engeki hyakka daijiten*, p. 378. *Oiemono* stories were known to be especially popular in the Osaka market during the Meiji period. *Kōdan: Date Hyōjō*, the transcription that ran simultaneously with Yūhō's novel in the *Osaka mainichi shinbun* was in fact an *oiemono*, and it seems not unreasonable to posit that Yūhō sought to compete by providing a modern *oiemono*. This is more indication that Yūhō felt discursive pressure from the oral narrative form.

Although I cannot follow this line of inquiry here, it would be intriguing to connect the special popularity of *oiesōdōmono* in the *bakumatsu* and Meiji periods to continuing anxieties about the locus of political authority.

34. "Kikuchi Yūhō," in vol. 61 of *Kindai bungaku kenkyū sōsho*, pp. 413–14.

35. Iwamoto Yoshiharu's ideas on women and the "home" are discussed in Chapter 1.

36. Peter Brooks, *The Melodramatic Imagination: Balzac, Henry James, Melodrama, and the Mode of Excess* (New Haven, CT: Yale University Press, 1976), p. 36.

37. Ibid., p. 91. Brooks is speaking here about plot elements found in the Romantic dramas of Victor Hugo and Alexandre Dumas, but his discussion centers upon what the Romantic theater shares with earlier melodrama, and so it should be permissible to attribute these particular elements to melodrama as well.

38. *Chikyōdai* comprises forty-eight chapters. My rough count shows that Kimie dominates twenty-nine chapters, while Fusae is the most prominent character in nine chapters. The remaining chapters either feature both women together or focus upon other characters.

39. Bertha Clay, *Dora Thorne* (New York: Hurst & Co., no date), p. 2.

40. Ibid., p. 4.

41. Ibid., p. 47.

42. Ibid., p. 55.

43. Ibid., pp. 76–77.

44. Ibid., p. 97.

45. Ibid., p. 107.

46. Ibid., p. 245.

47. Ibid., p. 116.

48. Ibid., p. 251.

49. A Japanese reader of the Meiji period would have instantly recognized the Earles' model of family continuity as following the *mukoyōshi* pattern, where an adopted son-in-law helps in carrying on the family line.

50. Clay, *Dora Thorne*, p. 263.

51. Letter from the imperial chamberlain Fujinami Akitada to Kenchō. Quoted in "Suematsu Kenchō," in vol. 20 of *Kindai bungaku kenkyū sōsho*, p. 21.

52. Letter from Kenchō to the empress's steward, Kagawa Keizō. Ibid., pp. 41–42. When he wrote this, Kenchō was conveniently forgetting his own crossing of status boundaries. Although he had been born to a rural landholding family of the *shōya* category, Kenchō was a man who knew how to take advantage of the social fluidity of the early Meiji period. He had learned English, then a highly marketable skill, and had managed to be sent abroad by the government to study at Cambridge. Upon his return, he had married the daughter of Prime Minister Itō Hirobumi and had become a member of the Diet and subsequently of the Cabinet. Along the way, he was admitted to the peerage.

53. Willful transformations of source texts were a common feature of Meiji adaptations of Western literature. For a study of this phenomenon, see J. Scott Miller, *Adaptations of Western Literature in Meiji Japan* (New York: Palgrave, 2001).

54. The term *chikyōdai* is usually written by combining the character for "milk" with the compound meaning "brothers." Yūhō has chosen a non-standard orthography in order to highlight the sex of his siblings.

55. It turns out later that the lieutenant is not technically an orphan—his mother is still alive, and he grew up without a father because of his parents' divorce—but Kimie's representation here is significant because it highlights the novel's investment in the discourse of orphanage.

56. *Kōtōjogakkō*, which was attended by only a small fraction of female students, consisted of secondary schooling spanning grades 7–11. It was thus equivalent to the male *chūgakkō*. The only more advanced public schools for women were the women's higher normal schools, which were extremely few.

57. Brooks, *Melodramatic Imagination*, p. 27.

58. Ibid., p. 34.

59. Ever the newspaperman, Yūhō gets in a plug for newspaper reading by noting: "The advertisement had been read by hundreds of thousands of people, but Ohama, who lived beside the sea in Shikama, did not subscribe to a newspaper" (107). If Ohama had been a subscriber, then, the drama would have ended before it began!

60. Brooks, *Melodramatic Imagination*, p. 44.

61. Ibid., p. 43.

62. Ibid., p. 44.

63. There are, however, numerous Meiji melodramatic novels where these observations apply in a straightforward way. In Kosugi Tengai's *Makaze koikaze* (Winds of evil, winds of love, 1903), the heroine, a poor female student, is beset by a wealthy suitor who would deprive her of her freedom and her chastity. And in Izumi Kyōka's *Onna keizu* (A female lineage, 1907), an orphan and a geisha are besieged by a rich family seeking social and political primacy at any cost. The binary of wealthy villains and poor but virtuous victims in these works shows sympathies that Brooks would call "democratic."

64. In fact, all of the female characters from Kansai, including the nursemaid Ohama, speak in a standard (or upper-class Tokyo) dialect. This is highly unrealistic, and the reader can only suppose that Ohama learned Tokyo speech while serving in the capital and that her daughters have picked it up through her and their schooling. This standard speech has the effect of narrowing the social gulf between a provincial family and the Tokyo aristocracy.

65. Brooks, *Melodramatic Imagination*, p. 31.

66. When Fusae comes into Ohama's care, she is three years old by the Japanese count, which would very likely make her two in ours. Thus, it is not unlikely that she too would have suckled at Ohama's breast.

67. Adopted siblings are not subject to the incest taboo if their union falls within the *mukoyōshi* pattern.

68. It will be remembered that, in *Hototogisu*, Kawashima Keiko holds the ancestral tablet before her son's eyes when she argues for the primacy of the *ie*.

69. Brooks, *Melodramatic Imagination*, p. 25.

Notes to Chapter 4

1. Natsume Sōseki, *Gubijinsō*, in *Sōseki zenshū*, vol. 3 (Tokyo: Iwanami Shoten, 1966), pp. 309–10, italics mine. The page numbers for further quotations from this novel are shown in parentheses.

2. Sōseki expresses this sentiment in a letter to Takahara Misao, 11/21/1913, *Soseki zenshū*, vol. 15, pp. 295–96.

3. Masamune Hakuchō, "Natsume Sōseki," *Sakkaron*, vol. 1 (Tokyo: Sōgensha, 1941), p. 203.

4. Hakuchō says the following about the moral sentiments in the work (when he refers here to "Kyokutei Bakin," he employs the penname for Takizawa Bakin

[1767–1848]): "The Sōseki who can be seen through *Gubijinsō* possesses a stiff, unwavering moral sense, and in this he is not unlike the Kyokutei Bakin who can be seen through *Hakkenden* (Biographies of eight dogs, 1814–42). Part of the reason that the ordinary reader (*tsūzoku dokusha*) of the educated classes cherishes Sōseki's work comes, perhaps, from the fact that this conventional morality (*tsūjō dōtoku*) forms the foundation of his work." "Natsume Sōseki," pp. 204–5.

5. Notably by Ochi Haruo, Hiraoka Toshio, and Takemori Ten'yū. In his *Sōseki shiron* (Tokyo: Kadokawa Shoten, 1971), Ochi explored the work's use of the concepts of "comedy" and "tragedy," and also analyzed Munechika and Kōno as two sides of the same coin, complementary characters who may have been split off from each other in the process of Sōseki's planning for the novel. Hiraoka may have been the first to call attention to the ideological functions of the novel's prose. In *Sōseki josetsu* (Tokyo: Hanawa Shobō, 1976) he argued that the *bibun* in the work constituted "the display of a subjectivity that clearly indicated its position on good and evil." In a tour-de-force of close reading, Takemori examines the novel's use of the image of the pocket watch in his article "*Gubijinsō* no aya: 'kindokei' to 'koto no oto,'" *Kokugo to kokubungaku* 65.8 (August 1988). The last section of my chapter has benefited from Takemori's article.

6. "'Otoko to otoko' to 'otoko to onna'—Fujio no shi," *Hihyō kūkan* 6 (July 1992): 158–77.

7. Mizumura's benchmark has been followed, among others, by Mizuta Noriko's feminist critique that views Fujio's death as being driven by the need to extinguish a threatening female sexuality, Ishihara Chiaki's double effort to analyze the semiotics of Kōno's "philosophy" and to delineate the commodification of value implied by the scenes set at the Tokyo Industrial Exposition, and Nakayama Kazuko's reading of the novel's misogynist morality. In English, Angela Yiu has pointed out the novel's sympathetic treatment of Ono and the suggestions of an incestuous sexual attraction between Kōno and Fujio. See Mizuta Noriko, "*Gubijinsō* ni okeru Sōseki no 'Fujio goroshi' ni tsuite," *Kokubungaku kaishaku to kyōzai no kenkyū* 42.6 (May 1997): 102–11; Ishihara Chiaki, "Hakurankai no seiki e—*Gubijinsō*," *Sōseki kenkyū* 1 (1993): 76–90; Nakayama Kazuko, "*Gubijinsō*—wūman heitingu to shokuminchi," in *Sutorei shiipu no yukue: Sōseki to kindai*, ed. Kumazaki Atsuko (Tokyo: Kanrin Shobō, 1996), pp. 21–33; and Angela Yiu, *Chaos and Order in the Works of Natsume Sōseki* (Honolulu: University of Hawai'i Press, 1998), pp. 14–31. Some of the most recent critical work on *Gubijinsō* appears in *Sōseki kenkyū* 16 (2003), a special issue devoted to the novel. This issue contains Seki Hajime's "Merodorama to shite no *Gubijinsō*," one of the first critical pieces to use the concepts made available in Japanese through Yomota Inuhiko's 2002 translation of Peter Brooks's *The Melodramatic Imagination*.

8. Masmune, "Natsume Sōseki," p. 206.

9. Ibid., pp. 205, 217.

10. Both *tsūzoku shōsetsu* (literally "common fiction") and *taishū shōsetsu* (literally "mass fiction") were terms developed in the 1920s, when there was an active critical discourse working to separate easily accessible commercial fiction from high-culture

art fiction. Although there was considerable semantic overlap, even interchangeability, *tsūzoku shōsetsu* originally tended to refer to popular fiction set in modern times, while *taishū shōsetsu* was more frequently used to refer to period fiction. The semantic range of the latter gradually broadened, coming to include genres with modern settings such as romance fiction and detective fiction, and it eventually became the general term used for entertainment-oriented popular literature. *Tsūzoku shōsetsu* is less commonly used today, probably because it carries a sharper pejorative edge, which is evident in Hakuchō's choice of the term.

11. In connecting *Gubijinsō* to turn-of-the-century fiction, I am preceded by Iida Yūko, who has argued for the need to think about the Sōseki novel in relation to newspaper fiction and the *katei shōsetsu*. See *Karera no monogatari: Nihon kindai bungaku to jendaa* (Nagoya: Nagoya Daigaku Shuppankai, 1998), pp. 132–55.

12. "Bungakudan," *Sōseki zenshū*, vol. 16, pp. 515–16. I was led to this passage by Mizumura's article.

13. Ibid., p. 516.

14. Mizumura calls attention to the moral contingency indicated by Sōseki's distinctive and repeated use of "preference" when speaking about morality. "'Otoko to otoko' to 'otoko to onna,'" pp. 175–76.

15. Peter Brooks, *The Melodramatic Imagination: Balzac, Henry James, Melodrama, and the Mode of Excess* (New Haven, CT: Yale University Press, 1976), p. 16.

16. Sōseki's plans were clearly at a preliminary stage when this chapter list was drawn up: the list shows only fourteen chapters while the completed novel contains nineteen. There has been considerable movement and adjustment among and within the chapters. The writer, however, had already determined the opening and the terminus of his novel; the work was to begin with Kōno and Munechika's hike on Mt. Hiei and end with Fujio's death. This last element is made emphatic through the use of the English word "death" in the jottings.

Although my discussion focuses on the kinship chart, it is also apparent, on the basis of the chapter list, that Sōseki was laying out his novel the way a playwright might block out a play. He was planning acts or chapters on the basis of which major characters interacted within them. This quality carries over to the finished novel, which is arranged as a series of discrete acts and whose tempo is driven by scenes in which dialogue is employed both for exposition and for advancing the plot. In the early stages of planning his novel, Sōseki appears to have recognized the drama in this melodrama.

In identifying the characters indicated by letters of the alphabet, I have followed the work of Japanese scholars who have deciphered the chart. See Ōkubo Tsuneo, "*Gubijinsō* ron nōto," in *Sakuhinron Natsume Sōseki*, ed. Uchida Michio (Tokyo: Sōbunsha, 1976), pp. 94–109. See also Ochi Haruo, "Kigeki no jidai—*Gubijinsō*," in *Gubijinsō·Nowaki·Kōfu*, vol. 3 of *Sōseki sakuhinron shūsei*, ed. Asada Takashi and Kimata Satoshi (Tokyo: Ōfūsha, 1991), pp. 47–62, originally published in Ochi Haruo, *Sōseki shiron* (Tokyo: Kadokawa Shoten, 1971).

17. The Meiji Civil Code was enacted after much discussion in 1898, just nine years before the publication of Sōseki's novel.

18. There is one instance where this pattern is inconsistent. Kōno's dead mother, shown as "C," has been left uncircled. Perhaps in this case the marking of the person as deceased has superseded the marking of gender.

19. Etō Jun points out the prevalence of single-parent families in the novel in his *Sōseki to sono jidai*, vol. 4 (Tokyo: Shinchōsha, 1996), p. 58.

20. I use "upper-class" because the Kōnos possess substantial wealth. They live in a house with a Western wing that fills Ono with envy and a garden spacious enough to contain a carp pond. The family's money has allowed Kōno to live comfortably without working for two years after graduating from the Imperial University. This wealth, in fact, is a key reason for conflict in the family: the existence of a family fortune large enough to nicely support its members means there is a great deal at stake in the struggle over succession, inheritance, and marriage. Status is also important to the Kōnos: there is a strong implication that they are of former samurai background and their high position in the status hierarchy has been maintained by the father's work in the diplomatic corps and by Kōno Kingo's graduation from Tokyo Imperial University.

21. Ochi, "Kigeki no jidai," p. 61n13.

22. Mizumura notes that the novel rests on a "promise to give or receive a woman" made between two groups of men. See "'Otoko to otoko' to 'otoko to onna,'" pp. 160–61. Nakayama, building upon Kamei Hideo, sees that a reciprocal exchange of Fujio for Itoko constitutes the most powerful potential transaction between men in the novel. See "*Gubijinsō*—wūman heitingu to shokuminchi," pp. 26, 31–32.

23. I am referring to a key "alliance" theorist when my larger focus is on dynamics within the *ie*, which, in anthropological kinship theory, has generally been regarded as organizing kinship according to "descent." The families in *Gubijinsō*, however, demonstrate that alliance and descent work hand in hand to determine gender and kinship relations in the *ie*. I am led to this view by the anthropologist Robin Fox, who regards alliance and descent not "as competing theoretical views, but as empirical components of all kinship systems. Put simply, whatever kinship systems do, they divide people into categories of kin and then define marriage-ability in term of these categories. They define descent, if you like, and legislate alliance." See *Kinship & Marriage: An Anthropological Perspective* (Cambridge, UK: Cambridge University Press, 1983), p. 2. I am grateful to William Kelly for contributing to my education on these matters.

24. Claude Lévi-Strauss, *The Elementary Structures of Kinship* (Boston: Beacon Press, 1969), p. 24.

25. Ibid., p. 115. The passage is quoted in full in Gayle Rubin, "The Traffic in Women: Notes on the Political Economy of Sex," in *Toward an Anthropology of Women*, ed. Rayna Reiter (New York: Monthly Review Press, 1975), pp. 174–75, and in part in Eve Kosofsky Sedgwick, *Between Men: English Literature and Male Homosocial Desire* (New York: Columbia University Press, 1985), p. 26.

26. Lévi-Strauss's formulations apply to other relationships discussed in this book. Namiko in *Hototogisu*, who marries a husband handpicked by her father, epitomizes a woman exchanged between men. The fictive father-son relationship

that develops at the end of the novel shows that her marriage and death have sealed male bonds. While things are not as clear in *Konjiki yasha*, Miya's marriage to Kan'ichi would have cemented the latter's ties to her father, Shigizawa Ryūzō, the younger man's benefactor. When she changes her mind, Shigizawa approves because of the advantages of having the wealthy Tomiyama for a relative. On both occasions, Shigizawa views his daughter's marriage as an opportunity to obtain a desirable alliance. Lévi-Strauss's theories do not apply to Kimie in *Chikyōdai*, a character who expresses female agency. But Fusae's marriage to Akisada at the conclusion of the novel reinforces Akinobu's bond with his adoptive (and her biological) father.

27. The Kōnos and the Munechikas are somewhat ambiguously posited in the novel as distant paternal relations (*tōi entsuzuki, shinrui* [392]). These two families are linked by male ties that are strong in affect but indeterminate on the level of kinship. A "marriage by exchange" would bind the two families together in powerful kinship relations.

Yiu's misidentification of Fujio and Munechika as "cousins" is significant because she appears to be anticipating the trajectory of the proposed union, which is to bring the families into closer kinship. See *Chaos and Order*, p. 27.

28. Sedgwick, *Between Men*, p. 26.

29. Rubin, "The Traffic in Women," p. 179.

30. Ibid., p. 179.

31. Ibid., p. 182.

32. Mizumura's perception that the work embodies a collision between a "world of men" and a "world of men and women" registers *Gubijinsō*'s foregrounding of gender.

33. Mizumura, "'Otoko to otoko' to 'otoko to onna,'" p. 166.

34. The best example of the snake image being used this way occurs in Ueda Akinari's "Jasei no in" (The lust of the snake), where the snake is associated with a rapacious and insatiable female sexuality that relentlessly stalks a male victim. The story is in Akinari's *Ugetsu monogatari* (Tales of moonlight and rain, 1776).

35. Brooks, *Melodramatic Imagination*, p. 27.

36. On powerless victims, see ibid., pp. 32, 44.

37. *The Civil Code of Japan*, trans. W. J. Sebald (Kobe: J. L. Thompson, 1934), Articles 748–750, pp. 169–70.

38. Ibid., Article 758, p. 172.

39. Kōno is the only other character whose inner life is made as vivid. His thoughts are made accessible, however, through quotations from his journal, while Ono's feelings are presented through inside views.

40. This differs significantly from the way other characters are portrayed. The text takes a less explicit approach to explaining how Kōno, Fujio, and Munechika have been formed by their social and family backgrounds.

41. *Nihon kokugo daijiten—dai-nihan*, vol. 6 (Tokyo: Shōgakkan, 2001), p. 713, contains no usage examples for these words prior to the Meiji period. There is a strong possibility that they came into being as translations for the Western legal concepts of the "illegitimate" or "natural" child. During the Edo period, the idea of

fatherlessness would have been expressed through terms such as *tete'nashigo*, literally "child without a father."

42. See *The Civil Code of Japan*, Articles 827–836, pp. 190–92. The Civil Code drew a distinction between *shiseishi* and *shoshi*, an illegitimate child who had been acknowledged by his or her father.

43. See ibid., Articles 733 and 735, p. 165.

44. Mizumura, "'Otoko to otoko' to 'otoko to onna,'" p. 165.

45. A son of Zeus, though mortal, Tantalus was occasionally allowed to join the banquet of the gods. Although there are numerous accounts of what constituted his crime, in many versions he is said to have angered the gods either by revealing their plans to men or by attempting to share ambrosia with other mortals. His transgression is thus connected with not knowing his place. This element of the myth resonates suggestively with Ono's situation.

46. The starting monthly salary for a civil servant in 1907 was 50 yen. Ono's income from tutoring would thus place him, in terms of earning power, in the new middle class. See "Kōmuin no shoninkyū," in *Nedan no Meiji, Taishō, Shōwa fūzokushi-jō*, ed. Shūkan Asahi (Tokyo: Asahi Shinbun Sha, 1987), p. 583.

47. Stefan Tanaka has written on the political and cultural effects of the introduction of Western timekeeping to Japan. See *New Times in Modern Japan* (Princeton, NJ: Princeton University Press, 2004).

48. Uchida Hoshimi, *Tokei kōgyō no hattatsu* (Tokyo: Kabushiki Gaisha Hattori Seikō, 1985), p. 143.

49. Ibid., p. 147.

50. Lewis Mumford, *Technics and Civilization* (New York: Harcourt, Brace, 1934), pp. 14–15. Mumford writes: "In its relationship to determinable quantities of energy, to standardization, to automatic action, and finally to its own special product, accurate timing, the clock has been the foremost machine in modern technics: and at each period it has remained in the lead: it marks a perfection toward which other machines aspire."

51. Uchida, *Tokei kōgyō*, p. 143.

52. Ibid., pp. 359–60.

53. Ibid., p. 154.

54. Seikō's first women's model, called "Laurel," was not introduced until 1913. Ibid., pp. 418–19. The gendering of consumer products such as pocket watches—which could functionally serve both men and women—is a topic that deserves further investigation.

55. I am grateful to Christopher Hill for helping me work toward this idea during a fruitful conversation.

56. Takemori Ten'yū has argued that the ticking of the desk clock in this scene "suggests freedom from time manipulated by the gold watch." See his "*Gubijinsō* no aya," p. 10.

57. Chapters 1 through 6 relate events during the week or so when Kōno and Munechika are in Kyoto, alternating between scenes set in that city and others showing the interaction in Tokyo between Fujio, her mother, and Ono. In chapters

7 through 14 the significant temporal span becomes days as the novel recounts the arrival of Kodō and Sayoko in Tokyo, and the few days following, during which the characters settle in the city, visit the Tokyo Industrial Exposition of 1907, and deal with the consequences that result when Fujio witnesses Ono walking with Sayoko. Chapters 15 through 17 take place on a single day as analepses relate events in the Munechika household, where Hajime ascertains Oito's love for his friend; in the Kōno household, where Kingo clashes with Fujio and then later fortifies himself in his study with Munechika; and at a meeting in the country, where Ono asks Asai to perform the dirty work of calling off the engagement with Sayoko. Chapter 18 mainly focuses on events during the next afternoon when Munechika forces his moral vision upon all of the other characters.

58. Takemori notes that, in this scene, Munechika's watch "relativizes and critiques" Fujio's "self-centered perception of time." "*Gubijinsō no aya*," p. 12.

59. The feat that he carries off here is analogous to just-in-time manufacturing.

Notes to Conclusion

1. Among the novels I wish I could have discussed are Kosugi Tengai's *Makaze koikaze* (Winds of evil, winds of love, 1903), which explores the social identity of *jogakusei*, or female higher school students, by focusing on the trials and tribulations of a virtuous heroine whose virtue is constantly challenged; and Izumi Kyōka's *Onna keizu* (A female lineage, 1907), which depicts a power-hungry *ie* and the hidden female lineages endangered by its machinations.

2. Peter Brooks, *Reading for the Plot: Design and Intention in Narrative* (Cambridge, MA: Harvard University Press, 1984), p. 63.

3. "*Kokoro* ni okeru hanten suru 'shuki'—kūhaku to imi no seisei," in *Kōzō to shite no katari* (Tokyo: Shin'yōsha, 1988), pp. 415–37. Although Komori has gone on to adjust his views of *Kokoro* in numerous later articles, I am limiting my comments to this brilliant essay. The critical controversy it ignited is discussed by Atsuko Sakaki in *Recontextualizing Texts: Narrative Performance in Modern Japanese Fiction* (Cambridge, MA: Harvard University Asia Center, 1999), pp. 31–53. My own earlier attempt to analyze *Kokoro* in this vein is "Writing Time in Sōseki's *Kokoro*," in *Studies in Japanese Literature: Essays and Translations in Honor of Edwin McClellan*, ed. Dennis Washburn and Alan Tansman (Ann Arbor: Center for Japanese Studies, University of Michigan, 1997), pp. 3–21.

4. The translations from *Kokoro* in this chapter are my own, although I cannot deny echoes of the McClellan translation, which I have read since my youth. The Japanese text I have used is in vol. 6 of *Sōseki zenshū* (Tokyo: Iwanami Shoten, 1966). Further page references are cited in parentheses.

5. Ueno Chizuko has pointed out that co-eating had a special place in *katei* ideology. See her *Kindai kazoku no seiritsu to shūen* (Iwanami Shoten: 1994), p. 107. For a brief history of the dining table in Japan, see the entry for "Shokutaku" in *Taishū bunka jiten*, abridged edition, ed. Ishikawa Hiroyoshi et al. (Tokyo: Kōbundō, 1994), p. 376.

6. Peter Brooks, *The Melodramatic Imagination: Balzac, Henry James, Melodrama, and the Mode of Excess* (New Haven, CT: Yale University Press, 1976), p. 6.

7. Ibid., p. 44.

8. Ibid., p. 45.

9. Komori, "*Kokoro* ni okeru hanten suru 'shuki,'" p. 429.

10. Ibid., p. 432.

11. Ibid., p. 437.

12. Ibid., p. 428.

13. Edward Said, *The World, the Text, and the Critic* (Cambridge, MA: Harvard University Press, 1983), p. 17.

14. Ibid., p. 16.

15. There is an implied protest against Okusan's exclusion in the younger narrator's sympathetic view of her, which highlights her suffering as a result of being denied any moral participation in the events that transformed her life and Sensei's. Here as elsewhere the narrator provides a counterpoint to Sensei's views.

Iida Yūko has convincingly argued that in *Kokoro* and other stories of its time women are marginalized in favor of a homosocial orientation, especially in comparison with turn-of-the-century *katei shōsetsu*. See *Karera no monogatari: Nihon kindai bungaku to jendaa* (Nagoya: Nagoya Daigaku Shuppankai, 1998).

Bibliography

Althusser, Louis. "Ideology and Ideological State Apparatuses." In *Cultural Theory and Popular Culture: A Reader*, 2nd ed., edited by John Storey, 153–64. Athens: University of Georgia Press, 1998.

Ambaras, David. "Social Knowledge, Cultural Capital, and the New Middle Class in Japan, 1895–1912." *Journal of Japanese Studies* 24.1 (Winter 1998): 1–33.

Anderson, Benedict R. O'G. *Imagined Communities: Reflections on the Origin and Spread of Nationalism*. London: Verso, 1991.

Bakhtin, M. M. "Forms of Time and of the Chronotope in the Novel: Notes toward a Historical Poetics." In *The Dialogic Imagination*, edited by Michael Holquist, 84–258. Austin: University of Texas Press, 1981.

Brennan, Timothy. "The National Longing for Form." In *Nation and Narration*, edited by Homi K. Bhabha, 44–70. London: Routledge, 1990.

Brooks, Peter. *The Melodramatic Imagination: Balzac, Henry James, Melodrama, and the Mode of Excess*. New Haven, CT: Yale University Press, 1976.

———. *Reading for the Plot: Design and Intention in Narrative*. Cambridge, MA: Harvard University Press, 1984.

Burns, Susan. *Before the Nation: Kokugaku and the Imagining of Community in Early Modern Japan*. Durham, NC: Duke University Press, 2003.

Chamberlain, Basil Hall. *Japanese Things: Being Notes on Various Subjects Connected to Japan*. 1905. Reprint. Rutland, VT: Tuttle, 1971.

The Civil Code of Japan. W. J. Sebald, trans. Kobe: J. L. Thompson, 1934.

Clay, Bertha. *Dora Thorne*. New York: Hurst & Co., no date.

Cohn, Dorrit. *Transparent Minds: Narrative Modes for Presenting Consciousness in Fiction*. Princeton, NJ: Princeton University Press, 1978.

Copeland, Rebecca. *Lost Leaves: Women Writers of Meiji Japan*. Honolulu: University of Hawai'i Press, 2000.

de Rougemont, Denis. *Love in the Western World*. Princeton, NJ: Princeton University Press, 1983.

Duus, Peter. "Whig History, Japanese Style: The Min'yūsha Historians and the Meiji Restoration." *Journal of Asian Studies* 33.3 (May 1974): 415–36.

Elsaesser, Thomas. "Tales of Sound and Fury: Observations on the Family Melodrama." In *Movies and Methods*, vol. 2, edited by Bill Nichols, 165–189. Berkeley: University of California Press, 1985.

Etō Jun. *Sōseki to sono jidai*, vol. 4. Tokyo: Shinchōsha, 1996.

Fox, Robin. *Kinship & Marriage: An Anthropological Perspective*. Cambridge, UK: Cambridge University Press, 1983.

Freud, Sigmund. "Family Romances." In *The Freud Reader*, edited by Peter Gay, 297–300. New York: W. W. Norton, 1989.

Fujii Hidesada. *"Hototogisu" no jidai*. Nagoya: Nagoya Daigaku Shuppankai, 1990.

Fujitani, Takashi. *Splendid Monarchy: Power and Pageantry in Modern Japan*. Berkeley: University of California Press, 1996.

Fukuda Mahito. *Kekkaku no bunkashi*. Nagoya: Nagoya Daigaku Shuppankai, 1995.

Genette, Gérard. "Introduction to the Paratext." *New Literary History* 22.2 (Spring 1991): 261–72.

Gledhill, Christine, ed. *Home Is Where the Heart Is: Studies in the Melodrama and the Woman's Film*. London: BFI Books, 1987.

Gluck, Carol. *Japan's Modern Myths: Ideology in the Late Meiji Period*. Princeton, NJ: Princeton University Press, 1985.

Hadley, Elaine. *Melodramatic Tactics: Theatricalized Dissent in the English Marketplace, 1800–1885*. Stanford, CA: Stanford University Press, 1995.

Hall, John W. "Rule by Status in the Tokugawa Period." *Journal of Japanese Studies* 1.1 (Autumn 1974): 39–49.

Hamada Keisuke. "Kanzen chōaku." In *Nihon koten bungaku daijiten*, vol. 2, 74. Tokyo: Iwanami Shoten, 1984.

Heilman, Robert. *Tragedy and Melodrama: Versions of Experience*. Seattle: University of Washington Press, 1968.

Heller, Dana. *Family Plots: The De-Oedipalization of Popular Culture*. Philadelphia: University of Pennsylvania Press, 1995.

Hiraoka Toshio. *Nichirosengobungaku no kenkyū*. 2 vols. Tokyo: Yūseidō, 1985.

———. *Sōseki josetsu*. Tokyo: Hanawa Shobō, 1976.

Hori Keiko. "*Konjiki yasha* no ranpon—Bertha M. Clay o megutte." *Bungaku* 1.6 (Nov.–Dec. 2000): 188–232.

Horie Shun'ichi. "Meiji makki kara Taishōki no 'kindai kazokuzō'—fujin zasshi kara mita 'yamanote seikatsu' no kenkyū." *Nihon minzokugaku* 186 (May 1991): 39–73.

Howell, David. *Geographies of Identity in Nineteenth-Century Japan*. Berkeley: University of California Press, 2005.

Howland, Douglas. "Samurai Status, Class, and Bureaucracy: A Historiographical Essay." *Journal of Asian Studies* 60.2 (May 2001): 353–80.

Hozumi Nobushige. *Lectures on the New Japanese Civil Code—As Material for the Study of Comparative Jurisprudence*. Tokyo: Maruzen Kabushiki-kaisha, 1912.

Hozumi Yatsuka. "Minpō idete chūkō horobu." Originally published 1891. In

Meiji shisō shū 2, edited by Matsumoto Sannosuke, 17–19. Vol. 31 of *Kindai Nihon shisō taikei*. Tokyo: Chikuma Shobō, 1977.

Huffman, James L. *Creating a Public: People and Press in Meiji Japan*. Honolulu: University of Hawai'i Press, 1997.

Iida Yūko. *Karera no monogatari: Nihon kindai bungaku to jendaa*. Nagoya: Nagoya Daigaku Shuppankai, 1998.

Ino Kenji. *Meiji bungaku shi*. 2 vols. Tokyo: Kōdansha, 1985.

Inoue Tetsujirō. *Chokugo engi*. Originally published 1891. In *Kyōiku no taikei*, edited by Yamazumi Masami, 408–46. Vol. 6 of *Meiji shisō taikei*. Tokyo: Iwanami Shoten, 1990.

Inuzuka Miyako. "Meiji chūki no 'hōmu' ron—Meiji 18–26 nen no *Jogaku Zasshi* o tegakari to shite." *Ochanomizu Joshi Daigaku jinbun kagaku kiyō* 42 (March 1989): 49–61.

Irokawa Daikichi. *The Culture of the Meiji Period*. Princeton, NJ: Princeton University Press, 1985.

Ishida Takeshi. *Meiji seijishisōshi kenkyū*. 1954. Reprint. Tokyo: Miraisha, 1992.

Ishihara Chiaki. "Hakurankai no seiki e—*Gubijinsō*." *Sōseki kenkyū* 1 (1993): 76–90.

Ishikawa Hiroyoshi, et al., eds. *Taishū bunka jiten*, abridged edition. Tokyo: Kōbundō, 1994.

Ishikura Michiko. "'Jō' no wandaarando—Ozaki Kōyō *Konjiki yasha* kō." In *Zoku Kōyō sakuhin no shosō*, edited by Senshū Daigaku Daigakuin Bungaku Kenkyūka Hata Kenkyūshitsu, 68–81. Kawasaki: Senshū Daigaku, 1993.

Ito, Ken K. "Class and Gender in a Meiji Family Romance: Kikuchi Yūhō's *Chikyōdai*." *Journal of Japanese Studies* 28.2 (Summer 2002): 339–78.

———. "The Family and the Nation in Tokutomi Roka's *Hototogisu*." *Harvard Journal of Asiatic Studies* 60.2 (December 2000): 489–536.

———. "Writing Time in Sōseki's *Kokoro*." In *Studies in Japanese Literature: Essays and Translations in Honor of Edwin McClellan*, edited by Dennis Washburn and Alan Tansman, 3–21. Ann Arbor: Center for Japanese Studies, University of Michigan, 1997.

Itō Mikiharu. *Kazoku kokka kan no jinruigaku*. Tokyo: Mineruba Shobō, 1982.

Izumi Kyōka. "Waga Ozaki Kōyō-kan." Originally published 1927. In *Ozaki Kōyō, Uchida Roan, Hirotsu Ryūrō, Saitō Ryokū shū*, 389–91. Vol. 3 of *Gendai Nihon bungaku taikei*. Tokyo: Chikuma Shobō, 1970.

Johnston, William. *The Modern Epidemic: A History of Tuberculosis in Japan*. Cambridge, MA: Harvard Council on East Asian Studies, 1995.

Kabashima Tadao, et al., eds. *Meiji Taishō shingo zokugo jiten*. Tokyo: Tōkyōdō Shuppan, 1984.

Kaburaki Kiyokata. *"Konjiki yasha" emaki*. Tokyo: Shun'yōdō, 1912.

Karatani Kōjin. *Origins of Japanese Literature*. Translated by Brett de Bary. Durham, NC: Duke University Press, 1993.

Kawashima Takeyoshi. *Ideorogii to shite no kazoku seido*. Tokyo: Iwanami Shoten, 1957.

Kikuchi Yūhō. *Chikyōdai*. In *Meiji katei shōsetsu shū*, edited by Senuma Shigeki, 89–240. Vol. 93 of *Meiji bungaku zenshū*. Tokyo: Chikuma Shobō, 1969.

Kinder, Marsha. *Blood Cinema: The Reconstruction of National Identity in Spain*. Berkeley: University of California Press, 1993.

Kinmonth, Earl H. *The Self-Made Man in Meiji Japanese Thought: From Samurai to Salaryman*. Berkeley: University of California Press, 1981.

Kinoshita Hiromi. "Kindai fujin-katei ron no tenkai—Sakai Toshihiko o chūshin ni." *Rekishi hyōron* 446 (June 1987): 78–88.

Kitani Kimie. *Ozaki Kōyō no kenkyū*. Tokyo: Sōbunsha, 1995.

Komori Yōichi. "*Kokoro* ni okeru hanten suru 'shuki'—kūhaku to imi no seisei." In *Kōzō to shite no katari*, 415–37. Tokyo: Shin'yōsha, 1988.

Kōno Toshirō. "*Hototogisu* shūhen." *Nihon bungaku* 6.11 (November 1957): 822–29.

Lebra, Takie Sugiyama. *Above the Clouds: Status Culture of the Modern Japanese Nobility*. Berkeley: University of California Press, 1993.

Legge, James, trans. *The Ch'un Ts'ew with The Tso Chuen*. Vol. 5 of *The Chinese Classics*. Taipei: SMC Publishing, 2000.

Lévi-Strauss, Claude. *The Elementary Structures of Kinship*. Boston: Beacon Press, 1969.

Masamune Hakuchō. "Natsume Sōseki." In *Sakkaron*, vol. 1, 201–48. Tokyo: Sōgensha, 1941.

Matsumoto Sannosuke. "Kazoku kokka kan no kōzō to tokushitsu." In *Kazokukan no keifu*, edited by Aoyama Michio, et al., 55–78. Vol. 8 of *Kōza kazoku*. Tokyo: Kōbundō, 1974.

———, ed. *Meiji shisō shū 2*. Vol. 31 of *Kindai Nihon shisō taikei*. Tokyo: Chikuma Shobō, 1977.

McClintock, Anne. *Imperial Leather: Race, Gender, and Sexuality in the Colonial Context*. New York: Routledge, 1995.

McDonald, Keiko I. *From Book to Screen: Modern Japanese Literature in Film*. Armonk, NY: M. E. Sharpe, 2000.

McKeon, Michael. "Generic Transformation and Social Change: Rethinking the Rise of the Novel." In *Theory of the Novel: A Historical Approach*, edited by Michael McKeon, 389–97. Baltimore: Johns Hopkins University Press, 2000.

———. *The Origins of the English Novel: 1600–1740*. Baltimore: Johns Hopkins University Press, 1987.

Miller, J. Scott. *Adaptations of Western Literature in Meiji Japan*. New York: Palgrave, 2001.

Miller, Roy Andrew. *The Japanese Language*. Chicago: University of Chicago Press, 1967.

Minear, Richard H. *Japanese Tradition and Western Law: Emperor, State, and the Law in the Thought of Hozumi Yatsuka*. Cambridge, MA: Harvard University Press, 1970.

Min'yūsha, eds. *Katei kyōiku*. Originally published 1894. In *Katei kyōiku bunken sōsho*, vol. 2, edited by Ishikawa Matsutarō. Tokyo: Kuresu Shuppan, 1990.

Mizoguchi Hakuyō. *Katei shinshi: "Hototogisu" no uta*. Tokyo: Tōkyōdō, 1905.

Mizumura Minae. "'Otoko to otoko' to 'otoko to onna'—Fujio no shi." *Hihyō kūkan* 6 (July 1992): 158–77.

Mizuta Noriko. "*Gubijinsō* ni okeru Sōseki no 'Fujio goroshi' ni tsuite." *Kokubungaku kaishaku to kyōzai no kenkyū* 42.6 (May 1997): 102–11.

Moore, Arlene. "Searching for Bertha Clay: Problems in Researching the Topic and Areas for Further Study." *Dime Novel Roundup* 60.1 (February 1998): 10–14.

Mosse, George. *Nationalism and Sexuality*. Madison: University of Wisconsin Press, 1985.

Mulvey, Laura. "Notes on Sirk and Melodrama." In *Home Is Where the Heart Is: Studies in Melodrama and the Woman's Film*, edited by Christine Gledhill, 75–79. London: BFI Books, 1987.

Mumford, Lewis. *Technics and Civilization*. New York: Harcourt, Brace, 1934.

Muta Kazue. *Senryaku to shite no kazoku: kindai Nihon no kokuminkokka keisei to josei*. Tokyo: Shin'yōsha, 1996.

Nagatani Ken. "Kindai Nihon ni okeru jōryū kaikyū imeeji no hen'yō—Meiji kōki kara Taishōki ni okeru zasshi mejia no bunseki." *Shisō* 812 (February 1992): 193–210.

Nakano Kii. "*Konjiki yasha* no hikaku bungakuteki ichikōsatsu: Bertha Clay to kanren shite." *Eibungaku to eigogaku* 24 (1987): 5–20.

Nakano Yasuo. *Roka Tokutomi Kenjirō*. Tokyo: Chikuma Shobō, 1972.

Nakayama Kazuko. "*Gubijinsō*—wūman heitingu to shokuminchi." In *Sutorei shiipu no yukue: Sōseki to kindai*, edited by Kumazaki Atsuko, 21–33. Tokyo: Kanrin Shobō, 1996.

Natsume Sōseki. "Bungakudan." In *Soseki zenshū*, vol. 16, 515–16. Tokyo: Iwanami Shoten, 1967.

———. *Gubijinsō*. In *Sōseki zenshū*, vol. 3. Tokyo: Iwanami Shoten, 1966.

———. *Kokoro*. In *Sōseki zenshū*, vol. 6. Tokyo: Iwanami Shoten, 1966.

———. "Meredith no fu." In *Sōseki zenshū*, vol. 16, 664–68. Tokyo: Iwanami Shoten, 1967.

Nihon Eigashi Kenkyūkai, eds. *Nihon eiga sakuhin jiten, senzen hen*, vol. 3. Tokyo: Kagaku Shoin, 1996.

Nihon Kindai Bungakkan, eds. *Nihon kindai bungaku daijiten*. 6 vols. Tokyo: Kōdansha, 1977.

Nihon Kokugo Daijiten Dai Nihan Henshū Iinkai, and Shōgakkan Kokugo Jiten Henshūbu, eds. *Nihon kokugo daijiten-dai nihan*. Tokyo: Shōgakkan, 2001.

Nihon Kokugo Daijiten Kankōkai, eds. *Nihon kokugo daijiten*. Tokyo: Shōgakkan, 1972.

Noguchi Takehiko. *Edo to aku—"Hakkenden" to Bakin no sekai*. Tokyo: Kadokawa Shoten, 1991.

Nolte, Sharon, and Sally Ann Hastings. "The Meiji State's Policy toward Women, 1890–1910." In *Recreating Japanese Women, 1600–1945*, edited by Gail Lee Bernstein, 151–74. Berkeley: University of California Press, 1991.

Nowell-Smith, Geoffrey. "Minnelli and Melodrama." In *Movies and Methods*, vol. 2, edited by Bill Nichols, 190–94. Berkeley: University of California Press, 1985.

Ochi Haruo. "Kigeki no jidai—*Gubijinsō*." In *Gubijinsō·Nowaki·Kōfu*, edited by Asada Takashi and Kimata Satoshi, 47–62. Vol. 3 of *Sōseki sakuhinron shūsei*. Tokyo: Ōfūsha, 1991.

———. *Sōseki shiron*. Tokyo: Kadokawa Shoten, 1971.

Ōkubo Tsuneo. "*Gubijinsō* ron nōto." In *Sakuhinron Natsume Sōseki*, edited by Ichida Michio, 95–109. Tokyo: Sōbunsha, 1976.

Ooms, Herman. *Charismatic Bureaucrat: A Political Biography of Matsudaira Sadanobu, 1758–1829*. Chicago: University of Chicago Press, 1975.

Ōta Samurō. "*Konjiki yasha" gafu*. Tokyo: Seibidō, 1911.

Ozaki Kōyō. *Konjiki yasha*. In *Ozaki Kōyō shū*. Vol. 5 of *Nihon kindai bungaku taikei*. Tokyo: Kadokawa Shoten, 1971.

Pierson, John D. *Tokutomi Sohō, 1863–1957: A Journalist for Modern Japan*. Princeton, NJ: Princeton University Press, 1980.

Poulton, M. Cody. *Spirits of Another Sort: The Plays of Izumi Kyōka*. Ann Arbor: University of Michigan Center for Japanese Studies, 2001.

Pyle, Kenneth B. *The New Generation in Meiji Japan: Problems of Cultural Identity, 1885–1895*. Stanford, CA: Stanford University Press, 1969.

Ragsdale, Kathryn. "Marriage, the Newspaper Business, and the Nation-State: Ideology in the Late Meiji Serialized *Katei Shōsetsu*." *Journal of Japanese Studies* 24.2 (Summer 1998): 229–55.

Roden, Donald. *Schooldays in Imperial Japan: A Study in the Culture of a Student Elite*. Berkeley: University of California Press, 1980.

Rubin, Gayle. "The Traffic in Women: Notes on the Political Economy of Sex." In *Toward an Anthropology of Women*, edited by Rayna Reiter, 157–210. New York: Monthly Review Press, 1975.

Saeki Junko. *Iro to ai no hikakubunkashi*. Tokyo: Iwanami Shoten, 1998.

Said, Edward. *The World, the Text, and the Critic*. Cambridge, MA: Harvard University Press, 1983.

Sakai Toshihiko. "*Hototogisu* o yomu." In *Sakai Toshihiko zenshū*, vol. 1, 72–73. Tokyo: Chūō Kōron Sha, 1933.

Sakaki, Atsuko. *Recontextualizing Texts: Narrative Performance in Modern Japanese Fiction*. Cambridge, MA: Harvard University Asia Center, 1999.

Sand, Jordan. *House and Home in Modern Japan: Architecture, Domestic Space, and Bourgeois Culture, 1880–1930*. Cambridge, MA: Harvard University Asia Center, 2003.

Sedgwick, Eve. *Between Men: English Literature and Male Homosocial Desire*. New York: Columbia University Press, 1985.

Seki Hajime. "*Konjiki yasha* no juyō to mejia mikkusu." In *Mejia, hyōshō, ideorogii—Meiji sanjūnendai no bunka kenkyū*, edited by Komori Yōichi, Kōno Kensuke, and Takahashi Osamu, 158–94. Tokyo: Ozawa Shoten, 1997.

———. "Merodorama to shite no *Gubijinsō*." *Sōseki kenkyū* 16 (2003): 111–25.

Sekiguchi Yūko, et al., eds. *Nihon kazoku shi*. Tokyo: Kazusa Shuppansha, 1989.

Sekikawa Natsuo. "Nisshin sensōgo no 'kane no yo.'" *Bungakkai* 48.1 (January 1994): 170–73.

Senuma Shigeki. "Katei shōsetsu no tenkai." In *Meiji katei shōsetsu shū*, edited by Senuma Shigeki, 421–30. Vol. 93 of *Meiji bungaku zenshū*. Tokyo: Chikuma Shobō, 1969.

Shōwa Joshi Daigaku Kindai Bungaku Kenkyūshitsu, eds. "Kikuchi Yūhō." In *Kindai bungaku kenkyū sōsho*, vol. 61, 411–91. Tokyo: Shōwa Joshi Daigaku, 1988.

————, eds. "Suematsu Kenchō." In *Kindai bungaku kenkyū sōsho*, vol. 20, 15–81. Tokyo: Shōwa Joshi Daigaku, 1963.

Shūkan Asahi, eds. *Nedan no Meiji Taishō Shōwa fūzokushi—jō*. Tokyo: Asahi Shinbun Sha, 1987.

Singer, Ben. *Melodrama and Modernity: Early Sensational Cinema and Its Contexts*. New York: Columbia University Press, 2001.

Sontag, Susan. *Illness as Metaphor*. New York: Vintage Books, 1979.

Sorokin, Pitrim. *Social and Cultural Mobility*. New York: Free Press, 1959.

Sypher, Wylie. "Aesthetic of Revolution: The Marxist Melodrama." In *Tragedy: Vision and Form*, 2nd ed., edited by Robert W. Corrigan, 216–24. New York: Harper and Row, 1981.

Takada Chinami. "'Ryōsai kenbo' e no hairei—*Konjiki yasha* no heroin o yomu." *Nihon bungaku* 36.10 (October 1987): 18–27.

Takagi Takeo. *Shinbun shōsetsu shi—Meiji hen*. Tokyo: Kokusho Kankōkai, 1974.

Takakura Teru. "Nihon kokuminbungaku no kakuritsu." *Shisō* 171 (August 1936): 76–88.

Takemori Ten'yū. "*Gubijinsō* no aya: 'kindokei' to 'koto no oto.'" *Kokugo to kokubungaku* 65.8 (August 1988): 1–15.

Takeuchi Yō. *Risshin shusse shugi: kindai Nihon no roman to yokubō*. Tokyo: NHK Shuppan, 1997.

Takizawa Bakin. *Nansō Satomi hakkenden*, vol. 2. Edited by Koike Tōgorō. Tokyo: Iwanami Shoten, 1927.

Tanaka, Stefan. *New Times in Modern Japan*. Princeton, NJ: Princeton University Press, 2004.

Tayama Katai. *Futon*. In *Tayama Katai shū*. Vol. 19 of *Nihon kindai bungaku taikei*. Tokyo: Kadokawa Shoten, 1971.

Tokutomi Roka. *Fuji*. In *Roka zenshū*, vol. 17. Tokyo: Shinchōsha, 1929.

————. *The Heart of Nami-San*. Translated by Isaac Goldberg. Boston: Stratford, 1918.

————. *Hototogisu*. In *Kitamura Tōkoku, Tokutomi Roka shū*. Vol. 9 of *Nihon kindai bungaku taikei*. Tokyo: Kadokawa Shoten, 1972.

Torrance, Richard. *The Fiction of Tokuda Shūsei and the Emergence of Japan's New Middle Class*. Seattle: University of Washington Press, 1994.

Tsubouchi Shōyō. *Shōsetsu shinzui*. In *Tsubouchi Shōyō shū*. Vol. 3 of *Nihon kindai bungaku taikei*. Tokyo: Kadokawa Shoten, 1974.

Uchida Hoshimi. *Tokei kōgyō no hattatsu*. Tokyo: Kabushiki Gaisha Hattori Seikō, 1985.

Ueda, Atsuko. *Concealment of Politics, Politics of Concealment: The Production of "Literature" in Japan.* Stanford, CA: Stanford University Press, 2007.

Ueno Chizuko. *Kindai kazoku no seiritsu to shūen.* Tokyo: Iwanami Shoten, 1994.

Uno, Kathleen. "Questioning Patrilineality: On Western Studies of the Japanese *Ie.*" *Positions* 4.3 (Winter 1996): 569–93.

Vicinus, Martha. "'Helpless and Unfriended': Nineteenth-Century Domestic Melodrama." *New Literary History* 13.1 (Autumn 1981): 127–43.

Walker, Janet. *The Japanese Novel and the Ideal of Individualism.* Princeton, NJ: Princeton University Press, 1979.

Waseda Daigaku Engeki Hakubutsukan, eds. *Engeki hyakka daijiten.* 6 vols. Tokyo: Heibonsha, 1960–62.

Weber, Max. *From Max Weber: Essays in Sociology.* Edited by H. H. Gerth and C. Wright Mills. New York: Oxford University Press, 1946.

Welter, Barbara. "The Cult of True Womanhood: 1820–1860." *American Quarterly* 18.2 (Summer 1966): 151–74.

Williams, Linda. *Playing the Race Card: Melodramas of Black and White from Uncle Tom to O. J. Simpson.* Princeton, NJ: Princeton University Press, 2001.

Yamada Yoshio. *Keigohō no kenkyū.* Tokyo: Hōbunkan, 1931.

Yamamoto Masahide. *Kindai buntai hassei no shiteki kenkyū.* Tokyo: Iwanami Shoten, 1965.

Yanabu Akira. *Hon'yakugo seiritsu jijō.* Tokyo: Iwanami Shoten, 1982.

Yanagida Izumi, Katsumoto Sei'ichirō, and Ino Kenji, eds. *Zadankai—Meiji bungaku shi.* Tokyo: Iwanami Shoten, 1961.

Yanagita Kunio. "Inaka tai tokai no mondai." In *Jidai to nōsei*, Vol. 16 of *Teihon Yanagita Kunio shū*, 28–50. Tokyo: Chikuma Shobō, 1962.

Yasuda Kōami, et al. "*Konjiki yasha* jōchūgehen gappyō." *Geibun* (August 1902): 86–138. Reprint 1968.

Yiu, Angela. *Chaos and Order in the Works of Natsume Sōseki.* Honolulu: University of Hawai'i Press, 1998.

Zwicker, Jonathan. *Practices of the Sentimental Imagination: Melodrama, the Novel, and the Social Imaginary in Nineteenth-Century Japan.* New York: Columbia University Press, 2006.

Index

Note: Figures are indicated by *f* following the page number.